THESE CRIMES MADE HEADLINES

Also by Leo Grex

MURDER STRANGER THAN FICTION
DETECTION STRANGER THAN FICTION
MYSTERY STRANGER THAN FICTION

MIX ME A MURDER
DEATH THROWS NO SHADOW
DIE—AS IN MURDER
THE HARD KILL
KILL NOW—PAY LATER
THE VIOLENT KEEPSAKE
THE BRASS KNUCKLE
TERROR WEARS A SMILE
LARCENY IN HER HEART
THANKS FOR THE FELONY
ACE OF DANGER
STOLEN DEATH (*filmed*)

THESE CRIMES MADE HEADLINES

by

Leo Grex

ROBERT HALE · LONDON

© *Leo Grex 1980*
All rights reserved
First published in Great Britain 1980

ISBN 0 7091 8602 9

Robert Hale Limited
Clerkenwell House
Clerkenwell Green
London EC1R 0HT

Essex County Library

Photoset by
Kelly Typesetting Limited
Bradford-on-Avon, Wiltshire
and printed in Great Britain by
Clarke, Doble & Brendon
Plymouth and London

CONTENTS

	Introduction	7
1	The Tangle of the Cameo Cinema Murders	9
2	The Incredible Brink's Robbery	24
3	The Austrian Poison Queen	38
4	Vibrations that Rang for Murder	53
5	Homicide and Honeymoons Rarely Mix	68
6	The Skyjacker's Conscience was Too Heavy	81
7	A Slow Train Brought Sudden Death	95
8	The Vanishing Millionaire	110
9	The Croupier Who Gambled on Murder	123
10	The Kidnapped Movie-Star	136
11	The Case of the Devoted Heart	150
12	Death was the Last Confessor	164

INTRODUCTION

The crimes in this book have in some instances made history and for that reason may be seen as a challenge in the sphere of significant crime.

Indeed, there are in this volume instances of crimes that can be considered as not only stranger than any fiction but larger than life as well. Although it is only fair to admit that most of them are murder cases, it is the quality and the choice of murder that are of value to any student of what is unusual. And in some cases the events covered are unlikely to have happened in the precise way in which they allegedly occurred.

For this very reason these crimes cannot be compared with fiction. On occasion these cases, which are world-wide in range and cover more than half a century in time, have a startling and even bizarre content of truth that seems to defeat the contrived ingenuities of the story-tellers. Once again, unsolved mysteries are mixed with patterns of human solution that seem subtly defiant of calculated analysis. Perhaps this is as it should be, for there are emotional depths to some crimes that cannot be calculated even if analysed.

For all such crimes it is the literary participation and narration that is of supreme importance and value—or, in simpler words, the story. This may, of course, evoke a number of mixed feelings.

It is to be hoped that all these cases are not only readable but worth the telling in such a collection.

1

The Tangle of the Cameo Cinema Murders

One of the most tangled and controversial arguments in a modern crime case occurred in Liverpool. Actually it was a brutal case of double murder which made it singular, and it certainly attracted a wide interest. Indeed, when the jury were unable to agree on a verdict, the trial, reputed to be the longest in British criminal history, had lasted for thirteen days—and then the judge ordered it to begin all over again.

It started a virtual marathon of legal endurance, with hold-ups and cross-examinations and fresh trials that developed into a Wavertree saga that was almost without parallel since the days of the Maybrick controversy, back in 1889, ninety years ago. Sixty years later, in March 1949, the whole of Liverpool and the surrounding district along the Mersey became involved in this crime.

The double shooting occurred on Saturday 19th March, in the Cameo Cinema in the suburb of Wavertree. The time was about 9.35 p.m., when the packed Saturday-night audience was agog and sitting enthralled in their seats.

The shooting in the cinema was the result of planned raid by two Liverpool men of Irish extraction—not that the raid was anything save an all-out affair of lethal and frenzied suddenness, but the consequences of the murderous act of violence were to linger for many months, and a man died for the paltry takings of a little over £50.

Over the shooting hung a grey pall of mystery which

hovered, thinned and then clouded over again like dark smoke caught in the cross-current of a changeable wind. However, despite arguments, acrimonious and otherwise, one fact emerged as inescapable. A few minutes after half-past nine Leonard Thomas, the cinema-manager, was shot and killed, and the assistant-manager, John Catterall, was also shot as he tried to stop the masked bandit, who fled to make his get-away.

In the course of the intensive investigation the police interviewed some 75,000 persons; they called at ten thousand homes and made and accepted twelve hundred phone-calls to and from members of the public who thought that they might hold a clue to the masked gunman's identity. Throughout these extended inquiries they rounded up and confiscated no less than thirty firearms, mostly revolvers, as well as several rifles and a shotgun. Fifteen individuals were prosecuted for being in possession of such firearms. Their disarming and the subsequent arrest of the persons responsible for the cinema murders were like a shadow of promised violence nearly twenty years distant.

However, one high-ranking police-officer who was tired of running rings around men who refused to talk called the shooting, rather bitterly, "a tangled crime". It may well have been, but it was the handiwork of someone who was a professional criminal.

For that reason most of those questioned clammed up and preferred to remain silent rather than help the police by making a voluntary statement. There were people in Liverpool who were scared to be seen talking to the police; for months a grim silence brooded over the city, and men known to have a record scurried away and conversed with one another only in whispers out of the sides of their mouths, while always they remained on the look-out for a blue-clad figure with a beckoning finger. They were uncomfortable days, and during this period crime could not be said to flourish along the Mersey. The police were too active.

They repeatedly visited the Cameo Cinema, the scene of the March shooting, on the offchance of coming on some overlooked clue. But they knew little more than the bare facts, which were that, on the Saturday night, shortly after half-past nine, a man, who had drawn a scarf over his face and was wearing a felt hat and a brown overcoat, crept up the spiral staircase to the manager's office in the Cameo Cinema in Wavertree just after the night's takings had been collected and the ticket-office closed. Later the money was found to be missing, and Thomas was sprawled in death. Then Catterall had collapsed. It appeared obvious that he had tried to stop the thief and killer.

Almost six months passed.

Then, on a squally day in late September, the police received a phone-call. It was made by a man named Northam.

"All right," he said, "I'm ringing to give myself up. But first I want to get one thing straight."

"What's that?" asked a police-officer who was making frantic gestures to his associates to listen in.

"I want protection. If I'm to co-operate, I need to be sure I'm safe."

Some minutes later, after receiving such assurance, James Philip Northam stopped hiding from the police who were looking for him and walked in to surrender.

The man who had given himself up was no mastermind of crime. He was a small-time crook. He was thoroughly scared, so scared he could hardly speak, though this may have been due partly to an impediment in his speech, for when he became excited he stuttered and was in consequence dubbed 'Stutty' by his associates.

According to his statement he and his girl-friend had been present at the initial planning of the Cameo Cinema crime, at 'The Beehive', a public house in the Mount Pleasant district of the seaport. (When the police checked the statement later, they found that the Cameo was a journey of fourteen minutes away by tram.) He went on to relate that he and his girl-friend had entered 'The Beehive' about half-past seven on the Saturday evening. They were living in Birkenhead and had come into Liverpool for a Saturday night out. They had enjoyed a few drinks, in the course of which they had met a man named Connolly. He was in his middle thirties, and Northam had known him on and off, as he put it, for some three years. Connolly had been at one time a merchant seaman but had given up the sea and become a labourer. For a quarter of an hour the newcomers chatted with Connolly, and then another man walked into the bar. He had quick, searching eyes and a tight mouth. When Northam nodded to him, he received a slow stare followed by another nod.

"What'll it be, Georgie?" asked Connolly, with an inquiring glance at the man he saw approaching but whose eyes had turned towards Northam and the latter's girl-friend.

They sat around and clinked glasses.

The newcomer was George Kelly, usually known to his friends and close associates as 'Georgie'. He had the reputation of a tearaway and was something of a leader among Liverpudlian toughs who lived by intimidation and violence. He had earned a brief renown for driving a hijacked lorry into a crowded bar, a wild, thoughtless act that had resulted in a man's death. He and his loose-knit gang lived by fear. On another occasion, when a gang-member had been compelled to talk to the police, a woman associate of the same gang had produced a straight-edged razor and slashed him in the face as he left the court building.

Kelly seemed to be waiting for someone when Northam saw him. It was a dark-haired woman who was late keeping the appointment—at which Kelly scowled angrily, though he cheered up later. The dark woman, who had bright eyes, was heavily made-up and kept stretching her lips as she applied a very red lipstick.

Suddenly Kelly broached a new topic—breaking into an arcade. Connolly was quick to take up the subject and suggested that 'Stutty's' girl-friend could very well act as a decoy. There was talk of hiring a taxi-driver named Harry whose past had earned him the role of stool-pigeon and who kept a well-filled pocket-book. When the low voices became heated, Northam's girl-friend suddenly had a change of heart.

"Count me out," she said brusquely. "I don't think it will work."

There was sudden silence, broken when Connolly said, "Look, there's this cinema. It's only a few minutes from Kelly's home in Cambridge Street, as a matter of fact. It should be easy, a real smashing place for a quick grab."

The new "smashing place", the Cameo Cinema in Wavertree, became the focus of interest, and the group

debated the prospect of making a quick raid.
Connolly became enthusiastic.
"It's practically a pushover," he said, warming up. "But it will have to be a quick job, a stick-up with either a real shooter or some dummy."
Then, according to Northam in his police-report, Kelly had looked at the dark woman and winked. He leaned sideways to remove a gun from his pocket. It was a 38-calibre weapon, long and heavy. In fact, it was a German gun with which officers had been issued. As he produced it, Northam's girl-friend had looked around quickly and snapped, "Put it away! Someone else might see it." But apparently that night Kelly felt he had to make an impression. Instead of putting the gun away, he opened the breech, clicked it shut with a loaded bullet and then pushed another into the magazine.
He hefted the gun, grinning and patting the girl with too much lipstick. He touched her on the arm. She looked a mite scared—particularly when Kelly put down the loaded gun and took out a white handkerchief, which he folded into a triangle over his face. The mask was too small, so the dark girl handed him a folded dark-brown apron which she kept tucked in her handbag. Kelly shook it out, refolded it carefully and nodded as though pleased.
Then he turned to Northam and asked, "You coming with us?"
The other hesitated before shaking his head.
"Not if guns are to be used," he said. "You know I've only just got out, and I don't like guns or the folks who use them."
Kelly and two of the others went out of 'The Beehive', the former carrying a brown overcoat he had borrowed from Northam. He and the dark girl went on with their drinks. Neither spoke. They were uneasy strangers who had nothing to say to each other.
Five or six minutes passed. Then the door opened again, and Northam's girl-friend came and sat down.
"I've changed my mind. I don't like it," she said.
Northam finished his drink and rose. Nodding to the dark girl, the pair left 'The Beehive'. They no longer felt that Saturday night held any attraction for them. They returned to Birkenhead.

According to the police-account, Northam read of the cinema murder the next day, Sunday. Around midday he called at 'The Star', a pub on Brownlow Hill which was customarily called 'Charlie's' from the landlord's name. There had been a loose agreement that after the cinema snatch Kelly and the others would meet and separate immediately afterwards. But the police were quickly following up what was believed to be a Kelly lead and were soon at the door of 'The Star' making inquiries.

This caused Connolly to get cold feet.

After the police visit he said, "Look, I'm getting out of the damned country."

Kelly had looked hard at him.

"You're a yellow bastard," he had jeered. "Just stay put, don't get in a panic, and keep your trap shut. You know nothing, remember. Not even each other." He glared around grimly. "That goes for all of you," he reminded the others sharply.

When the uneasy meeting broke up, Kelly handed back Northam's brown hat.

"You'd better burn this," he said, tossing the headgear and the brown coat at him. "Make sure they're not remembered."

In the meantime Northam became more jittery as the police probe continued, but he wanted to know what had gone wrong at the cinema. He felt he had a right to know. Kelly told him it was all Connolly's fault. He was supposed to 'keep douse'—to be the lookout and warn Kelly if anyone was coming. He had been expected to creep upstairs with the masked bandit in case the assistant-manager turned up unexpectedly. But at the last moment Connolly had refused to comply with his companion's instructions. He had flatly refused to accompany Kelly beyond the cinema's side-door.

According to what Northam told the police taking down his statement, Kelly had stood outside the cinema, waiting for the lights in the ticket-office to be switched off. As soon as they were, he sprinted for the side-door and up the spiral staircase. He was on his own since Connolly had held back. What then happened is explained in Northam's words at a later trial-hearing.

"Kelly said he got to the manager's office," he related, "and walked in. There was an old fellow sitting down. Kelly said he wanted the takings and pointed to the bag on the table. The man said, 'Don't be such a fool. Put that toy away,' and Kelly said, 'This is no toy and I want that bag.' The man then stood up and said, 'You can't take the bag. It belongs to the company. You can take some of my own money.'

"He then tried to brush the gun aside," went on Northam's narrative. "Kelly said, 'I couldn't be bothered with him any more, so I shot him.' He put the gun in his pocket, picked up the bag and started to make for the door. When he was a few feet away from the door, it opened, and another man came in and shut the door behind him. The man kept his hands behind his back and said to Kelly, 'What are you doing here?' The man then came towards him and made a grab at the bag, and the cash went all over the floor. The man tried to tackle him, but Kelly butted him. Kelly said the man then let go of him for a second, so he pulled out his gun and shot him in the chest. The man got up to his knees again and tried to tackle Kelly, so he shot him again."

In a quick review of the scene Northam went on:

"The man was stretched out by the door, and he had to drag him away so that he could try to open the door. He thought the man had locked it when he came in, so he shot the lock off. He rushed down the spiral staircase, and when he got outside, Connolly was not there."

In another part of the lengthy statement which was later produced in court, Northam said that Kelly claimed he had a cast-iron alibi.

"The police can't break it in a thousand years," had been his boast.

When the police called on him on the Sunday morning after the Saturday's shooting, he had his story ready-made. He said he had been drinking at his local, 'The Leigh Arms'. About ten past nine he left and went to another public-house, the Spofforth Hotel. He was looking for Doris O'Malley, who lived with him, but she was not there, so he stopped only to have a drink and then returned to 'The Leigh Arms', within a few minutes of half-past nine.

The inquiring police knew that, if what he had said was true, he could not be the man who had shot and killed

Leonard Thomas, for at the time of the shooting at the Cameo Cinema he had been about ten minutes' walk away, drinking with companions who would substantiate the claim. The police collected the names of these witnesses.

However, although Kelly purported to have this cast-iron alibi and clung to it, the Liverpool inquiry continued over months without let-up, and certainly Northam felt himself in danger as long as Kelly and Connolly shared his secret. So, jointly with his girl-friend, he composed an anonymous letter addressed to the police, including some of the truth mixed with fictitious claims.

The letter read:

Dear Sir,
This is not a crank's letter or suchlike nor am I turning informer for gain. It says in the papers you are looking for one man. I know three and a girl, not including myself, who heard about this plan for the robbery. I would have nothing to do with it, and I don't think the girl had. There was only two men went. The man he took with him lost his nerve and would not go in with him but said he would wait outside, but did not.

The letter-writer claimed to have met the murderer some days after the shooting. He told him that the murder weapon had been thrown into a park lake at Edge Lane, and then asked the police how he stood with them. Although he knew about the so-called job, he had not gone with the others, and he was particularly concerned about how he stood in the matter of turning King's Evidence, "or something like that", as he said. For he was a man with a record who might be 'framed' for something he had not done, and he was afraid of being charged as an accessory.

The police took the letter seriously and dragged the local lake but found no gun. They put an advertisement in the *Liverpool Echo*, as the letter-writer had suggested, when, in cautious terms, he offered to provide further details.

But this time it was Northam who had cold feet. He travelled to Manchester and changed his name, and he and his girl-friend separated. Then one day she ran into Kelly and was so shaken by the meeting that the man had to buy her a large double whisky to steady her badly shot nerves.

As he sat staring at her, he delivered a threat in grim terms.

"Say anything about what happened to anyone, and I'll knife you." He leaned closer to the scared girl to add, "What's more, if I don't, then someone else will. That's a promise."

Kelly then took her to Birkenhead. The meeting had badly scared her and left her brooding and morose. Soon afterwards she left to join Northam in Manchester. But they still argued about how safe it was to approach the police, for Kelly's threat to knife the woman was very real to her. She lived under its menace for weeks. However, Northam had seemingly overcome his personal jitters and made the first move to break away, though he did so in a doubtful way and certainly in a dubious fashion.

He telephoned the police. The date was 29th September.

On the 30th Kelly, who at the same time was trying to pose as an informer, was suddenly arrested. His reaction was one of savage shock. Connolly, who was seated next to him in the charge-room at the time, was equally dismayed.

Through tight lips Kelly warned him, "You don't know me, do you?"

Connolly shook his head vigorously.

"No," he muttered. "Never seen you before."

Some time after the two had arrived in Walton Jail, during an exercise-break, Kelly sidled up to a young man who was on remand. He said he wanted to pass a message from Connolly and then became talkative and appeared to brood. He whispered to the other that his life depended on five minutes. He went on to say he had got rid of the brown overcoat he had been given by Northam.

Eventually, after months of patient inquiry and the building of the case against Kelly and Connolly, the police felt they could proceed with it. But in a truly sensational manner, when the case came to trial, the Liverpool jury failed to reach agreement and could not provide the court with a verdict.

In the circumstances there had to be a re-trial.

This opened in February 1950 at the Liverpool Assizes.

The fresh trial was in the nature of things something of an

anticlimax. Already eleven months had dragged away since the shooting of Leonard Thomas and the intrepid John Catterall. The story of what had transpired at the Cameo Cinema on that fatal Saturday night had been sifted by both the police and the Press with resultant arguments and varied opinions. The theme was growing stale with over-use and repeating.

However, the legal stalemate was never an issue that was attractive to the judge who had to proceed with a re-trial before a freshly sworn-in jury. He was Mr Justice Cassels, who went on record with this expressed opinion:

"I've come to the conclusion that it is in the interest of justice that the jury, in a long case like this, particularly on a re-trial and on a capital charge, should not have to dissect evidence of individual witnesses and relate it to more than one person under trial."

He added:

"I don't think the defence is prejudiced. On the contrary, it may well be favoured by a separate trial in that there will be before the jury no evidence other than that relevant to the issues being tried concerning one person."

Accordingly Kelly and Connolly were this time to be tried separately.

The judge's announcement was accepted with surprise when he said, "The first defendant to be tried shall be George Kelly."

Thus a legal die had been cast.

Connolly's counsel made the requisite application, and Kelly's, Miss Rose Heilbron KC, strenuously opposed it.

In the first trial, heard before Mr Justice Oliver, the jury that was in disagreement had been told by the judge that they had a trio of questions to consider. Was Kelly the masked bandit? Did he fire the fatal shots? Was Connolly guilty of murder because he had agreed to the hold-up plan? Mr Justice Oliver averred, while summing up for the jury, that in the eyes of the law, if he knew that Kelly was armed, and furthermore knew that he would use the firearm, then Connolly was equally guilty. As he declared in severe tones, "He has helped to launch that murderer into that place; he has given him countenance and assistance and has encouraged him until it is

The Tangle of the Cameo Cinema Murders 19

too late to stop."

But when the jury returned, nearly five hours later, while a crowd of thousands packed the court and the streets around it, the longest trial in British criminal history had ended with the members of the jury continuing to agree to differ.

So in February 1950 Mr Justice Cassels had come to his own decision to hear the evidence separately, and Kelly was chosen to lead, with his mouth set in a tight scowl of disgruntlement. The most pertinent evidence, possibly, was that of James Philip Northam, given in his stuttering voice. To help him, the judge read aloud his own notes, taken down in shorthand, of which he had an easy flow, and then inquired if the witness agreed with what had been said.

Northam, after moistening dried lips, nodded slowly and muttered assent.

During this time there had been a bout of coughing in the court, for many of the public had a good quota of February coughs and colds, and a number were sneezing loudly. Irritated and annoyed by what he considered such unnecessary interruptions, Mr Justice Cassels broke off and turned round to stare over the assembly of Liverpool citizens.

"There's plenty of time between witnesses' going in and out of the box," he said somewhat wryly, "for people to have a really good cough."

He waited for silence, but when a witness left the box there followed a fresh round of coughing and throat-rattles. The Liverpudlian public somehow failed to appreciate the learned judge's difficulties! At times he had not been able to hear a witness's words at all clearly over the noises made in the public gallery.

However, in the course of the new hearing some additional points were made and underlined for emphasis. One dealt with the time Kelly was alleged to have appeared at 'The Leigh Arms' and Spofforth Hotel. He claimed to have left before nine-thirty, but the prosecution pointed out that when he returned some time after 9.45 p.m., he had deliberately ensured that he was seen by the people in 'The Leigh Arms'. He took occasion to tap a taxi-driver on the back and said loudly, "You can have a drink with me, pal. The best in the house." The driver, a man named Currie, who saw Kelly as a mere nodding-acquaintance, turned and asked him, "You been in the sun?"

Kelly's only tactic was to deny flatly anything said by other witnesses. He claimed he did not know Connolly or Northam or the latter's girl-friend, and what he had said to Currie was, in fact, "I've been having a go at the bevy." It was a 'scouse' expression for being 'on the beer'. Other witnesses, he claimed, had not acted in the way they said they had. But it was abundantly clear that Kelly was at last on the defensive. There were too many discrepancies appearing in his claims, and on one occasion the judge took the trouble to point something out to the jury. It was significant, and came about in this way.

Referring to the time when he was on remand with Connolly, Kelly said, "I couldn't see Connolly. That was impossible. But I could hear."

The judge looked at him.

"There was a prison-officer there?" he asked.

"Yes," said Kelly. "He could hear us, but not all the time."

Kelly then made to leave the witness-box, and he leaned nearer to the judge and stuck out a finger. He had drawn a rough line-map, indicating his cell and Connolly's. Mr Justice Cassels studied it with interest and came up with a question.

"Apart from the exercise," he wanted to know, "were you in your cells for the rest of the time?"

Kelly stared straight back at him and swallowed.

"Yes," he said in a rather subdued voice.

The judge nodded.

"That would be twenty-three hours out of twenty-four?" he inquired.

Kelly muttered a gruff affirmative that was not quite audible. The point the judge was making was not readily apparent until it came time for him to address the jury when he was summing up. Then he ruminatively reminded them of the point buried in his notes.

"Twenty-three hours a day is a long time to be in solitary confinement." He paused, fingering his notes. "Sometimes people want to talk and are very likely to talk."

The cross-examination of Kelly by the counsel for the

prosecution, Mr William Gorman, the Recorder of Liverpool, promised excited attention and a discontinuation of the persistent round of coughs. It was mid-afternoon when he rose to begin, and straightaway he began to attack by asking a series of fresh questions. Kelly seemed to be caught flat-footed by them, as though he had been unprepared. He appeared to be suddenly tense, and it was noticeable that he was not sure what to do with his hands, so he elected to keep them folded into fists. Hitherto he had been quick in his responses, almost chirpy at times, but at the Recorder's treatment his assurance flagged and crumpled. He answered with short jerks of his head when the prosecution asked him to repeat his words. In fact, the judge had to intervene somewhat testily.

"You must answer yes or no," he stressed. "The shorthand-writer cannot take down a shake of the head."

There was good reason for Kelly's nervousness, for the Recorder explained that the judge in the first trial, Mr Justice Oliver, had told the jury he intended to finish his summing-up the next morning, and shortly afterwards Kelly had received a visit from his brother Frank, accompanied by several friends.

"Don't forget, boys," he is alleged to have told them, "if I go down, it's up to you to do something about that Northam."

Kelly somewhat hesitantly agreed that he had made some such remark in front of the prison-officer who was present, but he claimed that it was not intended to be a threat. Thereupon Mr Gorman became bitingly disbelieving.

"Did you mean them to say merely to Northam, 'Please, Mr Northam, will you tell the truth?' Is that what you wanted?"

After a further exchange, Kelly was driven to assert, "All the time I've been in prison my brothers have threatened nobody yet."

It was a glaring mistake. The Recorder pounced and struck a verbal blow that made the other recoil and wince.

"What do you mean by that 'yet'?" he asked. "Is that something that's yet to come?"

Kelly was silenced. His case was folding, and Kelly knew it, for later Mr Gorman said, "If you're tired and want a rest, I will ask that you be given one, but I must ask you these questions."

There was no let-up. The hearing continued in a rather bitter fashion until the eventual summing-up, with Mr Justice Cassels making many points, both new and repeated, but one in particular sounded ominous as he asked the jury how, if Northam and his girl-friend had never met the defendant, as Kelly claimed, had he come to choose a public house well known to Kelly as their alleged place of meeting?

The jury at last retired, but they returned in less than an hour, to the surprise of many in the public seats. When the verdict was given, there was a dash to the telephone-booths, and the hundreds waiting in Lime Street seemed to get the result by bush telegraph.

Not for the first time had Kelly been found at a loss when asked formally if he had anything to say. He gulped and suddenly had as bad a stutter as his criminal associate 'Stutty'.

"I—I . . .", he started.

But he could not get the words beyond his teeth.

The judge, who had donned the black cap, began to pass the death-sentence but paused at Kelly's stumbling repetition. Mr Justice Cassels broke off. He reminded the prisoner, "The man who uses a gun to assist him in a robbery can expect no mercy."

Then he finished passing sentence.

Kelly had to be helped away by a couple of warders, who took him below. The trial was over.

A few days later Charles Connolly made his appearance in the same court. His plea was 'not guilty' of murdering Leonard Thomas and John Catterall but 'guilty' of robbing the former of £50 and also of conspiracy to rob. Thereupon Mr Gorman rose and announced that he proposed to offer no evidence on the charges of murder. A shaken Connolly drew himself up smartly (he had been a Territorial) and waited what was coming to him. The judge sentenced him to ten years' imprisonment for robbery and two years' for conspiracy.

In due course Kelly appealed, but the Court of Criminal Appeal decided against him and declared that he was not attainted under the Juries Act of 1870.

On 28th March 1950, a year after the Cameo Cinema

murder, six hundred people walked past the posted notice of Kelly's execution.

A strong March wind was blowing across the Mersey.

2

The Incredible Brink's Robbery

It was in the same year, 1950, when a man was hanged for the murder of a cinema-manager and his assistant, that another crime burst across the world, stunning the people of Boston with its outrageous nature, unlimited cheek and the very boldness that made it one of the greatest robberies of all time, certainly one to be bracketed with the British Great Train Robbers.

The consignment that was held up was the famous Brink's armoured-truck delivery in which millions of dollars changed hands. It was a crime that heralded a new departure in mobile assaults. The plotting and planning were executed with skill and unusual resourcefulness.

On a day when snow covered the New England countryside in the early days of a new year, seven men in warm leather peajackets, wearing heavy gloves covering their half-frozen fingers, assembled to offer a challenge to the Brink outfit. It was bitterly cold even for mid-January when they entered the North Terminal Garage, made their way towards the public car-park on the ground floor of a multi-storey park and then went up a short flight of stairs to the second floor. Here they came to a section of the sprawling building-structure that was operated by Brink's security firm, which had built up a wide and enviable reputation in New England. When it was dark, the muffled seven, who had come to know their way around the premises, moved to their allotted places, for they had grown familiar with routines as well as practices and had now reached a decisive deadline from which they would not retreat. They had come, in short, to remove a fortune.

When they approached a steel door, they had already made their choice.

The steel door was at the end of a corridor, which in turn was shielded by a bullet-proof turret strong enough to resist the attack of a tank. The turret was not manned or armed, and one of the smoothly functioning operators soon fell to picking the lock of the steel door. When the lock snapped open persuasively, the first part of the exercise had been accomplished: the steel door had been overcome. Grinning at each other under their peaked caps and thrusting their hands into their leather gloves, they made a concerted move in the direction of the door that led to the counting-house.

Once more they had to overcome obstacles, for two doors remained separating them from the vault where the money was stacked, but when it came to re-assessing the situation, they discovered that those doors were ajar.

They could scarcely believe their luck!

The way to the vault was unimpeded. They dumped three merchant-navy bags before the vault and opened one of them.

"Who'd have thought it, fellers?" laughed one exuberantly. "It's a piece of cake."

From the sailor-bag was extracted a rubberized type of Hallowe'en mask for each of them. The conspirators pulled the grotesque masks over their heads and then produced firearms, 38-calibre revolvers. Within a few minutes more they had worked expeditiously and arrived at a wired-off section of the floor.

They fell silent and checked their watches. It was now ten past seven in the early evening. They had been anxious to get ahead of schedule, so that a morning delivery by the Brink's trucks would not be held up.

They still could not believe their luck, for the vault door, swung open at their touch. They quickly fell to work raking aside and counting the stacks of money, which had been picked up by Brink's armoured trucks for the various banks in Boston. It was normal for a morning bank-delivery.

But this was no routine, and no one could call it normal—or

would later.

When the weighty vault stood open, the safe-breakers knew what they had accomplished. The vault was built into the massive rear wall of Brink's structure, and, as one man said later, "When one came to open the sacks, there was money everywhere, on tables and floor, in neat piles and simply tossed like loose change into baskets." One rough estimate of the amount of paper money stacked in that small compartment was that it must have weighed at least half a ton. But that was an estimate arrived at after the appearance of the guns, shortly after ten past seven.

It came about in this way.

The masked bandits had gone speedily about their operation, having timed everything meticulously, with constant re-checks as they proceeded into the strong-room premises. They knew that Brink's men usually dealt with last-minute cash-checks to prepare for the next day, so they were going to take a leaf out of their books. They hurried the procedure until they came to the moments before they would pounce. They knew precisely what they would do and where they would operate.

After finding the bank's doors swung open and unlocked, they knew they had taken the staff by surprise and that surprise would account for their success. Indeed, after donning their masks, gloves and seamen's jackets, they actually stood listening to the sound of Brink's men down in the vault stacking money for the delivery the next day. There were not only staff men but also guards, and no one was taking the trouble to be quiet. After all, it was something that had been done each day for a long time, and men and guards were armed.

The hold-up came close to achieving a quick, sharp and initial surprise. That was why the time of seven-ten became so fundamental in their precise as well as speedy calculations. What they were doing was certainly hurried, but they were not taking chances. They wanted to spring a surprise on Brink's men, and they did. As one reporter said, "It was the surprise of the century."

They caught the Brink's men with their pants not only lowered but straddling their feet very ignominiously.

Certainly the armoured-car men were left with flushed and bright red faces on this very cold January night.

What happened was like a television film.

As soon as the money was spilled and they knew what had to be done, there was no hesitancy. The man who gave the orders spoke only once behind his comic mask. That was when he suddenly appeared, brandishing a thirty-eight. The man who was transfixed by the sight was Charles Grell, a uniformed messenger who was about to leave the checking-table and walk towards the vault. He was suddenly rooted to the spot, staring goggle-eyed at the apparition that came towards him. There were six masked men standing in line abreast just outside the wire cage.

As Grell turned around, his mouth falling open, the leader spoke.

"All right," he said almost conversationally. "This is a stick-up!" He gestured with the thirty-eight, but there was no mistaking the abrupt meaning. "Open up."

Later it was recorded that he was the only bandit who spoke during the entire operation.

Before Grell could attract the attention of the others, they were standing as though turned to stone. Slowly they raised their hands. Thomas Lloyd, the chief cashier, had been about to walk out of the vault with Sherman Smith, one of the armed guards. A cashier, James Allen, and another guard, Herman Pfaff, were at a table on the left of the sorting-room. They had been concentrating on checking the deliveries to be made the next morning.

The scene was frozen.

Seven guns were levelled at the threatened men. They hitched their hands higher. Indeed, there was little else they could do, unless they wanted to die, for they were obviously in a position that had been very carefully calculated, for even if they had refused to open up, the wire cages stopped about eight feet from the ceiling, and a strong and muscular man could climb over the cage and tear the wire apart with his hands.

It was clear that the men behind the guns had come to rob the place, and everything had been planned. Watching Lloyd, the bandit leader nodded to Grell, who glanced at the chief cashier before nodding assent. The cage door swung open. Then the bandits moved with fresh speed. They tied up the hands and feet of the guards and cashiers, using stout strips of adhesive plaster. When they were securely taped and tied, the men lay prone on the floor and were rolled over on to their backs like so many joints of meat. After their mouths had been taped, the bandit leader issued a warning.

"Keep your faces to the wall," he said gratingly. "I don't want to see any of you looking up."

With that he dismissed them and turned to the work that remained to be done. A couple of the masked men reached over and took a pair of new submachine-guns from the sailor-bags. They then took up a position back to back at the door of the cage, while the others began collecting the money. They worked fast and for the most part in silence.

The pile of money-bags grew. Small bank-bags, filled with cash, were crowded into larger canvas coal-bags. These were recognized as being used by Brink's customers. A half-dozen of the coal-bags, each holding around forty of the bank-bags, were taken past the prone guards and piled in pairs outside the cage. Then hurriedly the bandits filled the seamen's bags. They thrust and shoved at the piles of paper money, not bothering about the spilled coins. Under their leader's guidance they worked with great concentration of effort, moving the stacked piles of money. There was no flippancy, no more threats. They were men at work and wanting to make a show of their labours, with heavy breathing.

Then, suddenly, as though at a silent signal, gunmen and money-stackers turned and with one accord left. The silence was almost eerie, until suddenly they could be heard dragging thousands of dollars along the floor, down the corridors and staircase and out to the street.

The taped men in the cage lay listening to the sounds of the incredible removal-operation, accomplished smoothly and utterly without panic of any sort. When the mammoth task was over, there was surprisingly little to show for it, for the gang left only a peaked cap, some thirty pieces of rope, of which ten had been bound around the employees, and five pieces of adhesive tape. The money they had collected amounted to the sizable sum of a couple of million dollars.

In retrospect it seemed as though they had been spirited away, for the entire operation had gone without a hitch. Thomas Lloyd and the others lay listening in the silence and at last decided to try to get free. Wriggling his limbs free, Lloyd tore off the tapes and rose to sound the alarm, given by a special buzzer, and then hastened to call the police and explain what had happened.

From the time when the masked men appeared at the cage until Lloyd was able to get himself free and raise the alarm only seventeen minutes had elapsed. Then one of the greatest manhunts ever staged in North America began. Police descended on the North Terminal Garage in droves, and the building's second floor was gone over inch by inch.

For days on end there was no police leave, and roadblocks were set up throughout Boston, sealing the city as effectively as if it were a tomb.

When the first news-reports of the robbery were announced, the estimate of the loss was given as a $100,000, but later in the day, when the cashiers got down to work with their calculators, the estimate was put at over a million. What was called a 'final audit' put the sum at $1,219,000. That was where the figure remained for four years. Then a routine court-report produced the amazing information that an extra $1,281,000 had been taken in negotiable bonds. This total brought the haul to $2,500,000.

There had been no such robbery in the United States previously. It was seen as something utterly fantastic, almost beyond conception.

For months the police chased clues without much promise of coming up with the successful bandits. There had been "an exchange of clues", as one senior Boston detective put it: the robbers had left behind a chauffeur's cap, pieces of adhesive tape and some lengths of rope in exchange for the firearms, the bags and the money—which was nothing like a reasonable swap. But police inquiries later produced the Hallowe'en masks and the get-away car. There was nothing for finger-print-experts to mull over, for the bandits had not bared their hands, but the rope went under the microscope and proved to be an average three-strand type of manilla used by housewives and tradesmen for blinds.

The peaked chauffeur's cap, with a glossy visor, had had the label ripped out and could not be traced, although hours were spent on the futile hunt, and the police came to the somewhat cynical conclusion that it was a 'plant'. The guns removed by the bandits were all the same calibre, thirty-eights, three Smith & Wessons and one Colt. Moreover, the serial-numbers were left on record. They had not been filed off.

But one of them appeared, three weeks after the robbery, in Somerville, a town about five miles north of Boston. Two youngsters had found a couple of guns on the shore of the Mystic River, but when their fathers took the guns home at night, they threw them away. A policeman who was checking back doors in a line of shops discovered one of them. The other was thought to have been lost under a pile of debris when the check was made.

However, while the police were sifting these clues, the hunt for the get-away car continued, and eventually they came upon three persons who had a recollection of seeing a canvas-topped car parked at Brink's at around the time of the robbery. The car they had seen proved by elimination to be a 1949 Ford with what is called a 'rack body'.

The police then checked every such body in the State of Massachusetts. All were tracked down until eventually only one remained to be accounted for, a vehicle which had been stolen from a Boston dealer in September 1949. However, three months after the robbery, when the lorry was found, its appearance had been changed. Someone had worked with an acetylene blow-lamp and cut it into scrap metal, which had been distributed around Stoughton, some ten miles south of Boston. In addition to the total destruction, all identification-marks had been burned off the engine and chassis.

As was to be supposed, FBI agents had been quick off the mark as soon as the robbery was reported and within a few hours were crowding into Boston. But it was to be four months before they came up with information that a local gangster had been in on the robbery.

He was a man whose police record went back for twenty years and was known as Joseph 'Specks' O'Keefe. He had, in fact, been one of the first men the police had picked up for questioning. He had a good story. He said he had been drinking at the Copley Hotel bar that night, and the police had not been able to prove otherwise. But they had kept checking on such an unsavoury customer, and it was possible that, for this reason, O'Keefe felt that he was being watched. At any rate, in July he decided to head south with a friend named Stanley Gusciora. As soon as he did so, he found two FBI men tailing him, and the pair of crooks did not get far beyond Pennsylvania's borders. They had reached the town of Towanda in that state when they were stopped by a state policeman for, of all things, speeding. When stopped, they were found to have in their possession some 150 rounds of ammunition. The shells had all been stolen from a local hardware store.

When O'Keefe was put into the local jail, he tried to bribe Towanda's chief of police, Dean Meredith, with $70,000, to be split between him, three members of the State Police and the two FBI agents he had observed. On instructions from the FBI Meredith pretended to go along with the offer of a bribe, but unknown to O'Keefe the call he made to a Boston law office was tapped. They heard him ask for the money, and then they heard a contact-man, as he was called, tell O'Keefe that he could not raise the sum he wanted by half.

This appeared to put the gangster in a dilemma.

He spoke to the contact-man and said, "Look, if it's any question of getting only one of us out, then get him out. He's the more important."

He was referring to Gusciora.

This was an undercover break-through, and the two men were arrested and convicted in a Pennsylvania court of violating a firearms law. Actually O'Keefe got three years and Gusciora a much stiffer sentence, but it was clear that the skids had been driven under the bandits. Indeed the FBI were still tapping the call when O'Keefe phoned to his own home and asked the woman who replied if she had been questioned by an FBI man. When she said she had, he asked a question that sounded hurried.

"Was anything found?" he wanted to know.

"No," said the woman sharply.

O'Keefe's voice came out in a kind of heavy sigh.

"Well, just take care of the baby," he said, and then he

stressed the message: "You know what I mean."

She certainly did, and so did the FBI.

Indeed, their understanding now was that the loot had been shifted to O'Keefe's house, which turned out to be in Stoughton. But after the lengthy hearing it was December 1952, close to another Christmas, before the gangster was brought back to appear before a Boston grand jury, as the American term has it.

Called as witnesses were a dozen men, including Joseph O'Keefe. In a solid phalanx, they promptly evoked the Fifth Amendment to the Constitution and refused to reply to questions on the grounds that by so doing they might incriminate themselves. Judge William H. McCarthy took a dim view of such a proceeding, and he sentenced six of these witnesses for contempt of court. They were given terms of up to a year in jail, but they could, they felt, not risk being questioned.

However, in the case of O'Keefe, his constitutional right to plead the Fifth Amendment was something no 'legal eagle' could deny, for he had by that time been accused of participation in the Brink's armed robbery. He remained in jail, being frequently consulted by his lawyers, for a further year. Indeed, it was January 1953—actually the 15th—and precisely two days before the statute of limitations on armed robbery ran out, that the grand jury is said to have handed the case back to the Federal men in a coffin.

It was returned with no indictments.

At the time, three reasons were given. One was the inability to get witnesses to talk; the second was that the participants were not successfully disguised, and the third was that there was a lack of eye-witnesses. But the greatest objection was the FBI's wiretapping, because it could not be legally employed, and while the Government had contempt sentences hanging over the heads of the witnesses, the appeal court ruled that the witnesses had been within their constitutional rights in citing the Fifth Amendment.

The FBI found themselves having to reconsider their position. Certainly the statute of limitations had seemingly run out in a slow trickle, but they geared themselves to bring a fresh case into court. This was on a conspiracy charge for armed robbery and receiving stolen money. In all, the ancillary charges numbered a half-dozen.

By this time the case was attracting wide interest because of its outcome, and a fresh name was added to the headlines in the Press. It was that of George O'Brien, a man with a reputation as an armed handit, though apparently he had not until recently been considered one of the Brink's suspects. There was a sound enough reason for this: he had been in jail in January 1950 when the action was reported.

But the FBI was trained to pick out discrepancies, and one they fastened on when the reconsidered O'Brien's position was the seeming difference between the man's accredited income and the $20,000 home he was living in at the time when the Federal men came calling. They asked him to account for that anomaly.

Accordingly one day in November 1953 O'Brien called on the Massachusetts Co-operative Bank. He wanted to make the monthly payment on his mortgage, which had been taken out some time earlier. A cashier making a routine check against the serial numbers discovered that several of O'Brien's bills, totalling some $50, matched the serial numbers of some stolen from an armed robbery in Danvers, not far from Boston, on 25th March 1952.

Earlier, FBI agents had followed O'Brien, who, they suspected, had known about the Brink's robbery. When the connection with the robbery in Danvers was discovered, O'Brien was arrested. When he was searched, his wallet produced forty-five $1-bills and one of $10. They were quickly traced to the Danvers job.

While O'Brien was in jail, his home was searched, and more marked bills came to light. More than $10,000 were found either on his person or in his home. Of this $9,000 were in new and clean $20-bills. The serial numbers of these notes were still in sequence.

The mills of the gods were now really grinding small, and they were chewing up the Brink's bank-robbers.

O'Brien's trial was slated for April 1954.

His defence was the time-dishonoured one of having won the money gambling, but he elected not to give evidence on his own behalf. Furthermore, he did not produce a single bookmaker from whom he had won even a dollar. In short, there was no record of money having passed through his hands. However, these were curious times, as a number of reporters were constrained to point out. The phenomenal Brink's robbery was back on the front pages.

For all that, the New England jury took their own strange line with the trial. They were out for nearly an hour and three-quarters considering their verdict, and then they reappeared with their faces set obstinately—for the best of reasons, as everyone knew when George O'Brien spread his face in a wide grin.

The jury had acquitted him.

But so mysterious are the ways of the underworld, and so darkly dubious are the paths they travel, that at least one reporter stated later that the armed robber would have been better in jail. He had only two months' grace after his release and freedom from the watchers of the FBI. Then one day he was found dead at the wheel of his car. In crooks' parlance, he had been 'rubbed out'.

So once again the Brink's robbery stormed back onto the front pages of the Press. By this time several deep features had been written about the bandits and the tortuous trail they had left for the police and the FBI men. Yet further developments were known to be approaching.

One was the release of Joe O'Keefe, better known as 'Specs', for obvious reasons. He had been released in February from the jail in Pennsylvania. But there was going to be no respite in the violence he and his friends had engendered. This time the peace lasted some four months. Then, one midnight a few nights before the shortest night of the year, the early-morning hours were shattered by the sounds of machine-gun fire, directed at an estate where O'Keefe lived. But the police arrived to be confronted by more mystery on 15th June. They found that a watch had been virtually shot off the owner's wrist, leaving a trail of blood leading to a corner of the estate. The watch was the property of Joe O'Keefe. Besides the bloodstains and some shredded leaves of bushes, the detectives found an empty forty-five. They decided that O'Keefe had no liking to be taken for a 'patsy', and as soon as the others opened up, he had fired back.

But he was not to be found readily.

His friend John Carlson volunteered some information, claiming that O'Keefe had called him around midnight. It was a cry for help. Carlson had hurried to join his friend and found him bleeding from both wrist and chest. It was a story in keeping with others the police had heard in the recent past, for when the detectives returned to question Carlson further, he too had gone missing. They found his car and discovered his glasses with the frames bent double. It looked as though there had been a desperate struggle.

Then, a couple of days after the mysterious shooting in the suburb of Boston, plain-clothes men arrived from New York with special bulletins. These concerned a certain Elmer Burke, at one time called 'Trigger' for his fondness for lethal hardware. He was known as a hired killer or contract assassin. The men from New York had been on the look-out for him for over a twelvemonth. When they had received a tip-off from an informer that Burke was in Boston, they travelled at speed to make the contact.

As is the way of real-life incidents, a strange coincidence marked the occasion: a young policeman who was off duty saw Burke standing on a street corner. Being young and keen, he grabbed the man, and Burke, very much to his surprise and consternation, was put under arrest. The police were summoned, and in Burke's room they came upon a miniature arsenal, including an unusual weapon: a paratrooper type of gun, capable of 'squirting' nine hundred rounds a minute. Tests proved that it had been the gun that had fired at the housing-estate. But more important were pencilled notes that indicated Burke had received a phone-call telling him to meet O'Keefe at the estate at midnight.

It was a case of a criminal's falling into the lap of the police looking for him.

After congratulating the New York men, the Boston police sent them home, believing that Burke was securely held, for possession of a machine-gun in the State of Massachusetts carries life imprisonment.

In the meantime the Boston police were still trying to flush out O'Keefe, who had gone to ground like a fox. This took another six weeks, by which time his scars had healed. By then

O'Keefe had been imprisoned for some twenty-seven months, which was the time a probation order was back-dated to 1945. In the interim he had been talking too much for his own good. It was his talking that had led eventually to the conviction of the Brink's men. O'Keefe in truth had reached the end of a very rough road. He had spent some twenty years in jail, apart from a term of thirty days. When he was at length rounded up by the police, it was merely to return to prison with a good many characters hating him and believing he had a loose tongue in his head, which was never silent for long.

In a continuing case of arrest and inquiry, the man wanted by the New York police, Elmer Burke, was indicted and lodged in the Charles Street jail in Cambridge. He too had made the headlines. His trial was set for the middle of September. However, he was always an impatient man, not only with his quick use of a gun. Before the end of August he broke out of the Charles Street prison.

That was on 28th August 1954.

The FBI promptly dubbed him 'Public Enemy Number One'. It was a distinction that had been shared by a long line of criminals.

He lasted a tempestuous year of violence and savage underworld rivalry, but his end came in the manner of Dillinger and other mob-leaders, in a furious battle with the authorities. Eight FBI operatives finally pinned him down and cut off any retreat. But he went down leaking blood and badly wounded. Then he was patched up and awaited mending in a prison hospital.

Finally came a trial that was a sensation throughout the United States. He fought for his life with the pugnacity of a man bred to terror and crime. But for once he was a loser. What was more, he was seen to be one. Even then, when he arrived in Sing Sing, reporters fed his vanity and played up to his ego. However, on 9th January 1958 he sat down for the last time in the green electric chair in Sing Sing while a late night audience watched him and waited for the switch to be thrown.

Suddenly he was seen to jerk and remain stiffened, his body straining against the straps binding it.

Nearly five years had passed since the day a group of men wearing fancy masks had made their way through the garage to hold up the Brink's men in Boston. When the news of the electrocution reached the streets, it was said that Joseph 'Specs' O'Keefe spent his first restful night in months.

However, nearly thirty years have now passed since the famous robbery that staggered a nation, with seven men in Hallowe'en masks making criminal history when they appeared at the North Terminal Garage. Over those three decades eight men were eventually sentenced to life imprisonment.

The wages of sin were becoming exceptionally heavy. Moreover, there was every indication that they were more and more being found out, as the story of the Brink's men showed. However, it still remains on record that the Brink's robbers had contrived what is probably to date the most audacious and daring of all robbery conspiracies—as it was the most profitable.

Just possibly it was too profitable, and for that reason they made what was to prove a fatal mistake in their calculations. They took with them too much money, which led a trail of evidence that could be followed.

It was a mistake made later by the notorious Great Train Robbers at Leatherslade Farm in Buckinghamshire, but for Arthur Biggs and the other robbers it could not be claimed that the hold-up of the Brink's bandits had been in the nature of what could be called a dry run.

Too many had come to grief.

3

The Austrian Poison Queen

One of the loveliest of blonde *femmes fatales* to be executed in Austria came to her gruesome end on a cold, rainy morning in early December 1938. When she suddenly stuck out her right arm in a rigid-muscle motion and gave what the world had come to learn was the Hitler salute, just possibly it was a gesture of derision.

Yet one could never be sure with a woman of the curious mental make-up of Martha Löwenstein, for she had certainly provided that her own strangely philosophical emphasis to life was rather mocking. But philosophy could not help her when it came to the brutal crunch. It was lacking in decision. The same could not be said of her death. That was grim and resigned.

Martha was slender and willowy, and had been from the age of fourteen, when she first attracted the opposite sex with her pale allure. She had a heart-shaped face, waved hair which she parted high on the left side, trimmed brows and brown eyes which a number of males had found 'melting'. Her nose was slightly too wide to let her be truly beautiful. On occasion she could contrive a bewitching smile, which caused many to turn and look at her with a second glance, and she had a quality of pose and distinction about her, with her high cheekbones and smooth-textured skin that placed her out of the ordinary. She was not tall, but of medium height.

Although Martha claimed to be Austrian, she was actually

Hungarian, having been born in Sopron. She was the daughter of an unmarried farm-girl, but her mother had removed her to Vienna at an early age, where she married Rudolf Löwenstein, who worked on the Viennese State Railways.

The stepfather made arrangements for Martha to take his name, but it was all he gave her, for there was little money to pay for a grubbing and grudging existence, as we are told. In fact, Löwenstein obviously considered he had contracted a poor bargain by marrying Martha's mother, and he gave serious thought to how he could improve his lot. He found that one way was to emigrate. So he left without telling the Hungarian woman of his intention and crossed the ocean to reach the United States, where he was not heard from again. He had not been in any sense a shining example of step-fatherhood, and his disappearance into the American continent came as a relief to Martha's mother, who felt she had made a marital mistake. In any case, she was not disposed to repeat it.

Frau Löwenstein gave her child into the care of a children's home situated in the countryside not far from the Austrian capital. But the life to which the young Martha was introduced was a great distance from the Strauss waltzes of the Vienna Woods. She was brought up in slovenly circumstances, in a home organized for the children of the poorer classes. Most of them soon became nimble-fingered thieves and pick-pockets, and Martha herself acquired a hardening of attitudes and accomplishments that turned her into little more than a practised vagabond, with light fingers and wheedling ways.

For six years the child grew up in the shadow that had been cast by the stepfather's taking himself off, and then, when she was thirteen, her mother decided she was required back in Vienna, where she should start to earn her keep and, with any luck, aid her mother to fend for her. They lived in cheap working-class lodgings, and the mother found means for Martha to bring in a wage, arranging for her to be employed to run errands for a dress-shop. One thing Martha had learned at the children's home: how to use a smile and play a part when it was to her advantage. She almost forced her employer to notice her, and when she did so, the thirteen-year-old was quick with a street *gamine*'s ways to make the best of herself, so that it was not long before the man was using her as a model for his dress-shop. Indeed, wearing good clothes regularly became part of her usual payment, as a good advertisement for the shop.

Her quick and nimble figure became a regular feature of the Viennese streets. People noticed her bright and smiling face, with her chin slightly lowered and her eyes looking upward encouragingly. She received nods and smiles from total strangers who approved of her trim appearance and deft mannerisms.

Martha took to catching a regular tram when she left work at the dress-shop, and one day a well-dressed man who was rather elderly and had a dignified appearance stopped to speak to her when she sat down before the tram started.

"Am I right in assuming, Fräulein, that you are employed at a dress-shop?"

Martha turned and looked at him.

"Yes, that's right," she said cautiously, "and I believe I have seen you before."

The man smiled.

"That's more than possible," he nodded. "I am Moritz Fritsch, and I own the department-store next to your dress-shop. You run errands, don't you? I've seen you hurrying past our windows. In fact"—he smiled—"you always seem to be hurrying. You seldom dally."

Martha's eyes brightened with interest as she returned the man's smile. She knew that Fritsch was reputed to be very successful. He was a man of some sixty years but looked a good deal younger. She had heard the local gossip that he was rich.

She found herself being encouraged to talk about herself and her life. The man listening to her asked many questions which she seemed keen and eager to answer, almost tumbling over her words in her readiness to be responsive. The elderly store-owner continued to smile indulgently at her and to listen to what he must have thought was her youthful prattle.

When the tram arrived at her stop, he alighted with her and to her surprise turned and accompanied her to her home, which he saw at a glance was very poor. He seemingly had some intention in mind, for he suddenly announced, "I'd very much like to meet your mother, Fräulein."

Martha, still clutching a dress she had brought home with her, flushed and looked pleased at what she thought was a compliment, so she introduced the Hungarian woman to the store-owner. Then, after a few minutes of Viennese chit-chat he raised his hat and took his departure, walking sedately to the next tram-stop. Mother and daughter watched him catch the tram and be trundled away towards a different part of the city.

After sitting up late over her evening meal, Martha went to her own small room, to ponder about the store-owner. When she retired for the night, she asked, "Why should he want to see you, Mother?"

Frau Löwenstein shrugged.

"Who can say what runs through a man's head?" she asked. "Especially when that head has looked at someone as pretty as my daughter?" she added with a thoughtful look.

A few days later Martha thought she knew the meaning of that look, as well as the answers to some of her questions, for there arrived a formal invitation for her to have lunch with Moritz Fritsch.

"Make yourself look your best," advised Frau Löwenstein.

It was advice Martha was quick to adopt, and when she met the store-owner he glanced at her appreciatively, for she made a demure and very pretty picture of youth and happiness. Indeed, Fritsch found her quite alluring.

"I've been remembering your smile," he told her. "In fact, I couldn't get it out of my mind."

He ushered her into a large restaurant and then, when she was settled and pecking at her food, suddenly came out with a direct question.

"How would you like to come and live with me in my villa?" he inquired.

Martha's smile became a trifle strained, for she had heard about old men who requested what they called 'favours' from young girls. But she had agreed with her mother that, if she took things carefully, she might well be on to a very good thing—something very much better than the dress-shop.

"Where is it?" she asked quietly.

"At Moedling. It's in the country and is a very pretty place. I'm sure you'd like it there, Martha, for I'd see to it that you would have every advantage. I'm a lonely man and have grown tired of being on my own."

By asking questions, Martha learned that he had been married young, but that he had been divorced. He said his children had grown up and had long ago left home.

"That is why I am lonely," he insisted, starting to urge her to agree to live with him. However, he did not get around to the subject of re-marriage. Martha played him along like a fish on a line, and the play became instinctive with her. She felt she would have no trouble in handling the store-owner. When he grasped her hand and became importunate, she knew he was hooked.

By the time the lunch was over, the oddly assorted pair had come to an understanding, and a few days later Martha left her mother's home in a low-class region of Vienna and moved into the store-owner's villa in the high-class suburb of Moedling, not far from the Austrian capital. There she settled down as though she were the mistress of the establishment, but in name only, for Fritsch was keen on his paramour's completing the formal education she had neglected, and in truth Martha was very ready to better herself in any way she could, realizing that in the long term it must be to her advantage.

For three years she continued her studies. In the vacations she travelled, to Britain and Italy and other parts of the Continent, acquiring culture by the easiest of means, with Fritsch paying the bills and settling the accounts, something he was happy to do when he saw how enviously other men looked at Martha. The attentions she received gave him pleasure, as much as though they had been earned. When she was seventeen and left finishing-school, she returned to live at Moedling.

Like many girls who have enjoyed easy living because of innate loveliness, she had become a character of vibrant moods. She was almost a person of two personalities, not exactly dual but able to change from one person to the other with her moods, just as she changed her dresses and fashionable footwear. She had certainly developed into considerable beauty, which enhanced her sophistication, and certainly when she was so disposed she could charm the birds from the trees—and there were quite a few trees in the Vienna Woods.

But Martha was careful not to give Fritsch any reason to regret his bargain. As a matter of fact, he came to think increasingly that it was the best bargain he had ever made, and so besotted was he that he continued to lavish clothes, jewels and furs on the young woman who had come to mean everything to him. If he was not in love with her, he was in love with the image of her, and apparently that was sufficient. They were seen at expensive hotels and restaurants, at the best night-spots and at first nights. Nothing seemed too good for the lovely creature who paraded at his side and was adornment in her own self.

But, in the way of the world, rumours about the pair and their way of life collected and grew, and the idyll became somewhat bruised and coarsened by repetition and usage. Stories about their unusual habits, of what the stationmaster at Moedling had seen and the different labels on their luggage, eventually became current and grew each time they were told. They became a scandal which was enjoyed behind closed doors. Fritsch became known as the girl's 'guardian', and Martha was termed his 'ward'. The sniggers did not reach the ears of either—perhaps they were not allowed to.

As Martha grew older, she gradually became more difficult to live with, and there were times when even Fritsch found her antics intolerable, especially when she took to screaming. He was forgiving, in his fashion, always remembering that there was some fifty years' difference in their ages, but he was not happy at the way things in his home were drifting. He was a man who liked order in his personal affairs, and that was something that was missing since Martha had come into his life.

He surprised her by announcing one day, "I've made a new Will, for I feel it is time I put my affairs in order."

Martha stared round-eyed at him and suddenly felt the stirring of a latent fear.

"Tell me about it," she said quietly.

"It's really straightforward," he said. "I'm leaving a third of my estate to Bette, whom I divorced. This is as the law declares. Then my children are to receive agreed sums. All else, including the villa at Moedling and my insurance, will eventually come to you, Martha." He looked at her and saw that a sparkle brightened the brown eyes. She gave him a swift kiss.

"Happy?" he asked her.

She shook her head, smiling and squeezing his arm.

"You mustn't talk about such things," she told him in a way that passed for fondness. "I forbid it. There's nothing wrong with your health—or is there? Tell me," she urged, the brown eyes regarding him closely.

He gave a short laugh.

"No, there is nothing wrong with my health. Sometimes I think I'll live to be a hundred."

The new Will was forgotten—or at least not discussed, but gradually a change came over Martha. Fritsch's 'ward' took to leaving little notes explaining why she would be away visiting her mother. The frequency of these visits puzzled the storekeeper. He found himself forced to spend lonely nights at the villa. He never questioned Martha's absences, but he considered it somewhat strange that usually after visiting her mother the girl appeared to be in high spirits and cheerful.

Then, rather suddenly, at the age of seventy-four, Moritz Fritsch died. He suffered only a brief illness, and Martha was at his bedside, full of attention and plumping up his pillows and straightening the bedclothes. When the sheet had been drawn over the dead face by his physician, a Dr Pollack, Martha became distraught and seemed to collapse.

The doctor shook his head as she dried her tears.

"I fail to understand what happened. He seems to have suffered a paralysis of his general system. It's quite remarkable, and I fail to find a reason for it."

It was a subject he returned to when the Will had been read in the presence of Bette Fritsch, who was now the owner of a popular Viennese café. She took the doctor on one side.

"I'd like to speak to you privately," she said. "It was Moritz's intention, after we were divorced, to leave the estate to me and the children. As you know, he was much older than I. Why did he draw up a new Will?"

Dr Pollack seemed uncomfortable under the woman's direct gaze.

"As a matter of fact," he said, "I was a witness to the new Will. He was very keen that it should be made."

"Then that creature of the streets is at the bottom of his mysterious death," she declared angrily. "I'm sure of it."

The doctor stared aghast at her.

"I'd like to have the body exhumed," she said firmly.

The doctor made little plaintive noises suggesting she reconsider what she was saying.

"Exhuming a buried body can involve you in many regulations and brings in its train considerable publicity—usually of a most unwelcome kind. It wouldn't be pleasant for your family."

"Nevertheless," said Frau Fritsch obdurately, "that is what I propose."

"In that case I'll make inquiries," said the doctor, "but the outcome could be ugly."

He shook his head dolefully and after the woman had left took occasion to talk to the lawyer who had drawn up the new Will. The latter invited Fritsch's son to call at his office, accompanied by the physician.

Fritsch's son explained that his mother was, as he put it, "insanely jealous" of his father's so-called ward.

"She was very bitter about his changing his Will," he told the professional pair, "but for my part I'm quite satisfied that my father's death was perfectly normal. What's more, despite what my mother says, I don't intend to have my father's bones disturbed. Such a thing is highly distasteful to me and the family, and I would be grateful if you would let her know how I feel. Indeed, my mind is made up. I want no publicity or scandal."

"Certainly I am quite prepared to let the death-certificate stand," said Dr Pollack.

"It would certainly seem best for all concerned," muttered the lawyer. "There have been more than enough idle rumours."

"Precisely," nodded the doctor.

So Frau Fritsch was talked out of her intention to have her ex-husband's bones removed from their recent interment, and a family scene was averted in the name of publicity—or the prevention of it.

The years drifted by in a slow progression, and Martha duly received her inheritance, though her expectations were less than she had expected. She continued to live at the villa and usually dressed in well-fitting black, which set off her fair skin and hair.

The neighbours at Moedling, taking an interest in the young woman, observed that she left the villa several times a week. Sometimes she returned accompanied by a young man with dark hair who was invariably dressed neatly and without any display of ostentation. Then, a few months after Fritsch's death the people of Moedling heard that Martha had married the man and had settled down with her husband in the villa. The news percolated that his name was Emil Marek. He was younger than Martha, twenty, while she was twenty-three. He was an engineer working at the Vienna Technical Institute, but his studies came to a swift end with the advent of Martha into his life and their subsequent marriage. As though conscious of his youth, he grew a full beard.

Marek turned some of the rooms in the villa into a laboratory for scientific experiments. Soon he interested the Austrian Government in a project for electrifying a province known as Burgenland. The scheme marked time for more than a year, then the authorities came up with a suggestion: if Marek would put up half the capital, they would raise a similar sum. Marek expected a show of enthusiasm from his wife, but she poured cold water on the Burgenland project.

"I can't afford the money," she stated roundly. "I've been poor in the past, and I intend never to become penniless again, so I'm not investing my own money. If the Government want the project, let them find the cash. I don't intend to."

However, she apparently modified her views, for towards the end of May Emil Marek seemed to be a happy man, making an application to the Anglo-Danubian Lloyd Company of Vienna for life insurance. They considered the application and in due course insured Marek's life for a sum equivalent to £25,000, though the policy contained a clause that stipulated that in the vent of his suffering a permanent disability he would be paid four times that sum. The first month's premium became due on 11th June.

Two days later Martha made an urgent phone-call to the insurance company. Her husband had had an accident and was being rushed to the Moedling Hospital. Herr Moeller, the Anglo-Danubian official who had approved the terms of the insurance, consulted Herr Swoboda, a branch-manager, and they informed the police, who had been summoned. Inspector Ludwig Peternell explained that Marek had been chopping some wood with a sharp axe when the blade slipped. It caught him a slicing blow which almost severed his leg below the knee.

"If it had not been for his wife's presence of mind in tightening a tourniquet," said the senior surgeon at the Moedling Hospital, "he would surely have bled to death."

It was the insurance-man Swoboda who raised doubts as to whether the smashed leg was indeed an accident.

"He had made only one down-payment on his policy. In the exceptional circumstances, I feel we should have the leg examined by the Vienna Medical Institute." He and Moeller exchanged a long glance. "We must speak further with Inspector Peternell."

In due course they joined the inspector, and when Martha led them to a back garden, they saw the lengths of firewood and dried pools of blood.

"It was shortly before midday," Martha explained, "and I was gardening when I heard Emil's cries for help. I hurried to him and saw the blood. The axe had missed its stroke and smashed his leg. I got a maid to fetch Herr Doorzak from the fire-station. He helped me to tie up the leg until the ambulance arrived."

But it was a very subdued Frau Marek who left with her visitors. The axe, according to the Vienna detectives, must have been wiped clean. It held no fingerprints.

The next day Herr Moeller received a report on the severed and smashed leg, which had been cleanly amputated. Professor Meizner from Vienna had examined the leg, which showed three distinct axe-blows. He asked how Martha could have seen her husband slip three separate times, with the blade landing in the same place. "I can't imagine," was all she said, and then she was allowed to return home.

But the Inspector Peternell had another conference with Herr Moeller, at which he suggested that the 'accident' had been deliberate. The insurance official seemed shocked at the suggestion.

"You're implying that Marek and his wife acted in collusion? By heaven, that's terrible, Inspector!"

It was indeed, for at the end of a further day the Mareks were placed under arrest on charges of attempted fraud on the insurance company. They were given bail, Marek in his hospital bed, Martha under custody at the villa. Overnight the case had become a sensation throughout Austria, but the blonde wife of a self-induced cripple provided additional sensation of her own when the trial was still some weeks away. She summoned reporters and told them that she had positive proof that the insurance company had been conspiring with the hospital to cheat her husband out of the money due to him.

"The surgeons," she claimed, "arranged it so that the leg would appear to have been severed by three blows. I know this because a hospital-worker overheard the insurance-officials talking to the medical staff, and later he told me he saw a surgeon handling the leg when my husband was unconscious and before the amputated leg was dispatched to Professor Meizner."

The name of the hospital orderly who had overheard the men was said to be Karl Mraz.

The following day large headlines spread the report and Mraz's name, but within a few hours there was a blistering denial of the libellous story. When he was confronted by Inspector Peternell, the orderly grew apprehensive and nervous. It did not take the inspector long to discover that Martha had bribed Mraz to say at the trial that he had seen the leg being tampered with. The orderly left under close arrest. Then Peternell confronted husband and wife with the story. Marek remained silent, enduring his pain stoically, but Martha was vehement in her denials.

"I haven't even heard of this Mraz or set eyes on him," she asserted. "The whole thing is a figment of his imagination."

But she was lodged in a woman's prison, where her cell-mate, by some extraordinary chance, was a woman awaiting trial for poisoning her husband, whose name was Lichtenstein. The poison she had used had been thallium, which was both tasteless and odourless, and it is thought that the information given Martha by her cell-mate provided her with more than the germ of an idea for what happened subsequently.

When the Mareks came to trial, it was to find that public opinion firmly supported them, and for a time they were toasted and won approval throughout Austria, for few people could believe that Martha had swung the axe at her husband's leg. After a long hearing there was a split decision: the Mareks were found not guilty of attempted fraud for insufficient evidence, but guilty of trying to bribe the hospital orderly, for which each was sentenced to four months in prison, though because of the time they had already spent in jail they were summarily released. Mraz went to prison for six weeks, though few understood why or wherefore.

Meanwhile, the lawyers of the Anglo-Danubian Lloyd Company had worked to get the Mareks to agree on a settlement. When there was even a hint that Moritz Fritsch's body might be exhumed, Martha urged her husband to make a very modest settlement, as little as the equivalent of £1,500.

The publicity of the case resulted in the Austrian Government's no longer being interested in Marek's scheme for Burgenland. He bought an artificial leg and invested in a fleet of taxis which went broke. Then he interested several Austrians in a project for manufacturing cheap radios for the Algerian market, and Martha sold her villa, and she and Marek journeyed to North Africa. There things went wrong from the start, and they were glad to return to Vienna, where they settled in cheap rooms in the suburb of Heitzing.

The one-time proud beauty was reduced to helping on a vegetable-stall in a market, and poverty seemed to cling to the couple, to whom two children were born, Alfons and Ingeborg. Then Martha's mother died.

In Germany the Nazis had come to power, but politics were nothing to interest Martha. She was more concerned, when in early July 1932, Marek became very ill and lost weight. He told his friends that his legs had become numb, that his sight was failing and that he had difficulty in swallowing. A doctor said he appeared to be in an advanced state of tuberculosis and should immediately go to hospital. He entered a charity institution, where he seemed to fade before his wife's moist brown eyes. He died on the last day of July. A little over a month later, his daughter joined him. Her unexpected death was given as due to natural causes.

A friend of Martha's took care of the boy Alfons, and for the first time in years the blonde woman, who was now over thirty, felt free of encumbrances. She donned her best clothes and called on Suzanne Löwenstein, the aunt of her mother's husband who was quite well off and who seemed delighted to see her after so many years. Over a cup of coffee Martha agreed to become Frau Löwenstein's companion. She had not been with her long when she took to going out at night, while the older woman was sleeping. She became a typical Viennese *boulevardière*, circulating and enjoying the bright lights and listening to the music.

Curiously Frau Löwenstein's health started to fail, quite inexplicably. In June 1934 a doctor was called. He promptly ordered the older woman to bed on a special diet, which Martha cooked and served to the patient. But the aunt's illness grew worse; she began to lose her hair, and her sight began to deteriorate progressively. On 11th July 1934 she died, and the doctor who had attended her duly signed the normal death-certificate.

By Frau Löwenstein's death, Martha inherited a fair sum in cash and insurance as well as costly furnishings. She at once moved to a large apartment in the fashionable Kuppelweisergasse, and she gathered a new circle of friends, who were content to live on her until her money was about to run out.

Then she met Jeno Neumann, an insurance-agent and widower of nearly fifty, who took over the lease of her apartment. Martha also advertised for someone to share her home, and thus met Felicitas Kittenberger, a seamstress, with few resources, who was easily persuaded to insure her life. A couple of months after the policy was signed, and very much to Neumann's surprise, for he had advised Martha about the policy, Frau Kittenberger became ill, with familiar symptoms, and died on 2nd June 1936. When her son Herbert arrived and called Martha a murderess, she, taking the bull by the horns, summoned the police and told them of Herr Kittenberger's charge. They pacified the angry son, and when he learned from his mother's doctor that she had died of natural causes, his anger evaporated.

Then, like a bolt from a very deep blue, on the last day of October in that same year, 1936, Inspector Peternell received a phone-call from Martha.

When he arrived at her flat, she pointed to bare places on the walls.

"My pictures and tapestries have been stolen," she announced rather grandly.

"Were they insured?" Peternell inquired.

"Yes," she declared. "My agent, Herr Neumann, had taken that precaution, Inspector."

The inspector left with a list of the stolen articles, but he remembered Martha Marek and when he returned to headquarters had another detective, Josef Gunacker, make further inquiries. Through him a removal-man was found who had, on 30th October, rather late at night, taken some rolled-up packages to a warehouse in Vienna. Further questioning and checking of the address of the parcels resulted in Martha's arrest, again on a charge of attempting to defraud an insurance company. A fresh scandal washed over the city, and when the newspapers reported it, one of the first persons to hurry to the police was Herbert Kittenberger.

"I'm now sure my mother was poisoned by the woman," he declared, "so I'm insisting that you exhume her."

Thus in a very roundabout way Martha Löwenstein got her deserts. Kittenberger's insistence meant that the authorities had to take notice of his demand, and one by one Emil Marek, Ingeborg Marek and Suzanne Löwenstein were disinterred. A lethal amount of thallium was found in their bodies.

Only prompt action on the part of the police and medical authorities saved the life of young Alfons Marek, for he had already been doctored with lethal poison, and in the Viennese hospital where he was rushed he confided to a nurse that he was soon going to heaven to join his father. The Austrian public who had earlier shouted encouragement to Martha now turned against her and villified her.

She was brought to trial on 2nd May 1938, eleven years after her first. Two months earlier Hitler had crossed into Austria and established the Greater German Reich, to the acclaim of the populace. It was a harsh time for justice, but Martha adopted a philosophical attitude to her fate. She of course denied everything and calmly faced a hostile crowd in court as the prosecutor, Herr Wotawa, declared her to be another Lucrezia Borgia. Then she broke down and sobbed, but all her appeals failed. She seemed impervious to the fact that young Alfons was recovering from her ministrations.

A few days before Christmas 1938, she was led to the execution-shed with a cold, wintry rain falling. She gave the Nazi salute, then she was bound and forced down to meet her end with the axe. There was a dull thud as her neck was severed. Then some sand was sprinkled over the ground and a squad of Nazi guards turned and goose-stepped away.

She was the first woman to be executed in Austria for sixty years.

4

Vibrations That Rang for Murder

Just over twenty years ago, in October 1956, there was growing gloom in Pinewood, a small South African town which was really a suburb of Durban and where the Atken family had their pleasant home. The gloom was occasioned by the failure of the daughter to return home. Her parents were understandably worried and more than a little apprehensive, for neither Fred Atken nor his wife Isabel could remember an occasion when their daughter, Myrna Joy, a smiling girl of eighteen, had not come home at her usual time, shortly after five o'clock, when her Durban office closed.

Now it was after eight o'clock.

That was why the Atkens were becoming worried. In fact, Fred was growing more concerned than he cared to let his wife perceive. For one thing, Joy's office was only a twelve-mile ride from Durban; the girl had given her mother no reason for supposing she would be late, and normally she was considerate and thoughtful and understood that her being several hours late would cause her mother to grow anxious about her and her safety. Also she knew that her brothers would become worried, as well as her parents, for the Atkens were a close-knit family, very much involved in each other's lives, sharing both pleasures and problems.

Colin, the elder brother, was a man of twenty-eight, who was very fond of Myrna Joy—or simply 'Joy' as she was customarily termed. He looked upon her as his kid sister and would have done anything for her. His brother Graham was younger by some four years.

They all fell silent as eight o'clock passed, and the elder son kept glancing at his mother, while studiously careful not to catch his father's eye. Isabel Atken was constantly turning to the clock, as though she felt she must continue to stare at its face, willing the hands to move slowly. At the same time her fingers plucked at her mouth, only to fall after a few tremulous seconds into her lap, where her hand remained listless, although it jerked nervously. She and Joy had intended to join a dancing-class that evening, and they had both talked over the prospect as something new in their lives.

Suddenly she gave a little cry.

"Oh, why doesn't she come home?" she said tearfully to her husband.

He took hold of her hand and patted it encouragingly.

"Gently," he said soothingly. "After all, there may be a very simple reason for the delay. You mustn't get panicky, Isabel. That's not going to help anyone."

But they were words easier to say than to live through, and when half-past ten showed on the clock, and still no word from their daughter, he suddenly rose and squared his shoulders as though he had made a swift resolve. The others looked up at him expectantly.

"I'm going to notify the police," he announced. "I'll have a word with Sergeant Grobler."

Grobler was a police-sergeant who had known the family from the time Joy herself was a little girl.

Atken crossed to the telephone and picked up the instrument. Impatiently he toyed with the flex. He was put through and spoke hurriedly. Then he cradled the phone and broke the connection as he turned around.

"Grobler's coming," he said shortly.

His wife looked relieved that such a stalwart as Sergeant N. J. Grobler was about to find out why Joy was so late in coming home.

At eleven o'clock the sergeant arrived and was shown into the living-room, but he had time only to ask a few questions before the phone pealed. Colin was prompt to pick it up.

"Hallo," he said. "Is that you, Joy?"

Vibrations That Rang for Murder

A few moments later he shook his head at the others. The caller was a girl called Ivy who worked in Joy's office. She was ringing up to inquire why the Atken women had not turned up at their dancing-class.

"You mean to say that Joy hasn't been home at all?" she asked in some alarm. "But she left at five in the normal way. I saw her getting into a car." Then she paused uncertainly. "As a matter of fact, I can't remember seeing it previously. But I think it was a Ford Anglia and fairly new. It was certainly some pale colour."

Grobler moved across to ask if she had noticed the driver or what he looked like, but she had not. She had been kept answering some questions at the office, and when she had looked again for the car it was gone.

"Can you tell me," inquired the sergeant, "if you know of any of Joy's men-friends who would be using such a car?"

But Ivy said she had no idea.

"You don't know the car's number?" Grobler asked.

"No," she said.

After a few more questions the sergeant rang off.

"It's getting on for midnight," he said, "and I've got some further inquiries to make. I suggest Isabel gets a good night's sleep."

A tearful wife accompanied her husband to bed, but there was little sleep for the Atkens for what was left of the night. The next day was Wednesday 3rd October, a bright spring day in Natal, and by halfway through the morning the police had checked on the missing girl's friends. Several of them somewhat reluctantly said that Joy had sometimes spoken of being restricted at home.

"She said," reported one, "that she was thinking of leaving home and supporting herself, but I don't know if she really meant it, or if it was just talk."

Grobler and a detective named Caspar Nel took this information rather seriously. They told the Atken family that it seemed likely that Joy had gone off on her own quite suddenly and unexpectedly.

"You mean she's run away from home?" asked a perplexed father. "But Isabel and I and the boys would have done anything for her, given her anything. She had only to say."

"I'm sure that was so," said Grobler, "but one cannot always think the way a young girl does, so when we find her, you have to be patient with her. Is it possible that she has eloped?"

The question was asked almost casually, but the Atkens' immediate reaction to any such suggestion made the sergeant fear he might be near to the truth.

Fred Atken said that any such suggestion was ridiculous.

"If Joy was thinking of eloping, it would have been with young Hugh, and I saw him only this morning, so that answers your question."

But Grobler felt less sure, and he knew Hugh Finlayson had already been questioned and cleared by the police, as had the other young men Joy had dated in the past few months. Grobler returned home and conferred with Nel, and the detective started several new inquiries, hoping to discover what had happened to the missing teenager. One thing was clear: so far as both men knew, the girl had not become mixed up in a fast clique that sported flashy cars and whose choice in women might be just as flashy.

On Friday the 5th they interviewed the girl Ivy, to find out if she could remember anything she might have forgotten earlier. They took her through the days since 24th September and, after reaching that day, continued hour by hour through each business day of that last week of September. It was a process that jogged Ivy's memory several times. On one occasion, on Friday the 28th, in particular, she and Joy and another girl were sitting down at lunch-time eating their sandwiches when a smiling stranger with a breezy and easy manner appeared before the girls, who stopped chewing as he said loudly, "Hallo, cookie!" Ivy had looked up startled, but the hail was apparently meant for Joy, for she greeted the stranger and gave him a broad smile.

Ivy told Casper Nel that the unknown was a man in his mid-thirties, as she supposed. He was of medium height and had well-brushed brown hair that was combed back. She thought his eyes were either light blue or grey. He was neatly dressed.

"But you couldn't say he was a dandy, if you know what I mean," she said. Then she turned to the detective, and her manner became more earnest. "Still, there was something about his ears," she added.

"How do you mean?" asked Nel.

"My impression was that they were too big, making his face seem odd."

"A very good point," the detective approved and with Grobler went over the various details again.

It was this constant repetition that caused Ivy to recall something else now. In the middle of the afternoon on the day she disappeared, Joy had received a phone-call. Such personal calls were not encouraged by the firm's management, and Joy's produced some jokes among the other girls. One asked if it was "Hello, cookie" ringing, but Joy had made no reply, and the subject of the phone-call was dropped. Joy did not appear to welcome the jokes.

"About what time was the call made?" asked Nel.

Just before four, he was told. But Ivy could not provide any further information, and Nel and Grobler left to join Major Norman Parker, their divisional chief of police in Natal, who asked about the progress they were making. Nel, who was the spokesman, told him that her family claimed she had not eloped.

"In fact, her father considers any such notion quite inconceivable," he told Major Parker. "Frankly I'm inclined to agree and so is the sergeant," he said, nodding to Grobler.

"That leaves us with murder," retorted the major. "In which case she has been killed by her abductor—or have you any other suggestion?"

Nel shook his head, but he did not look happy.

"So the chances are," went on the Natal police chief, "that as recently as last Tuesday her killer or abductor was seen to be driving a Ford Anglia, and from your checking it would seem that he either owns it or else borrowed it from someone, perhaps a friend. Well, we must go on checking, especially Ford Anglias."

After the discussion with Major Parker, the first report of significance came in. That was on the Saturday. It was received at Amanzimtoti, many miles out in the bush, where Constable Nienaber had seen an Anglia parked in a section of paved streets with built-up houses. Being an alert officer,

Johannes Nienaber had walked over and spoken to the Ford's driver, a man of about thirty-five. The man spoke agreeably and gave the constable a ready grin. He said he had been driving and felt hot and tired, and had parked to cool off and, if possible, catch what breeze there was.

"But I don't seem to be in luck," he smiled.

The Anglia started up and drove off. However, later that day Nienaber saw the Ford again and spoke to the driver, who said he still felt tired and 'rinsed out'.

Next a Durban man attached to one of Parker's squads was able to trace a witness who remembered seeing a pretty girl who was in her late teens and had a vivacious manner. She was in a Ford that might have been an Anglia. When the witness was located, he said he might have seen Joy Atken with the sand-coloured car. He was asked if he could place the time. He said about quarter past five on Tuesday 2nd October. However, his most vital piece of evidence was the name of the Ford's driver. He said he had actually recognized the man as Clarence van Buuren.

This was a considerable leap forward.

Major Parker's men were soon checking records, and they found that he was a man who had been several times in trouble with the police. In fact, he had a record dating from 1939. Then the police found the name of his employer, who ran an electrician's firm and radio outfit. He employed van Buuren as a salesman who worked on radio-repairs in his spare time. The employer, when the police called on him, said that van Buuren had gone off on a job for him sometime around midday on 2nd November, but there had been an extended silence. Nothing had been heard of the radio-repairman for fifty hours or so. On the Thursday van Buuren had phoned in and said he was not feeling well but promised to report again on the Friday.

"I told him to return the firm's car," his employer told the police, "and he agreed to do so, but when I arrived at the office, there was no sign of him, though our beige Anglia was parked outside and the car-keys had been dropped through the letter-box."

The employer said he had examined the car and found some live ammunition in the glove-compartment. When he held out the cartridges, Sergeant Grobler took them and chinked them in his hand. Van Buuren's address was out of date, but his employer had his recent one. When he handed it over, Grobler had a surprise: it was a town apartment in Pinewood, only a quarter of a mile from the Atkens' home.

Grobler and Nel found another surprise when they visited the Pinewood address. Van Buuren had a wife who was living with him. Her name was Yvonne, and she was the mother of two small children. She had her own woeful story to tell: she had not seen her husband for the past week.

"I've no idea where he is," she said tearfully as she told her story to the police-officers. "I don't know where he's gone or why. He's kept me in utter ignorance."

Later the same day forensic tests on the Ford Anglia brought up some minute bloodstains. But there was nothing to point directly to murder, though the police continued their intensive search for the part-time radio-repair man.

At the same time Colin Atken decided to undertake a curious mission of his own, largely because he and his family seemed to be making no progress with the police investigation, and he was impatient to know what had happened to his sister. So he called to see a man named Nelson Palmer, who was a widely proclaimed spiritualist of repute throughout Natal, and indeed in other parts of South Africa. For more than thirty years he had been a solver of problems for persons who came to him in mental distress and wanting his advice and assistance.

When Colin Atken told the spiritualist of the mystery concerning his sister and her strange disappearance, he asked Palmer quite openly, "Can you help me?"

The spiritualist frowned and considered his reply.

"I very much hope I can," he said softly. "Tell me, do you think your sister is dead?"

"That's what I fear," said the young man. "Otherwise she would have contacted us."

The spiritualist nodded and then took Colin Atken into the study of his own home, where his wife and son collaborated in holding a séance. When all were seated around a table, and the room was in darkness, the medium sank into a trance, first relaxing then noticeably stiffening before his lips moved.

When his voice came, it was abrupt and terse, quite unlike his normal voice. The words were short. When the medium spoke, he said quite clearly so that anyone listening could hear: "From fifty to sixty miles south. In a culvert. Over two hills, and in a culvert. Near water, lots of water—hills and bush and water."

Then he sighed and stopped, as though the spoken words had dried up on mental blotting-paper. As Colin Atken described the experience later, it was uncanny. When the spiritualist emerged from the trance a little later, he was unable to repeat the words he himself had spoken in a different voice, but Colin remembered them quite clearly. They were imprinted on his memory, and the experience was one he would never forget.

At once he was anxious to round up a party who would start searching for this culvert and the wide sheet of water. A group of searchers in two cars drove through Natal to the region of Umtwalumi, which was only about two hours away. They arrived, accompanied by the Palmers, at about two o'clock. The date was 10th October.

It took some little time to locate the precise place recalled by the medium in his trance, but suddenly Palmer stopped and held up a hand as a signal.

He said, "I feel we are close now, because I felt familiar vibrations, which are quite distinctive. I am sure we are now on the right track, and we should find your sister, Colin."

The group spread out, widening the area of search. At length they came upon the culvert, almost buried under the Natal Coast Road, about a mile and a quarter north of the village of Umtwalumi. When the medium saw it, he again pointed.

"That's where we shall find her," he announced quietly.

He stood unmoving and not trembling as he continued to indicate the place he had found.

The culvert lay some ten feet under the coast road. When the seekers climbed down into the dip, they soon came upon a piece of bloodstained petticoat, and after another search of the culvert Nelson Palmer came upon something that made him quiver. It was a pair of female legs. Investigation revealed that a naked body had been thrust firmly and brutally into a narrow hole head first. But it had apparently become wedged and was sunk no more than a foot from the outer rim.

As Colin Atken was able to state, it was the remains of his murdered sister. The young victim had been savagely mutilated after being shot in the head several times. Later it was to be established that parts of her crotch area had been too badly cut about for a medical examiner to be able to establish whether or not she had been sexually assaulted.

The discovery of the misused body of their sister sent the Atken brothers post-haste to bring the police. The news of what had been found sent shock-waves through the local community, and the police were quickly on the scene, angry that such a crime had been perpetrated in such a brutal manner.

The police, who now searched the culvert region closely, soon came upon a floral dress covered with mud and stained with splotches of blood—a dress which a trembling and shocked Isabel Atken identified as the one her daughter had worn on the morning of 2nd October. When the police had finished their preliminary examinations, they removed the body, which was taken to Durban for a post-mortem examination.

The examiners in the forensic department found that five bullets had been fired into the victim's body. They were bullets from a 22-calibre Beretta pistol, two of which had lodged in the brain. The time of death had to be fixed officially, and this was later given as sometime between eight and nine p.m. on the day the girl had disappeared.

In short, during that evening when the family waited for the girl to return home, she was actually lying dead and naked. The whole family had been buoying themselves up desperately against the inevitable, but now they gave way to a truly tragic grief. The house in Pinetown became a home of mourning for a brutally murdered daughter and sister whose bright and cheerful personality had been snuffed out by a deliberate act of savagery.

One of the first persons to be affected by the news from Pinetown was a young mother: Yvonne van Buuren collapsed under the news given to her by the police. The murder left her shattered, with her life in ruins spread around her. She refused to see reporters, and a police guard had to be put on her home. She sat through days with the curtains drawn, trying to live through the long and hopeless hours.

Through them all the hunt for her husband continued with no let-up. Almost a hundred police-officers were searching for him by the evening of the day of the terrible discovery of the body in the culvert, where the ground was being examined and sifted for possible clues. For one thing was certain: the public were anxious to increase their knowledge of the crime and the criminal. Within hours of the séance's being held in Nelson Palmer's home and its incredible outcome, the newsmen of Durban had a story that would hold the headlines for weeks.

On the day following the find in the culvert, a sharp-eyed African servant noticed a man who seemed to fit the police description of the now urgently wanted man. He saw him creeping through some bushes on his master's property, and, ducking to one side without being observed, he hurried away to warn the police.

His excited, shining face was presented to Sergeant Grobler, who saw at once that he brought news. He did indeed, for on his way to the police station the hurrying African had run full tilt into Sergeant van Wyk, accompanied by a constable.

"What's the hurry?" asked van Wyk.

The man panted his news, pointed through the trees and bushes and was quickly sent on his way to tell Grobler of the changed situation.

The two police-officers turned around and started a fresh search for the wanted man. They saw him trying to evade capture and searching the undergrowth and greenery. A branch snapped under van Buuren's foot, startling him, and he spun around and saw the police half screened by the close vegetation.

Sergeant van Wyk shouted and pulled his gun. He cut loose with a warning shot, clipping the leaves from some trees. The gunfire startled a woman who lived across the road from the police-station, not far from the Atken home, and pretty soon she heard rustling sounds as van Buuren pushed his way through the undergrowth where it was thickest. Other shots were fired, and the now thoroughly scared woman bundled her two children into a room where they were playing and turned the key in the door. She sat listening with her heart pounding.

It was as well she had taken the precaution to lock the door, for a few moments later van Buuren came bursting out from his cover and brandishing a firearm. He was making straight for the back door of the house which the woman had locked against him. He rattled the door furiously but could not force it open. He turned and ran round the side of the house, then took a flying leap and vaulted the garden wall, only to come face to face with Sergeant van Wyk and the constable, who had also turned to cut him off.

With levelled guns pointed at him, the fugitive knew he had no chance of getting away and escaping. He had dallied too long. He threw up his hands in quick surrender and called out, "I didn't do it! I swear I didn't!"

The sergeant and the constable seized him, taking his small-calibre Italian pistol and searching him for other weapons. As the arrested man started another tirade of protestations, the sergeant snapped, "Save it, van Buuren. Keep it till later."

They did not handle the man with particular care, but they did remove the nine rounds of ammunition he had had secreted in his pocket, and then they pushed him along to the police-station, where Sergeant Grobler was already coming out to meet them, watched by the wide-eyed African.

When Joy Atken was buried in the cemetery at Pinetown, almost the entire town turned out to pay tribute to the girl whose life had been cut short in her teens. It was Friday 12th October, only a few hours after her suspected killer had been rounded up. A man who remained in the background, wanting no publicity at the funeral, was Nelson Palmer. He had been sought avidly for his views by a number of reporters who had travelled a considerable distance to interview him, for the case of the murdered teenager and the startling development and outcome of the séance held by Palmer had been broadcast throughout the whole of South Africa.

It was not until well into the New Year that the man who had become thoroughly loathed throughout the Union was brought to trial. That was on Monday 11th February 1957.

The court was crowded for the occasion, with most persons hoping to catch a glimpse of Nelson Palmer, the spiritualist who had truly divined the whereabouts of a girl whose body lay concealed in a culvert in a lonely place in the Natal brush.

In the course of the trial the prosecution introduced some surprise witnesses, including the boys who said that van Buuren had given them a lift in the Ford Anglia on 3rd October. That was within a few hours of Joy's disappearance. They claimed that Clarence van Buuren had boasted of using a revolver, which he had actually shown them. But the prosecution finally had to concede that the gun found in van Buuren's possession when he was arrested in Pinetown might not with certainty be identified as the weapon used to shoot the teenager.

The evidence of the girl Ivy was equally crucial. She related to the court how during the time of a tea-break the prisoner had accosted Joy Atken with a smiling, "Hallo, cookie!" Joy had appeared surprised, and then she had smiled and taken the incident as a joke. But seemingly the man who had singled her out for attention was attracted to her ready smile and easy way of getting along with people, Ivy explained to an attentive court.

"But then Joy was easy to make friends with," she told the men listening closely to her recital. "I include men-friends," she added, as though wishing to make a point in fairness. She did not look at the defendant. Her eyes were averted, but it was clear that the girl was close to tears and prevented herself from breaking down only with a supreme effort that was costing her a good deal of anguish as she recalled the past. The judge led her gently over a bad patch, and neither the prosecution nor the defence (for very different reasons) was anxious to be seen to prolong her ordeal. When she stood down, it was as though the persons in the public seats emitted an overcharged sigh of relief.

The summer days during that February in 1957 were close and humid. They felt still more close to the man in dark glasses in the dock, for whom the days were drawing in. His dark blazer with its metal buttons and bright club badge, and his carefully knotted, colourful tie, were seen as a façade of cheerfulness, for he did not smile. Indeed, for long periods he remained with tight lips and did not show his teeth. His hair, parted low on his left, remained each day without a hair out of place, but at times he removed his lenses and wiped his eyes. He stared at nothing. When it came to giving evidence on his own behalf, he appeared to go through the motions and responses as though in a dream or as if he had something else on his mind—as indeed he very well might have had.

But his words, delivered in an even voice, gave the lie to proven fact, which did little to help his case.

He related how on Tuesday 3rd October he had given Joy Atken a lift, intending to be helpful. But giving her a lift was not his idea: it was hers, he claimed. He said she had asked him to drive down the coast road, arriving at an area of coast with an expanse of beach. With the sun pouring over them, the smiling girl had stretched her arms as though she was enjoying the break from the everyday. She had said nothing about joining her mother in a dancing-class.

He had thought it was the thing to do to invite her to go into a nearby hotel for a drink, but she had declined, still with a smile. He said she had preferred to stay outside in the Anglia, which had its windows down and was drawing an ocean breeze. When he asked her if she was sure, she nodded quickly, and so he walked alone into the hotel bar and ordered a drink.

He could see Joy sitting in the car, he said, and then he claimed that he had become inattentive, turning around and looking at the others who were having a drink. When he had finished it, he rose leisurely, intending to take the girl to where she wanted to go, but suddenly he saw that both Joy and the Anglia were no longer there.

His first feeling, he said, was one of annoyance, and he walked across to where they had gone. He thought she had gone off for a short spin alone, and instead of waiting for her to return he had decided on another drink. When he came out again, he saw the car about fifty yards away from where it had been parked originally. But he could not see the girl. He was puzzled by this and hurried over the shore to look for her. He flung open the car door, and then he saw her.

She was crouched down with blood on her face, which was why he had failed to see her before. He felt for her pulse, but there was none, and suddenly he felt scared, knowing that he was a man with a criminal past which the police could soon check.

According to his story, it was this fear of the police that haunted him and made him drive around the countryside at night without going home and without removing the dead girl from his car. He worked himself up into a frenzy, jettisoning one story after another, until in a kind of grim despair he had thought of a solution to his problem. It came to him in a flash, as he put it. He would hide the body in the culvert to the north of Umtwalumi.

"But she was fully clothed and had not been mutilated," he insisted.

More brokenly he resumed after a lengthy pause, claiming that, after returning the car to his employer, he had tried to get home to his wife and family. Then he added, "Or to my mother's." But he found both houses being watched by the police. Presumably he was expected. So he again wandered off, not sure where to make for or whom he could call on for help. He spent days sleeping rough, yet always being drawn towards his home.

His pretence of ignorance of the crime deceived no one, although the unhappy women in his life stood by him loyally, backing up his threadbare story, and both of them, his mother and his wife, cried heart-brokenly before they were led away by an unhappy policeman. There was a strange and sympathetic silence after they had given their evidence, but everyone in court knew that the outcome was inevitable, and the prisoner's story had been a waste of time and had availed him nothing.

For two weeks in February the trial was debated, and then the jury was asked to give their verdict. They did not take long, and in the afternoon of 26th February they heard the judge declare:

"The unanimous verdict of the court is that the accused is guilty."

The defence made a strong attempt to win for the accused man a measure of clemency, but public opinion, as well as the court's, was against him, and on 10th June 1957, at Pretoria's Central Prison, a hempen noose was fixed around his neck.

With the sun sinking in the evening sky, Clarence van Buuren was hanged, after one of the strangest cases ever recorded in South Africa.

5

Homicide and Honeymoons Rarely Mix

Somehow Saturday is the last day a person expects to find murder. Why this should be is quite inexplicable, except that any day that is a holiday somehow seems free of the inclination to murder or be murdered. But one such Saturday in the blazing August of 1969 became an exception to the run of everyday things, including weekends and holidays.

It was on 23rd August that two little girls who had rented mounts from the Gold Creek Riding-Stables went out for a Saturday ride. They were both eleven years old, and their home was in Washington State, in the north-west of the USA. Somewhere between the towns of Woodinville and Redmond they came upon a gruesome discovery. They were riding across the countryside of King County, a suburb of Seattle with plenty of fields and brush, and nearing a black-topped road when one of the horses shied and both shook their heads and tossed their manes as they slowed to a halt. That was when the girls became aware of an unpleasant smell.

They looked about them and found the apparent cause, a stinking piled-up mound of fir branches and pieces of brushwood. The nearer they approached, the more fetid the smell became and the more skittish the horses acted, trying to rid themselves of the obnoxious stench. They plunged and kicked their hooves and jumped aside, so much that one of the small girls found herself having difficulty in controlling her mount. Then the other called quite suddenly, "What's that?"

She was pointing. "There, through that pile of leaves." She was staring at something white through the brushwood and firs. By this time the horses were anxious to get away from the stink, and the girls turned aside.

"Probably a dead calf," called the one who had pointed to the pale patch. "We'd better ride back and report it. Come on."

Both girls knew it was not unusual for a heifer or calf to become tangled in brush, and frequently there was a reward offered by farmers for reporting a dead animal. The girls continued to the riding-stables, where they excitedly told the owner what they had seen and about the stench that had greeted them.

"OK," he said, "I'll ride back towards the wood and take a look for myself, but I've got several things to do before I can leave and ride over."

With that the impatient youngsters had to be content. After they had put up their hacks and helped in the grooming of them, they left. A short while later the owner of the riding-stables mounted and rode off in the direction mentioned by the eleven-year-olds. He came to the place where the pile of fir branches and brush was heaped and was immediately accosted by the repugnant smell that seemed to come from the centre of the heap. He dismounted and, holding his hand to his face, approached inquiringly. He moved the brush pile and was suddenly staring aghast at a human arm. He quickly remounted and rode over to report his find to the police and to the King County Department of Public Safety.

A group of detectives hastened to the place where the arm had been found. They were soon joined by Dr Charles Fontan, the chief of the King County Crime Laboratory. They removed the smelly brushwood and collected the limbs of the victim, who was in an advanced state of decomposition.

As soon as he could, Chief of Detectives Tom Nault issued a preliminary statement to the Press.

"Frankly," he told them, "at this point we don't even know if the victim was a man or a woman. The hair was long, making us think that, if a male, the body might have been one of the hippies who attended the Rock festival held in Woodinville during the last week in July."

Nault, who yet had to establish the cause of death, was already thinking of the possibility of murder having been committed. His men searched for traces of identification but found none. There were no personal effects or distinctive clothing, and after the remains had been removed for a post-mortem examination by Dr Fontan, the detectives spread out and searched the vicinity but came upon nothing in the nature of a clue. In short, all means of identifying the victim had been removed.

"The body could have been left lying there for all of three weeks," said Nault.

So far he and the other officers had no way of telling whether the victim had died from an overdose of drugs or had been 'removed' more sinisterly. The King County Medical Examiner helped Dr Fontan with the post-mortem. For the record, the victim was stated to be male, 5 feet 11 inches in height and about 12½ stone in weight, of muscular build and possibly between twenty and twenty-five years old. His death was the result of murder, for three bullets had been found in the grisly head, having caused wounds in an eye as well as a temple and a cheek. Two thirty-eight slugs had been recovered.

It had not been possible to take fingerprints, but Paul Foster had peeled the skin from the tips of the fingers and mounted it on slides with a special preservative. These he dispatched to the FBI for an examination by their own laboratories, which have possibly the world's best facilities in this area of research. But naturally such research took time, and the men awaiting the outcome spent days going over the same ground and widening the area of search, awaiting word from Washington DC, thousands of miles away.

When finally the word was received, it was conclusive.

The victim was now known to be Karsten Knutsen, a twenty-four-year-old Norwegian who had been in the United States for seven years. He had an address in the Ballard region of Seattle.

As one detective said, "This has blown the hippie theory. Hippies don't leave calling-cards or addresses."

The Ballard district of Seattle, spread along the shore of Puget Sound, is known as 'Little Scandinavia', for many people of Norse extraction have settled in the region, and they are said to have a strong and abiding sense of community. However, the calling detectives found that Knutsen was not known at the address they had been given. The owner had almost forgotten the Norwegian's name.

"True, I stood sponsor for him when he came to America seven years ago," he said, "but I haven't heard from him for years and can't remember what he looks like."

Inquiries revealed that the Norwegian had obtained work with the fishing-fleets that cruised the waters of the North Pacific, but the man seemed something of a drifter. However, when the police searched the Seattle Police Department's files, they had a curious success, for Knutsen had indeed been reported missing about a week before the discovery of the body in the brush. He had been due to sail, and when he had not reported for duty, the police had been notified. The man's skipper said it was not like Knutsen to miss a sailing-date, which is why he had asked the police to help in locating him.

The local detectives were told by the skipper that Knutsen had returned to Seattle from Alaska during the first week of August. He had been working on a crab-boat in Dutch Harbour and Adak.

"Of course," he said, "he might have returned to Ballard"—in which case he could not account for what had happened, for there had been no trouble with other members of the crew.

Nault's detectives realized that they had come to a full-stop and that the only thing left for them to do was start fresh inquiries around Ballard. But pounding pavements and making inquiries was a time-consuming occupation and intensely frustrating. In the meantime Nault asked the Alaska State Police to check what they knew of Knutsen's last trip with the crab-boats.

While the detectives in Ballard continued an exhausting round of inquiries and showing the picture from Knutsen's passport, often covering familiar ground to make sure, they were rewarded by a totally unexpected recognition. When one of them asked a man in a bar if he had seen Knutsen before, he turned casually and said, "Sure. He comes in here a lot. Least, he does when he's in Ballard."

"Remember when you saw him last?" asked the detective.

The man turned round to the woman who accompanied him.

"About three weeks ago, wasn't it?"

"Must have been," she said, and then broke off to say, "I remember now, it was a Sunday. Must have been 10th August."

"That's right," said her husband. "He was with a pretty blonde."

His wife said sharply, "It was Audrey Ruud."

The detectives exchanged glances, for the woman had spoken positively, and they had caught an odd note in her voice.

"What do you know about her?" asked one.

The man looked at him, then shrugged.

"Just that she was supposed to be going steady with Pat Fullen," he muttered uncomfortably.

"How steady?" pressed the detective.

"She had shacked up with Fullen," put in the wife in a reproving tone. "That's how steady they were, if you must know. Yet, when she and Karsten Knutsen came in here on that Sunday night, it was sort of as though Karsten had taken Pat's place." The wife frowned, recalling the incident. She went on. "Pretty soon Pat Fullen came in, and immediately Audrey went over to him and began acting as though she hadn't seen him for a long time. I felt sick."

"The rum part is," said the men who had recognized Knutsen's passport photo, "that Pat didn't say anything or ball out Audrey for playing fast and loose with him. After a few words he drifted over towards us, and then shortly afterwards he left. About a quarter of an hour later Karsten and Audrey also left. But it was damned odd, say what you will."

The detectives agreed and inquired where Audrey Ruud and Pat Fullen lived.

"Somewhere on North-West Fifty-third Street, I believe," said the woman quickly, but her husband was frowning intently.

Both said they had not seen either Audrey or Pat since that Sunday night. The detectives nodded. It was a break-through of sorts.

The following day the Alaska State Police reported that there had been no trouble between Knutsen and the crab-boat men. In fact the last they had heard from him was that he had received a tax-rebate from the Alaska inland revenue. The cheque had arrived on the last day he had spent in Alaska and was for $40. The sum had been cashed and a receipt given in Knutsen's name, but the Alaska police came up with a discrepancy which was rather puzzling: when their handwriting experts had checked the receipt, they felt that it had not been signed by Knutsen. It was a forged signature, and they were inclined towards the opinion that it had been forged by a woman.

At last the case was growing tentacles. They were spreading out and groping.

In the meantime detectives traced Fullen's address, which they located at Fifty-third Street. It was number 821, a house divided into apartments, in a very long street. The landlady viewed the call with suspicion, but when her feelings had been reassured and smoothed over, she readily answered the questions of the two Washington State police. She agreed that the couple had lived at the apartment at number 821 until August.

"They moved out suddenly," she announced, "on the 11th and they left without giving me notice, as they were expected to do legally. What's more, they didn't clean up the place as they should have. It was like a pig-stye."

She was a woman who had no time for the late occupants, whom she had not taken to for reasons she did not bother to explain to the detectives, who felt they could be treading on delicate ground.

"Was it let as a furnished apartment?" asked the senior, whose name was Steinauer.

The landlady shook her head.

"No," she said, "they had their own furniture, but they didn't take the pieces. They had some friends arrive a few days later and clear everything out for them. It wasn't done by a regular removal firm, I know that." Then she tapped her mouth with the spread fingers of her hand. "Just a minute, I've remembered something—something I saved when I cleaned up and found it in the bathroom."

She produced a bowl with a piece of shiny metal in it, which she had found in the bathroom. She had tried to flush it down the lavatory, but it was too heavy, and she had had to fish it out.

"I kept it for some days, then threw it out."

The detectives started, but she smiled.

"Afterwards," she went on, "I got it back before the next collection of garbage. See? It looks like a bullet, doesn't it?"

Steinauer and his colleague bent over the mis-shapen piece of metal and saw that it was a fired bullet of thirty-eight calibre. Then they started to check the apartment room by room and found that a screen-door and a ceiling had been damaged by what seemed to be several bullets. When they checked an interior staircase, which led down to a basement, they found some dark stains that could have been blood. This area overall was quite small, but the detectives scraped away some of the wood that had been stained, and they pocketed the pieces for testing in the laboratory.

After delivering the scrapings, the detectives returned to continue their inquiries. Both men felt encouraged by the episode with the landlady.

It was Steinauer who found a fisherman with an interesting enlargement to the developing case. He told the detective that there had been some rumours "flying around", as he put it, ever since the police had found that Knutsen was the dead man buried under the pile of pine and fir boughs and inquiries had got under way. One was to the effect that Knutsen and another man had shared a savings-account, which they owned jointly.

"We do that," he explained, "so that if one partner is up in Alaska, say, on a trip and needs money urgently, then the other can draw it out in Seattle. Anyway, the story goes that the other man checked the account and found most of the cash gone."

After further questioning of the man, the detective was given an address in Ballard, where he found that someone had indeed drawn $750 from the joint account, and on 11th August, which Steinauer knew was a significant date. He accordingly made inquiries at the Ballard branch of Knutsen's bank and was shown the records. Someone had signed a withdrawal-slip with Knutsen's name at the Stoneway branch of the bank. The accountant at the Stoneway branch had made sure that there was sufficient money in the Ballard branch and then paid out the sum requested.

When the local detective explained, the withdrawal-slip was officially released. It was then passed to an identity-technician, who was already grappling with the clue of the thirty-eight bullet and blood-samples scraped from woodwork in the flat. But the blood-samples proved to be too minute; the bullet had been too battered for comparison with slugs taken from the victim's head, and a great many hands had certainly fingered the withdrawal-slip. But while the technicians worked at the problem, word was received from a totally unexpected quarter.

The Clark County sheriff's department in Las Vegas had picked up another rumour, to the effect that Ruud and Fullen had made a journey to the city of bright lights and gambling in the early days of August. As a result, the Nevada and Washington State detectives made distant contact and found that on 1st August in Las Vegas Audrey Laurel Ruud and Patrick Joseph Fullen had been married.

"A real turn-up for the book," one Seattle detective explained, for Fullen was guilty of bigamy. His colleague had found the current Mrs Fullen, and she was not Audrey Ruud. She had petitioned for divorce, but it still had not been finalized.

Then an even more surprising piece of news came from Detective Chief Nault. His identity-technician had succeeded in lifting and identifying a single perfect fingerprint from the much worked-on withdrawal-slip. When the loops and whorls were seen clearly, they proved to be those of Audrey Ruud.

No time was lost in swearing out a warrant for the woman's arrest, and teletyped requests to eleven Western states were dispatched immediately. However, both she and Fullen had vanished, and it was now known by the police that Fullen's two-year-old Ford convertible was well laden when it left Seattle on 11th August.

Once more it was Detective Steinauer who doggedly followed official changed-address forms over a long trail, trying to catch up with the fugitives. He crossed North Dakota, swung towards Kansas City and then went eastwards towards New York. But all this took time. A dossier was prepared on the missing couple for the National Crime Information Centre in Washington DC, for dissemination by every law-enforcement agency in the USA.

Then on 17th September there was another unexpected development.

On that day Dave Wooster, a resident Deputy on Sanibel Island, Florida, answered what seemed to be a routine call near the Gulf resort. There had been trouble at a local motel, and when he arrived, the deputy was greeted by a screaming blonde whose angry face was contorted and convulsed as she pointed a trembling finger at the man who was the object of her rage and contumely. As soon as she saw the deputy, she shouted, "He killed a man in Seattle, I tell you! He committed murder!" Her voice rose to a shrill peak.

The Florida Deputy, aware that this was no run-of-the-mill quarrel, pinched his eyes half shut at that word 'murder'. It rang an alarm-bell in his mind. He was a man who thought quickly and whose reactions were fast. He read the quarrelling couple their rights and had them sign waiver-forms before they could cool down, which was as well, for the story the woman poured out was so grim that it would shock all who heard it.

The woman repeated that the man had committed murder, and he kept waving his hands and declaring that he was glad to get it all off his chest. The past weeks had got him down. They both said they had gone to Las Vegas to get married, and afterwards he had lost all his money gambling. When they were broke, they had returned to Seattle. Their intention was to get a man drunk and roll him for his money. But Fuller had been smoking marijuana and was feeling high, and that was when things, in his own words, "got out of hand". He had shot the man he had robbed at the apartment, and the woman had stabbed him several times. Then they had removed a savings-bank book from the dead body and withdrawn some $700 from the man's account on the following day. After the money had been banked, they had removed the victim's clothes and taken the body to Woodinville.

Homicide and Honeymoons Rarely Mix 77

It was as though floodgates had been flung wide open: both the man and the woman seemed very ready to tell what they had done, and the woman wrote her name and the date of the killing on the back of one of the waiver-forms. At that the Deputy breathed easily, for he realized that he now had two confessions to murder and had to make urgent contact with his superiors. In due course Ed Jones, the investigator for the Lee County sheriff's department, and Captain Ted Smith hurried to the Gulf island and took the couple to the Lee County jail, where they learned for the first time that Fullen had once sold insurance in nearby Fort Myers, so that escape to Florida had been no accidental choice. When the jailed couple arrived in Florida, they had had only $200 left.

The Lee County authorities soon made contact with the National Crime Information Centre and requested that a message be sent to the King County police. They wanted information on which to hold both Patrick Fullen and Audrey Ruud.

"Seattle wants them," replied the National Crime Information Centre. "Hold for further communication."

The news of the arrest spread throughout the North-West, where the murder and the investigation that followed had been followed with avid interest. The next day Chief Nault and a sergeant took off for the flight to Florida, where they entered a different world of palms and tropical waters.

When Fullen's Ford convertible was searched at the motel, he had handed the Florida men a thirty-eight revolver, which he said he had normally kept under the front seat. Another weapon found in the search was a switch-blade knife, which the woman had kept in her handbag. By then Fullen had admitted to the Seattle sergeant that he had shot Karsten Knutsen.

"I'm sick of the whole thing," he growled. "Everything went wrong for me."

When the formalities in Florida were completed, the prisoners started the long journey back to Seattle to await trial. Then ensued months of waiting, during which the prisoners suffered a change of mind and outlook. Lawyers got to work on them and induced them to request separate trials in their own interest. These were eventually granted by the court, with the compliance of both prosecution and defence counsels, and thus in due course the pair faced different juries in what were to be consecutive trials. The first began on 4th February 1970, before Superior Court Judge James W. Mifflin.

The prosecutor, Nick Marshall, who had been an FBI agent at one time, was reported by the Press to have made a strong case against the defendants. He kept Steinauer, who had journeyed so far and done so much legwork, at his table as a consultant throughout the hearing which continued for days in a crowded court.

The woman's trial opened first.

The good-looking blonde was drawn and pale, without the tan she had acquired in the Florida sun. In fact, she appeared pale and rather nervous, as though enduring strain. In a whisper she related the events of the violent days of the previous August and admitted that previously she had worked as a prostitute in Seattle for two years. Because she and Fullen were broke, she had reverted to the same work to obtain money.

But when it came to the actual murder, she had insisted that she had not stabbed Knutsen, as had been related in earlier accounts of the crime, and in a somewhat louder voice insisted, "There is no way that I had anything to do with the murder."

At this there were some exclamations in court.

Then she resumed to say that she had pleaded with Fullen not to shoot Knutsen or herself. That opened a number of eyes very wide, for hitherto there had been no suggestion that she might have been in danger, and she went on to claim that the Norwegian was not shot in the apartment but in the boot of the Ford after they had arrived in Woodinville. She had waited in the car while Fullen concealed the nude body with boughs.

The jury did not look much impressed by the story she was telling, nor did they when she came to tell of the alleged wedding in Las Vegas, which she said she knew was not legal, but the marriage so-called had been celebrated to spite a relative of the 'bride' who had been critical of her. Afterwards the lengthy honeymoon, which had been paid for by the victim's work as a fisherman, had been what she termed a "terror trail" and at times a nightmare. She insisted that she had remained with Fullen only through fear.

"I was afraid for my life," she averred.

But the jury remained stone-faced and impassive, and it was seen that her gaze remained averted as Dave Wooster gave his evidence about what had transpired on 17th September. There was little hope for her in his words or throughout the three days of her trial. Then, in the middle of an afternoon, it was over, and the jury filed out and remained deliberating until an hour before midnight, when they returned to say that they had reached a unanimous verdict.

It was one of "Guilty of murder in the first degree"—shattering but predictable.

On the following day another jury was sworn in, and it was Pat Fullen's turn to face a hostile hearing. But, as it turned out, he had conveniently misplaced his memory. In fact, he claimed that he was unable to recall anything clearly since the time when he had started smoking marijuana on the night of 10th August until he woke up in the Seattle apartment at number 821 North-West Fifty-third Street "feeling guilty" about something, as he said.

Then he went on to explain that he had found a bloodstained revolver and a switchblade knife in the flat, and said that on the day of the killing he had drunk beer and vodka as well as consuming narcotics. However, his defence counsel suggested that his knowledge of the crime stemmed from what he had been told by Audrey Ruud, and Fullen himself hotly denied that he had had any intention of robbing the Norwegian fisherman.

However, the prosecuting attorney interposed to remind his listeners that voluntary intoxication could not be considered a valid defence in a trial for murder, and he somewhat scathingly pointed out how convenient was Fullen's form of 'amnesia', for his memory appeared normal until the time of the murder and returned after the body had been disposed of. He suggested that Fullen had gambled away his ill-gotten gains in a spirit of easy come, easy go.

"Robbery was the motive for this crime," the prosecutor declared loudly, and then in a lower voice he went on to explain how the couple had practised forging the Norwegian's signature until they were ready to present it to the bank.

All the same, the jury was out for seven hours arguing the facts of the case. Fullen had told them, "I am very sorry for what happened. Nobody's life is worth a few dollars," and presumably his regret for what he had done was seen to be genuine—certainly as genuine as the comments he had made in the motel on Sanibel Island, many hundreds of miles away. But when the arguments petered out as the hours crept on, the jury returned to find the prisoner guilty as charged.

Three weeks after the trial started, on 25th February 1970, the convicted killers appeared before Judge Mifflin for sentencing. They heard the judge sentence both of them to life imprisonment, with a recommended twenty-year term in the case of the man but with no similar minimum term recommended for the woman.

But if Audrey Ruud felt judicially rebuffed, she gave no sign and was her usual buoyant self when she and Fullen left the court with newsmen clustered around and a photographer hovering nearby to get a good shot. She turned to the latter and asked pertly, "Are you going to take pictures?"

"Sure," he said.

"Well, wait," she retorted, waving the detectives back. "Take us together, mister."

She smiled into Fullen's face, posing, although he continued to wear a worried frown. It was the last-remembered moment of a strange time she liked to think of as a 'honeymoon'. Then the camera clicked several times, and the detectives waved the Pressmen back and crowded the couple into a police car, to start serving the long years of deadly daily monotony.

6

The Skyjacker's Conscience Was Too Heavy

That October there were some bitingly bitter winds blowing squalls across the Île-de-France, a region that includes the French capital.

As well as high winds there was a good deal of drenching cold rain that made certain travellers huddle in their seats and turn up the collars of their coats, then think ahead with pleasure to the expected sunshine of the Côte d'Azur. On 18th October, despite the chill raindrops blowing in their faces and squelching under fashionable footwear which was anything but substantial, those travellers made their way shortly before mid-morning through the bay of No. 12 gate at Orly Airport. There were 110 of them registered for Air France Flight 409, preparing to wing south towards the sun and warmth. For those of them who played mental guessing-games with numerology, 409 added up to a sinister thirteen, but the chances are that no one even thought about that as they embarked in the big Boeing 727 and watched the rain trickle down the plastic panes of the aircraft. They were scheduled for a flight to Nice, where, if all went as expected and according to the time-tables, they were due to make a landing within eighty minutes.

One passenger was doing a considerable amount of thinking as the time to depart approached. She had held herself somewhat rigidly when the customary immigration search was held and the inspection of the passengers' luggage conducted by an electro-magnetic scrutiny, intended to find hidden weapons. Though in such weather the search was seen to be cursory, it was not in any way lax, but rather very experienced in the tricky art of getting travellers through Customs and Excise with the least delay and harm to tempers.

When at eleven forty-five, the Boeing trundled across the runway, ready to take off, it was only some fifteen minutes late. Ponderously the mechanical bird rose through the curtain of rain. As it did so, the voice of the French air-hostess welcomed her passengers aboard and then asked them to unbuckle their seat-belts.

Among the eight travellers journeying first class was the woman who seemed very thoughtful, as though she had something on her mind which she had to debate with herself. She had a quick smile when she caught the eye of the air-hostess, and was a slender young woman, who appeared rather petite, certainly well-groomed and chic. Across her shoulders she clutched a pastel-tinted mink coat which she wore over a pair of plum-coloured silk slacks, very much in the mode. Her small features made her look about thirty, and there was no gainsaying she wore a distinctive air and was a person of considerable charm, carrying her small body with grace and ease, qualities which she seemed well aware she possessed. She had a small lapdog who had made himself comfortable in her mink lap, a detail that pointed to her obvious social status. In fact, both the dog and his mistress belonged to the travelled 'jet-set'.

She calmly received the smiles of Jacky Lapoussière, the tall and handsome steward, when he attended to them, but when a champagne bottle was uncorked with a decided pop, Marie Vaillant, the red-haired air-hostess, had to soothe dog and owner as the latter looked around startled.

"Nothing to alarm you, Madame," she said quietly and smiled. "Vintage champagne can go off like that, just like a bullet sometimes, unless it is smothered by a napkin."

The woman who answered to the name of Madame Cravenne murmured, "Of course. How silly of me to be so jumpy!" She returned smile for smile and sank back in her seat with the high head-rest and then turned her eyes towards a bearded Briton who occupied the next seat. He threw her a grin, seeing the woman in purple trousers as someone who was a little on edge but, in his own description, "thoroughly normal and quiet", as he was to recall later.

Her other neighbour was someone who appreciated the picture she made with her smooth creamy skin, delicate complexion and emerald eyes, which were in sharp contrast to her jet-black hair, worn loosely and at shoulder-length. But she gave neither of her male neighbours any opening for talk or chit-chat and remained seemingly content to contemplate the thoughts behind the green eyes and absentmindedly to tickle the fur of her small griffon's ears.

At a quarter past twelve the good-looking steward pushed open the door of the first-class compartment and began passing round dainties for a light lunch of three courses, which was accompanied by a ruby-red half-bottle of a quality Beaujolais. By the time the meal had been served, the jet-liner had passed over Clermont-Ferrand, near Vichy, in the centre of France, and the Air France captain, Michel de Savoye, had finished climbing to his maximum height along the flight route and was beginning very slowly and gradually to begin the descent towards Nice and the Mediterranean beyond, with cloud constantly crossing the view as objects came into sharper focus and perspective and Provence was spread out like a patchwork quilt below.

Then, while the jet was flying over Montélimar, Madame Cravenne, her lunch finished, made a seemingly natural move to leave the first-class compartment. She was carrying a large holdall, which an observant female passenger thought was an overture for preparing for her toilette before landing at Nice airport. Sitting next to the rear door, this passenger was a dog-lover who, when she saw the small griffon's nose poking out of the holdall, stretched out a hand and stroked the dog's hair, smoothing it out of its beady eyes. Then dog and chic owner vanished into the port lavatory.

Some time later the woman who liked dogs felt that a long time had elapsed without the woman with the stylish mink appearing, and she began to grow anxious. She tapped at the lavatory door and inquired solicitously, "Are you all right, Madame? Do you feel ill at all?"

There was a long moment's silence, but the door was not

opened. Instead a low voice replied, saying, "I'm quite all right, thanks, but I should be pleased if you would be so kind as to send the stewardess to me."

The woman looked for a moment at the closed door and then moved away.

"Very well, Madame," she said, but she was still wearing an anxious look when she summoned the air-hostess with the red hair.

Marie Vaillant went to answer the summons at once. When she reached the door, it opened without waiting for her knock. At the sight of a levelled gun, she did a quick double-take and gulped.

The gun, which was a twenty-two rifle that had been put together from parts carried in the dog's holdall, jerked authoritatively, and the air-hostess was told in a voice that had dropped several tones, "You'd better not scream. Simply do what I say and take this letter to the captain. Tell him he had better come here quickly and bring the steward."

Marie Vaillant's forehead was suddenly moist, and her legs felt tottery as she saw another abrupt gesture with the slim rifle. She turned and retreated as the door closed behind her. Then she broke into a hurried scamper to reach de Savoye with the momentous news she bore.

The captain looked up as the words spilled from her. There was no need for him to inquire if anything was wrong. It was plainly very wrong, as Marie Vaillant shouted, "There's a woman skyjacker aboard, Captain, and she's got a rifle. She's in the first-class lavatory."

The pilot heard the words as through a daze. At first their meaning failed to register with real impact. He and the others in the cabin were immobile for seconds while the import of the hostess's words suddenly took meaning and life as he unfolded the three pages of the letter Marie Vaillant held out to him.

Like his fellow-officers peering over his shoulder, he had at first been inclined to believe the letter was a joke and not in the best of taste. But as he continued to wade through the words, certain names leaped out at him, those of Pierre-August Messmer, the Prime Minister of France, Raymond Marcellin, the Minister for Home Affairs, and Marcel

Dassaunlt, an aircraft-designer and manufacturer. These and others named were taken to task and indicted in scathing terms for, as Madame Cravenne had written, "promoting wars through their indiscriminate sales of heavy armaments and supersonic jets to under-developed lands".

As the crew of the Boeing perused the letter, one growled, "She must be a nut-case," for he read that the writer was blaming the French Government for not bringing to an end the Arab-Israeli war, as though it were something that could be turned off like a tap. Then the writer made a demand for a 'motorless' day, when drivers must halt their cars and lorries. But the demand became a threat when she issued it in these words: "Bring a halt to the whole automotive industry throughout the country—or else!"

When de Savoye had finished reading the letter, he turned with a puzzled shrug to the air-hostess.

"I'm baffled by it," he said. "Is it written by a lunatic, or is there some verbal smokescreen? And has she any confederates among the passengers?"

He looked up inquiringly.

"Somehow I don't think so," said the air-hostess, who had had some extra seconds for considering the letter and re-reading it. "I agree that she might be a nut-case. Only someone who is mad would skyjack a Boeing 727 with a lapdog in tow—certainly not a normal person, Captain."

Lapoussière had by this time joined the others in the cabin and was reading the letter. He waved the pages.

"My God, she must be the first female skyjacker to make such an attempt on her own—utterly solo!" he declared with a note of grudging admiration in his voice. "Even Leila Khaled made her attempt with the help of three or four others."

He referred to a Palestinian woman skyjacker who had previously shocked the world—apparently Madame Cravenne was in her intrepid way a trail-blazer, out to make an original score. One of the crew debated whether she could indeed be a Palestinian, for with the letter she had given the captain a Cairo address for its destination. He thought this odd. But the steward had no doubts about the woman.

"She's not a Palestinian," he said firmly. "Not with her accent. She's from Paris, no question of it. There's no doubt about her being French." He turned to the air-hostess. "Come, Marie, we'll try reasoning with her. That'll give you time, Captain, to think over the situation and decide what you want to do."

The captain nodded, and the air-hostess and steward went out of the cabin. Michel de Savoye returned slowly to his own seat, a man sunk in thought, for he was beginning to feel his responsibility for the plane-load of 110 passengers and crew carried by the Air France Boeing. He contacted his control-tower at Marseilles-Marignane and saw that the time was twenty-five past twelve.

When radio-contact was made, he announced an alert:

"This is Air France Orly–Nice Flight 409. There is an armed woman among our passengers. Her voice sounds as though she may be deranged, and her demands and reasons are not clear for doing what she has. We are trying to persuade her to allow us to land the other passengers at Marignane. Over."

He spent some short time in further explanation and then put the automatic pilot on and climbed out of his seat. He stood some moments pondering how to deal with the problem of the female skyjacker. He realized that she had manoeuvred herself into a position where she could menace anyone between two lavatories with her rifle. She had obviously chosen the place deliberately. As he approached, he could hear the air-hostess and the steward arguing with her, but she was being obdurate. However, he saw that the majority of the plane's passengers had no notion that anything was at all untoward and were chatting normally.

Then he approached the lavatory, and the voices became clearer. His crew-members drew back, and he was faced by the obstinate woman with the rifle.

"Madame . . ." he began gently, but he was given no time for a rational argument before she became heated. The flight captain had a duty to perform, and he had to make his voice heard. Helped by the two members of the crew, he pointed out that the Air France jet had not sufficient fuel to fly non-stop to Cairo, and he began an argument as to whether they could accordingly land at Marseilles-Marignane where they could pump in a necessary 3,500 gallons of aviation-fuel to complete the Mediterranean flight to Cairo. They tried to be patient with her, but by this time she was seemingly obsessed with the nature of the demands which had been put down in the three-page letter.

In her low-pitched voice, and with her green eyes glittering in bright hostility, she constantly repeated phrases from the letter, as though she had memorized them and had them on record; she repeatedly referred to 'war on want' and the Government's having at its disposal batteries of 75s and 155s "which are on sale everywhere". Then she switched to the subject of her purchase of the twenty-two rifle and also a thirty-two automatic, with plenty of ammunition. She seemed to become infuriated by the gunsmith, from whom she had made her purchases, having asked her, "And what else, madame?" It was obvious that she was becoming more excited the longer the talk was prolonged, and there was considerable danger of words being translated into sudden shooting and death. It was the air-hostess who reminded her that there were children aboard the plane.

"It is not my intention to hurt anyone, least of all children," she declared.

In a moment when her attitude had seemed to soften somewhat, the captain explained that in such circumstances it might be as well for her to allow the passengers to disembark at Marignane. This got the flight personnel into a further argument with the woman, but at the steward's suggestion she agreed to release the air-hostess, keeping as hostages the captain and the steward himself.

With this uneasy truce being played out in the clouds scudding across southern France, the captain returned to the cockpit at twelve-forty to contact the Marignane control-tower, where a radio-line was being kept open, usual in such an emergency, and from which the aircraft was provided with flight-directions. This was done without alarming the passengers, who were aware only that there had been a change of plan. The woman still huddling between the two first-class lavatories, with the dog crouching against her and the rifle pointing at the air-hostess, remained in the same position as the minutes ticked away and the Boeing was throttled back. Then, through what seemed an interminable time of waiting, the aircraft touched down, slowed across the tarmac and came to a halt. Almost at once the after-door of the Boeing was opened, and the passengers were directed by the crew to leave. There was no semblance of panic or even hurry. For most of the passengers it was a normal evacuation for technical reasons outside the control of the flight-planners.

In fact, it was said that the first time the first-class passengers were aware of the skyjacking was when the Boeing arrived and they disembarked at Marignane instead of Nice. A fresh Air France plane was taxied into position and prepared for the passengers to continue with their interrupted flight, but by this time a cordon of police was thrown around the skyjacked Air France Boeing where the strange drama was still being enacted.

One of the first to hear of the skyjack was the Marseilles prefect of police, informed as soon as Captain de Savoye gave his radioed news. The prefect and his chauffeur drove at speed to the airport, followed by three cars filled with marksmen of an anti-gang special squad, who took up roof-top positions over the chamber of commerce freight-hangars. An official of the airport police walked to within hailing-distance of the grounded aircraft. He knew he risked being shot at, but there was no shot—possibly because de Savoye was still engaged on the intercom and posing as a reporter who had to answer questions. Indeed, the Marseilles prefect quickly understood the subterfuge and readily agreed to fall into the role of a newsman out to get an exclusive interview, which certainly fitted in with the skyjacker's mood and plans, for she had been brought to the verge of hysteria.

She was by this time shouting, "Keep clear, everyone, if you don't want to get a bullet in the belly!"

Afterwards Lapoussière told how he at one time scarcely believed that he would live through the next couple of hours, while he and the others who had been selected as hostages talked to a woman who was becoming hysterical. Round and round the argument circulated, until all were dizzy except the skyjacker. Her tirade was broken three times by the captain to relay various messages by radio-telephone. Afterwards she resumed her harangue, always accompanying her words by gestures with the aimed rifle.

As the arguments and the hours wore away, the flight personnel grew very tired and a little despondent, for none of them could see how the strange business could end. Certainly they could not excite the woman's animosity, and patient and prolonged reasoning was having little effect. Then, at three o'clock in the afternoon, a massive petrol-tanker moved alongside the grounded plane to pump in the required fuel for the agreed flight to Cairo. When the big tanker was hooked up, the hostages began another round of pleas, trying to talk the obsessed woman out of her plan—whatever it was, for they did not know what was in her mind and what she intended doing. They put up arguments that President Sadat of Egypt was already taking steps to try to bring an end to the hostilities between his country and Israel, but seemingly any words of rationality were wasted, for she still spoke with heated insistence and continued to gesture with the rifle, poking it at the men's chests.

"Don't treat Danielle Cravenne like an imbecile," she cried, waving their protests to silence, "and stop trying to talk me out of what I intend to do." She drew herself up to her short height, and the green glint in her eyes became impressive, seeming to strike fire as she again became agitated. "Don't forget that my husband is one of the top men in France in public relations."

It was true that Georges Cravenne was a person of considerable significance in his own world of creative films and public "creations", but the men watching the female skyjacker were not recalling the husband's successes. They were intent on observing his wife's trigger-finger.

Then suddenly there was another interruption on the intercom. It was the voice of the Marseilles prefect, who was posing as a reporter. He spoke again to inquire if the woman wished to continue her flight to a possible alternative destination. This was an obvious ploy to deflect her interest in a fresh direction.

"You have only to say, Madame," he said. "It can easily be arranged."

But this verbal trick received nothing in the way of true satisfaction, for she retorted, "Just do as I say and no one will be hurt."

Yet still the woman had not said what she was planning or described her intentions when the departure for Egypt was finally agreed—if anything could be agreed in her flexible state of mind, hopping from one consideration to another. She was constantly changing her demands, but never to anything specific, simply nagging in general terms about an alleged armaments race which she saw as immoral. The prefect, like the crew-members, continued to engage her in discussion likely to keep her attention occupied and her interest fixed, but the longer the process continued, the more tired everyone was becoming from the strain. They were wondering how long it could continue before something—or someone—snapped.

Then the incredible interview suddenly changed direction.

Over the intercom her purpose was elicited. It was her intention to drive to Marseilles and halt the showing of an Israeli film titled *The Adventures of Rabbi Jacob*, a comedy that saw the Jews in a harmless light and was devoid of propaganda and political views. Madame Cravenne now declared her intention of exchanging her hostages for a ransom, the money to be received by a Catholic charity called 'The Brothers of Men'. Then once again she changed her disturbed mind's direction sharply, claiming that "her clever husband Georges" would perhaps see this as a stunt on her part, and so she "must sacrifice her life to shock the world's conscience against social evils and war".

She was by this time becoming really obsessed by the theme of social evil leading to war. Then she became quiet as a fresh thought crossed her mind. There was silence in the aircraft as the two men stared at her, for she made an announcement that staggered both of them. She said she had been intending to nose-dive in a suicide attack on Nice Airport. This brought a wide-eyed reaction, until she changed her mind again.

"Since that might mean the death of children, and I'm a mother myself," she went on, "I decided to change the target to the large oil-refinery at Berre on the Étang de Berre, not far from here, but then I thought of the ideal target, the uranium-plant at Pierrelatte, which is only about 20 kilometres from Montélimar. That's where the H-bombs are made, you know."

While this dangerous but exaggerated talk was flowing, the

marksmen on the roof of the freight-hangars were keeping their fingers crooked around the triggers of their rifles, waiting for a chance to shoot without risking an innocent life.

Half an hour later the opportunity arose, but not in the way they had imagined.

Madame Cravenne suddenly rose and said she would like something to eat and drink. "I only toyed with my lunch," she said.

Her request was speedily granted. It was felt that the risk of hitting Lapoussière at close quarters was too great, so a detective dressed as a steward, carrying a tray, made his way towards the rear of the plane. He was accompanied by two marksmen, who carried a hose of large diameter for servicing the fuel tanks. Things were going smoothly until the woman suddenly became suspicious and pointed with her rifle.

"Put down that tray at once!" she ordered peremptorily.

However, the detective in the uniform of a steward continued to walk towards her as though he had not heard. She raised her rifle and fired. It was a signal for the detective to bring out his concealed gun from under the tray and return her fire—"in self-defence", as it was described later.

Madame Cravenne was hit twice by the heavy police slugs, once in the head and again in the chest, and the crazed idealist who was bitterly opposed to war was bowled over like a rag doll between two rows of seats. Blood flowed over the plum-coloured slacks and soaked into the pastel-shaded mink. Her little dog began to bark furiously.

It was as though a television drama had somehow lost its thread of continuity.

Madame Cravenne was rushed to an ambulance but was dead before she reached a Marignane hospital. The drama had vanished like powdered chalk in a high wind.

However, the shooting of the deranged skyjacker was merely the genesis of a controversy that was to continue with rumblings and repercussions for a long time, for in a curious way Madame Cravenne had become something of a heroine for what her perplexed mind was trying to establish, and to many in France she was seen as a martyr sacrificed on the altar of war. Perhaps the green-eyed woman who was fond of toy dogs and had two children of her own whom she wanted brought up in the ways of peace and concord, and who enjoyed the sleek feel of mink and silk trousers under her finger-tips, was less a fashionable sybarite than a person seeking desperately in her own mind to change the course of the world. She saw it plunging into self-destruction encouraged by the men who had been termed 'merchants of death'. Since the emergence of the super-powers, the term had fallen into disuse, though one would suspect that, for Danielle Cravenne at least, it had more meaning than ever up to the time of her death.

The police of Marseilles came in for a good deal of criticism and many strictures for the manner of her death and how the whole case was handled. It was called "a summary execution" by killers who had faced a mentally unbalanced woman who had armed herself and behaved with complete lack of restraint, with a wild and surging hatred of the social conditions she fervidly desired to change. To this end she had plotted and connived, while keeping her own secret counsel.

The controversy about her death waxed intensely the more it was discussed. The two heavy bullets that bowled her over were considered in detail by ballistics experts, and there seemed to be no lack of evidence that the police marksman had shot to kill. In the first police version of the affair the disguised marksman had shot three rounds "in self-defence", but only two in later reports. This discrepancy became something the Marseilles police had to live with. Many people wanted to know why the police marksman was in such a hurry to shoot down a woman who was behaving erratically. Certainly her small-bore rifle was not a weapon expected to be used with deadly effect. In normal circumstances she would have been talked out of her intentions and a resort to firearms, but when it came to her facing a possible return fire she was not accorded the time. The twenty-two bullet she discharged was not found.

To the average Frenchman Madame Cravenne had brought about her own death by opening fire on the police and also threatening to commit a kamikaze-style suicide, although she did not know how to fly a jet!

Undoubtedly the prefect was extremely upset by her threat to destroy the Pierrelatte uranium plant in a suicide attempt.

Though it is now known that Danielle Cravenne existed on a diet of bluffs, the fact that she had purchased the firearms meant that she had to be taken seriously.

But to what extent?

That is what the French Press continued to ask a harassed prefect. The captain and the steward were certainly unhappy about the shooting of a distraught woman with distorted ideals, and had they been aware that the police were about to open fire, they might very well have protested, but when the woman herself fired, it was thought that the Marseilles police had received instructions to shoot to kill in such a contingency, if only because other lives were involved. So an element of misunderstanding might be said to have crept in.

It is possible that the prefect had been surprised by the message recorded at Marignane and had been caught unprepared by the approaching climax. He was certainly not given time to report an approved course of action, such as getting in touch with a medical man or a psychologist who might well have prescribed a tranquillizing drug for the excitable woman driven on by her fears for the world's future. That would certainly have allowed Georges Cravenne time to reach her side and calm her down.

The tragedy was all the more poignant because time was running out for the misguided woman. Guy Villatte, the principal private secretary to the Minister for Home Affairs and a friend of the Cravenne family, was actually in Marignane at the time of the shooting. Had he been apprised a few minutes earlier of the drama that was taking place, the outcome of the tragedy might have been very different.

So mixed up in her mind was Danielle Cravenne that she had even forgotten that her husband, a well-known Paris impresario who had sponsored films and spectaculars and public celebrations, some of which might be classed as 'stunts', had been interested in furthering the fortunes of the film *The Adventures of Rabbi Jacob*, a character played by Louis de Funes, a leading French comedian. Madame Cravenne was known to have considered the comedy in poor taste when Jews were fighting against Egyptians, and she had tried to get it withdrawn, but without success—hence the point of much of her letter to the airline captain. Her husband had considered her efforts no more than some peculiar prejudice but had sent her to Vence, not far inland from Nice, to recover from a near-mental breakdown. This could have triggered her emotional upsurge until alone she could not control it.

So comedy had been superseded by stark tragedy, and a loving mother with two small children and a toy dog had found herself unable to cope with the continuing pressures imposed on her by a modern world in which her own innate concern for others had grown into a private horror which destroyed her very mind and the peace she had known.

The bullets that landed in her chic Parisienne body dressed in a coat of mink that had become a shroud ended her life in October 1974. Fittingly it was a dull day with almost no brightness in the southern sky to which she was journeying.

In the recent sharing of a Nobel peace prize by the presidents of Egypt and Israel, one may spare a thought for some who fell by the wayside in the cause and pursuit of peace. One such was Danielle Cravenne, whose tortured mind craved for a lasting peace such as perhaps only death can bring.

7

A Slow Train Brought Sudden Death

The late Chief Inspector William Gough of Scotland Yard once delivered himself of what he termed a "considered opinion about railway murders". He thought they were the most tricky of all murders for a detective to solve. He spoke with feeling and knowledge, for he had once accused a man of killing his small son on a train journey. In the outcome the man was cleared of the crime, but the impression of the case remained embedded in Gough's memory as a shadow that haunted him through his later days.

What he said in retrospect was this: "It is the considered opinion of past and present chiefs of the Criminal Investigation Department that the train murder forms the most difficult of all the categories of homicide." However, he added a short sentence that that might well be disputed today, for times have changed, as has the emphasis on murder. He claimed: "The major percentage remain unsolved."

There can be no disputing the passage of events that comprised the mystery of what happened to little Willie Starchfield. He was strangled and his body left lying in a third-class railway-compartment with his laced tunic and curled hair sprawled in diminutive death, his eyes popping and his tongue lolling as his killer exerted increasing pressure on his chubby neck until it became bloated extravagantly and suffused the face with deep colour.

Gough saw the face a short while later and was saddened by

the destruction of a promising young life.

Indeed, the case made such an impression on the Scotland Yard detective that, in a number of ways, he allowed it to influence his whole career. Perhaps it was the dead five-year-old boy lying in a mortuary that presented a challenging picture to Gough's sharp eyes. It was a pathetic scene which, once viewed, could always be recalled instantly in its poignancy and stark brutality.

A photographic fashion of the early years of the present century was to dress boys in 'Little Lord Fauntleroy' suits, their hair waved and curled, especially when it was fair. One such child was Willie Starchfield. His knee-length knickers and long jacket were of a style that disappeared in the First World War. He had serious eyes that stared inquiringly at the world, and rather full pouting lips. In one photograph he stands sideways, not quite comfortably, his right hand pushed away as though he wanted to make a gesture of some sort.

On 8th January 1914 his girlish-looking body was found lying under a carriage seat on a North London railway-train. The rough usage his small body had received and the savage bruising of his throat bore ample evidence of a killer's ferocity. He was found dead at Broad Street Station on a cold wintry day. A station official alerted the police to the discovery and was immediately connected with Scotland Yard. At the time the late Sir Basil Thomson was the Yard's Assistant-Commissioner. Always a man of decision, he had a clear mind and was to be notable during the approaching war for speedily adopting the role of the first British 'spy-catcher', in which he achieved a number of remarkable successes and captures.

Such was the man who summoned William Gough into his office on a bitter winter's day early in 1914 and pushed a brief report across his blotter. After giving the detective time to scan and digest the lines it contained, he said, fingering his trim military-style moustache, "I want you to switch to this new case that has just come up, Gough. A child's body found in a railway carriage—it could get plenty of attention from the reporters and the general public. So locate this fifteen-year-old errand-boy who found the body and get what he can tell us."

A Slow Train Brought Sudden Death 97

A few minutes later, when Gough closed the door of the Assistant-Commissioner's office, he left Basil Thomson brooding as his lowered neck crushed the tips of his winged collar. He was already re-reading the brief report and reaching for the telephone.

Gough himself related the opening of a case that was to intrigue thousands for months to come and was at one time to overshadow his own career. He said:

"I found that a fifteen-year-old errand-boy had entered a third-class compartment of the train at Mildmay Park soon after four o'clock. As the train approached the next station, he noticed a small hand protruding from beneath the seat. He was too terrified to examine it. When the train stopped at Dalston, he tried to attract the attention of a porter but failed."

The detective continued: "At the next station, Haggerston, the boy, very shaken and unable to stand the strain any longer, fled. Once in the street he recovered himself and went back and told the stationmaster what he had seen. The train had already started, but by telephoning to the next station the stationmaster had a search made, and the body was found."

By this time the winter's day was drawing to its close, and lights were appearing through the deep dusk. It was dark when Gough arrived and took charge of the inquiry.

"As I examined the body," he later reminisced, "I found all the appearance of death from strangulation. The face was intensely dark and suffused with blood, both lips were bruised, and on the neck were marks indicating the recent application of a narrow constricting band with sufficient force and for a sufficiently long period to cause a marked groove."

After examination the pathetic body was removed to the mortuary, and some while later Dr Bernard Spilsbury—later to be knighted for his brilliant work as a pathologist—checked his findings with the Yard man and agreed with them. Later, at the post-mortem, he provided Gough with some additional information of a somewhat startling nature.

Spilsbury claimed that the dead boy was in a condition of '*status lymphaticus*', which meant in effect that Willie Starchfield was more likely than a normal healthy boy of his age to die if he was subjected to any sudden and violent shock.

In short, the boy's chances of living a full and long life were fairly remote with what he had got weighed against him.

He was the son of John and Agnes Starchfield. The father had been a soldier. He was burly, dark, with a broad head and what some people considered over-prominent eyes, rather like a frog's, and he favoured a full moustache. Daily he occupied a pitch, as it was termed at the time, for the sale of newspapers outside the Underground at Tottenham Court Road on the Central Line. He was in no sense a striking personality, but he was usually quite affable and was later said to have a fondness for children and animals. He had become quite well-known for a singular reason which for a time had brought him to local prominence.

In the autumn of 1913 a deranged Armenian named Stephen Titus had run amok in front of the Horseshoe Hotel at Tottenham Court Road quite near Starchfield's newspaper pitch. The man had been armed and had started shooting. He had killed the manageress of the hotel and wounded a barmaid. The news-seller had heard the shooting and had tackled the Armenian, closing with him after the man had levelled a gun at him. He was wounded but helped in overpowering and disarming the Armenian. The incident had created a stir, and as a result Starchfield had been awarded £50 and a weekly allowance of £1 by the Carnegie Fund for his heroic display of tackling a frenzied madman.

At the time of the publicity it was learned that Agnes Starchfield, who was younger by some years than her husband, was living apart from him and was in furnished rooms with her little boy. One of the mysteries of the Starchfield case that was never resolved was the reason why the family had split up, and what were the grounds for the separation. It was generally assumed that there was no deep-seated grievance but more an accepted incompatibility of temperament—or perhaps temper would be a more appropriate word, for it was believed that Starchfield was a man who 'enjoyed his glass' and could get into an argument, when he was known to appear somewhat heated in his views and opinions.

"If the skeleton in the domestic cupboard," wrote one reporter of the case, "was of a more grim and grisly type than is represented by occasional matrimonial bickerings, the fact never came out. If affection between the two languished and died, if a mild dislike on her part and an indifference on his caused them to drift apart, nothing ever transpired to make one suppose that their differences had any bearing on the dreadful event of 6th January 1914."

Starchfield was certainly not a spendthrift. Indeed, he was careful with his money. The allowance he gave his wife was very small, but she made out by working as a seamstress. The modest income from the Carnegie Fund was put aside for her son, and she always ensured that Willie was kept neat and tidy and above all what she considered "presentable and respectable". There can be little doubt that Agnes Starchfield was very fond of her son. But money remained an increasing problem in the broken household, and an indication of this was the husband's cessation of the weekly allowance he made for her and the boy. Indeed, there were formal maintenance-proceedings against Starchfield which were continuing at the time of the murder. It would not have been a happy Christmas for Willie.

Gough went over the evidence. He found that at eleven o'clock on the morning of 6th January, the traditional Twelfth Night, Agnes Starchfield had left her lodging in Kentish Town to go in search of a job. Willie was in the care of the landlady, a motherly woman who looked after him when his mother was away working. When Mrs Starchfield returned home, the landlady was in some distress.

"Willie's disappeared," she announced. "I can't find him anywhere. I sent him out on an errand just after one o'clock, and he hasn't been back since. Nearly two hours have gone by, and I can't think where he's got to."

At times Willie was left to play with other boys in the streets around Kentish Town, but when he was sent on an errand, he was usually left within call. With the dark winter day closing in, nearly a couple of hours had passed since Willie had been sent on his errand. For some reason Agnes Starchfield jumped to the conclusion that something must have happened to her son.

"You go and search the streets in case he's wandered off on his own," she said to the landlady. "I'll wait for him in case he comes in. But be quick. It's already getting dark."

Three hours later it was quite dark, and the anxious mother decided to go to the police.

"He's not coming back," she wailed to the landlady, drying moist eyes. "I've got a feeling in my bones that something has happened—something dreadful."

By this time both women were in tears. They entered a period of waiting and sharing the continued absence of the small boy.

In the interim Willie's strangled body had been found by the fifteen-year-old boy, and within a short time Gough was making his own inquiries. As soon as he had identified the victim, he had to face each of the separated parents.

The Starchfields had only the one child, and since his parents separated Willie had been living with his mother in the house of a Mrs Longstaff in Hampstead Road, which is a northern continuation of the Tottenham Court Road, where the father had his news-vendor's pitch. Gough learned that Willie had been sent on an errand to a stationer's shop. The time when he had gone was fixed at twelve-fifty, and medical evidence placed the time of death between the hours of two and three. Gough worked out a relevant time-table for the trains between Chalk Farm and Broad Street.

The schedule ran:

    4.14—train left Chalk Farm Station.
    4.17—train left Camden Town.
    4.19—train left Maiden Lane.
    4.21—train left Caledonian Road.
    4.23—train left Highbury.
    4.25—train left Canonbury.
    4.27—train left Mildmay Park.

With the exception of the additional minute between Chalk Farm and Camden Town Stations, there was a regular two-minute interval between stops. As Gough said, "I had to assume that the body had been on the train during its earlier journeys, but how many?" His investigation at this stage turned up one clue. A Camden Town signalman had caught a brief glimpse as the train shuttled past at 2.14 of a man leaning over someone in a third-class compartment very near to the engine.

Gough lost no time in starting to work on a theory of his own. If the murder had been committed during the journey timed to leave Chalk Farm at 1.59, it would have arrived at Broad Street at 2.21. In that case the body had been driven back and forth between stations twice before it was found, and around midday, when the train was almost empty, one could assume that it would remain undiscovered.

Of course the murder could have been committed somewhere else and the body transported in a bag or suitcase, but close inquiries failed to find any justification for this possibility. On the following day, when the line was searched in daylight, a police-officer found a piece of cord not far from Shoreditch Station. It was string for securing bundles of newsprint, and it could have been dropped from the window of a passing train.

Spilsbury examined the cord, which was compared with the groove made in the victim's throat. His opinion was that it was probably the cord used to strangle Willie Starchfield, though this could not be entirely conclusive.

Gough said, "I spent considerable time endeavouring to trace some motive for this murder, without result. True, there were domestic differences between the parents, but both were devoted to the child. I had accounted for all the movements of the mother, but all I could guarantee about Starchfield himself was that at intervals during the day he was selling his newspapers in Tottenham Court Road. It was at this stage that we began to collect evidence which incriminated Starchfield to a considerable extent."

One of the first witnesses to come forward was a traveller named White, who said that a few minutes before two he saw the victim with a man at Camden Town Station. Another was a Mrs Wood, who said she had been in Kentish Town Road soon after one, when she observed a man leading a little boy by the hand. The boy was eating a slice of currant cake, and she said she particularly remembered his light curls. The post-mortem contained some verifying evidence, for it revealed that Willie's stomach contained an ounce and a half of partially digested food containing currants.

Starchfield, who was lodging in Long Acre at the time of the murder, was questioned at considerable length by Gough, but during this ordeal he did not betray anxiety or any positive sign pointing to guilt. He claimed that he had remained in bed until three-thirty in the afternoon, when he rose and had some tea at an eating-house at the corner of Endell Street, after which he had walked along to take up his pitch near the Underground. He had threaded his way between the costers and their laden barrows of produce in the Covent Garden area.

At the inquest doubt was cast on Starchfield's statement, when Mrs Clara Wood made a dramatic identification. When shown a photograph of Willie, she at once declared that he was the child she had seen with the man walking beside him.

The foreman of the coroner's jury asked her, "Have you seen this man again?"

The court was silent as the woman's eyes flashed and her mouth straightened in a thin line.

"Yes," she said clearly.

"When and where?" the foreman inquired.

She took her time before replying, looking round at the faces in the coroner's court. Suddenly a finger jutted out, pointing to a man of about forty, rather short—in fact less than average height, a man with dark hair and a swarthy complexion. He had a heavy dark moustache and wore a soft felt hat.

"That's him," she said sharply. "That's the man I saw."

Most people turned to stare at the man to whom she pointed. John Starchfield jerked his head up like a marionette, trying to stretch his inches. Then he bounded to his feet with an alarmed cry.

"Me, lady?" he shouted.

But after the first sound his throat had gone dry, and the couple of words he uttered came out as a croak in his mouth. Then he struggled with his throat-muscles and swallowed hard. But it was seen to be an effort.

"Yes," said the woman as Starchfield made to overcome his erratic breathing and find his normal voice.

But his denial came out as a shout.

"It's a lie!" he yelled.

There was a long moment when no one spoke. All seemed gripped in a trance until the next words were spoken by Mrs Wood quite firmly.

"It certainly isn't," she said resolutely. "It's the truth. I recognized him as soon as I saw him standing outside the court this morning."

There was considerable hubbub and confusion as Starchfield made to resume his seat.

"That woman's swearing my life away!" he shouted.

However, he was persuaded to sit down, and the witness left the box to take a seat near the door of the court. But the atmosphere continued tense and electric. An engine-driver was called to give evidence about a dark man with broad shoulders bending over a seat as though he was tying a parcel. The man had been in the fourth compartment of the second carriage from the engine. But he was indefinite about the time. He claimed that it was in such a compartment that Willie Starchfield's body was found.

Another railway witness, a signalman, had glanced into the compartment. This man was from St Pancras and had caught a glimpse of someone dressed in dark clothes bending down. He said that he had noticed that a child, whose head was moving, lay on the carriage floor. When pressed by the coroner, he said the child was Willie Starchfield. But then the witness became hesitant, and he rubbed his lips nervously. He said he had formed the impression that the person bending over the child was a woman.

At this there was fresh hubbub and nodding of heads on the public seats, and the coroner had to rap for attention. When the inquest continued, several witnesses were called in support of Starchfield's claim that he was not the killer of his son Willie. He called as one witness the porter of the lodging-house where he lived. This man declared most positively that he had seen John Starchfield in bed at ten to one in the early afternoon of the day of the murder, and then again, some two hours later, when he was about to get up. The other witness was a street vendor, who said that when he got up at half-past two Starchfield was still in bed.

"He still hadn't come down at three o'clock," he told the coroner.

However, at this stage in the proceedings the coroner was seen to be frowning, as though he could not agree with what he had heard. He was observed to speak to Gough, who nodded in agreement on some point. What this was became very apparent when, to the "general surprise and consternation of the jury", as one account termed it, the coroner brought in a verdict of "wilful murder against John Starchfield". This was duly reported amid great excitement and with raised voices.

Then William Gough rose and took John Starchfield by the arm.

"What's this?" the news-seller asked and tried to tug away, but Gough was not a man to release something he wanted to hold.

Starchfield was very soon told. He was being charged with the murder and was formally arrested and then cautioned. However, it is fair to assume that Gough himself was not happy in the task that had been assigned to him, and it is thought that his superiors at the Yard had themselves weighed the chances in the case and had already decided on Starchfield's guilt. Gough was not so sure. He would have felt better if such a summary arrest had not been made. He was a man who was known to weigh the pros against the cons and to prefer a balance to be struck visibly. He had a niggling feeling that justice would not be served by hurrying things through a coroner's court to reach a solution in this case.

It was tidy, but not so tidy that it did not have loose ends protruding, and some of them were questionable. One line of reasoning that worried Gough was this: if Starchfield was not guilty, then who was? It was a question to which he knew he could not reply, but he felt that he deserved a positive answer, and this was what he found both unsettling and indecisive.

Years later Gough told how he felt at the time Starchfield was charged. He told a reporter who had studied the case: "The arrest of John Starchfield was a most thankless task, and in all my experience no murderer was ever so lucky as the real slayer of Willie Starchfield, for from the moment breath left the child's body every possible circumstance conspired to facilitate his escape from justice."

In short, upon reflection over the intervening years,

William Gough was at no time convinced that Starchfield was guilty. Further, there was little doubt that the inquest was not conducted soundly and impartially. The whole procedure was rather hit or miss, as though a decision had been taken too readily. While some of the jury might have demurred at what they looked upon as undue and even unseemly haste, it was certainly clear that the foreman was a man of decision, supporting the contentions of the coroner, and Gough was in no position to make headway against the verdict delivered. A few thinking members of the jury believed that the foreman had helped to dragoon them in their penned-up box into arriving at their overall vote and that they had been intimidated by his insistence that it should be unanimous.

But that can be an outcome for tidy decisions. They can lead to second thoughts, always providing that a die has not been irrevocably cast. It was so in the case of John Starchfield. Some of the depositions had been taken in what was claimed to be irregular fashion, unsound in law. Too much latitude had been allowed some witnesses who had given their evidence in good faith. For this very reason the complexion of the inquiry had indicated that the little boy's father might have been the author of the nauseous crime.

There had been notable cases in the past when a coroner and his jury, in circumstances of murder, had merely served in the long run to confuse the actual issue that was under serious debate. Unjustifiable suspicions against innocent persons had indirectly enabled a guilty man to escape the very justice intended and sought.

While he remained in a remand cell, John Starchfield was constantly loud in his protestations of innocence. Gough, given no choice by his superiors, worked hard to support a case that he had developed about the piece of string or cord found beside the railway line. During this probing a fresh witness came forward to make a startling announcement. After saying that he knew John Starchfield well, he claimed that shortly before 2 p.m. on the day of the murder he had seen him in Kentish Town Road.

Gough started with genuine surprise.

"You're sure it was Starchfield you saw?" he questioned the man, to make sure there was no mistake.

"I'm sure," said the man who had come forward.

"Very well. What was he doing?"

"He was holding Willie's hand. I saw him stoop and speak to him."

Gough had a question.

"Why have you come forward now? Is it because you know that a reward has been offered?"

The man flushed but shook his head.

"No, it's nothing like that, Inspector," he said in protest.

"Then what is it like?" Gough asked cynically, watching the colour recede from the other's face as he moistened his lips and glanced around him furtively, as though he was afraid of being overheard.

He leaned nearer and said huskily, "To tell the truth, Mr Gough, I'm scared."

The Yard man stared at him, taken aback. He knew that no man coming forward in this way could be indulging in an ill-timed joke.

"Of what?" Gough wanted to know.

The man hesitated before speaking again. Then he said, "I think I may be threatened and that my life could be in danger."

Gough opened his eyes wide as his face-muscles contracted in a frown of frank disbelief. What he had just heard was something completely surprising, for which he had not been prepared. However, although he questioned the other closely, the man would not admit to anything further. But Gough saw that the man was perturbed and, underlying his obduracy and refusal to impart anything further, thoroughly scared by what he believed. Still he refused to enlarge on what he had meant by saying that his life could be endangered by what he knew, and Gough was finally driven to believe that the man was being both fanciful and fantastic. It amounted to something like an hallucination—at least mentally.

John Starchfield came before the Old Street magistrates, and Archibald (later Sir Archibald) Bodkin appeared for the Crown, Mr Margetts for the defence. Mrs Wood repeated the evidence she had offered in the coroner's court. Certain evidence asked by the defence was found to be assailable in a number of particulars—for instance in the matter of Willie's playing about near the booking-office "round about two o'clock" while the man believed to be his father was collecting the train-fare. The man who came forward was a very hesitant witness and created a poor impression. Mr Margetts adopted a firm line. He insisted that the killer of Willie Starchfield was a woman, not a man, and that John Starchfield was innocent and in bed at his lodging at the time the strangling took place. A telling point was made by a defence witness who stated that, just before one o'clock on the day of the murder, he had observed a woman with a little boy standing outside a public house in Camden Town. It was only five minutes' walk from Willie Starchfield's home.

He described the boy and his clothes with great detail, making expansive gestures with his hands to indicate the woman's clothes, and he added that he had seen the woman before in the same neighbourhood.

"But I didn't see her with this boy," he said. "That was the only time I saw her with him."

"Did she move away from where she was standing with the boy?" the defence counsellor inquired.

"Yes, I saw her take him by the hand, and then she was tugging at him. I don't think he wanted to go with her. That was my impression."

It was enough to set frowns on the faces of several listeners, who craned forward to catch the witness's words. What was offered as confirmatory evidence was then made by a bus-conductor, who lived in Walworth, South London. He stated that he had picked up a woman with a small boy. The two had been standing at a bus-stop, and when he rang the bell he had chanced to get a good look at the boy. His route passed through Camden Town. The statement he made was confirmed by John Markham, the driver of his bus.

However, such evidence allowed plenty of room for a reasonable doubt, and despite a strong plea by the defending solicitor, the magistrates found that there was a case for John Starchfield to answer.

He was accordingly committed for trial at the Old Bailey.

It was on 9th March that the trial opened at the Central Criminal Court. The next day there were fresh headlines in the Press, for the man Gough had questioned about going in fear, possibly of his life, suddenly made an attempt on his own life.

The effect of this tumult was that Mrs Wood, who hitherto had been a staunch and sound witness, suddenly cracked under cross-examination, and when the judge, Mr Justice Atkin, intervened, she was so undecided that she could not remember having seen Starchfield's photograph before identifying him. The judge spoke sharply to her, which increased her confusion as she sat in the witness-box, and she could not give a clear impression of the clothes the defendant had been wearing on the day of the alleged crime.

In the circumstances, Mr Justice Atkin turned to the perplexed jury and asked them if they were prepared for the hearing to continue.

"From what I have heard of the case and seen of the jury's demeanour," he told the court, "I feel satisfied they would not say the case had been left so as to remove all possible doubt from their minds, and I feel that in the circumstances you will be exercising a proper discretion if you say that the prosecution will not continue."

He had also some strong words for the coroner.

"In addition," he stated harshly, "I find that the depositions were not taken at the time by the coroner, or, at any rate, they were not read over to the witnesses. Then apparently the coroner's officer who took them round to be signed was permitted to allow the witnesses to correct them. That procedure seems to me to be an entire mockery and an abuse of the duties entrusted to any coroner."

In short, justice had to be seen to be served. But it had not happened so in this case. The judge therefore instructed the unhappy jurymen that in such circumstances the only recourse was to bring in a verdict of 'Not guilty'. This was done in somewhat sheepish fashion, and John Starchfield found himself released from custody, something he was not expecting.

The killing of little Willie remained formally unsolved, and his father took to brooding over his recent unhappy past. To anyone who would talk to him he claimed that his son's strangling was an act of revenge for what had happened outside the Horseshoe Hotel when he had tackled the

Armenian, but few wanted to listen.

Some months later came the rape of Belgium, the attack on France and, after the famous retreat from Mons, the dour and bloody commitment by the British to years of trench-warfare. Two years later, in April 1916, John Starchfield died in St Pancras's Infirmary, affirming to the last his innocence of his son's murder.

8

The Vanishing Millionaire

The first intimation that the Zürich police had that anything was amiss was when Inspector Hoffmeier had a call from a worried young man. The latter was Arthur Hoffman, who was phoning to report that his father had not been seen for a week.

"He was supposed to go to Munich a week ago," he reported, "but I haven't seen him or heard from him since."

Hoffmeier took down the particulars usual in a reported case of someone missing and asked the customary questions, but he was suddenly startled when young Hoffman inquired, "Do you have anyone in Zürich who can analyse handwriting?"

That took Inspector Kurt Hoffmeier by surprise.

"You mean a graphologist, Herr Hoffman?"

"Why, yes, if that's what he is," said the young man. "You see, Inspector, something may have happened to my father, and I've a feeling that anything in the way of what he wrote may be important."

"I suggest you come in and see me," said the inspector, "and we can go into things in more detail."

Nearly twenty minutes later Arthur Hoffman was shown into the Swiss inspector's comfortable office, with its wide view over the lake, and the inspector saw a worried-looking young man who was obviously much concerned about why his father had disappeared in Germany. The inspector was young, one of the rising generation of career policemen employing technological data and statistics. He endeavoured to set his visitor at ease from the moment he began talking.

"Your father is also Arthur Hoffman. Is that right?" he began.

"Yes, we have the same name. As I explained, my father went to Munich last week to visit our plant, but he hasn't been heard from since, though I know he was anxious to discuss a business matter with a friend of his, Karl Angst. I phoned Herr Angst, but he hasn't heard from my father either."

He went on to explain to the attentive Swiss detective that the Hoffmans owned a manufacturing company in Zürich and a branch in Munich. They made telephone equipment, and at regular intervals the elder Hoffman went to Munich to check on things there and look over the factory management. But this time he had failed to return, though it was the younger Hoffman's understanding that his father had planned to return the next day.

There had been occasions in the past when the older man had been held up through some business that took longer than expected, but he had always phoned his son to say that he was delayed.

"Now," said Hoffman, "he has been gone a week, and I can't account for his absence. Nor can his secretary. My father always tells her where and when he is going, mainly because he prefers to know he can be reached at any time. All his secretary knows is what he told her, that he was travelling to Munich and would reach the German town on 17th June. But, as I said, that was a week ago."

"Since then you have received no word from him?"

"Only this, Inspector."

Hoffman held out a postcard.

"You see what it says. He's enjoying himself, and all is fine. But that doesn't sound like my father. He doesn't say when he is coming home."

Hoffmeier took the card, which had been posted in Stuttgart, and read the message.

Suddenly the visitor spoke, and his frown deepened.

"I've also a letter which I know is in my father's writing. You can compare the letter and the postcard. The postcard looks as though it is written by him, but I feel I can't be sure, and I'd like your expert's opinion, Inspector."

"Very well," said the Swiss detective. "This shouldn't take our crime lab long. Wait here."

He went out and was gone for a quarter of an hour. When he returned, he was smiling.

"I'm told that both letter and card were written by the same hand, Herr Hoffman."

The young man's frown lightened only a trifle. He took the postcard and put it into his pocket, then rose to leave.

"You've been very helpful, Herr Hoffmeier. Perhaps I'll get news soon."

He was shown out by the detective, who saw that his visitor was still uneasy about his father's unusual behaviour, and told him not to hesitate to ring if there were any fresh developments. The young man said he would.

The following day Hoffman received another postcard from his father. This too bore a German postmark. It had been posted in Munich and contained merely an abrupt admission of the fact that he was still in Germany, with no enlargement and no reference to his likely return. For a man who was approaching sixty, this seemed a piece of peculiar behaviour to his son, who had invariably found his father predictable and certainly reliable in all matters pertaining to business.

More postcards arrived during the ensuing few weeks, all presumably in the father's handwriting and all couched in the same terse, almost cryptic style. The strangeness of such a procession of missives eventually sent Hoffman on a return visit to the Swiss detective, who heard him out patiently but pointed out that in the circumstances there was little he could do. The senior Hoffman was an adult who was not answerable to anyone.

If he wanted to take time off without his family, that was his privilege. As long as he had a valid passport, he was not breaking the law.

"But of course," said the inspector, "if anything leads us to suspect that a crime of any kind is involved, that will be a very different matter."

The tense young man suddenly blurted out, "I think he has been kidnapped!"

The Swiss detective tried not to show his surprise. He countered by asking quietly, "In that case, surely you would have received a ransom demand? After all, kidnappers are always concerned with money."

That was logical, but the young man went away again without feeling he had achieved anything. After leaving Zürich police headquarters, he called on his father's solicitor, who was an experienced lawyer. The latter suggested that he consult a private investigator, Erich Blau, who handled some cases for him in the past and was sound in his judgement and to be trusted. The younger Hoffman called on him, and later the investigator was dispatched to Germany to pick up the trail of the elder Hoffman.

Before leaving for Munich, Blau, who had been well briefed in the Hoffmans' affairs, got in touch with Karl Angst, Hoffman's business associate. Apparently he had called several times to make inquiries about the absent manufacturer. The two men, Hoffman and Angst, had been engaged in exploiting an invention which the latter had called a 'biofiltre'. This was a machine to help to break down waste products that could be used as fertilizers for impoverished soil. Both men were expecting to make a small fortune from the process. When he saw Angst, the private detective found him to be a man somewhat older than Hoffman, nearer seventy, a man who appeared well dressed and lived in a good neighbourhood.

Angst explained that the biofiltre experiments had not been conducted in Hoffman's Munich factory but in a separate manufacturing plant at Oberhausen, in the Ruhr.

"He was expected to visit the Oberhausen works," Angst told Blau, "sometime in the middle of June. But he didn't arrive, and although I've tried to contact him, I have not been successful. As you may know, that was my reason for ringing his son. I wanted to know where his father was."

This supported the information that the junior Hoffman had given, and after the interview Blau left for Munich, about a couple of hundred miles away, where he made an appointment to see Hoffman's secretary at the plant, a trim Bavarian woman whose manner was very efficient.

"Herr Hoffman left here," she said, referring to a desk

diary, "on 17th June. He said he would be going to the works at Oberhausen."

"Journeying by train or car?" asked Blau.

"Train," said the secretary. "He was scheduled to return the next day, the 18th." She spread her hands in a helpless gesture and let them fall in her lap. "Since then there has been no word from him, as the younger Herr Hoffman can tell you."

Blau told her about the postcards, which she found puzzling.

"It's all so unlike Herr Hoffman," she said in a frowning pout.

Erich Blau occupied the remainder of his day with inquiring about the manufacturer to the other persons he employed, but they could tell him very little about the man's personal habits, so Blau took his inquiries into the centre of Munich, expecting to get a line on Hoffman's eating-habits, the cafés he visited and favoured, and if anyone had seen him at the railway station. But each inquiry drew a blank, and Blau was forced to return to Zürich with a negative report for the younger Hoffman.

"What do you make of the mystery?" Hoffman asked. "For it is a mystery, and it's growing."

"No hint of blackmail or a kidnap plot?"

"Just silence."

"I think I should go to Oberhausen," said Blau. "Perhaps I can get a lead from there. I'll let you know if I turn up anything."

The private detective started for Oberhausen, travelling by train. He questioned railway staff and restaurateurs and then took a taxi to the outskirts of the town, where the driver said the factory was situated. As he rode through the modern town Blau was depressed by his still having nothing to report to his employer in Switzerland, but when the taxi pulled up, he found a surprise awaiting him: not only was the factory a new-looking structure and modern, it was locked and deserted.

The Swiss investigator was a man of resource. He found a key that opened a gate and inside saw several parked motors with electric engines and what were presumably some uncompleted biofiltre machines in various stages of development. The place looked deserted.

Going through the plant, the shrewd Swiss got the quick impression that few books were necessary. The bills he went through and the letters in the few files he found bore the stamp of being old. True the bills had all been paid, but the dates on them were several months old, which was rather extraordinary. Then he came upon a date that was recent.

11th July 1968.

That was barely a week earlier!

Moreover, it was an invoiced sale for a carboy of sulphuric acid and was for a quantity that made the private investigator's eyes pinch together: 15 gallons. Quite a lot! Then he looked at the invoice again and saw that as yet it had not been receipted, so it was possible that the sulphuric acid had not been delivered to the Oberhausen factory. Blau found nothing else remarkable in the layout or contents of the German factory, and after relocking the gate he returned to his hotel near the station and put through a call to the younger Hoffman.

"I haven't found your father," he said, coming to the point, "but I'd like you to send on to me a photograph of him and then get a photo of Angst and send that with the other."

"Why?" asked the son.

"To help me determine if your father really reached Oberhausen after leaving Munich, and if he did, was it Angst who met him?"

"I don't pretend to understand, Herr Blau."

"I'll explain later," said the private detective. "Just be sure the two photos are sent."

"They'll go off today without fail."

While awaiting the arrival of the photographs, the private detective made inquiries in Oberhausen about the two men. About Hoffman he could find out nothing, for apparently no one had heard of him, but people in the town had heard of Karl Angst, who was known as a rich inventor. He also had the reputation of being a man with strange ways.

"I'd call him eccentric," said one person Blau spoke to, "but I don't know much about what he does."

A garage-owner told Blau an interesting story about Angst.

Some five or six weeks earlier, towards the end of May, Angst had told some of the people he employed not to take any notice if they heard what sounded like shots coming from the plant. He was experimenting with some explosive charges. The garage-owner lived next to the plant.

"I remember hearing what sounded like a couple of shots," he told Blau, "but that was weeks ago."

"Could you pinpoint the time more closely?"

The garage-owner shrugged and did some reckoning.

"I could have been mistaken," he said. "It was later. Around the middle of June."

When Blau received the posted photographs, he spent time interviewing taxi-drivers and finally found one who remembered both Hoffman and Angst, saying that he had driven them to the address of the biofiltre plant on the town's outskirts.

"That's what made me remember it. I hadn't been there before," he said.

So it could be proved that Hoffman senior had arrived in Oberhausen. At the same time, Karl Angst had patently lied to the man's son. The detective hastened back to Zürich with what he knew, and the son was soon calling on Inspector Hoffmeier, who was impressed by what he was now told.

"I'll have my sergeant call on Angst," he said. "He should be back in half an hour."

When the elderly man who claimed to be an inventor arrived with Hoffmeier's sergeant, he was expansive and very understanding and seemed to be completely unworried by what he had been told.

"You know, I warned Arthur. I said his son would make inquiries," he told the police.

"I think you should amplify your meaning, Herr Angst," said the Swiss inspector cautiously.

"Of course," nodded Karl Angst. "Actually I have been worried about Hoffman."

He went on to admit that he had not seen the elder Hoffman in Oberhausen but had readily agreed to his request to say nothing about where he had gone. The man had disappeared for some reason of his own, and his partner had respected his request.

"I am not one to pry, *mein Herr*, you understand. But it is time he came home," he continued, nodding. "The summer is wearing away, and we must get on with the biofiltre project. We can't delay much longer, you know."

Hoffmeier stared back at the elderly man who seemed to be speaking reasonably and without any sign of anger or annoyance, and there was no evidence that he had not told the truth, except in the matter of his request to his partner.

At the close of the interview Angst left.

"You know, Sergeant," said Hoffmeier slowly, as though he was weighing his words, "I think we should make a thorough investigation into Karl Angst. I've got a feeling, now I've spoken to him, that something about him is too good to be true. It may be just policeman's instinct, of course, but something in the picture isn't right. Let's dig for a few facts."

They did, and what they mined, proved that Herr Angst was not what he appeared to be. He was smooth and amiable, but he glossed over discrepancies. For one thing, in three days of close inquiry, they found that Angst was neither an engineer nor an inventor. He was no more than a part-time electrician. But he had been passing himself off as an inventor for the past forty years by his smooth performance as an actor.

"He's a fake," said the sergeant. "He has been posing as a technician and an inventor and bamboozling everybody. That's what it comes down to. He's no more than a glorified con-man."

He felt incensed and outraged by the deception but then cooled down when Hoffmeier pointed out that for forty years the alleged con-man had got away with his act, deceiving a good many people. He grinned wryly when he said, "Even his so-called 'biofiltre' wasn't anything that originated with him. It was something started by a Swiss engineer."

"Yes," grunted the sergeant, "a man with the same surname as myself who couldn't make a go of his invention for large quantities. Now he's dead. But what about Hoffman?"

He looked at his superior.

"It's the disappearance of that man seven years ago that I find of particular interest," said the inspector. "Make us a cup of coffee and let's go into the facts once more."

The disturbing facts to which they alluded concerned a man

named Mader, who was close to seventy and had invested the equivalent of more than £2,000 in one of Karl Angst's ventures, hoping to make a fortune by his old-man's dream. Apparently Mader had quite suddenly taken a trip into Yugoslavia and never came back, although inquiries were made by both Swiss and Yugoslav authorities in their efforts to trace him.

But the strange thing about the Mader disappearance was that for months his family continued to receive postcards from him.

"It's too much for coincidence," the inspector decided. "Maybe he is an old man and given to repeating himself. So!" He shrugged. "It's time we found out, Sergeant."

Apparently the cards sent to Yugoslavia had all been penned in Mader's own hand, which was a feature of the case the Swiss inspector distrusted.

When the sergeant called on Angst, the man was not to be found, but he was traced by phone to Interlaken, a resort in the Bernese Oberland, especially popular in the summer months. But he reported to the inspector that he had found nothing at all untoward except a concrete patch in the garage cement floor.

"It looks fairly recent," he explained on the telephone, "but Angst claims it is a drainage repair, and we'll have to compensate him for the damage if we dig it up."

"He could be bluffing," said Hoffmeier. "Tell him we'll compensate him for any damage caused."

Then came anticlimax. A couple of hours later there was another call to Zürich. This time the sergeant's voice sounded rather dispirited.

"All we found was a drain-pipe," he recorded with disgust, and later, when he returned to Zürich, a somewhat scathing Karl Angst accompanied him.

"I tell you I know nothing about Albert Mader's disappearance in Yugoslavia, Inspector," he told Hoffmeier. "Anyway, it was years ago."

But the Swiss inspector had now got a bone between his teeth and proceeded to worry it—and the sergeant. He sent the latter to Oberhausen, to contact the local police and also the taxi-driver who had driven Blau. But although local inquiries produced nothing new, something else did. The large container of sulphuric acid had been delivered but then returned because there was no one to take in the delivery.

It was a German inspector who discovered something additional of almost exciting interest: no less than a bill for work on a cement patch of flooring done on 5th June, some twelve days before Arthur Hoffman senior had vanished. The invoice for the work was listed somewhat laconically as 'Drainage'. The German detective traced the man who had done the repair-work. He said that he had done cementing to three places required in the floor, two in the front and one more under a large piece of equipment.

"I'd like to be shown the places where the work was done," said the German detective.

He left with the other man, who, as soon as he saw the cement patch under the larger piece of equipment, said, "This isn't how I left the job. This is an amateurish piece of cementing." He pointed to a piece of protruding pipe. "Who would want a ventilation pipe?"

But the pipe was plugged.

When the German detective removed the plug, he recoiled from the stench.

Some hours or more later, after workmen had smashed the cement patch in the floor, they uncovered the remains of a male body. The Oberhausen doctor said the remains had been buried for about two months. Later, after some dental charts had been flown to Oberhausen from Zürich, the German police confirmed that the body under the cement floor was that of the senior Arthur Hoffman.

Eventually a full post-mortem report revealed that the corpse had been shot in the head, and the German medical man found evidence of strangulation, though he could not be sure because the state of decomposition was too advanced.

However, by this time Karl Angst had been formally charged with murder. Despite the evidence of what had been found under the factory floor, the old man stoutly continued to deny that he knew anything about Arthur Hoffman's death. All he would say was that Hoffman had disappeared for his own unexplained reasons.

When Hoffmeier questioned him, he received no satisfactory answers. The older man insisted that he knew nothing about Hoffman's plans or what had happened to the man he had had as a partner and colleague. Then Hoffmeier came to the crunch question, asking the man if he had poured the carboy of sulphuric acid into his partner's grave to hasten decomposition of the body.

The older man simply stared at him blankly, but his response, hitherto quick and voluble, this time was slow in coming. He muttered a short denial.

"That's not true," he said slowly and not very distinctly as he shook his head.

He firmly stuck to this denial, and continued interrogation did not make him change his mind. He continued obdurate and obstructive in his answers to questions. Hoffmeier saw that he was getting nowhere with the man, whose mind seemed firmly made up, and he was showing signs of being stubborn in his denials of the truth.

But Angst was opposed by a detective who could be equally stubborn and even more determined. Hoffmeier was fully aware that he had achieved nothing that pointed to Angst's being concerned in the other's real business, for both men, Angst and Hoffman, had by nature been secretive and unwilling to share all they knew about each other and their business activities. What particularly concerned the Swiss inspector was that he could not find a way of proving precisely how the older man benefited from his partner's death. In his consideration, motive was paramount—or lack of it, for in effect he could not discern any avenue of profit for the onetime partner.

All the same, both the Swiss detective and the dead man's son were certain that Hoffman had paid out a number of sizable sums towards the biofiltre's development, but it was well-nigh impossible to establish that the man now unmasked as an arrant fraud and possibly as a murderer could have his guilt proved.

However, by constantly turning over each scrap of evidence, the Swiss investigators eventually proved that Angst had continued to draw Mader's pension for months after the man had supposedly vanished. So the receipts of the payment-slips had to be forged.

Karl Angst continued his denials despite being confronted by visual evidence to the contrary. His story remained consistently the same and was direct in its lack of variation. He insisted that he knew nothing except what he had already admitted to the Zürich police, and despite almost daily interrogation he maintained this for an incredible two years, while his life was wearing away in a slow-motion procedure that was becoming a dull routine. But he found himself ranged against an obduracy that more than matched his own.

So it was that three months later he came to terms with the law, if not with his own dented conscience. He confessed.

It was on 14th September 1968 that Karl Angst confessed to the murder of his partner in the biofiltre project. He did not suddenly go to pieces but remained cool and very calculating of what he considered his chances of beating the rap, just as he had been throughout interrogation that had become almost a daily occurrence for more than two testing years. He found himself required to sign a confession.

He now claimed that Hoffman had tried to cheat him out of the money his invention would have earned. Consequently he had no other recourse but to shoot the man who, he decided, wanted to cheat him of what was his. After he had shot his partner, he had buried the body and poured wet concrete over it, intending to pour acid down the plugged pipe to remove all traces as well as the stench.

However, one admission he refused to concede. He continued to claim that he knew nothing about the postcards sent to Hoffman after his partner's death. So the sorry business of obtaining the ultimate truth had to continue. Then, suddenly, on a late April day in the following year, he announced, to his hearers' surprise, that he was prepared to make what he called a full statement.

He said he knew that Hoffman was trying to take over the control of the partnership, and he had decided to kill him. So he told him that a Dutch firm was interested in the biofiltre and would pay a million guilders for it. "I said he should go to Oberhausen immediately," Angst said, and then went on: "I fired once, but he didn't fall, and I thought I'd missed. I hadn't, and a minute later he crumpled."

Angst hauled the body to the prepared pit, then mixed the

cement and poured it over the body. It was later that he built a cement platform, leaving the air-vent through which to pour the acid, as he said, "to make double sure".

On 13th May the elderly killer was found guilty of murder and sentenced to the maximum penalty of life imprisonment. But the case was not one Inspector Hoffmeier could view as having an entirely satisfactory outcome, for he had discovered no clues that pointed to what had really happened in the other case, that of Albert Josef Mader, who had presumably once made a trip to Yugoslavia from which he never returned.

9

The Croupier Who Gambled on Murder

Joseph Hayes and his wife Elsie, both in their middle sixties, had a ship-repair yard at Barking, Essex, and it was their normal practice to draw out the money for payment to their employees on Thursday of each week.

"I like paying my people in cash," Hayes would argue. "It's more personal than a slip of paper called a cheque. After all, they can spend money at the weekend."

Each Thursday night before the evening meal he and his wife would make up the individual pay-packets, ready for distribution to their employees on Friday. Husband and wife were known personally to the people in their employ, and there existed a very good relationship between employers and employees, which continued for years.

But on a summer night in 1963 the routine of making up the weekly pay-packets was interrupted, and very violently. The date was 23rd July. It had been a sultry day, and the evening was settling into a close night, the heat humid and rather steamy. At their usual Thursday-evening time, a quarter past six, the Hayeses climbed out of their parked car in Longbridge Road, and the husband said, "Feels a bit sticky, Elsie. Maybe it's time to think about holidays." His wife made some comment which was lost as she passed to her husband an attaché-case containing the £2,000 in notes and coins that had earlier been collected from the bank. She carried it into their house and put it down on a table in the kitchen. Shutting the door of their Ford Zephyr, Joseph Hayes followed his wife indoors, and after securing the front door, both got down to the business of making up the pay-packets before preparing their evening meal.

They had just got down to this regular weekly chore when there was a ring at the front door.

"Now who can that be, I wonder," said Hayes, rising and pushing back his chair, while his wife started counting the bag of cash and notes.

He walked to the front door and opened it part way, to be confronted by a rather tall young man with dark hair who was a stranger. The young man held a newspaper in his right hand.

"Yes?" said Hayes inquiringly.

With a quick thrust, the young man pushed his way into the house, past Hayes, and turned to reveal a snub-nosed revolver hidden under the folds of a newspaper. Quickly he reached out and closed the door.

"I want the money," he said menacingly and jerked the gun in his hand.

From the kitchen came Elsie Hayes's voice.

"Who is it?" she called. There was a sound of her rising to answer her own inquiry. She found herself staring at a stranger holding a gun. She opened her mouth, her eyes goggling with sudden terror as she fought to get her breath.

Suddenly the gunman fired, and the bullet caught Hayes in the chest. He reeled back against a wardrobe chest in the hall, falling against it. Elsie Hayes screamed and leaped to help her stricken husband, but the gunman pushed her back.

"Stand away," he snapped. "Just get me the money."

Elsie Hayes took no notice of him, concerned with her husband, whereupon the gunman seized her, and a struggle began beside the stairs. She was beaten over the head with the butt of the gun and fell back towards the kitchen, with the intruder crowding her.

Then, when he saw the attaché-case with the money spread out in little piles of coins and bundles of notes, the man became vicious. He raised his gun and shot the tottering woman in the chest. He grabbed the case of money, snapped it shut and hurried out of the Hayeses' house, slamming the front door shut. He ran to the Ford Zephyr, climbed in and started up the engine. In a matter of seconds he was driving away, without anyone in Longbridge Road knowing that anything unusual had happened.

Elsie Hayes was fighting desperately to bring help to her stricken husband, bleeding copiously in the hall. She dragged herself to a kitchen window and succeeded in smashing the glass as she raised her voice in a desperate scream for help. She was heard by a young female servant next door, who hurried to the house of Mrs Hayes's sister Pearl, who was preparing dinner. Mrs Pearl Clough quickly dropped what she was doing when the servant-girl came running to her and started for the Hayes house. When she reached it, she found her wounded sister and brother-in-law with blood over them. Hayes seemed to be in a bad way, for his wife continued trying to rouse him without success.

Mrs Clough left her sister, with blood pouring from her wound, and rang the police on the kitchen telephone, summoning an ambulance. The police radio-car arrived almost at the same time as the ambulance, but the doctor needed only a glance at Hayes to learn that the man was dead. The killer's bullet had torn through an artery just below the heart.

The doctor then turned to the sobbing Elsie and gave her a sedative. She was placed on a stretcher, and an ambulance sped both unconscious wife and dead husband to the local hospital, accompanied by a tearful Mrs Clough. At the hospital it was learned that a bullet had passed through Mrs Hayes's arm and entered her chest before coming to rest against her spine. She was in a serious condition. Her son, who had been apprised of what had happened by his aunt, rushed to his mother's side but was not allowed to remain with her for long.

Then Detective Superintendent Jack Williams, chief of the East Ham CID, arrived with Inspector James Rutland, and after initial explanations and inquiries Elsie gave a whispered account of what had happened. She said the gunman was a young man, possibly in his early twenties, who was tall and had dark hair with a thin face, but she could not say whether she had seen him before. However, she was able to continue a whispered description of the man's appearance. He was dressed in a blue suit, she said, struggling to recall the young man's face, as though she wished to fix it permanently in her mind, but then she roused to make a fresh inquiry about her husband.

"You must rest now. That's important," said the superintendent, who had been told by the doctor not to tell the woman of her husband's death.

The Yard pair returned to the house in Longbridge Road, where a forensic crew and other detectives were already engaged in the early stages of a murder investigation with a mobile crime-laboratory. An alert had already gone out in the East London area, which included Dockland, for all police to be on the lookout for Joseph Hayes's Zephyr.

Among the first clues found were some fingerprints on the railing of the stairs. They were presumably those of the killer, but they were too badly smudged to be of real value. However, the fingerprint-man found a clearly made palm-print.

"This should help to identify any suspect you pick up," he told Jack Williams. "Meantime we'll run tests on this newspaper, and we may be able to bring up some latent dabs."

Searching detectives came upon a felt-lined leather case with a spring clip, which could have carried a man's sunglasses on a belt. As the Yard superintendent saw, this case had been slit down the side to make what could be a holster. It had presumably slipped from him during his struggle with Mrs Hayes. Then Williams got down to asking Mrs Clough some questions while his men continued searching the house in Longbridge Road.

Pearl Clough said that the Hayeses were devoted to each other, and both were very much involved in their business activities. They hired many men for working on ship-repairs, which was casual labour, and they always paid them on Friday. The men never had to wait for their money. She described the Thursday-night ritual of preparing the paypackets.

"The murderer must have known about this," she said to Williams.

"It looks that way, Mrs Clough," the Yard man agreed.

However, no one in Longbridge Road had seen a stranger looking at the house, and when the inquiries in Longbridge Road had been completed, the Ford Zephyr had still not been reported. Superintendent Williams sent the home-made holster to the Yard's crime lab and later to detective teams in the East End and the neighbourhood of the Docks, but no description fitted the man who had shot Joseph Hayes and his wife, and this inquiry drew a blank. A number of tallish dockworkers were held and questioned, but it seemed that no one had seen the stranger.

By the time the post-mortem was received the Yard knew that it was a thirty-eight aluminium bullet that had killed Hayes. It was a type of bullet rarely seen in Britain, a flat-nosed slug of foreign manufacture that could have been used in target-practice. But it was a scene-of-the-crime squad that found the small piece of metal which Williams recognized to be a piece of trigger that had been broken off during the struggle with Elsie Hayes. A ballistics expert later reported that the broken piece of trigger was from an American new-style handgun made by Smith & Wesson. It fired 'flat-nosed wad-cutter bullets'. The ballistics man said he had seen only three such bullets. Immediately the area of search was extended to include seamen and others travelling to and from the United States.

While this lead was being pursued, the Metropolitan Police found Hayes's Zephyr. It had been abandoned in the East End in a side-street and had been locked. The police towed it away and started work to examine it, but they drew a blank, for the killer had carefully removed anything that could have provided a clue.

While this work was continuing, the Yard experts were studying a fresh report on the home-made holster. It appeared to have been made from the case of a pair of sun-glasses, thought to have been of American make, not currently available for sale in Britain. When he received this report, Superintendent Williams posted the sun-glasses case to the Federal Bureau of Investigation in Washington, and within three days he received a report from the FBI. They said the case was of American make and had originally been designed to carry sun-glasses with beachwear. They even narrowed the manufacture to Florida, pin-pointing the actual locality to Miami!

In the interim Mrs Hayes had undergone an operation to remove a bullet from her spine. This was done successfully, and when the woman was recovering her strength and was able to answer further questions, she told Williams that the gunman's accent was definitely British.

"He was not an American," she stated positively.

But when the Yard man asked her if the killer looked tanned from the sun, her eyes suddenly brightened with renewed interest.

"Yes, he did. Now I recall he had a deep tan."

Gradually a picture was emerging. It was of a young Englishman who had been to Miami Beach. Then the fingerprint chief phoned Williams to tell him the latest news.

"We've brought out latent dabs with iodine fumes, enough for classification," he told the superintendent.

Some minutes later Williams was in the Criminal Records Office, which houses a couple of million fingerprints. He saw the fingerprint-man continuing with the work of matching up the sets of prints. It took a little time, but when it was completed, he stood staring at the prints of a man known as Ronald John Cooper.

Cooper's last known address was in Trinity Road, Barnes, to the south of London, famous as the Thames-side locality where the annual Boat Race was run. Cooper was twenty-six and had only one previous conviction, for participating in a Notting Hill race-riot. But that had been five years previously. Since then Cooper had served his prison term and been released. Nothing was known about him until his name now emerged in a murder-inquiry.

When Cooper's photo was shown to Elsie Hayes, she recognized a face she had cause to remember.

"That's the man," she nodded gravely. The few words were spoken with a quiet assurance.

The next move in a lengthening chain of inquiry switched to Barnes, to which Williams and Rutland drove to find the man's former address. They discovered that Cooper was quite well known in the Barnes district, particularly in the pubs. They learned from local inquiries that he was unmarried and lived with his parents. But he had been a merchant seaman, which confirmed Williams's suspicions.

One man in a local bar told the Yard men that Cooper had made a number of short trips to Denmark and Scandinavia, but the same man shook his head when Williams inquired if Cooper had ever gone to the USA.

"I never heard of him going that far," he said, "but I did hear that he had been going to school."

He grinned and waited for the Yard man to react. Williams obliged.

"What sort of school?"

"To learn to become a croupier," said the man. "He wanted to get a job as a professional gambler. Seemed very keen on it, but that was some months ago. He seemed full of it at the time. All he could talk about was becoming a croupier."

The informant told the Yard man that he had seen Cooper about two weeks previously.

"It was a Saturday, I remember. He came in for a Scotch, but he didn't stay long and said little. Seemed to have something on his mind."

Closer questioning revealed that it was during a busy period on 18th July that Cooper had come in. That was the Saturday before Joseph Hayes was shot dead. Williams left Barnes and set to work to prepare a list of schools for croupiers. He soon had a phone-call from a gambler who was anxious to remain on the right side of the police and had a record of Cooper's attendance at a school.

When he spoke to the Yard man, he said he recalled Cooper very clearly.

"A tall man with a deep tan, as though he had been out in the sun a good deal. He was anxious to become a croupier because he thought it would mean a different sort of life. Anyway, he claimed that his father and some friends were intending to open their own casino. Cooper was going to be their croupier. I remember him as a quick young man, eager to learn, and he seemed to be a good mixer, which is essential if one's going to get on. But it means long hours."

The croupier paused and looked at the Yard man.

"I must also tell you this, Superintendent," he said somewhat hesitantly. "The father's plans fell through, and the son seemed very disappointed. He asked if I knew of anyone who would help him to start up as a croupier. Well, it so happened I did."

The man explained that the job Cooper obtained was in the Bahamas. When he said he was ready to start work at once, the West Indies management agreed to pay his plane-fare, so, as the West End teacher said, "They seemed keen to get him."

"How long ago was this?" asked Williams.

The manager of the gambling-school reflected.

"About a twelvemonth, I'd say, and so far as I know he's still there. He's made good all right. His tips, I'd say, should double his salary."

"And where is this job he found so quickly?" inquired the Yard man.

He was told it was at the Lucayan Beach Hotel and Casino, in Freeport, on the Grand Bahamas Island, which held the reputation of being a fabulous resort to which the wealthy and free-spending community thronged. It was only a short airflight from Miami, so it attracted many moneyed Americans wintering in the Florida resort.

But Williams had a hunch that Cooper was no longer in that mecca of gambling. A certain murder had occurred to interrupt his pleasant sojourn, though he still retained his tan to show how recently he had travelled to hotter climes.

When the manager of the gambling-school left, the superintendent joined other high-ranking officials from the Yard in a conference about procedure. They agreed that, first of all, a call had to be made at the Barnes house in Trinity Road. In effect they were proceeding to sweep up as they went along.

Trinity Road was a thoroughfare of modest houses, some of which had been converted into flats. When the superintendent rang the doorbell, it was answered by a middle-aged man. He gave Williams and Rutland a sharp probing look, as though sensing the kind of trouble such unsmiling men brought with them. It could be given in a single word: police.

He sniffed loudly.

"My son isn't in," he said flatly and in a dull voice. "Don't tell me he's in trouble," he added as he led the way into the house, closing the door after the two Yard men had stepped inside.

Neither of the plain-clothes men spoke until the father had sat down. Then Williams began asking what kind of job the son had found. After clearing a frog from a husky throat, the father said his son had been employed for some time as a croupier in the West Indies.

"You mean the West Indies, and not the West End of London?" inquired Williams, as though he felt entitled to sound dubious.

"The West Indies. Freeport, Bahamas." Again he cleared his throat. "But he said he was returning by air on 9th July," he went on, glancing from one Yard man to the other. "Something about getting into a fight with his boss, for which he was dismissed on the spot. But that's Ron. Never could bite his tongue when he should. Always wanted to have his say, and he could be a bit wild when his temper was roused. Then he didn't care what he said."

"How long was he with you, Mr Cooper?" Williams asked.

"Just on a fortnight," said the father, not looking at all happy. "Said something about intending to get a fresh job in England as a croupier." He seemed to hesitate before he plunged on, speaking more quickly. "Then one day he was just gone. No word or message. Just up and left without collecting his clothes or anything. But that's Ron for you. Here one day and gone the next. I don't know where he's gone this time, but I can't help being worried about him."

The Yard men retained impassive faces. This was no time to inform the father that his son could be wanted for murder. Williams had no wish for the father to break down. By cautious inquiries he led round to the subject of 23rd July—without alluding to the Hayes murder, although this had been prominently displayed in the national Press. By claiming to be making a routine check on someone who was a ticket-of-leave man, he obtained formal permission to be allowed to look over the son's things.

"Go ahead," said the father, extending a hand invitingly.

The Yard men mounted to a rear bedroom, where they found in a suitcase an airmail letter written on 18th July from Freeport. The letter was on Lucayan Beach Hotel stationery and was penned by a certain Judd Casey, who was apparently a musician playing at the time in the hotel orchestra. He wrote to say that he was a friend of Ronald Cooper, for whom he had words of advice. It would seem that another friend, named Marie, was dating a good many men in Cooper's absence. Casey went on to give Cooper a word not only of advice but of warning.

"I still think you are crazy not to break with her for good, because you know she is out of your league," he continued. "But if you still want to marry her, all I can say is you'd better get back here fast before someone else gets her."

The letter in its way provided a roundabout motive and revealed that Cooper was involved in a possibly amorous adventure with the unknown Marie. Williams now felt that enough time had been lost. He left Barnes and returned to the Yard, from where he phoned London Airport, where a check on flights revealed that Ronald Cooper had booked a passage to New York on the morning of 24th July, the day after Joseph Hayes's murder.

Obviously Cooper was in a hurry.

After consulting his Yard chiefs, Williams put through a transatlantic call to the police of the Bahamas and requested them to provide information about Cooper, so that he might be arrested pending the arrival of detectives from Scotland Yard.

A phone-call from the Bahamas the next day informed the Yard man that the local police could find no record of Ronald Cooper's return to the Bahamas. But in the circumstances they were keeping a lookout for the wanted Englishman. Williams also asked the local police to question the man's musician friend, Judd Casey. Another call was put through to the FBI, who were now asked to help in tracing Cooper after his arrival in New York.

On 15th August Williams received an airmail letter from the Bahamas police, who had diligently compiled a dossier of dates and facts relating to the wanted man. Cooper had quickly settled down to living in luxurious surroundings, where as a croupier he had his own Hawaiian-style 'cottage' and lived well and was friendly with wealthy patrons. Occasionally he flew over to Miami to visit friends. He had bought a large American car.

However, the local police reported, he was a man who had eyes for only one woman, a cocktail-waitress who was employed in the casino. This girl, Marie Cusset, was French. She was aged twenty-four and exceedingly attractive; although she was working as a cocktail-waitress, she had studied in Paris, where she had obtained a degree in philosophy. Then she had gone to the USA, and afterwards she had gone on to the Bahamas. She was believed to be out to make a good marriage, according to Judd Casey. Ronald Cooper was said to be very much in love with the black-haired entrantress and wanted to marry her, but she was holding off, looking for an older man—"more mature", as she said. He had even tried to win her affection by demonstrating that he could become 'mature'. He had attempted to start saving, instead of throwing his cash about. Then he had quarrelled with the casino management and been dismissed; under the terms of his contract with them they were obliged to pay his return fare to England.

However, according to the Bahamas police, he had told his girl-friend that he would return for her, and when he did they would have plenty of money. Then he could marry her. It was a grand illusion, and one based on murder, as Superintendent Williams appreciated grimly. He now had a case with only a few loose ends.

He cabled back to the Bahamas police.

Almost at once came word from the FBI in Washington. They had picked up Cooper's trail. He had registered in a *de luxe* hotel and spent three days visiting a former British girl-friend who lived on Long Island. At the end of this visit he had taken a flight to Miami.

When the FBI lost his trail, they contacted the Miami authorities, who picked it up with strange alacrity, for Cooper had been held for questioning on a charge of drug-smuggling, though after photographing he had been released. However, one of his associates had been found by the Federal men, and from him they learned that it was Cooper's intention to fly to Jamaica. In fact, he had booked a passage to Kingston on 11th August.

Once more Williams phoned the Bahamas police. This time he wished to alert them to be watching for incoming flights from Jamaica. There followed a wait of a few days, until the police in Nassau, Bahamas, rang Williams and told him that Cooper had arrived from Kingston the day before. He had been arrested and held at the airport, and a Nassau magistrate had ordered his detention to await the arrival of Williams and Rutland, who left by air on 17th August.

Before arriving in Nassau, the Yard men made a call at Freeport. Marie Cusset was awaiting them on the beach near the hotel, very anxious to help the Yard men, as she explained. Although she was fond of Ron Cooper, she said, she did not feel that he was a man to settle down with and marry.

"He was too keen on having a good time, while I wanted security—and eventually a home."

It was much the same story when the Yard men met Judd Casey, a forthcoming man with a frank manner. He told Williams quite openly, "I told Ronnie he should forget the girl, but you know how it is with some men, he just didn't want to listen to advice. He was certain he could get enough money to make her want to marry him, and he had this way-off idea about a smuggling-ring for handling dope, but I told him he'd just better steer clear of that sort of trouble. In any case, I was sure Marie wouldn't have anything to do with any shady transactions. Anything like that, and he could forget her."

Then the two Yard men went on to Nassau, where they were greeted warmly by their opposite numbers in the Bahamas force and were told that Cooper had been granted the right to consult a solicitor while he remained on remand. On 23rd July Williams formally arrested him on a charge of murdering Joseph Hayes.

When they confronted Cooper in his cell, the Yard men found him cool and composed but very alert and watchful. He flatly denied any knowledge of the killing, and when Williams inquired how he had obtained the money to fly back from England, he had a quick answer ready.

"I won it at a gambling-club in the West End. You know how it is. I had a run of luck. But now I want to get something straight," he went on. "You characters have got the wrong man. I haven't committed any crime, and I'm staying put until I'm extradited. My lawyer's told me of the procedure."

The position was that the arrested man was prepared to stall for time, for it would take all of six weeks to get the extradition petition finally cleared for Cooper to return to Britain, and in that time, as he well knew, some political changes were in the offing around mid-October. These included a Bill for the abolition of the death-penalty.

Cooper arrived back in Britain on 5th October, a chilly autumn day, and his British solicitor started to work at once to earn an additional delay in the courts. Thus it was not until December 1964 that Ronald Cooper at last stood in the Old Bailey on trial for the murder of Joseph Hayes. It was a bare three weeks to Christmas.

The prosecution had a case that was almost unassailable, for Cooper was identified by the victim's wife, and when Mr Justice Megaw came to sum up, he had to resolve very few problems of law to the jury, who after a short trial found the defendant guilty.

The judge sentenced him to death.

However, the sentence had become a mere ritual, and the stay of execution by the Home Secretary was another, for capital punishment was in process of being abolished by not very easy stages.

Ronald John Cooper's sentence was almost automatically commuted to life imprisonment as the last changes in the law were made. But the man who had gambled on murder faced long years of contemplating whether the gamble had really been worthwhile.

Only he could say.

10

The Kidnapped Movie-Star

Another case that concerned an emotive consideration of all aspects of capital punishment occurred ten years later in the early 1970s. It became a deep and abiding issue in the Philippines, and no case divided people and focused attention more strongly than that in which a lovely and popular film-star, known to millions in the Philippines as 'Maggie', became the centre of a revolving controversy.

Feeling ran high at the time, and Magdalena de la Riva was starred in a bout of publicity she had not invited. But she had good cause to feel that she had been deeply wronged and that those responsible should be made to pay the price of the humiliation that had been accorded to her.

At one time she feared that her career might have been jeopardized, but she was a person of firm resolve who had a will of her own, and once she set her mind on a course of action, she did not falter—which possibly explains why she had come as far as she had in a profession in which so many founder.

The great drama she was forced to play began on a June day in the year 1967.

On the night before she had appeared in a television show on Roxas Boulevard, a long thoroughfare running alongside the shore of Manila Bay. She had a video-recording session in one studio, and at another she had to complete a different programme at a quarter to four in the morning. By the time she had finished, she was ready to leave the studio for her home.

She had parked her car some distance away and was walking towards it, accompanied by her maid, when she was suddenly accosted by a couple of young men. They were well dressed and smiling. One called her by name. She smiled but tried to move away when they spoke to her rather familiarly. At that time of night the streets were deserted, and Maggie de la Riva could not imagine that anyone would want her autograph at such an hour. She hurried her step in time with her maid and hastened to reach her car. Of course it could be a case of some young men having had a drop too much alcohol.

She and her maid climbed into her car, and Maggie started the engine and moved away from the kerb. But soon after they had started their drive to Maggie's home, in a suburb of Quezon City, she glanced round and saw that she was being followed. She became annoyed when the rear lights of a red sportscar were seen to twist this way and that, following persistently; then the sportscar closed up as they approached Maggie's home and slowed. Suddenly the red car cut her off by a deft manœuvre, and she was forced to the kerb. There was a screech of rivets as she had to brake sharply to avoid hitting a wing. Both women were thrown back and then jerked forward, and Maggie's anger was roused by what she considered churlish conduct. But before she could open the car door to make a protest, it was forcibly opened for her.

A hand reached in and covered her mouth. Then she was seized and dragged from behind the wheel rather brutally. She had a momentary impression of three men, bareheaded and with lean faces. Two of them, one on each side of her, forced her to get into the sportscar, and she had a sudden awareness that she was being abducted.

It seemed impossible that it could be happening on the streets of Manila. It was something out of a wild American movie and was surely not really taking place except as a fantasy in her mind.

Maggie's maid was frightened by this abduction of her mistress, as well she might be. The woman crouched back against the car's upholstery, choking with dry sobs, and stared as a voice told her, "If you're nice, you won't be hurt. Just be quiet, or you'll regret it."

The speaker managed to make it sound like a sinister promise.

It did nothing for the maid's composure when she heard her mistress suddenly scream. But the sound was pinched off, and she remained with turbulent thoughts whirling in her head. Her dry sobs had ceased. She was utterly bemused by what had happened in front of the home she shared with Maggie and her widowed mother.

Again Maggie screamed. The sound was broken off short by a heavy punch in her midriff, which left her gasping and striving to recover her breath. Then she felt the sportscar travelling, and a low voice told her she had better remember what had happened to a Filippino girl named Lucila Lalu. At the mention of the name she went numb with shock, for the case was one that had appalled Manila fairly recently. Lucila was a pretty Filippino who had run her own beauty-shop. She had been raped by several unknown men, and afterwards her dismembered body had been thrown into various dustbins and similar receptacles throughout Manila.

Mention of the murdered girl's name silenced any complaint and protest Maggie was about to make. The words choked in her throat. At last she understood what her captors planned for her, and fear overcame her sense of outrage. She resorted to pleading with her captors to let her go.

"Release me, and I'll say nothing about this," she urged hopefully.

Instead of acquiescing, the driver increased the sportscar's speed.

"Shut up," one said roughly.

She had been forced down to the car's floor, so she could not see in which direction she was travelling, and when at length the car slowed and came to a sudden stop, she was blindfolded and half-dragged, half-pushed, into a room and a bolt drawn. She was left without any sense of direction as she heard a man breathing close to her. It seemed he was excited by her presence, but he still had a caution for her.

"Let this blindfold slip, and it'll be curtains for you, baby. You'd better believe me."

Then the men in the room really ganged up on her and

started a multiple rape in which she suffered many indignities besides cruel usage and was put through many sexual humiliations. The whole ordeal seemed to her to continue for hours. She suffered spells when she was not fully conscious.

Then she was tossed loose in a street at around six-thirty. She was found walking uncertainly and slowly by two cruising policemen. She was only two streets from her own home in the fashionable Twelfth Street district of Quezon City.

When the early-morning patrol came upon the tottering woman, they recognized her familiar features.

"It's Magdalena de la Riva!" shouted one. "What's happened to her? She looks as though she's drunk or been mugged."

But the truth was vastly more terrifying, and the publicity received by the case meant that it became a *cause célèbre* within a few hours. Indeed, it remained for years an outstanding topic of conversation for Filippinos until the whole grim affair had run its inevitable course and justice had been seen to be done by the outraged movie-star.

After Maggie's maid had heard the kidnappers' sportscar drive off, she had lost no time in running into the house and rousing the widowed mother and the other occupants, telling them of the abduction. The police were called, and in a little over a quarter of an hour the maid was explaining to Colonel Ernesto San Diego, the Manila detective chief, what had happened to her mistress. The maid thought the driver of the car was a girl and that there were three men, none of whom she could describe clearly and whose features she could not remember.

"But they were rough and in a hurry," she related.

Colonel San Diego asked the maid what sort of car the kidnappers had, and she said it was a sports model, she thought fairly new, and it was red. After a good deal of cogitation, she thought the model was a hard-top Pontiac.

The investigational wheels were put in motion, and some of them sped very rapidly. An alert went out for the red Pontiac, while a visit was made to the television studio where Maggie had worked late, in the hope that the sportscar was known. But Colonel San Diego very much feared that he already knew the motive for the crime. There had been a spate of kidnappings and rapes of young girls in Manila, and indeed the crimes were on the increase. The young men who perpetrated them had become known as 'sex gangs', and few good-looking females were free from intimidation and being molested if they appeared on the streets unaccompanied.

There was a veritable orgy of such sex-crimes being committed throughout the Philippines at that time, and the perpetrators and their victims were receiving a great deal of headline publicity, while the police were coming in for much criticism for not being able to clean up the youthful gangs, who sometimes seemed to roam at will, especially when they had spent a late evening carousing and imbibing. They were known to be capable of turning vicious. Some had driven their victims to motel rooms and continued the assaults for days on end. One reason for the rash of kidnappings and assaults on good-looking women was the relatively light sentences imposed by the courts. This was a feature of the crimes Colonel San Diego deplored, as he told a Press conference soon after this latest outrage on Magdalena de la Riva.

In the meantime, after Maggie's discovery in the early hours wandering in a distressed state, she had been driven home by the angry police, and a doctor had been summoned. He was very disturbed and closed the door on his patient's room, where he remained for a full hour. By this time the reporters had learned of the abduction. When the doctor emerged from the room where he had been closeted with his patient, his face was grave as he met the detective chief's eyes.

"Miss de la Riva has undergone a very grim and quite harrowing experience and is in a state of severe shock," he announced. "Her body has been ill-used and subjected to grave criminal indignities."

As the reporters scribbled away, he went on to explain that his patient could not speak coherently, and she must be accorded complete rest and quiet for a number of days. She had no recollection of how she had made her way towards her home until the patrol found her weaving an erratic path like a woman who was drunk. In fact, that was what the police patrol thought she was at first, a woman who had imbibed too well. Only when they had stopped their car and then climbed out had they realized that the woman was in distress, and when they had first recognized her, their immediate reaction had been one of profound shock.

The doctor explained to the assembled police and reporters that his patient had, very fortunately in the exceptional circumstances, suffered little in the way of really serious physical injury. But he spaced the last four words as though to underline them, and he quickly vetoed any suggestion that Maggie could be interrogated formally about her experience at the present time.

"She needs rest and quiet and to be given a chance to recuperate," he said firmly, "and I would ask the Press kindly to accept what otherwise might be a hazard to Miss de la Riva's health."

However, after this session had closed, Colonel San Diego phoned his opposite number in the Quezon City force, Tomás B. Karingal, and explained the situation that had arisen. Between them the two police-chiefs undertook to acquaint newspaper editors personally that any account of what was termed Miss de la Riva's 'driving mishap' was to be kept to a bare announcement, promising that later they would release a full statement of what had occurred, "in the public interest".

But when the Quezon City police chief phoned a short time later, he took occasion to point out to the medical man that rape was, in the Philippines, what was termed 'a private offence', as compared with a criminal one. It could be prosecuted only with the consent of the victim, and in this regard he felt he had to add a warning.

"If your patient chooses to avoid the degrading publicity that would attend the capture and subsequent prosecution of the men involved, that is her right. In that event," he went on to state, "the police would have no option but to drop the case and any prosecution."

Seemingly in the Philippines it was a matter of relevant legalities. The doctor thought about what his patient would elect to do, which at the moment was nothing.

During the three days that Maggie de la Riva was recovering, Colonel San Diego was unable to make any real progress with the case, but when these had passed he was called by her doctor to say the patient wanted to make a statement to the police. The colonel hurried to her home.

He found Maggie sitting up in bed, pale but with a look of dogged determination on her smooth features. She started speaking. She confirmed her maid's account of what had taken place when she was forced into the red Pontiac, and, speaking slowly and distinctly, as though she still had a good deal to consider, she said that the men responsible were not street hooligans. They had been well dressed, spoke like educated men and presumably came from good families.

She was able to tell the colonel that the driver was not a girl, as her maid and she had first supposed because of his longish hair, but another of the young men. His hair was not only long but fair, and he was presumably proud of it, for it was certainly distinctive enough to be outstanding. After she had been blindfolded, she had been taken some distance to what might have been a motel, because, as she remembered, the door seemed to open directly into a bedroom. But at no time was her blindfold taken off or removed, although her clothes had been taken off when the men began to handle her.

During her ordeal she had become very distressed, and it could have been for that reason that the young men ended the rape. She was told to get dressed. She did so with the blindfold still over her eyes, so that she had to feel what she was doing. When she was dressed, one of them led her away and held her arm until she reached a wide street. It was then that he removed the blindfold. As she stood swaying and blinking in the morning sunlight, she heard a voice saying, "Don't look behind you."

It was a menacing warning.

But out of the corners of her eyes she caught a glimpse of "a man with a Beatle haircut". She would always remember that man and his face. Then he pushed her forward towards the street. When a taxi came, the young man gave the driver the direction, "To Gilmore Street." That was a street not far from Maggie's home.

When the taxi drew up, her captor let her out and he went on with the taxi-driver. A short while later she was found by the early-morning patrol.

Asked by Colonel San Diego, Maggie said it was possible that she would recognize her abductors again, but that she now wanted to forget the whole incident.

"I feel I've gone through enough," she said bitterly, "in fact too much to prolong this business. All I want is to be left alone."

Both police chiefs could only respect Maggie de la Riva's feelings and wishes.

Then, some hours later, Maggie herself underwent a change if not of heart, then certainly of mind. She told Karingal, who had warned her about the effects of publicity, that she had indeed changed her mind. Indeed, it might be said that she had undergone a 'chemical' change. Anyway, it was quite revolutionary, for the iron had seemingly entered her soul, and iron can be a great stiffener of resolve. She now made a sworn statement to the Filippino police, and later she had phoned directly to the Philippines' President, Ferdinand E. Marcos. He was shocked by what she told him, and he ordered the police to concentrate on the case.

This was taking off the wraps and laying bare the assault and Maggie's ordeal. She was suddenly bathed in the brash limelight of glaring publicity, and headlines announced the rape in large type. A great and concentrated manhunt began, to find the perpetrators of this act on a film-star of such distinction.

At one such conference called by President Marcos, the actress said she was now determined to see that her kidnappers were brought to justice for what they had done to her, and she encouraged public opinion to join her in condemning such acts on other young women who had become the prey of ruthless men. By such statements she helped to organize a strong body of formidable opinion, and in case any move was made against her by terrorist tactics, she and her family went to live in a house that was guarded by the Filippino military, outside Manila. It was suddenly as though war had been declared.

The police-chiefs now concentrated their attention on trying to identify the taxi that had picked up the film-star. They believed that the motel where the rape had taken place was somewhere in the district of Pasay City. They questioned scores of taxi-drivers and checked on all red Pontiac cars. This investigation was handed to San José, a captain with a good reputation for obtaining results.

The colonel joined the captain in studying a large-scale map of Pasay, a suburb reputed for wild parties that had an unsavoury record. It was not long before the taxi-driver was found. He claimed to be innocent of any attack on the popular film-star, but, when questioned about the young man with a Beatle haircut, he said he had taken him to Beundia Avenue, in Makati, a modern suburb. There the young man had tipped him and walked away. San Diego sent a squad to Makati, and they made inquiries of all petrol-pump attendants, but it was a slow process and could not be hurried.

While this was absorbing time, the police-chief studied again the description of the youth, apparently the leader of the sex-gang, who had punched the film-star with a heavy blow to the body. The description obtained was that he was hard-handed and tough and had a swaggering manner, like a man who was very sure of himself—and equally of others. He was in his mid-twenties and acted at though the world was his oyster and he was having no trouble at all in getting to the pearl. It was when Colonel San Diego was going through a file of sex-offenders who were known to the police that he decided that he might have found the man for whom he was searching. There had been a charge against a man for raping a young television starlet the previous autumn. He was currently out on bail and was awaiting trial. With another man he had been a suspect in an unsolved fatal shooting of a police-officer in an argument outside a night-club.

In the police file the suspect's name was given as Basilio Pineda, known familiarly as 'Boy'. His father owned property and was a former police-chief of Pasay City. That was the region where the stripping and rape of Maggie de la Riva had taken place.

While the colonel was digesting these unpleasant facts, Captain San José had succeeded in locating a petrol-pump man who had identified the driver of the Pontiac sportscar as one Jaime José, whose father was a doctor. The sporty red car belonged to the youth's mother. He was the leader of a small dance-band combination and was reading a news story about Maggie and her ordeal when he was suddenly arrested and brought by the police to confront her. He became agitated when he saw the film-star and said he was not one of her abductors. In ice-cold but blistering tones she said she would never forget any of the faces seared in her memory—whereupon the youth, who was just over twenty, broke down and blubbered like a child.

When he had ceased sniffling and feeling sorry for himself, he made a statement to the police and signed it, admitting that the actress had been kidnapped in his car but refusing to make any admission that he had taken an active part in the abduction. He also refused to name his companions.

The next police move was locating the 'Swanky Motel', where a room-boy was induced to talk about a so-called party that had been held in Room 8 on the night the film-star was kidnapped.

"Did you see a naked and blindfolded young woman?" asked San José.

At this question the room-boy looked scared.

"I daren't tell you what I saw," he told the captain. "My boss owns the motel, and I'm scared of him and what he might do to me if I talk."

But the truth was eventually extracted. Basilio Pineda was the motel-owner. He had given the alleged party.

The room-boy was asked for the names of the others who had assaulted Maggie de la Riva. He was very reluctant to provide them but finally yielded under pressure and continuous questioning. He named the others as Edgardo Aquino, the son of a Manila lawyer, and Rogelio Canial, son of a retired headmaster. Then the room-boy was taken to police headquarters, where he formally identified Jaime José.

Later President Marcos warmly congratulated the police on discovering the identities of the much-publicized 'sex-gang' so rapidly. Mingled with the congratulations was an exhortation:

"They must be rounded up quickly," he told them urgently, "and an example made of them."

When this latest piece of news broke, Maggie received a phone-call. A gruff voice informed her that her face would be disfigured by acid thrown into it, and she would be otherwise mutilated, unless she accepted a sizable sum to close the case and call off the police. This threat was terrifying, but the film-star, although shocked by the lengths to which her kidnappers would go, duly reported the details to the police.

However, the police had already taken the precaution of monitoring all incoming calls on Maggie's new number. They moved speedily, but when Pineda had been traced to a public call-box in San Miguel, he had vanished.

But by now he was a much-wanted man, and the hunt was stepped up.

A new dragnet was started, and a fresh operation brought the news that the wanted man had made a call to Lipa City. The police were told to be on the lookout for a white Mercedes. Within twenty-four hours the news was received that it had been sighted, and on 1st July, at about seven-thirty in the evening, the wanted man walked into an ambush. Both he and Canial were captured in the home of a Lipa City businessman when nearly fifty police moved in and surrounded the neighbourhood. Under close questioning they said that Edgardo Aquino had plans for driving to Taal and hiding out there.

Then a large force of detectives and police in uniform started to close in on the last member of the sex-gang, while the film-star was brought to confront the others. The expression on her face was one of loathing as she pointed to Pineda, and her finger trembled as she said in a voice of hate, "That's the man who punched me in the stomach. He was their ringleader."

In the circumstances there was little Pineda and Canial could do except claim that the whole idea was José's. He was the one who had suggested that they follow Maggie and kidnap her. Then they told the police the order in which Maggie was raped after being stripped naked and blindfolded.

José was the first to rape her, Aquino the second, Pineda third in the sexual line-up, and Canial fourth.

It was now only a matter of time before Aquino was rounded up in the police dragnet, and he was caught and captured on 5th July in Batangas. He was a college student, working for a degree in journalism, and he had already phoned his father's solicitor about the police hunt. He was rushed to police headquarters, where an excited crowd of reporters awaited him, but the doors closed before any additional statement could be made.

Aquino had had time to think about the statement he would

make, and he came up with something both startling and novel. After admitting that he had been in the red car with the other youths, he claimed that Maggie de la Riva had gone with them willingly after they had promised her a sum of money for doing a strip-tease for them. He also refuted any suggestion that he had taken part in any assault on her, sexually or otherwise.

However, such a bold attempt to deny his complicity only earned bolder headlines, which angered the Philippines' President. Both he and the public prosecutor were now demanding a severe penalty for the rapists if they were found guilty.

The trial was brought forward to early October. By this time millions of words had been written about the case, which was the most sensational of its time. Even the sex of the judge was sensational: she was a woman.

Judge Lourdes P. San Diego was approaching sixty and viewed the world with the eyes of experience as well as a sound knowledge of the law. She was the mother of seven children, and grandmother of nine. She was a veteran of Filippino justice, a member of the Court of Appeals, and her name and record were familiar to all.

The judge gave permission to have the trial-proceedings broadcast live from Quezon City. Once those proceedings had started, it was as though the quartet of rapists suddenly awoke from a deep sleep to reality of the grave position in which they stood. They saw themselves in danger of earning a death-penalty.

Pineda had already pleaded guilty but sat throughout the proceedings like a man in a trance, and he remained in that state although he had not been sentenced. Canial retracted his confession, and this encouraged the defence to contend that the film-star had been willing to put on a private strip-tease show for 1,000 pesos. But the judge held that such a defence was not compatible with the facts. She accordingly refused to admit it.

The peak moment in the trial came when the star herself told her own story of events. It was a moment when millions listened to their radios with rapt attention. The story Maggie told was simple and concise, but it was thoroughly nauseating, and she did not flinch when calling a spade a much-mired digging implement, though a number of her listeners were heard to gasp audibly when unpleasant facts were disclosed. Despite what the effect of her testimony might do to her career, she firmly denied having gone willingly with the members of the sex-gang who had assaulted her.

As it turned out, both Press and public were sympathetic to her throughout, and indeed for the duration of a two-months' mammoth trial one columnist after another argued for the maximum penalty possible. One Manila writer went so far as to declare roundly that electrocution was too clean a death for such animals. In his opinion they should be spread out and pegged down on an ant-hill and left to be devoured and rot in the sun. Many felt much the same way, for feelings were running high against the men.

By the time the trial was in its closing stages, there was little doubt as to what the outcome would be, and it could have given the defendants no encouragement.

On 14th October 1967 Judge San Diego gave her final ruling to a packed court. Her decision occupied nearly sixty pages, and the silent throng listened to her words avidly and attentively until the last page was read. The judge found all the defendants guilty, and the sentence for each was death in the electric chair.

In a statement read out when the victim was not present, the judge said: "Not all the money in the world can repay her for all the fear, the indignity, the ignominy, the humiliation that her sordid experience with these men had piled upon her. Not all the money in the world will ever wipe away the excruciating memory of that event."

Magdalena de la Riva is said to have wept when she heard the verdict.

"This is a triumph of justice," she declared, "and a vindication of my name and honour, and I hope it will be a deterrent to sex-maniacs."

At the close of the trial the quartet of prisoners was removed to the National Penitentiary in Muntinlapa, to the south of Manila. Two of them, Pineda and Aquino, had also been convicted of abduction and rape in yet another case, which earned separate death-sentences. Jaime José was convicted of a further case of rape. In this instance, however, the imposed sentence was commuted to imprisonment for life.

In short, there had been a clean sweep of the notorious sex-gang, but although Judge San Diego had moved with commendable speed, Filippino justice was invariably slow, and it was some years before the Supreme Court made its final review of the case, while the convicted men waited in the slim hope of a different outcome. But on 6th February 1971 the Supreme Court finally confirmed the trial's sentences. Then came an announcement that President Marcos had suspended capital punishment in the Philippines, prior to the possible abolition of the death-penalty.

However, one of the quartet had not waited. Canial was already dead. He had committed suicide in December 1970 by drinking doped hair-tonic, a very unpleasant end. It was thought that he had been overcome by feelings of remorse and shame that had preyed on his mind until he felt he had to end the sorry business.

The death-penalty continued as something hotly debated pro and con, but on 17th May 1972 the remaining trio of convicted rapists went to their much-delayed death at three in the afternoon, after attending Mass. The first to be executed was Jaime José, who was praying as he died in an old electric chair when the current was switched on. The 'chair', with its dangling straps and fixed electrodes, had been imported from the USA in 1923 during the so-called gangster era.

Pineda and Aquino followed him in that order, repeating his prayers with closed eyes and muttering lips.

The lengthy and prolonged case was at last concluded, and justice was seen to be observed, but the previous five years had brought about many changes, and there was the promise of others to follow. Not least was that the victim was growing into an older woman who, in quiet times when alone, still recalled some bitter memories.

11

The Case of the Devoted Heart

This is a case in which amorous prejudices interposed to end in tragedy, but there are no rules for such prejudices nor for tragedy, so that both are wildly and widely unpredictable. It was so in this Irish case, which involved the slaying of a young girl who was vivacious, responsive and lively, a girl whom many had found to be enchanting.

The case achieved some of the largest headlines ever accorded a murder in the Irish Republic, for it not only held the public's rooted attention and interest throughout every corner of the Emerald Isle but sustained them as talking-points for a considerable time to come because of its unique quality.

It was a truly gruesome case which affected a number of basic allegiances as well as those that were primarily religious. By the time it came to trial in Dublin's "fair city", there were unusual factors to be considered by the police and Gardai, the least of which concerned the identity of the youthful killer who had slain a good-looking Irish girl. The motive was something the Irish police had to frown over and constantly re-assess.

The case could be said to have opened on a warm August day in 1963. It was about two in the early afternoon, and a couple and their two children were walking along Harcourt Street in Dublin. As they came level with a restaurant with venetian blinds and striped awnings, in which green was very much a favourite colour, the woman espied tendrils of smoke curling upward from an iron grille in the pavement. She slowed her step, stared and was about to blame someone for being careless with a cigarette-stub when she sniffed afresh.

"Smells like something's burning," she said to her husband as she wrinkled her face. A whiff of acrid and pungent smoke reached her nostrils. She came to a halt and watched the smoke rising through the grating. She gestured to her husband, half turning away.

"Think you should tell them inside?"

The husband nodded and crossed to the restaurant door but found it locked when he pressed. He rapped to draw attention to the locked door, while his wife went to a side-door and pressed a bell. She kept the bell depressed, and the sound continued inside the restaurant.

At length the door was unlocked and opened. Framed in the doorway was a dark-skinned man with quick, darting eyes, who glanced curiously at the Irish pair with their children. The Irishwoman took the man to be from the East Indies.

Then he spoke.

"You saw some smoke?" he asked questioningly. His English was accented but very clear. "It's nothing to be worried about, nothing at all." He flashed a good mouthful of teeth in a smile. "I was cooking some meat and some fat caught alight. The burning doesn't smell too good, does it?"

It was an easy explanation, and the woman drew back.

"In that case I'm sorry I bothered you, only I thought it could be something serious. Sorry," she repeated as she drew back.

The dark-faced man closed the door. He did not seem ready to linger and chat. But as the woman turned away, she saw that the smoke rising from the grating was growing thicker. Not only that: it was rising in gusts. She returned to where her husband waited with the children.

"Something's odd," she said, "and that young man was very nervous."

"Oh, come on now," said her husband, "you're imagining things."

But the smoke was still rising, and it was certainly smelling unpleasantly. The Irishwoman had very much a mind of her own, and she could make it up quickly.

"I'm going to phone to fire-brigade," she decided. "If something's caught fire, it could be dangerous."

Not far from the restaurant in Harcourt Street was a phone-box. She alerted the fire-brigade, and within a few minutes engines from the Tara Street station were sounding their alarm-bells. Within a quarter of an hour the engines drew up, and the escape was lowered, ready to rescue anyone in need. After the commotion of the engines' arrival, the dark young man, who at closer glance seemed to be an Indian, appeared with his face wreathed in a wide smile. He was wearing a pyjama jacket over his jeans.

"Why has the fire-brigade come?" he asked. "There's no fire, as you can see."

However, the fire-officer who had moved forward looked rather dubiously at the writhing coils of smoke that still mounted between the bars of the grating.

"Looks to me as though there's a fire in the basement. Anyway, we'll go down and make sure it's safe."

He pushed past the Indian, and a couple of his men followed him. Then the fire-officer turned and inquired, "What's your name?" He watched the young Indian lick his lips, he thought rather nervously.

"I am Shan Mohangi," said the young man. "I'm a medical student, but I work part-time as a cook in the restaurant and have a room on the top floor." He hesitated and then went on, "I was cooking in the basement kitchen, and some rags caught alight. A few sparks from the electric grill. Come, I'll show you."

He hurried below to the basement with the fire-officer. By this time the basement was filled with choking fumes. Shan Mohangi indicated an electric grill, on which some burning rags still emitted smoke.

"I'd like to speak to the manager," said the fire-officer, indicating that his men should stand back, as there was seemingly no immediate danger of a serious fire spreading.

The young Indian said the restaurant was closed for the weekend, and the manager was away.

"What's his name?" asked the fire-officer.

The Indian told him, but he seemed oddly reluctant to give the information.

At another nod to his men the fire-officer started them walking towards a door leading to the rear of the basement. The Indian quickly sprang to stand in front of it.

"There's nothing behind that door," he said. "It's only a storeroom."

He opened the door part way and closed it again to demonstrate the truth of his words. But the fire-officer pointed out that leaving refuse in such an underground place constituted a fire-hazard. The place should be cleaned up. Mohangi readily agreed with him.

"I've been meaning to get round to cleaning up," he said.

By this time the smoke was thinning. The fire-officer took another look at the grill, switched off the current and prepared to leave the restaurant premises, outside which a small crowd had collected. They dispersed as soon as the firemen started back to the fire-station. The whole incident was summed up in two words by an onlooker:

"False alarm."

More than two hours passed. Another Indian student, who lived in the same building as Shan Mohangi, arrived home at five o'clock to find a pervading odour of oily smoke clinging to the hall.

"What's this stink?" he asked.

Mohangi tried to pass off the incident.

"Oh, I burned some meat," he said casually. "But you know how some smells cling this hot weather. It'll soon be gone."

Two hours later, about seven o'clock that Saturday evening, Desmond Mullen and his girl-friend arrived by car to visit the Indian medical student. Mohangi let them in. He was dressed in a suit and looked very spruce.

"Hazel arrived yet?" asked Mullen.

He was referring to his sister, with whom he had arranged to have a dinner-party for the four of them.

"She phoned to say she couldn't make it," said Mohangi, spreading his hands. "We'll just have to eat without her."

Mullen thought this very odd.

"Didn't she say anything about why she couldn't keep her

date?" he asked.
The Indian student adopted a sad expression.
"Perhaps she had another date. Well, let's go ahead and enjoy the food."

In the circumstances there seemed little else to do, but Desmond Mullen failed to understand what had come over his sister. Normally she was keen to enjoy a dinner-party, especially if the food on the table was good, for Hazel liked eating out. He was surprised, too, that she had found an alternative date on a Saturday and ran over in his mind the friends she might have contacted. But at the present time he thought Mohangi would head any list. In such circumstances her refusal to join her brother and his girl friend for a dinner-party with the Indian student was even more perplexing.

Hazel had been very friendly with Mohangi for about a year. She was only fifteen, but, as Desmond knew very well, she was often taken for three years older than her actual age. This had been part of her attraction for the medical student.

While the meal continued, Desmond Mullen kept shooting puzzled glances at the Indian. Mohangi was twenty-three and a native of Natal, in South Africa. He had saved enough money to get to Ireland two years before, and in Dublin he had become a medical student at the Irish Royal College of Surgeons, possibly attracted by its enviable reputation. To help towards his overhead expenses he had taken several jobs, the latest as a part-time cook at the restaurant in Harcourt Street. For the past year Shan Mohangi had been paying court to Hazel in a sort of desultory on-and-off fashion, for the Mullens were something of a straight-laced family in which improprieties were neither allowed nor encouraged and certainly not indulged in these days of permissiveness. The mother was a widow with half a dozen children, and the family lived in the Shankhill district of the Irish capital. Desmond was the eldest.

"You're too young, Hazel," she had said to her daughter. "There's plenty of time to think of getting married. No need to be in a hurry. Besides, Shan isn't a doctor yet."

That had put the entire concept of marriage in abeyance. The Indian student was welcomed as a good friend of the family, but in the mother's eyes he was something less than a suitor or potential life-partner for her daughter. Of course, if he passed his exams and became a doctor, as she reminded the family, that would be different, though Hazel was still very young. In that case she could not object to her daughter's husband being an Indian.

"Colour is only skin deep," she reminded her family whenever the subject was broached.

On this particular Saturday when Desmond had dinner with his girl-friend and a lonely Shan Mohangi, who was acting as host, the brother's thoughts were very mixed, for he had an unaccountable feeling that things were not as they should be.

After the chicken dinner was cleared away, Mullen left with his girl-friend to attend a dance. The original arrangement had been for both couples to go to the dance, but since Hazel had apparently broken the date, Mohangi said he would not go.

"I'll wait for you to get back, Desmond," he told the brother, "but please don't cut any dances on my account."

So the couple left for the dance. When it was over, Desmond took his girl-friend home and drove back to Mohangi's to spend the night as had been originally arranged. By this time it was shortly after two in the morning. Desmond had just got back to Harcourt Street when the phone rang.

It was a worried Mrs Mullen calling to ask where Hazel was. She sounded very anxious. Mohangi said he did not know and then explained about the broken date and how it had come about.

"By the way, Mrs Mullen," he said, "Desmond's here now. Have a word with him."

"Yes, but what's happened to Hazel, that's what I want to know?" continued the mother before the Indian could put the phone down. "She's never been out this late before."

Then Desmond broke into the conversation.

"I'm coming home straight away," he said hurriedly, "and Shan's coming with me." He looked at Mohangi, who nodded quickly. "I'm on my way. Shan't be long."

He hung up.

The Dublin streets were deserted at that hour, and the pair made good time on the journey. As she heard the car draw up, Mrs Mullen flung the front door open expectantly. But the youths had not brought Hazel home, as she had half hoped. No one had heard from the missing girl.

The Indian spent the night at the Mullen home and slept in Hazel's bed. The next day he and Desmond were up soon after daylight, making inquiries about the girl. They called at the Shankhill police-station, where an officer named Donaghue took down particulars. He learned that Hazel worked in the Bank of Ireland and had planned to spend the Saturday with Mohangi and her brother, but she had called off the engagement.

"Didn't she explain why?" asked the Irish police-officer.

"No, she rang off," said the Indian.

On the Sunday afternoon the two youths drove back to Harcourt Street, where they continued their inquiries about the missing girl with people who might have seen her. Then, with Sunday evening approaching, they called in at the Harcourt Terrace police station and told the story once more, saying they had already been to the Shankhill station.

Detective Inspector Matthew Kennedy listened to the narrative. He asked some pointed questions.

"Just how friendly are you with Miss Mullen?" he asked. "Do you sleep together?"

Mohangi reacted strongly.

"Certainly not. She is a nice girl, and we are planning to be married, as I have told her mother."

The calm Irishman stared at the troubled eyes of the student, while Desmond kept biting his lips, not liking this turn in the inquiry. Kennedy's stare broke when he lowered his eyes.

"Tell me about the broken date," he asked.

When it was related again, he rose and suggested that they should join him in a short trip to the restaurant. But he received an unexpected objection from the Indian.

"There can't be any reason for going to my place," he said rather heatedly. "After all, she didn't arrive there."

The Irish inspector's eyes narrowed as he pursed his mouth, nodding.

"All the same," he said smoothly, "I think we should take a look. What did you say the place is called?"

"The Green Tureen," said Mohangi, who seemed to have

calmed down as he saw both the inspector and Desmond looking at him. "I'm sorry," he muttered. "This thing has upset me."

They went to the restaurant and met the other lodgers who lived in the building. One young man, another Indian, said that he had seen Mohangi meet an Irish girl about midnight, but she left alone.

"I saw her climb the stairs," he said.

Matthew Kennedy asked him, "You're talking about Hazel Mullen, I take it?"

"No," replied the other. "I know Hazel. This was another girl."

Kennedy became interested. He was told that this girl was several years older than Hazel. The lodger had seen her calling on Mohangi several times. She was on one occasion dressed in a white uniform.

"I think she is a nurse," he added.

After taking notes, Kennedy left, but the next morning he went to the College Green branch of the Bank of Ireland, where he continued his questioning. He learned from a bank employee that she had walked with Hazel Mullen as far as Trinity College, and then Hazel had turned towards Grafton Street, but she had given no indication of where she was heading, though it could have been in the general direction of Harcourt Street. The inspector headed in that direction, questioning people in shops, but he got no affirmative response until he came to the local Woolworth's, where he talked to a bright girl with red hair, who readily said that she knew Hazel Mullen, who frequently called in.

"Do you know if she was here on Saturday about twelve-thirty?" asked Kennedy.

"She was," said the salesgirl. "She bought a lipstick."

"Any idea where she was going?"

"Sure. She had a date to see her Indian boy-friend. She told me that was why she'd bought the lipstick."

Kennedy walked away from Woolworth's with a frown on his face. He did not like what he was now forced to consider. He returned to Harcourt Terrace police-station and remained closeted with Superintendent Bernard McShane for a long time. At the end of their discussion McShane phoned another policeman with superintendent's rank. This was Pat McLoughlin of the Dublin Technical Bureau. The men agreed to conduct a search of the restaurant premises.

While the police were coming to this decision there had been developments in Shankhill, where an old-time friend of the family had told Mrs Mullen he was in a good position to say where Hazel was, by what he called 'divination'. He told the girl's mother that she would be discovered roving about in the Crumlin district of Dublin.

Such homespun divination was akin, in the eyes of some sceptics, to reading tea-leaves in a cup—and about as likely to get a true result. But Mrs Mullen, with Mohangi, set off to look for Hazel in the Crumlin district. They trudged from door to door, an odd-looking pair of inquiring callers, a middle-aged Irishwoman and a youthful Hindu. The search came to nothing, and Mrs Mullen, in tears, was forced to return to Shankhill, while the young Indian turned back towards Harcourt Street.

The Monday was wearing away. Mohangi was seen washing out a shirt in a tub, and some time later a Mrs O'Connor, who was a vegetable-cook employed at 'the Green Tureen', arrived to begin work after the closed weekend.

She went down to the basement and was at once struck by a strong odour of disinfectant, which seemed to come from a closed partition-door. She opened the door and saw some rubbish and newspapers and what she took to be a hambone, which she wrapped in a newspaper and threw into the dustbin. But having found the source of the unpleasant smell, she looked further and came face to face with Mohangi, who told her he was about to clean up the place. Mrs O'Connor was quite ready to leave the task to the young Indian. Some while later, after the heat of the August afternoon, the dustmen arrived on their Monday round, and Mohangi hurried out to add his quota of refuse to the collection.

In the evening the owner of the restaurant arrived from a stay outside Dublin and was surprised by two unusual occurrences, the news of the fire-brigade's appearance there on the Saturday and the strange odour traced by the vegetable-cook. He went down to the cellar himself, puzzled by what he had heard, and when he came up again, he called in to see Mohangi and soon was listening to his account of the Irish girl's disappearance.

He came to a quick decision.

"Look, Mohangi, I'll drive you to the police-station," he offered. "But get this thing cleared up."

However, the medical student insisted that he had done nothing to interest the police, and he was clearly reluctant to take up his employer's offer. During the warm hours of the August night the man decided he had not been firm enough. He phoned the police himself and asked them to go over the premises thoroughly.

The police came early, about five o'clock in the morning, and there were three of them. As they arrived at the top floor, to work their way down to the basement, they found that Mohangi's room was locked. From it came an unmistakable odour of gas. They broke it down to find Mohangi sprawled fully clothed on a couch with gas-jets turned on and the gas-fire unlit.

He was still alive, but unconscious. He had emptied a pill-box and scrawled a message on cardboard, declaring that he left everything to a girl-friend, who was not Hazel Mullen. He was rushed to St Vincent's Hospital by ambulance. The news alerted Inspector Kennedy, who was joined by the pair of superintendents, McLoughlin and McShane. Then a descent was made to the restaurant basement. On top of the rubbish-pile was the bone found by Mrs O'Connor. The technical man recognized it at once.

It was a human thigh-bone!

When the door leading to the storeroom was opened, it was seen that a piece of plywood was propping it up. When this was removed, a whitish mass was revealed. The officers shone their torches on the unsavoury pile. In the bright glare they picked out a hand, pieces of a female body and a forearm.

The State Pathologist, Dr Maurice Hickey, was summoned. He found seventeen parts of a young female brunette who was in her teens. Her body had been dismembered by someone with anatomical skill and a couple of sharp instruments—he thought they were a honed butcher's knife and a meat-cleaver. But the head was missing, as were most of the internal organs.

When a search was made of the gas-cleared room on the top floor, some bloodstained jeans and a handkerchief were found, and tucked behind the gas-fire were some pieces of flesh. In other corners of the room were a woman's shoes, an umbrella and a wristwatch.

Later Dr Hickey began a post-mortem.

By this time the news of the murder had brought crowds out onto the Dublin streets to gossip and mill around and speculate. There was a vast quantity of dark stout consumed during licensed hours.

The Indian student recovered from his attempt to commit suicide and eventually arrived at Mountjoy Prison. There he made a statement to the effect that he had loved Hazel Mullen and wanted to marry her, but her mother had forbidden her marrying until she was seventeen. One day she had admitted kissing another boy. He had been furious and struck her but afterwards apologized most abjectly and begged her forgiveness.

Then, on 17th August 1963, the pair had reached a crucial stage in their courtship. Hazel had arrived at one o'clock and as she had never been down to the basement, he had taken her down to see the cooking-equipment. Their close proximity resulted in hugging and kissing, and then Hazel had felt emboldened to make a confession. According to Mohangi, she admitted having had sexual relations with another man. At that the Indian went berserk.

"I don't know what happened to me," he said in his statement. "I always loved and worshipped her. I thought she was different from other girls. But she turned out to be like all the rest. I was in a rage at the time. I caught hold of her and put my hands around her neck. Before I knew it, it was the end."

He claimed that the last thing he had intended was to kill Hazel.

"It was an accident," he told the grim-faced men from Dublin, who had heard the like many times before.

With a dead girl on his hands, the medical student had proceeded to dismember the body. He had difficulty in burning the head and some of the girl's clothes which were wadded together—hence the telltale tendrils of smoke from the grating, which had become thicker and more voluminous. Then the couple with their children had arrived. He had got rid of them, but they had summoned the fire brigade. However, the interruptions in his gruesome task of destroying the girl he had claimed to have loved were unnerving, and by the time Desmond Mullen and his girl-friend arrived, Mohangi was having to struggle to continue the grisly charade and the brutal deception.

When the statement was finished, he was shown the piece of cardboard on which he had written a brief Last Will and Testament.

"Who is she?" asked McShane, tapping the cardboard.

"A nurse I knew when I first came to Ireland."

"Where does she work?"

The Indian hesitated, while the police waited.

"Meath Hospital," he said grudgingly.

"Wasn't she at your place on the Friday before Hazel Mullen's death?"

Mohangi dropped his chin. The police did not press the point. After all, they could now join up the loose threads. They had their case.

One of the loose threads to be tied concerned Mohangi's relations with other women. It was becoming plain that Shan Mohangi was more deeply involved than he had cared to admit. So were his various relations with other women. Indeed, some of the Irish investigators began to suspect that Hazel's death might have been carefully planned a good time before, when he had grown tired of the Irish girl. It was an old story on an older theme.

Suspicions were strengthened when Dr Hickey said, in the post-mortem report, that he had been unable to find the real cause of Hazel's death, for her throat had been cut away, thus removing any fingerprints as the result of the alleged strangling. Moreover, parts of the girl's genitals were also cut away, so that it could not be determined whether or not the teenager was a virgin. All this evidence was presented by McShane to the State Solicitor's office, with the result that Shan Mohangi was charged with murder and confined to Mountjoy Prison.

His trial opened on 10th February 1964, with crowds being

turned away from the court buildings. Mohangi's mother had flown in from South Africa for the trial, which had created a great deal of public excitement and speculation. Her son, neatly garbed in blue serge and wearing a white shirt with a striped tie, appeared to be at ease in the dock.

Niall McCarthy opened for the prosecution, stating that Mohangi had been a victim of apartheid, but when he came to Ireland he found himself mingling with whites and non-whites quite freely and possibly because of this he quickly took up with an Irish girl. He went on to say that, in the case of Hazel Mullen, Mohangi had admitted seizing the girl by the throat and, because of her alleged infidelity, had wilfully strangled her and carefully removed any evidence of what he had done.

Mr Condon for the prosecution further contended that Mohangi had wanted Hazel Mullen dead because she stood in the way of his warmer feelings for another woman.

"Miss Mullen," he added soberly, "died from a determined strangulation attack resulting in asphyxia, after which the accused attempted with cool deliberation to conceal the bloody evidence of his crime."

It seemed an open-and-shut case, but Mohangi's defence strove strenuously in the full tradition of Irish law.

"The defence in this case," said Mr Fahy, "is nothing more and nothing less than accidental death."

His fellow defence counsel, Mr Bell, considered that Hazel Mullen's death was not so much due to strangulation as to what he called "vagal inhibition". In support he cited a prominent witness, Dr Alan Thompson of the Irish Royal College of Surgeons, who testified that any pressure on the throat, even if it was unintentional, could well cause death by a reflex heart-stoppage.

Once again the medical experts were in contention and opposed. It was a legal confrontation that had occurred many times. Dr Thompson said that individuals differed in this and that certainly all persons did not appear to be susceptible to death through vagal inhibition, "but that Miss Mullen might have been one who did".

The defence went on to quote a long letter from Shan Mohangi in which he quoted some verse, which ran:

> There never will be a heart so true
> For I am devoted to you, my love,
> And for ever will be true.
> I love you, Hazel.

Mohangi's 'devoted heart' had to spend eight hours in the witness-box, while he was examined and later cross-examined, but his composure remained throughout completely unruffled, and the creases in his tie continued in place—he was "bloody cool", as one member of the public said with grudging admiration for a remarkable performance that lasted for the eleven days of the trial.

It ended on 21st February. Within three hours the foreman rose to say that the jury were ready to give their verdict. They found the defendant guilty of murder.

There were audible gasps from the public galleries, where a number of women called their disagreement, while some wept openly.

When Mr Justice Teevan asked the defendant if he had anything to say, Mohangi shook his head emphatically.

"No, nothing at all," he said firmly.

So the judge sentenced him to death.

But it was not a popular verdict, and many people started a movement to have it set aside, which grew in momentum. In a little more than six months the man with the 'devoted heart' was deported to South Africa, where all trace of him has been lost.

12

Death Was the Last Confessor

It was on a Sunday night in late November 1943, halfway through the Second World War, that the 'John Barleycorn' public house in the blacked-out docks region of Portsmouth was broken into. The pub was kept by an elderly licensee, Rose Ada Robinson, who was not a person with great faith in banks and similar institutions. It was customary for her to keep both her own money and the cash of the bar's takings in two stout handbags, which she slung around her ageing person and which were rarely out of her sight.

In fact, Rose's bags were known throughout the 'Pompey' docks area. They were on display most nights and certainly on that Sunday night of 28th November 1943. The 'John Barleycorn's' clientèle were not a particularly choosy collection of Sunday-night drinkers, and trade was limited to beer in bottles and casks. The somewhat run-down pub was really only an ale-house, patronized by the thirsty and those with a more than average intake of beer; no spirits were dispensed across the bar.

It was usual for the rule about closing-time to be promptly observed once the traditional call for "Last orders, please," had been voiced. Ten o'clock was closing-time on a Sunday, and it was usual for the front door to be locked and bolted within a very few minutes of that hour after the only barman had gathered up his glasses and bottles, swept up perfunctorily and seen Mrs Robinson, accompanied by her two large handbags, climb the stairs to her room. Presumably she settled down for a normal night's sleep, but on 28th November little was normal—at least, not in the small hours.

It was sometime during those hours that a light-sleeping neighbour heard the sound of someone breaking into her home. She was petrified, and although she lay still, she must have made a noise which disturbed the intruder, for shortly afterwards she heard distinct sounds of his leaving by the way he had entered. She lay awake wondering if she could have imagined the incident.

A little later she knew otherwise.

It was around three in the morning when her attention was again caught by an unusual sound. It was of breaking glass. The sound so startled her that, although it was a cold morning of mist, she pushed aside the blackout curtains and peered out. What she saw made her hold her breath. She saw the outlines of four men getting into a car close to the 'John Barleycorn'. The car then drove away.

Five hours later, at 8 a.m., Mrs Robinson's regular cleaning-woman arrived and could get no reply to her continued knocking. Being a woman of some resource, she continued down the street to the home of a naval stoker, whom she roused. He climbed in and opened the door for her, but there was no sign of Mrs Robinson, despite the noise and knocking made in entering the public house. The stoker and the woman cleaner went upstairs, where they found Rose Ada Robinson lying dead on the floor. Spread across her face was a piece of cloth. The bedroom was in upheaval and had been ransacked, with the blackout curtains torn down and left lying in a bundle. Of the money there was no sign.

The police were hurriedly summoned, and one of their first discoveries was a broken window at the back of the house. They dusted the sill with graphite powder, but the prints they brought up were very smudged and could not be used for purposes of identification. However, on the lower ledge was found a button with a thread of cotton affixed.

Later, after the local police had examined the premises and the 'John Barleycorn' had been closed, a post-mortem on the victim was held by Dr Keith Simpson, who reported that Mrs Robinson had been manually strangled. It appeared that only the right hand of the killer had been used to take her life, as there was a mark of thumb-pressure on the right side of her throat, while fainter marks appeared on the left side.

The post-mortem examination clearly pointed to murder, but there were indications that the dead licensee had put up a struggle, during which she was thought to have struck her head, most likely in the middle of the forehead and features. Her inert body had fallen on her back towards the left. Then the murderer is believed deliberately to have knelt on her and choked her to death.

The medical evidence revealed signs of senile change. From this it was deduced that it was possible that she might have collapsed unexpectedly. There was a small mark where the skin was broken, like a nail-scratch. This was found on her throat, along with two or three others, rather similar. They could have been occasioned while she was threshing around to free herself of the pressure on her windpipe. But after the post-mortem the police were left still searching for a vital clue.

The local Press played up the murder of the elderly woman, who was in her sixties, and although it was approaching winter and enemy air-raids were still threatened nightly, both police and reporters joined in the hunt for anything that could be considered a clue.

The process continued for three weeks and drew a blank.

Then, just before Christmas, on 21st December, they had a break. At four-thirty in the morning of a dark winter day a man was arrested in Kennington Cross, in South London, not far from the local police-station. He was picked up for trying to sell a pair of shoes which were supposedly stolen. When arrested, he was found to be a man with a record. He was forty-seven and had spent more than half his life in jail. While on his way to a cell, he suddenly made an admission which was quite unexpected.

"I am wanted for other things far more serious than this," he told the South London police. "The Yard wants me. It is the trapdoor for me now. I am glad you picked me up." He stopped speaking and observed the officers watching him. As a gesture he held out a cigarette-case. "Here is a Christmas box for you. This will be my last Christmas, I know."

Then he began to grow maudlin, and after one of the

police-officers had taken a cigarette from the case in his hand, he went on in a strangely hollow sort of voice, as though he were making a confession.

"I'm glad I'm in," he went on, with a touch of what could have been wonder in the words, as though he could not really believe what he was saying. "I've been through hell for the last three weeks. I've been a bastard all my life, and I'll finish as I lived. I was sorry for it the moment I had done it. I've had no sleep since. It's preying on my mind."

After a longer pause he resumed.

"She must have had a weak heart, poor old girl. But I had to stop her screaming, though I didn't mean to kill the old girl. You know what it is when a woman screams."

He appealed to his listeners, who sat like statues.

There was another longish pause as he added, "This is the end for me. I want to say that I done the murder job in Hampshire about fourteen days ago."

In this broken fashion the story of a crime was told.

The man who had confessed was Harold Loughans. He was not only maudlin, he was depressed about the prospect of dying. That may have been his reason for saying that most of the stolen money, which was about £250, was in a suitcase.

"I've left it with a girl-friend," he told the silent police who had been taking down his words, though they were confused, even a little perplexed, by what he had called 'the murder job in Hampshire'. In the welter of police notices and reports a relatively minor provincial murder which had not made the national headlines had been overlooked, and as yet the Yard had not been called in.

However, the statement made by Loughans on that dark morning just before Christmas meant that the Portsmouth police would have to be contacted. Following an urgent phone-call, a couple of CID officers arrived from the port and had a session with the arrested man, who now made a more detailed and fuller statement. Loughans continued to make statements under careful cautioning, adding to the overall story piece by piece.

In one he admitted: "I heard a customer say the old lady had about £2,000 in the house. I thought this over and went to the pub. I climbed over the wall and, as far as I can remember, got through the kitchen window." He then went on: "I saw a woman about sixty and told her to keep quiet, and I put my hands round her throat. She became quiet, and I think she had fainted. I left her lying on the floor in the bedroom. This is how she was found."

Yet another piece of enlarged explanation followed:

"She started to scream, and I grabbed her by the throat with my right hand. She fell down near the window, and as she fell, the blackout fell down from the window. I held her down on the floor. She looked awful, so I covered her face. Did the old lady have a weak heart? I cannot understand it as she went quiet right away."

He had found the button missing from the cuff of his jacket, so had cut off the remaining buttons. He said that Mrs Robinson had not worn any rings, and she had left the two large handbags on the dressing-table under a glass top.

When the last of these statements had been initialled and signed, Loughans was driven back to Portsmouth. There, in the local charge-room, he heard himself charged with the murder of Rose Ada Robinson.

One feature that helped to identify the man who had spent most of his life in the pursuit of crime was that his right-hand fingers had been mutilated. They were little more than knuckle-stumps, which made the hand grotesque, for the thumb was large enough to fold over the stumpy ends. The loss of his finger-tops had occurred when he was about fifteen, employed in a brickyard.

Not only did the police go thoroughly into Loughans's story of the murder but a detective journeyed to the police laboratory at Hendon to check and examine articles of clothing and bedding from the 'John Barleycorn'. One exhibit was a hair caught in one of the empty handbags. Some time later the forensic scientist was also able to check out the thread of the button that had been torn from Loughans's coat. It was of real interest, for it was thread that had been used in the tailor's shop in Parkhurst Prison, on the Isle of Wight. That was where the habitual criminal had served his last prison sentence.

However, among the fifty or more exhibits, such as bits of fluff, small eiderdown feathers, scraps of mats and some other hairs and fibres, there was none that was truly significant in the murder investigation.

After Christmas the committal-proceedings were opened by Loughans's having a change of mind. He now strongly denied having murdered Mrs Robinson and retracted his confession.

"I did not murder the old lady," he insisted, surrounded by a ring of raised eyebrows.

It was plain that the old lag had had not only second thoughts but also a change of heart—if, in the circumstances, that is not a misapplied term. The magistrates heard his plea but in due course decided that he had a case to answer in a higher court. He was duly sent for trial to the Hampshire Assizes, which took place in March 1944, three months before D-Day was to be announced.

The prosecution was led by the late J. D. Casswell KC and J. F. F. Platts-Mills, and the defence by John Maude KC and G. W. Willett. Loughans claimed he had made his confession merely to annoy the police. In that case a very pertinent question arose: how could he explain his alleged innocence of the crime when he knew so much detail about it?

He provided a glib answer. He insisted that he had read all about the murder in a newspaper and that on the night of his arrest the police officers themselves had provided him with additional information, piece by piece.

Not unnaturally the police vigorously denied that such information could have been obtained in that way. For once, the old adage that it is best to keep mum until a suspect's lawyer arrives was proved empty and void. Loughans could be said to have taken the police very literally for a ride. He had certainly talked, but with deep and conniving purpose, like an old lag who knew precisely what he was saying and why. It might even have been considered that he was getting back in this way at his long-term enemies, the police.

In evidence Dr Keith Simpson said he had not examined Loughans's mutilated right hand, and he explained on a later occasion that he felt it might have been improper for him, a pathologist, to make an examination of a living hand. That, in his considered opinion, was something to be undertaken by a clinician. However, he believed that the stumpy hand could have made the marks on Mrs Robinson's throat. But details of medical evidence were swept away by the defence, who had a really penetrating arrow for their boy: a strong alibi.

There was certainly a sensation in Winchester Crown Court at this, for the news came as a shock to the Crown, who were taken out of their legal stride. They appeared dumbfounded as they watched and heard five independent witnesses testify to Loughans's being in their company in Warren Street Underground air-raid shelter on the night of the murder.

The five witnesses acted as though very sure of themselves and their story. They were three women and two men, London Transport employees, resolutely unshakable in their testimony about both time and date. In fact one of the London Transport men produced a 'record of works' sheet for the night of 28th–29th November to show that the Sunday night was the only one that his colleague had been at work in Warren Street Station. Such a demonstrative alibi was something the Crown could not circumvent. Eventually it came time for the judge to sum up, but he could only leave the jury with an unsolved problem in view of the alibi.

In the circumstances, the foreman felt he had to make a gesture. He did so rather objurately, by inquiring of the judge if the prosecution had made any attempt to test the alibi. After considering the request, the judge patiently informed him that the jury should not reject an alibi solely because the fact had not been disclosed early enough for it to be tested. The foreman nodded and went back to his fellow-jurors. When he returned to the jury box, it was to report to the judge that he and the others were unable to agree on a verdict. At that a fresh hubbub broke out. A hung jury meant a re-trial.

So the case had to be heard again, this time at the Old Bailey.

The change of venue had not produced a change of faces. The same barristers were lined up in opposition, and the prosecution produced the same evidence, but when Keith Simpson was called in cross-examination, the defence started to examine more closely than previously the apparent failure not to test out Loughans's right hand. In fact, John Maude then made great play with telling words. He conceded that his client was not someone an upright citizen could be proud of, and he was certainly a liar to boot, but he had not committed this particular crime. The words rang like nails being driven into an obstinate boot.

Maude remained on his feet as he faced the judge, and his voice rose a little in emphasis.

"My lord," he said, "I propose to call certain medical evidence. I shall call Sir Bernard Spilsbury."

That was like throwing a gage to an old opponent, and there was a good deal of rustling and other movement in court as well as some *sotto voce* muttering behind guarded hands.

Spilsbury rose and took his place in the witness-box, and John Maude led him to the point where he testified that in his opinion the defendant had not sufficient strength in his right, mutilated hand to strangle the victim. As he put it, 'contractile power' was all but completely lost. Again the prosecution was, as it were, caught flat-footed, but they rallied in further cross-examination to suggest that the doughty scientist might have been 'hoodwinked', presumably by a prisoner who knew that his life depended on the outcome. So it was at least possible that Loughans had made out that his right hand was much weaker than was actually the case.

Spilsbury would have none of it. He shook his head firmly in denial. He was a man who stood by his opinions when he gave them, and only very seldom varied them. When he left the witness-box, he knew he had blown the Crown's case to smithereens.

Desperately the prosecution sought as a last resource to apply to the judge for permission to call rebutting evidence. But when Mr Casswell turned to do so, he was told by the judge that he should have called it earlier. It was too late for him to do so now. For a moment he appeared flabbergasted by the ruling, for in the circumstances he had no further argument. The case had folded flat, and there was very little the jury could do except to find the defendant not guilty.

In the strange and curious tussle with the law the old lag had won a memorable battle of wits and decisions. He was grinning widely when he walked out of the Old Bailey a free man.

But his newly won freedom lasted for only a few yards. The police were waiting for him. They arrested him for a robbery with violence, this time at St Albans, in Hertfordshire. For this crime he was sentenced to seven years' imprisonment, with a further seven years of 'preventive detention'. As a certain cynical student of the crime observed, during this violent robbery the old lag found that "his right hand was serviceable enough for him to have tied an old woman to her bed with the flex of an electric fire".

So the elderly recidivist, who was now pushing his years, yet again disappeared behind the locked and guarded gates of one of His Majesty's prisons, and his criminal saga was adjourned for a further lengthy bout of years 'with porridge'. But in the interim he did more than merely contemplate his wasted life: he took to thinking about the future and the parade of personalities who had crossed the crowded arena of his criminal life. He was a man who read avidly about legal lights and luminaries, especially when they touched upon his own career. Indeed, he consumed with great interest a serial version of J. D. Casswell's memoirs, particularly references to himself and the case he had helped to make a legal landmark. The serial was published in a national newspaper with a considerable coverage, beginning in November 1960. It was issued in book-form the following year, entitled *A Lance for Liberty*. One chapter of the book was devoted to the case featuring Harold Loughans.

However, it was the serial version that interested the man who had been in gaol most of his years. He soaked up the retold story of the murder at the 'John Barleycorn' years before and scrutinized through frowning eyes pictures of Mr Casswell and others who had been featured, as well as the rear view of the Pompey pub. He was disappointed when an episode he had expected to read the following week did not appear, and he made inquiries about it, but he had to wait for some time until the hardback volume eventually appeared on the bookstalls. When that version appeared, Mr Casswell had written a new piece about the murder that had occurred twenty years before.

In this he related how, between the pair of trials, he had divined how that alibi barrier could be removed and much of its weight challenged in rebuttal. Ruminating over the case after the lapse of years, it had occurred to him, quite dramatically, that only one of the defence witnesses had claimed to have seen Loughans between the significant hours of twelve-thirty in the early morning and a quarter-past five.

As the barrister recalling the past considered the former evidence, it seemed to him that possibly this woman witness might have been mistaken about the date. If she was, then the tight alibi had vanished. There were nearly five hours to be accounted for by a witness who had been the only person to see Loughans. In a packed Underground air-raid shelter, with many persons stretched out or lying in unusual postures on a cold winter's night, there could have been a mistake.

Mr Casswell felt he had to consider the possibility that Loughans, in those hours, could have driven or been driven on a journey to Portsmouth and back, in which case the all-important alibi appeared very shaky, for certainly there was evidence to show that Rose Ada Robinson's killer had both arrived and left by car, and despite the wartime blackout restrictions on travel, the return trip could, he felt, still have been done in the time. Furthermore, a couple of local detectives had actually driven a police car from Warren Street to the 'John Barleycorn' and returned within that time: the double journey had taken four hours and forty-five minutes. They had stated they had done this within a reasonable margin of time, for they had spent half an hour in Portsmouth, allowing for time in the pub. This was indeed the vital evidence that the prosecution had desired to call but which was not allowed. All the same, the writer was at pains not to give the impression that Loughans had been in any way wrongly acquitted.

Mr Casswell expanded on his feelings:

"I did not want to dispute this finding by the judge," he said, "nor for a moment do I wish to impugn the complete and utter vindication, as the result of which no further evidence was called, that Loughans subsequently received by the verdict of 'not guilty' returned by the jury."

But this was careful writing after the publication of the newspaper series, which had been frankly ghosted by a staff-writer keen to make his work readably acceptable and interesting to a public who enjoyed reading about famous lawyers and their trials.

In the newspaper version there had been a paragraph about halfway through the article which posed a question: "Could it be possible that the alibi was purely a carefully contrived cover?" Later in the article the writer reminded his readers: "But Harold Loughans was found not guilty of the odious crime for which he twice stood trial." Then, speaking in the first person and addressing Mr Casswell directly, the newspaper memoirs went on: "It may be that the views I have on the exclusion of my additional evidence are of little consequence now. But I can assure you that they are very strong indeed."

This article first appeared in December 1960, when Loughans was in Wormwood Scrubs serving his period of preventive detention. As he said some time later, he was shown the article by a prison warder, who had suggested it was "like accusing him of a murder he hadn't committed". The warder had said to him, "You should do something about it."

Perhaps that is what happened. Anyway, Loughans wrote to his MP, the late Sydney Silverman. In an account of the incident, Silverman, known as a stalwart champion of wrongs, pointed out that the article was actionable. Be that as it may, Sydney Silverman, who was a solicitor, ultimately brought an action on Loughans's behalf for libel.

Early in July 1961 the first legal moves were made in a further development of the case that had purportedly begun with the murder of Mrs Robinson. There was more squaring up to legal opponents in the libel action that ensued. The hearing began towards the close of January 1963. Mr Justice Gorman was the judge, Patrick O'Connor QC and Stanley Waldman had been selected as the plaintiff's counsel, and J. T. Molony QC and Hugh Davidson had been chosen for the defence. The court was crowded to hear both the evidence and echoes of a case that had its roots hidden in the past, before the Second World War was over.

It started with Loughans's evidence, which went over much old ground, and it went on to the lengthy cross-examination of the plaintiff, which continued for quite a while and was directed towards proving that Loughans was not a man whose bare word could be taken on trust. As one reporter said, "I don't think one can believe a word he says. The man's a congenital and pathological liar, though I'm not to be quoted."

In a progression of evidence there was also reference to the case of the attacked woman in St Albans. For this assault it was sought to show that Loughans was, despite his fervid denials to the contrary, a man who had lived by a violent code of conduct. This opened up the evidence in a manner that could not have occurred in a criminal trial. The chief witness for the defence was the editor of the publishers of the book, *A Lance for Liberty*. The serial rights had been disposed of for a sizable sum previously, but between then and later a 'disclaimer' had appeared in a revised passage.

However, something very material had happened between the earlier two trials and the action for libel: Sir Bernard Spilsbury had committed suicide in University College Hospital in 1947. As a consequence he was unable to provide further cross-examination. Instead Mr Harold Harris FRCS a well-known surgeon, and Professor Francis Camps were called and went through the process of testing Loughans's mutilated fingers' grip. They concluded that the manual grip was too weak to have provided sufficient stranglehold, but they entertained provisos. For instance, Professor Camps agreed that the photographs of Mrs Robinson's throat revealed what he termed "a classic picture of an ordinary right-handed strangulation", but the strangling with Loughans's right hand could not, in his opinion, have occurred in the precise way in which Mrs Robinson was strangled.

However, they were men who were forced to give their opinions nearly twenty years after the murder.

The evidence began to accumulate in volume, as is the way with such civil cases, until nearly a fortnight later Mr Justice Gorman was in a position to sum up and the jury retired to consider what they had heard and to render a verdict. When the judge himself retired he left two prime questions with the jury: "Did the words mean that the plaintiff was guilty of the murder of Rose Ada Robinson?" and again, "Were the words true in substance and fact?"

To both questions the foreman gravely said, "Yea," in a quiet, rather flat tone.

There was a suppressed gasp of surprise in the public seats, for the soft affirmations meant that the case had gone against Loughans, who had found that the third time was in no sense lucky for him. Or perhaps it was a case of having gone too often to the well.

Of course, he had been acquitted in 1944 of the capital charge and consequently could not be put in peril of his life even if found guilty. All the same, it has been pointed out that the case was unique because there had not previously been one in which a civil jury had, in effect, found a man guilty of a murder of which a criminal jury had acquitted him.

However, within a very short time the final curtain was to be run down on the drama that had extended over a couple of very changeable decades.

It was towards the end of May 1963 that the ageing but nimble-witted criminal who had used up his life, as it seemed, uselessly in the pursuit of crime, often with violence, went to the offices of a national newspaper and told a member of the editorial staff that he had only a short while to live. Then came the bombshell. He claimed he was ready to confess to the 'John Barleycorn' murder. Sitting in a rumpled mackintosh and in need of a haircut, with his eyes sunken and his clean-shaven face gaunt and worried-looking under furrowed brows, he wrote out the words of his confession in pencil, clutching the stumps of the fingers of his right hand. There was a haunted look about him.

Silently he spelled out what had happened in Portsmouth those two decades before. He said he had arrived in the port in a stolen jeep and after the murder drove it back to London. No enlargement was required, for it was all in the various records.

The appearance of the confession created a stir in the newspaper world, for whether Loughans was believed this time or not made no difference. He was a man living on borrowed time who wanted, it was claimed, to put the record straight. In October 1965 he died in Hammersmith Hospital.

He still had a prison sentence to work out in a technical sense, but in another he had cheated the law, which might have provided him with wry amusement. But he could not cheat the cancer that killed him.

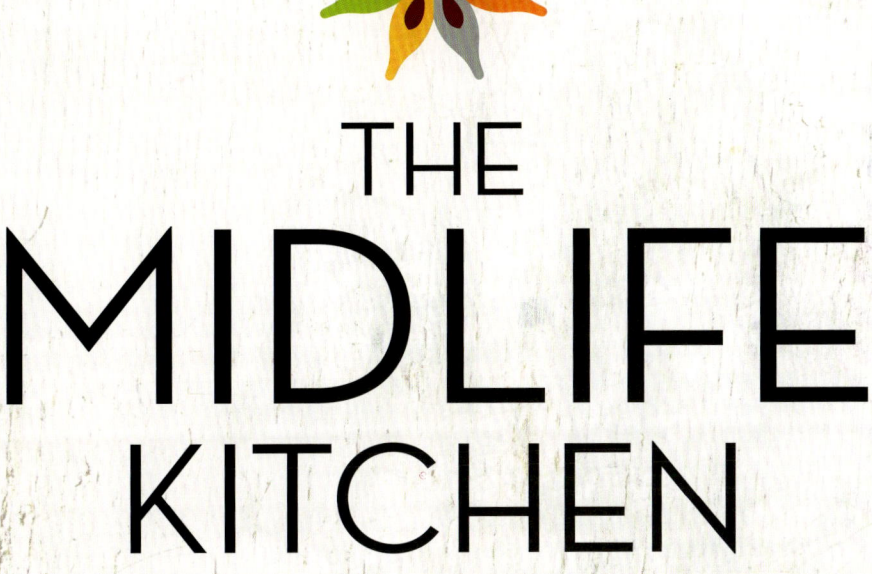

THE MIDLIFE KITCHEN

HEALTH-BOOSTING RECIPES FOR MIDLIFE & BEYOND

MIMI SPENCER & SAM RICE

Nutritional consultants Sarah Schenker and Claire Baseley

MITCHELL BEAZLEY

CONTENTS

- **4**   Welcome to the Midlife Kitchen
- **16**   40+ for 40+ the Key Ingredients for Midlife Health
- **22**   Midlife Must-haves
- **36**   Breakfast & Brunch
- **84**   Salads & Soups
- **136**   Healthy Mains
- **186**   Sides & Snacks
- **216**   Midlife Extras
- **246**   Good Sweet Stuff
- **282**   Drinks
- **298**   Index
- **303**   Acknowledgements
- **304**   About the Authors

Welcome to the Midlife Kitchen

It's hard to believe that Sam and I started thinking about The Midlife Kitchen almost a decade ago. We wrote it to service our own requirements about what best to eat as we hit our middle years, chiefly because such a book didn't exist. We answered our own questions about how to protect and benefit our bones, our hearts, our hormones, how to support digestion and boost immunity, how to retain muscle mass and maintain memory as we aged. What emerged from a lot of research and a good deal of joyous cooking was a complete manifesto for healthy eating – a holistic and integrated approach which has since become the norm.

Back then, as now, we wanted to respond to a time in life when health starts to become more of a priority. We wanted to pick a clear path through the endless and ever-changing noise of food headlines, to find a sensible route for eating in the interests of health, happiness and a long life. Our focus has always been on foods for which there is an overwhelming body of evidence supporting their nutritional CVs, updated for this new edition by registered nutritionist Claire Baseley, with each ingredient selected for the midlife benefits it offers. We also know that busy lives require simple, sustaining recipes which incorporate health-giving ingredients without too much fanfare or fuss, so everything here is quick to prep and produce.

At its heart, The Midlife Kitchen is about eating a diverse range of gorgeous ingredients in the most delicious combinations to give yourself the best possible odds for a healthy future. The recipes are intended to be rejuvenating, restorative and reviving, a way of future-proofing your life through your forties, fifties and beyond. As we both look towards our not-so-distant sixties, the message is all the more valid. We hope you find inspiration in these pages to mark a new chapter in your relationship with food, one where you can cook fantastically tasty dishes, safe in the knowledge that they're also doing you the power of good.

OUR STORY

When we first had the idea for *The Midlife Kitchen* more than eight years ago, we were in our perimenopausal mid-forties, suffering restless nights, achy hips if we sat too long and baffling bouts of brain fog. Since then, we've run the gamut of the menopause, so it's perhaps a fitting moment to reflect on our journey.

We met nearly 20 years ago when our children were mere dots, and we were surviving on coffee and carbs. We recognized kindred spirits in our sleep-deprived semi-stares and started a conversation that didn't stop for the next couple of decades.

At that time, in our late thirties, although we felt 'old' we really weren't – we were just tired. The next five years passed in a blur of kids' activities, raucous dinner parties (yes, we still had dinner parties back then) and burning the candle at both ends. Nutrition was not a top priority.

In 2013, Sam and her family decided to spend a year in Bali, and loved it so much they stayed for five. It was here, during one of Mimi's visits, that we found ourselves bemoaning the symptoms of perimenopause, from feeling tired all the time to inexplicable bouts of anxiety. It was time to act, and our diets seemed the best place to start. Bali, with its vibrant health food scene, provided the perfect inspiration and *The Midlife Kitchen* was born.

Back then, the midlife movement was in its infancy, but our fabulous publishers shared our vision and their gamble paid off. The book was an instant *Sunday Times* bestseller; we'd hit on something! There were thousands of menopausal women out there who felt just as we had and wanted to be seen.

The landscape has changed much since the first edition of this book – you could say the menopause has gone mainstream – but we remain incredibly proud of *The Midlife Kitchen* and are beyond excited with this revised edition for a whole new wave of midlifers.

HITTING THE MIDDLE

Among the upsides of ageing is the fact that we're all going through it – or we will do, one of these days. Perhaps your hair is greying, or you've noticed you don't metabolize alcohol as you did in your thirties. It could be that you don't sleep as well as you once did, or that your energy levels have dipped as your metabolism slows. For many of us, like it or not, it's our mother's face that looks back from the mirror. Hormonal shifts may well have redistributed body fat to accumulate stubbornly around the middle (typically, we put on up to a kilo a year in middle age). So, small alarm bells ring and something tells us it's time to act.

And act we can. For most leading causes of death, our genes account for only part of the risk; the rest is directly in our control. It's worth taking a moment to digest that fact: the ways we live, and particularly the foods we consume, have the powerful potential to reduce our risk of age-related disease. It may sound like a fridge magnet, but we really are what we eat.

The idea that the building blocks of our diet have a direct and measurable effect on health as we age is something that has been truly assimilated into our thinking over the last decade. Indeed, since *The Midlife Kitchen* was first published, attitudes to diet and nutrition have pivoted towards so many of the concepts articulated in these pages. Most of us now recognize the importance of eating a rich variety of ingredients to support health and wellbeing on a wealth of measures. We are well aware of the fortifying power of protein, the spiky dangers of sugar, the empty nothingness of a plate of beige carbs and the come-hither menace of ultra-processed foods. We're rehearsed in the importance of probiotics, prebiotics, ferments and fibre in supporting a healthy gut biome. Concepts that might once have seemed esoteric – antioxidants, polyphenols, the 'gut biome' itself – are widely understood; ingredients which once seemed exotic – kefir, fresh turmeric root, sour cherries - are now firmly installed in the nation's consciousness and larders.

We've imported and absorbed plenty of the healthful global culinary traditions that influenced the recipes in *The Midlife Kitchen*, foods from places like Bali, Japan and Peru, which have long recognized the potent symbiosis between health and nutrition. You can now find jamu shots at Pret A Manger, kimchi in Tesco, as well as sauerkraut, sprouted legumes and bircher pots at every turn. Recently, we were offered an (alcohol-free) Mother Root Switchel at a swish bar, for £11.50, cocktail umbrella included. We've come a long way. And we know more. So much more. Post-pandemic and with the rise of AI, we're more attuned to our own health metrics than ever, thanks to calorie-gauging apps and activity trackers, gene mappers and wearables, ingenious ways to notice the effects of a doughnut or a 5K run around the park.

Fortunately for us, modern midlife isn't the clandestine burden it once was. The age itself has, organically, gradually found itself redeemed. Indeed, when this book was first published, the word 'menopause' was still something spoken only in hushed voices in GP surgeries, or perhaps in slightly louder voices among girlfriends after a few glasses of wine. The intervening years have seen a tremendous change in public perception, together with a glut of new research and information, which means that the menopause and its accompanying curiosities and challenges is now a welcome part of everyday conversation. All of this means that there's something about midlife – its experience, its wry understanding of the world, the fact that we now know and appreciate these singular bodies of ours – that demands we rejoice, not lament. And while we can't turn back the clock, we can, with small changes and minimal effort, stay healthier for longer. The Midlife Kitchen concept is therefore concerned with 'health span' rather than lifespan – extending the number of fit and 'functional' years ahead. With that in mind, this book is categorically PRO-ageing, not anti-ageing. We don't fear growing older. We want to embrace it in the knowledge that we are as healthy as we can be.

When we get to 40 and beyond, though, things do change. As Sam and I mosey through our fifties, we have both found that our palates have shifted; whether that's down to changes in our sense of taste, an understanding of the fundamentals of good eating, or simply because our bodies are telling us that they require certain nutrients to function properly, we've found that where once we craved pasta we now prefer an interesting salad; the sweet tooth of our youth has diminished as the need for intensely savoury, texture-rich foods increases. Alcohol just isn't as interesting as it once was. One glass of lovely wine is worth far more than a mediocre bottle.

Indeed, in midlife, our nutritional needs are very different from those of our twenties and thirties; we need greater fortification from foods full of vitamins and minerals to support cellular health – important for all metabolic and physiological processes, from turning food into energy to manufacturing hormones. We need more lean protein, too, vital for maintaining muscle mass and bone health. This is especially important in perimenopause and menopause when hormone changes mean we start to lose bone density and strength. Eating enough protein, together with bone-friendly micronutrients such as vitamin D, calcium and magnesium, can help counter this. We also require a moderate quantity of 'good' slow-burn carbohydrates from wholegrains, and plenty of gut-friendly prebiotics and probiotics. In perimenopause, we typically have less diversity of friendly gut bacteria which can adversely affect digestion and immune function – all the more reason to eat plenty of fibre from a wide range of sources as we age. Women can also benefit from eating foods high in phytoestrogens, especially soy products such as edamame and tofu, which can help with perimenopausal symptom management. We can also afford to eat fewer calories (the World Health Organisation estimates that our Basal Metabolic Rate decreases by 2% every decade), so those calories should ideally be good ones: nutrient-dense and satiating.

But there's no need to make any of this stressful or performative. Much of what you'll find in these pages could be described as 'stealth health' – fresh food that tastes so good you'll hardly notice its protective and supportive credentials. The trick is to get these vital building blocks onto your fork in the tastiest way possible, in recipes that make you feel good about eating them, with no denial, no deprivation, no big deal. After all, there's little point in forcing yourself to eat anything you don't enjoy; far better to choose foods that really appeal. This is our commitment on every page.

We think of The Midlife Kitchen as an MOT, a time to fine-tune your daily diet to access peak performance for the years ahead. It may be that optimum health is your goal, or you're interested in supporting your metabolism through the menopause. Or perhaps you're just bored with the same-old meals in your repertoire and want inspiration for interesting recipes that will breathe new life into your cooking. Either way, we hope you find plenty of inspiration here to spark your appetite.

The Midlife Manifesto

The world of nutrition moves at lightning speed, new research and studies appear every day, and the food noise gets ever louder and more confusing, yet the essence of what constitutes a healthy, balanced diet hasn't changed. Our Midlife Manifesto, which we devised as a set of basic principles to guide us when creating our recipes, remains as relevant now as it did when this books was first published. We're still wary of buzzwords, so you won't find references to superfoods, detoxing, 'free-from', or restriction, and rather than overpromise, we prefer a simple, assured and – as befits our years – grown-up approach. So here it is.

1.

VARIETY IS VITAL

Restrictive diets aren't just a bore; they reduce gut microbe diversity and can lead, in turn, to all manner of health issues. Indeed, the prevailing wisdom is that we need to eat 30 different plant foods a week for optimum gut health, including fruit, vegetables, grains, pulses, nuts and seeds… even those humble herbs and spices count. So, our banner is inclusion, not exclusion, a welcome sign not a keep-out notice.

2.

THE WHOLE TRUTH

A diet rich in whole foods (such as fresh produce, whole grains, nuts and seeds) and low in ultra-processed foods and refined sugars, is the most effective long-term health insurance and current best advice. We therefore maximize the use of natural, whole plant foods in every Midlife recipe.

3.

LESS SUGAR, BETTER FAT, GOOD CARBS

We now know that sugar is the one to watch, so we intentionally use very little, and where possible from fruit sources. Healthy fats, notably the omega-3s from oily fish, extra virgin olive oil and, yes, even a little butter, are all welcome at the Midlife table. As for carbs, there's good evidence to suggest that sticking to slow-burn, complex carbohydrates that are rich in fibre can help control blood sugars and improve insulin sensitivity, which lessens the risk of developing type-2 diabetes. That's one reason why our recipes embrace wholegrains such as brown and black rice, quinoa and oats.

4.

TASTE COMES FIRST

It's worth reminding ourselves that just because something is healthy, it doesn't mean we have to eat it. The point of every recipe in this book – each one honed through experience, experiment and quite a lot of tasty research – is that you'll want to come back for more (we know we did).

5.

EASY DOES IT

Do you know what people tell us is their biggest barrier to healthy eating? Time. We're not in the business of adding to the pressure that already exists around food, so our recipes are purposefully simple, speedy and practical. Midlife is no time to soak lima beans, we really have better things to do.

6.

SMALL CHANGES, BIG DIFFERENCE

When it comes to healthy eating, there's no need to reinvent the wheel. Most dishes can simply be tweaked to improve their nutritional credentials. With this in mind, you'll find twelve Midlife Must-haves on pages 22–35. This is our 'capsule kitchen', a set of store-cupboard essentials you can prep in advance and which crop up in a number of our recipes. But you can also freestyle with them, like adding some Midlife Spiced Seed Mix to a salad or your morning eggs, ensuring a mega Midlife health boost with every bite.

7.

SOMETHING OLD, SOMETHING NEW

We know how off-putting a long list of weird ingredients can be, so we've gone out of our way to make our recipes comfortingly accessible. We want these recipes to become part of your everyday life, not a one-off where ingredients then languish hopelessly at the back of the cupboard. So most items can be found on the shelves of your local supermarket. But, if we believe an unusual ingredient will make a difference to how you feel in midlife, we've included it, with a clear explanation of why it's there. Most items are easy to come by, and less common ones are listed in The Midlife Larder, see page 14.

HERE'S HOW…

In midlife, health is no longer something peripheral that we can take for granted. It is central to the quality of life that we enjoy. We want all of our recipes to be utterly delicious and full of goodness, so we are wholeheartedly ingredient-led. We have researched the health-giving properties of most of the foods you can think of, plus a few newcomers, too, and cherry-picked the best of these to form the basis for our recipes. For our list of key Midlife ingredients, see our 40+ for 40+ list on pages 16–21.

Nutritional advice does, of course, tend to be in constant flux, with new theories, discoveries and opinions often conspiring to cloud the view (sometimes depending on who is funding the study). At the Midlife Kitchen, we're also sensitive to experiential evidence – for example, where particular ingredients have been used as traditional remedies for generations. We take a pragmatic 'best odds' approach, based on 'weight of evidence': if there is plenty to suggest that an ingredient has certain health benefits and it tastes great, then we think that's a good enough reason to eat it!

Our icon for Midlife health is the star anise, a wonderful spice that has long been used in Asian cooking for its health-giving properties. We have devised a colour-coded system to support and improve health and wellbeing in eight categories, each represented by a star anise seed. If a recipe features that colour seed then it has known benefits in that category.

Our Star Anise Rating

DIGESTIVE HEALTH

The gut may lack glamour, but it has a hand in so many important aspects of our health. During menopause our microbiome diversity can reduce, so it's important to keep it boosted with a diverse array of plant foods (the current recommendation is to aim for 30 different plant foods a week). At the Midlife Kitchen, we love our guts; that's why you'll find plenty of recipes in these pages incorporating soluble fibre from beans, seeds and oats, spices to aid digestion such as the traditional remedy ginger, plenty of leafy greens loaded with vitamins and minerals, bioactive enzymes and prebiotics from onions, garlic, leeks, asparagus, bananas, apples and berries.

The bright red seed shows you where to find recipes which support digestion.

BLOOD-SUGAR BALANCE

We all know that type 2 diabetes has become a major health concern of our age, driven in part by our modern lifestyles. It therefore makes sense to eat a diet rich in slowly digested, sustaining foods, that is high in fibre and with low glycaemic load carbohydrates. Include plenty of foods such as wholegrains, especially oats, nuts, seeds and legumes. Some spices such as cinnamon, cumin and turmeric, plus our Midlife favourite, apple cider vinegar, have shown some promise in regulating blood-sugar levels (research is on-going!). In any case, they taste delicious so they're staples in the Midlife Kitchen!

Look for the brick-red seed.

HORMONE HARMONY

Our hormones have far-reaching effects on health – among many other things, they keep our skin supple, our bones strong, our minds alert – and it is age-related hormone imbalance that can lead to common midlife health issues, whether it's flagging energy, low libido, poor sleep or dry skin. The Midlife Kitchen incorporates plenty of hormone helpers which might be able to help manage symptoms of perimenopause and beyond; phytoestrogens in foods like soya and flaxseeds, tryptophan in oats and legumes and plenty of good fats in avocados and oily fish. Women, in particular, may need some decent unrefined carbs from whole grains and beans to maintain their endocrine balance.

Look out for the orange seed on recipes that are particularly helpful for hormone harmony.

ENERGY BOOSTING

While our metabolism does gently slow as we get older, if we eat well there is no reason to be 'tired all the time', that common refrain of our age. The link between diet and energy is direct; food is fuel, so it makes sense that consuming foods such as almonds, pumpkin seeds, oats, quinoa, beans, sweet potatoes, yogurt and oily fish – which provide slow, sustaining energy – will help us feel (sometimes literally) full of beans. B vitamins are key for the release of energy from our food, so eating plenty of wholegrains, eggs, lean meat, fish, green veg and pulses will keep us firing on all cylinders. We also need adequate hydration to maintain energy levels, so drinking plenty of water is essential to feeling more alert and alive.

The blue seed leads the way to increased stamina.

SKIN, SENSES & IMMUNITY

A robust immune system is vital for staving off illness as we age, and we can strengthen our defences by eating fresh foods rich in essential vitamins, minerals and antioxidants. Healthy skin, hair and nails also rely on an adequate supply of vitamins – A (for cell renewal and repair) in carrots, sweet potatoes and spinach; C (for collagen formation) in berries, red peppers and kale; and E (to defend against free-radical damage) in almonds, seeds and broccoli – together with essential fatty acids from foods like avocados and oily fish. Iron and zinc are critical for supporting the immune system. Iron is found in red meat, pulses, and green vegetables. Zinc is in meat, fish, dairy foods and wheatgerm. Flavonoids and carotenoids, found in brightly coloured fruit and veg, are particularly useful for maintaining supple skin, sharp senses and healthy hair.

The yellow seed indicates recipes that are particularly beneficial here.

BONE & JOINT HEALTH

In our middle years, and particularly during perimenopause and beyond due to inevitable hormonal changes, bone density can diminish, so it makes sense that the Midlife Kitchen includes foods containing bone-supporting nutrients. We all know that calcium – from dairy, leafy greens, nuts such as almonds and fish (canned with their bones) – is the building block for bone structure, but we also need vitamin D (in oily fish, butter, egg yolks and mushrooms) to aid its absorption. Our joints can also start to cause us problems as we move into midlife and keeping inflammation at bay is key. Anti-inflammatory foods are those containing omega-3 fatty acids, such as oily fish, chia and flax seeds, and walnuts which are all important for promoting healthy joints.

Look out for the bright green seed.

HEART HEALTH

In peri- and post-menopause our risk of heart problems increases, as key supporting hormone levels drop. So, it's especially important to eat foods with a nutrient profile that lowers the risk factor for cardiovascular disease. We recommend whole grains, nuts (walnuts and Brazils are excellent), legumes, especially soy beans, oats, oily fish, avocados, dark berries, turmeric and loads of leafy veg in the Midlife Kitchen.

The dark pink seed indicates our heart-friendly recipes.

MIND, MEMORY & MOOD

It's essential to maintain cognitive function as we age, and there are plenty of foods thought to help with memory, mood, mental alertness and concentration. Our recipes incorporate many ingredients rich in omega-3 fatty acids or containing specific vitamins, minerals and antioxidants to help keep your brain in tiptop condition. Midlife brain-boosters include oats, nuts, seeds, dark berries, leafy greens, oily fish, extra virgin olive oil, turmeric and dark chocolate (yes!).

Look out for the pale green seed.

OUR STAR ANISE RATING

WHY US?

Mimi: My early career was spent as a fashion journalist for *Vogue*, the *Evening Standard* and then as editor of *ES Magazine*, followed by stints at national newspapers and magazines writing lifestyle features, particularly at *The Times*, and as a columnist for *You Magazine* and *Observer Food Monthly* Magazine. I went on to co-author *The Fast Diet* with Michael Mosley – the book which introduced the concept of 5:2 intermittent fasting – and wrote several subsequent cookbooks including *The Fast Diet Recipe Book*. As a result, I developed a keen interest in nutrition and health, particularly concerning our changing requirements as the years go by, culminating in creating *The Midlife Kitchen* with Sam in 2016.

Since *The Midlife Kitchen* was first published, I have retrained as a ceramicist, and a yoga teacher running regular retreats, which include meals based on the health-promoting principles in this book. I discovered a couple of years ago that my pesky 'alcohol issue' is in fact histamine intolerance, which means I have to think carefully about everything I eat or drink in order to avoid crippling headaches. It has allowed me a deeper understanding of the physical impact of every morsel we consume, and a profound empathy for people who struggle with allergies and sensitivities. Like most 57-year-olds, I'm a bit wiser now. David Bowie, said it best: 'I think ageing is an extraordinary process whereby you become the person that you always should have been.' Midlife really is our moment. Let's love it and live it well.

Sam: My career could best be described as a series of curveballs, none more so than when I moved to Bali with my family in 2013. I had just completed a demanding three-year wine course with the intention of setting up as a wine buyer, but the wine industry in Indonesia was, sadly, non-existent. There was, however, a flourishing health food scene, from raw vegan cafes to experimental local cuisine, and I was keen to get stuck in.

At this time, I was re-prioritising my health after the loss of both my father in 2008 from a sudden heart attack, and my youngest brother in 2012 from complications arising from type-1 diabetes. I had become acutely aware that my genetic heritage, combined with a lack of attention to my general health was not exactly a recipe for longevity.

Inspired by how much better I felt when eating well – lots of tropical fruit and veg, fish, and fabulous fresh local food – a new passion for nutrition was ignited. *The Midlife Kitchen* was just the beginning. I have since written two more books on the subject, *The Midlife Method* in 2020 and *Supercharge Your Diet* in 2022.

The pandemic sadly curtailed our Asian adventure, and these days I live in beautiful Bath. I am the nutrition expert at *the Daily Telegraph*, and I'm pursuing a master's degree in clinical nutrition which has further underlined for me the importance of taking care of these precious midlife bodies of ours.

All nutritional information in this edition has been reviewed by registered nutritionist Claire Baseley. If you have a particular medical concern please consult your doctor. Otherwise, grab and fork and dig in. You'll be doing yourself the world of good.

The Midlife Larder

Most ingredients in our recipes are familiar and will already be on your usual shopping list, but there are some, listed here, which we use in abundance or are just a bit unusual. With these in stock and your Midlife Must-haves to hand, there isn't much in this book that you can't make without the addition of a few fresh ingredients.

BOTTLES

- Light olive oil spray
- Extra virgin olive oil
- Apple cider vinegar ('with the mother')
- Rice vinegar
- Thai fish sauce (nam pla)
- Date syrup or nectar
- Pomegranate molasses

CANS

- Chickpeas
- Butter beans
- Kidney beans
- Black beans
- Coconut milk
- Pumpkin purée
- Peeled cherry tomatoes
- Anchovy fillets
- Sardines

DAIRY

- Natural unsweetened yogurt (see page 20)
- Feta cheese
- Goat's cheese
- Ricotta
- Parmesan

DRIED

- Lentils (green, brown, red, Puy and Beluga)
- White and red quinoa
- Brown basmati rice
- Wholegrain couscous
- Black glutinous rice
- Jumbo oats
- Desiccated coconut
- Medjool dates
- Dried figs
- Apricots
- Cranberries

FROZEN

- Cherries
- Mixed berries
- Blueberries
- Cranberries
- Shelled edamame beans
- Petits pois peas
- Root ginger

JARS

- Jalapeño peppers
- Cornichons
- Capers
- Brown rice
- Miso paste
- Tahini
- Harissa paste
- Dijon mustard

MISCELLANEOUS

- Lemons
- Unsweetened almond milk (7%+), see page 296
- Coconut water
- Dark chocolate (minimum 70 per cent cocoa solids)
- Dark chocolate chips or raw cacao nibs
- Date sugar
- Xylitol
- Clear acacia honey
- Nori seaweed sheets
- Sushi ginger
- Vietnamese rice-paper wrappers
- Sea salt flakes
- Matcha (green tea) powder
- Dried hibiscus flowers
- Chai teabags

PACKETS

- Flaxseeds
- Pumpkin seeds
- Sunflower seeds
- Chia seeds
- Sesame seeds
- Almonds (whole, with skin on, blanched, flaked and ground)
- Walnuts
- Brazil nuts
- Cashew nuts
  buy nuts raw and unsalted

READY-COOKED POUCHES

- Lentils
- Quinoa
- Mixed grains
- Brown or red rice

SPICES

- Cinnamon (ground and sticks)
- Cumin (ground and seeds)
- Coriander (ground and seeds)
- Fennel seeds
- Mustard seeds
- Cardamom pods
- Star anise
- Ginger (fresh and ground)
- Nutmeg
- Turmeric (fresh and ground)
- Dried red chilli flakes
- Garam masala
- Vanilla pods (or a vanilla bean grinder)
- Vanilla extract
- Ras el hanout
- Herbes de Provence
- Black peppercorns

40+ for 40+

FRUIT

THE KEY INGREDIENTS FOR MIDLIFE HEALTH

Think of this as your checklist for healthy eating in midlife: just 40 or so ingredients (or ingredient groups) to keep in mind when shopping, cooking or choosing from menus. We've picked each one for the benefits it brings, with particular reference to the health categories designated in our Star Anise ratings. Of course, the list is not exhaustive, and no single ingredient can be a 'super food' magic wand; it is your overall dietary pattern of diversity and inclusion that will determine your health. This list will give you basis for a vibrant diet, full of variety and vitality.

APPLES

An apple a day... it's true: apples, fresh or cooked, are a great source of health-boosting antioxidants and pectin, a water-soluble fibre that improves digestive health, lowers cholesterol and helps balance blood sugars. They're also heart-protective and can help guard against osteoporosis, thanks to the boron they contain.

BLUEBERRIES & OTHER DARK BERRIES

We swear by these. Blueberries, blackberries and cherries (and cranberries, goji berries and blackcurrants) contain anthocyanins that can help protect against cardiovascular disease, lower blood pressure, improve cognition and memory and support eye health. There's lots of lovely vitamin C in them too, which will support your immune system. Keep them in the freezer for a year-long dark-berry bonanza.

DATES

A firm fixture in the Midlife Kitchen, dates – particularly the fat, sticky Medjool variety – deliver natural sweetness but have a low GI, so they won't spike your blood sugars to the same extent as refined sugar. Better yet, dates are high in insoluble fibre – great for the gut – and magnesium, which benefits bones, muscles and the nervous system. It can also help improve sleep and help with night cramps.

FIGS

Not just beautiful to behold, figs are also full of good things – including calcium to benefit the bones and fibre to aid digestion. Try them fresh and pink in a salad, or baked in the oven until soft and sticky.

LEMONS & OTHER CITRUS FRUIT

In the Midlife Kitchen, a bowl of (unwaxed) lemons sits right next to the salt and pepper; we consider them the third seasoning and you'll find that many of our recipes involve lemon in some form. Lemons are full of vitamin C, while their plentiful phytonutrients support the heart, immunity and skin health, guard against osteoarthritis and aid iron absorption.

POMEGRANATES

Who doesn't love jewel-pink pomegranate seeds scattered on a salad? But they're more than just a pretty ornament – they contain vitamin K for the bones and folate for healthy blood, while plant compounds in pomegranates may have an antioxidant effect.

VEGETABLES

ASPARAGUS

Asparagus is a Midlife favourite, not only for its unique flavour, but also as a great source of vitamin C which supports collagen production and vitamin K to keep bones strong. Asparagus contains the prebiotic fibre inulin which can help support your gut microbiome.

AVOCADOS

Avocados are indispensable in the Midlife Kitchen. It's all about those heart-healthy good fats, which also enable nutrient absorption from other foods. Avocados are also known to support the immune system, and skin and eye health, on account of the vitamin E they contain.

BEETROOT

Brilliant beets crop up time and again in this book. There is a good body of evidence for beetroot being beneficial for blood pressure, brain function and digestive health.

BROCCOLI

If pressed, we'd choose broccoli as our top Midlife ingredient, thanks to its incredible phytonutrient profile: vitamin C and K, folate, beta carotenoids, sulforaphane, lignans, iron, zinc, phosphorus, calcium, potassium and indole-3-carbinol. Studies have shown that eating foods rich in these nutrients might help protect bones, joints, eyes, skin and hair. Many of the nutrients found in broccoli may also enhance brain function, digestion, immunity and energy levels, support the production of red blood cells, lower blood pressure and reduce the risk of many chronic diseases associated with ageing.

CARROTS

It's easy to overlook carrots, but they're brilliantly rich in beta-carotene, lutein, lycopene, potassium and fibre, which can support the heart, skin, digestive function and eye-health.

CHILLIES

Chillies not only add glorious heat, they also provide vitamin C and antioxidants which can support immune function and skin health.

FENNEL

Fennel's aniseed bite comes from the aromatic compound anethole, which is thought to have anti-inflammatory effects. For this reason fennel has been linked with benefits for the heart and immune system as well as brain and eye function.

GARLIC

Allicin is the wonder stuff here. Found in abundance in garlic, it supports immunity, protects against heart disease and improves blood circulation. Garlic is a prebiotic, and great for gut health.

KALE

If you are suffering from 'kale fatigue', give it another try – it's cheap and easy to prep, and it really is a health powerhouse. Kale is nutrient-rich, containing vitamins C and E, plus selenium and beta-carotene to help support immunity. It's also a source of plant-based calcium to help support bone health, and boasts compounds which may protect against heart disease and cancer.

PUMPKIN & BUTTERNUT SQUASH

It's the beta-carotene in orange squash and pumpkin – converted to vitamin A in the body – which is such a bonus for vision and skin. Vitamin A, also known as retinol, is involved in the development and function of a range of immune cells. All good news for our middle years.

RED CABBAGE

Again, the clue is in the colour: red cabbage is particularly beneficial, thanks to an abundance of anthocyanins, all working to protect the brain, skin and vision; the plentiful vitamins, minerals and fibre in red cabbage will benefit the immune and digestive systems, and help support bone health.

VEGETABLES CONTINUED

RED ONIONS

We specifically choose red onions over regular white ones because they contain more antioxidants, in particular anthocyanins that give them their beautiful colour, helping to lower the risk of all manner of age-related diseases. Red onions are also a source of vitamin C, which can help support immune function.

RED PEPPERS

Vitamin C, beta-carotene and lycopene are the big hitters here, protecting the eyes, skin and heart, they may play a role in the regulation of blood sugar and blood pressure.

SPINACH

Spinach is an absolute Midlife gift, full of vitamins (C, E, K and Bs) and important minerals such as iron, magnesium and zinc. So this little leafy green has plenty of clout: it will support bone and tissue health, aid cognitive function, and its high fibre content is good for the gut. It also contains carotenoids to benefit the eyes and skin.

TOMATOES

The backbone of the Mediterranean diet, tomatoes are stacked with health-giving goodness; they contain lycopene in abundance, together with vitamin C and plenty of fibre, which is all good news for the heart, bones, gut and skin.

WATERCRESS

Among the most nutrient-dense plants on the planet, and happily available on every supermarket shelf, watercress contains plenty of calcium to support bones and muscles, iron to help cognitive function and relieve tiredness, and a whole host of antioxidants and other phytonutrients which can benefit blood pressure, skin and eye health.

LEGUMES

BEANS

Beans, beans, good for the heart... yes, and they're also brilliant for digestion and blood-sugar regulation. They're a prime plant protein food and an excellent source of sustained energy. Their plentiful B vitamins will help with mood and memory too, making beans a Midlife no-brainer. We use butter beans, kidney beans, pinto beans and black beans – the more the merrier. The darker ones contain antioxidant anthocyanins, which bump up their health credentials.

CHICKPEAS

Full of protein and fibre, chickpeas are an essential (and inexpensive) Midlife ingredient; their mineral content makes them good for the hair, nails and energy levels, and they help stabilize blood sugars too.

LENTILS

We could live on lentils. An excellent source of protein and fibre, they also contain nutrients that help support the digestion, hormone system, brain and nervous function. As part of a diet low in saturated fat and sugars, they can help to lower cholesterol and balance blood sugars. Great in dhals and soups, but we also love them served cold in a salad. Our favourite? Black beluga lentils – it's those anthocyanins again.

SOYA

A complete plant-based protein, soya is known to be protective for your heart and bones, and effective at balancing hormone levels; it contains tryptophan, which supports serotonin production to boost mood, soothe anxiety and promote good sleep. Tofu, tempeh, miso and edamame beans all feature in the Midlife Kitchen.

GRAINS, NUTS & SEEDS

NUTS

The vitamins, minerals, protein, fibre and good fats in nuts make them a simple way to sustain energy and maintain optimum nutrition. Nuts contain tryptophan too, an essential amino acid required for growth and development, and for the production of serotonin, a neurotransmitter thought to enhance sleep and stabilize mood.

Almonds provide fibre and protein as well as vitamin E, which is great for the skin and cellular repair; they're a key non-dairy source of calcium, helpful for maintaining bone density.

Brazils provide magnesium which helps support bones and muscles as well as psychological function. Magnesium is beneficial for sleep, and Brazil nuts are also rich in selenium which is an antioxidant that supports skin and hair.

Cashews contain nutrients that support immune function, eye, skin and hair health. They're also great for the heart because they are rich in health fats.

Walnuts help protect against heart disease and age-related cognitive decline; they benefit the skin and have anti-inflammatory properties.

OATS

Oats are so good for the old grey matter that they are known as the 'grain for the brain. Oats contain a type of soluble fibre called beta-glucan which has been shown to be effective in reducing cholesterol. Oats are also an excellent, high-fibre, low GI energy source – a perfect way to kickstart the day. You'll find plenty of oat-y recipes in our Breakfast & Brunch chapter.

QUINOA

We're keen on quinoa for good reason: it's packed with B vitamins, iron, magnesium, zinc, fibre and protein. With all that going on, it's no surprise that it has multiple health benefits for the brain, digestion, bones and joints; it also helps keep blood sugars steady.

RICE
(wholegrain brown, red, black & wild rice)

Like other whole grains, rice is an excellent source of B vitamins, manganese and fibre. It contains slow-release carbohydrates and plenty of fibre, so can help regulate blood-sugar levels and aids digestion. The B vitamins can help support energy release and psychological function, and the manganese is good for bones. Not bad for a little grain.

SEEDS

They may be small, but seeds are a potent addition to a diet, thanks to the fibre, vitamins, minerals and omega-3 fatty acids they provide, plus more mood-soothing tryptophan. Scatter them on salads, soups, porridge, yogurt, cakes and puds… or just open a pack and snack.

Chia seeds are fibre-packed and provide heart-healthy plant-based omega 3s; they contain calcium for healthy bones and fibre to improve digestion.

Flaxseeds are a wonder-seed for midlife: they can can help ease menopausal symptoms alongside other phyto oestrogen-rich foods like soy. They also contain bags of omega 3s and fibre which are heart healthy and help digestive function. They'll also protect against heart disease, type 2 diabetes and stroke risk, while supporting digestive health, nervous function and collagen production.

Pumpkin seeds are great little energy-boosters. They also contain plenty of zinc which is crucial for immune function, heart and prostate health, and promote relaxation and restful sleep.

Sesame seeds are excellent for cellular health, good skin and strong bones and teeth.

Sunflower seeds contain polyunsaturated fats that can help lower cholesterol. These nutritional heavy hitters also contain iron and vitamin B6 which can support the brain as well as magnesium for bones and muscles.

EGGS, FISH & DAIRY

EGGS

For pure nutritional power, nothing beats eggs. They provide vitamins A, D and Bs, plus essential minerals, choline, lecithin and easily assimilated protein. This catalogue of qualities makes them excellent for tissue repair, muscle maintenance, bones, heart health, sustained energy and psychological function.

OILY FISH

It's the omega-3 fatty acids in mackerel, sardines, salmon and trout that make them especially good for heart health, reducing cholesterol build-up in the arteries and lowering blood pressure. Oily fish will also help maintain healthy joints, skin, hair and eyesight (if you eat the tinned ones along with all the little bones), boost brain function and help circulation. They're also an excellent source of protein which can help us stay fuller for longer – in fact, a simple tin of sardines would probably be our desert island food.

YOGURT

Plenty of dishes benefit from a good dose of yogurt, and there are convincing reasons to eat it. Recent research has found that people who eat natural unsweetened yogurt every day have a lower risk of developing type 2 diabetes, while it has also been shown to help lower blood pressure. Yogurt is a source of vitamin B12, as well as calcium and iodine. B12 is needed for energy release from food, supports the immune system, aids psychological function and can reduce tiredness. Calcium is needed for bones and muscles. Iodine is found in very few foods, milk and dairy products being prime examples. It supports the thyroid, skin and nervous system as well as cognitive function. Live yogurt, which we heartily recommend, also contains probiotic bacteria (these good guys are not present in heat-treated yogurts), which can enhance immunity, improve vitamin synthesis and assist digestive function.

HERBS & SPICES

We use plenty of herbs and spices in the Midlife Kitchen to bring bags of fabulous flavour to our recipes. As they are used in relatively small amounts, the health benefits are hard to quantify, but we do know they provide a range of phytochemicals, some which have been prized for their health benefits in traditional cuisines. They also provide that all-important diversity when it comes to including as many plants foods as possible to support our gut health. Here are our favourites:

HERBS

Basil contains vitamin K to support bone and heart health.

Coriander, a digestive aid, will also help lower blood sugars and LDL cholesterol levels.

Dill strengthens bones and supports the digestion.

Mint is an excellent digestive aid and decongestant, with antiallergenic properties.

STORE CUPBOARD

Parsley aids oxygenation of the blood, which can help reduce fatigue. Its vitamin K benefits the bones.

Rosemary improves immunity and digestion, and is known to support brain health. **Sage**, great for short-term memory, protects the brain, benefits circulation and aids digestion. It can also lower blood glucose and cholesterol levels and help alleviate menopausal symptoms, especially hot flushes.

SPICES

Cardamom helps aid digestion and boost immunity and mood; it's also known to lower blood pressure and support bone and cellular health.

Cinnamon helps regulate blood-sugar levels, while supporting liver and gut function, heart health and bone density. It lowers cholesterol, reduces joint pain and can aid sleep.

Cumin is excellent for digestion and can also help with blood-sugar control.

Ginger aids digestion and reduces inflammation (one of the main causes of arthritis). It also lowers the risk of heart disease and type 2 diabetes.

Star anise, anti-inflammatory and antioxidant, is also oestrogenic – so a good hormone helper. It's great for the digestion too.

Turmeric: anti-inflammatory and antioxidant, turmeric is particularly beneficial for the brain and heart; it can help prevent age-related conditions including arthritis, and play a role in regulating blood sugar. Keep fresh turmeric in the freezer until required – just like root ginger.

APPLE CIDER VINEGAR

While some of the health claims made for apple cider vinegar recently may have been overstated, we still love it for it's flavour and the probiotic compunds it contains (buy the one with 'the mother'). It's the star of our Midlife Dressing on page 33, but ACV even works as a drink – try our Switchel on page 294 – you'll be pleasantly surprised...

DARK CHOCOLATE

Few of us need any excuse to eat more chocolate, but the dark stuff (70 per cent cocoa solids) provides plenty of health-giving compounds: mineral-rich and high in antioxidants, cocoa is good for the brain, nervous system and heart. And let's not forget, eating should be for pleasure, too, and there's nothing like some chocolate at the end of the day to lift your mood.

GREEN TEA (MATCHA)

Green tea is full of antioxidants which, when consumed alongside a healthy, balanced diet full of colourful plant foods, can reduce your risk of a whole range of non-communicable diseases. All excellent reasons to go green.

OLIVE OIL

We all know that a Mediterranean diet has significant health benefits – and that's thanks in part to the use of olive oil, which promotes heart health by lowering cholesterol and helping to control blood pressure, particularly when it is used to replace saturated fat in the diet. It also contains Vitamin E which is a key antioxidant, helping to scavenge cancer-causing free radicals in the body. For a vinaigrette, choose extra virgin, which has more flavour, nutrients and antioxidants than standard oil (keep it in a cool dark place to maintain its freshness). Try a light olive oil spray for quick cooking.

MIDLIFE MUST-HAVES

WHY WE LOVE IT

We believe spices deserve a far greater role in our cooking – but somehow, for many of us, they seem to languish at the back of a dusty cupboard awaiting an occasional curry. The solution is to make our Midlife Spice Mix in advance and keep it on hand to add instant flavour, depth and a pinch of goodness to all manner of dishes. You'll find this delicious mix cropping up with satisfying regularity in many Midlife Kitchen recipes.

Midlife Spice Mix

MAKES APPROX. 5 TBSP

1 tbsp ground fennel seeds
1 tbsp ground coriander seeds
1 tbsp ground cumin
1 tbsp ground turmeric
2 tsp ground cardamom

Combine all the ingredients and store in an airtight container for up to 6 months.

Midlife Hack: Spices lose their potency (and some of their health benefits) over time, so don't keep them longer than 6 months.

Health Tip
This combination of spices draws on Ayurvedic principles, using turmeric, cumin, coriander, fennel and cardamom to enhance digestion and boost the metabolism. Spices may have health-boosting antioxidant and anti-inflammatory properties.

WHY WE LOVE IT

The health benefits of seeds are beyond doubt – they're stacked with heart-healthy fats, gut-friendly fibre, mighty minerals, vital vits and energy-boosting protein (seeds, of course, provide the starting blocks for the next generation of plants, so it's not surprising that they are such a complete food). Clearly, these small wonders pack a hefty nutritional punch, but they can often sit in a cupboard, unloved and overlooked. We've found that the best way to introduce more seeds into our cooking is to have a seed mix like this to hand. Add them to wraps, eggs, soups, salads, puds, breads and bakes.

Midlife Raw Seed Mix

MAKES APPROX. 9 TBSP

3 tbsp pumpkin seeds
2 tbsp ground flaxseeds
2 tbsp sunflower seeds
2 tbsp sesame seeds

Combine all the seeds and store in an airtight container for up to 2 months.

Midlife Hack: Because of their high fat content, seeds soak up pesticides, so it's wise to choose organic.

Health Tip
Flaxseeds are a rich source of plant lignans, phytoestrogens that help regulate the body's oestrogen production. This makes them a great Midlife hormone helper. Eat them alongside other phytoestrogen-rich foods like soya and oats in perimenopause and beyond.

WHY WE LOVE IT

This is a big bang of health-boosting taste and texture to jump-start a salad, soup or wrap. It uses our Midlife Raw Seed and Midlife Spice mixes – so although there seems to be lots of ingredients, it takes mere minutes to assemble and will transform a humdrum bowl of leaves into something spectacular. Try using this mix instead of croutons on soups and in salads.

Midlife Spiced Seed Mix

MAKES APPROX. 8 TBSP

4 tbsp Midlife Raw Seed Mix, see page 25
2 tsp nigella seeds
2 tsp mustard seeds
2 tsp poppy seeds
2 tsp extra virgin olive oil
2 tbsp Midlife Spice Mix, see page 24
1 tsp chilli flakes or smoked/sweet paprika
sea salt flakes and freshly ground black pepper

Place the raw seed mix in a large, shallow frying pan and dry-fry over a medium heat for several minutes until it starts to colour and pop, adding the remaining seeds for the final minute or so, taking care not to burn them.

Tip the seeds into a bowl and add the oil, spice mix and the chilli flakes or paprika (add more or less according to your liking for heat). Season with salt and pepper.

Transfer the mix to an airtight container and store for up to 2 weeks.

Health Tip
Pumpkin seeds and sunflower seeds contain healthy fatty acids, which can help boost heart health, which is important after the menopause when women's cardiovascular risk increases.

WHY WE LOVE IT

Australians swear by this homemade mix of ground linseed, sunflower seeds and almonds and it's hard to argue. LSA is a simple and versatile way to catapult omega-3s, protein, minerals, vitamin E and fibre into your recipes, so it makes sense that it's one of our store-cupboard essentials in the Midlife Kitchen. Use LSA as a coating for falafel or simply add it to bakes, smoothies, porridge, yogurt...you name it.

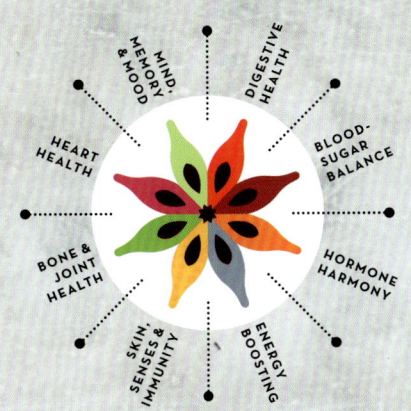

Midlife LSA

MAKES APPROX. 12 TBSP

6 tbsp flaxseeds (another name for linseeds)
4 tbsp sunflower seeds
2 tbsp whole almonds (skin on)

Simply use a 3-2-1 ratio of L-S-A. Using a coffee grinder or spice mill, pulse the seeds and almonds in batches until finely ground.

Transfer the mix to an airtight jar and store in the fridge for up to 2 months.

Midlife Hack: It's tricky to buy LSA in the UK – and you're better off making it at home anyway, as the oils shouldn't be heat treated (which would destroy their potency). Due to the high oil content of ground flaxseeds, LSA should be kept in a dark jar in the fridge to prevent it turning rancid.

Health Tip
This combo is rich in antioxidants, vitamin E and a host of good-for-you minerals. Flaxseed is a tough little dude, so it is best consumed in its ground form, which breaks down the shell and releases the nutrients within.

Midlife Power Porridge

WHY WE LOVE IT

This is porridge with wings – you're getting the usual slow-burn carb-y goodness of oats, but with the added bonus of flaxseeds, almonds, sunflower seeds and oat bran, which turns a very good thing into something truly great. Prep a batch in advance and it will be to hand when you're in a rush and in need of something filling and fast. This is the essence of the Midlife Kitchen: stacking up the health benefits with minimal effort, for maximum taste.

MAKES 600G (1LB 5OZ)

FOR THE BASIC MIX

400g (14oz) rolled or jumbo oats

100g (3½oz) Midlife LSA, see page 27

100g (3½oz) oat bran

TO SERVE

125ml (4fl oz) milk of your choice (cow's, almond, soya or oat) or coconut water (for a lighter bowl of porridge)

sea salt flakes (optional)

Health Tip
Oats are loaded with dietary fibre, have a range of cholesterol-lowering properties and are also an excellent slow-release energy source, making porridge a brilliant way to start the day.

Combine the basic mix ingredients and store in an airtight container for up to 3 weeks.

To make a simple porridge, place 30g (1oz) of the basic mix in a saucepan, add the milk or coconut water (we also like to add a pinch of salt) and cook over a low heat for about 5 minutes, stirring frequently, until thickened to your liking.

Try This…

The mix makes a creamy, mildly nutty porridge that works as a comforting base for all kinds of Midlife extras such as:

* Chopped or grated apple and cinnamon, which will boost the antioxidant count of your breakfast bowl
* Banana and Midlife Sweetener, see page 31
* Dried fruits, such as cranberries, raisins, golden raisins, apricots, prunes or goji berries
* Fresh fruit, such as chopped pear, blueberries, raspberries, strawberries, kiwi, mango or cherries
* Canned fruit, such as crushed pineapple, apricots or peaches
* Rhubarb compote or Midlife Apple Sauce, see page 244
* Raw jam, see page 242
* Chopped toasted nuts
* Spices, such as nutmeg, vanilla, grated fresh root ginger, cinnamon or cardamom and a dash of rose water
* Raw cacao nibs

MIDLIFE MUST-HAVES

WHY WE LOVE IT

We have a love-hate relationship with granola. We love the delicious nutty crunch it adds to a breakfast bowl, but we hate the fact that most shop-bought versions are stuffed full of sugar. So, in devising this one, we have gone completely sugar-free – a grown-up granola, if you like. Ours still delivers the requisite extreme crunch, but rather than achieving it by baking with masses of oil and sugar, here egg whites do a much lighter and healthier job. Sprinkle on yogurt and add a dollop of raw fruit jam or some dried fruit and you'll have all the sweetness you need.

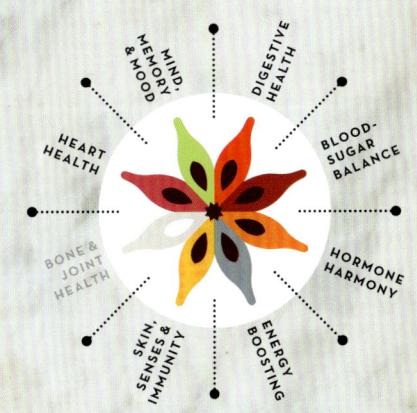

Midlife Grown-up Granola

MAKES 300G (10½OZ)

50g (1¾oz) unsalted cashew nuts
100g (3½oz) jumbo oats
50g (1¾oz) Brazil nuts, chopped
50g (1¾oz) flaked almonds
25g (1oz) flaxseeds
25g (1oz) amaranth
1 tsp ground cinnamon
a good pinch of sea salt flakes
3 egg whites

Preheat the oven to 150°C (300°F)/Gas Mark 2. Line a baking sheet with nonstick baking paper.

Roughly crush the cashews with the back of a spoon, then mix with the remaining dry ingredients.

Whisk the egg whites until stiff peaks form, then add to the dry ingredients, stirring thoroughly with a metal spoon until all the ingredients are fully coated.

Spread the mixture on to the prepared baking sheet and bake for 40 minutes, stirring after 20 minutes to break up the granola a little. Leave to cool completely.

Transfer the granola to an airtight container and store for up to 3 weeks.

Health Tip
Similar to quinoa, amaranth – which means 'everlasting' in Greek – was a staple of the Aztecs. Richer in protein than most other grains, it is also packed with fibre, B vitamins, iron, calcium, magnesium, zinc and omega-3s.

WHY WE LOVE IT

Intensely savoury, deeply nutritious, mildly exotic – this Egyptian dukkah really sums up what the Midlife Kitchen is all about, delivering on taste, texture and versatility with incredibly little effort. Park this in the fridge and reach for it every time you want a flavourful health boost.

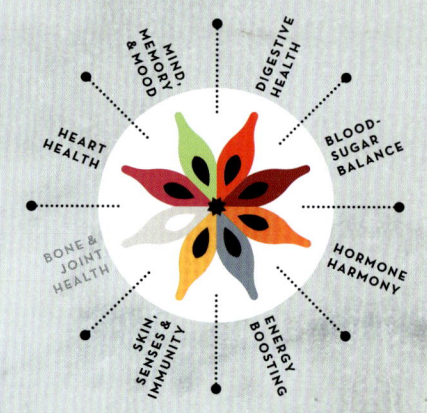

Midlife Dukkah

MAKES APPROX. 10 TBSP

- 2 tbsp whole almonds, blanched or with skins on
- 2 tbsp pistachio nuts
- 2 tbsp sesame seeds
- 1 tsp cumin seeds
- 1 tsp coriander seeds
- 1 tsp fennel seeds
- 10 black peppercorns
- 10 pink peppercorns
- 1 tsp sea salt flakes

Place all the ingredients in a large, shallow frying pan and dry-fry over a medium heat for a few minutes until the nuts and seeds start to colour and pop, taking care not to burn them. Leave to cool.

Tip the mixture into a coffee grinder or spice mill and pulse until it resembles the coarse texture of a 'dry rub' seasoning. Alternatively, pound the mixture using a pestle and mortar.

Transfer the dukkah to an airtight container and store in the fridge for up to 1 month.

Try This...

* Sprinkled on soft-boiled eggs or fried eggs, in an egg mayonnaise or as a coating for peeled hard-boiled eggs
* As a topping for salads and soups
* With steamed asparagus, cauliflower, spinach or tenderstem broccoli, or scattered over grilled veggies
* As a rub for chicken or meat, a coating for falafel, folded into hummus or on a baked sweet potato topped with natural yogurt

Health Tip
If you're trying to eat 30 plants a week, this will provide you with 8. The more diversity of plants you eat, the more benefits for gut health.

WHY WE LOVE IT

We all need a bit of sweetness in our lives, but you'd have to be living under a rock not to know that too much sugar is bad news. This is our answer. Yes, dates contain natural sugars, but a little really does go a long way. And, since it's a whole-plant food sweetener, our date syrup is also packed with antioxidants and fibre. Better yet, it takes minutes to make and keeps in the fridge for 3 weeks.

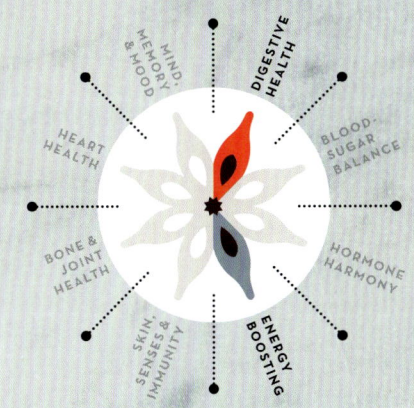

Midlife Sweetener

MAKES APPROX. 10 TBSP

200g (7oz) pitted Medjool dates

2 tsp lemon juice

300ml (½ pint) water, plus extra if needed

Place all the ingredients in a food processor or blender and process until completely smooth, adding a little more water as necessary – you're looking for something with the consistency of apple sauce.

Transfer to a sealed jar and store in the fridge for up to 3 weeks.

Health Tip
Dates are an excellent source of dietary fibre which is required by the digestive system to function properly. Fibre protects against constipation and can help lower blood cholesterol.

WHY WE LOVE IT

An excellent 'semi-salt', this seasoning includes sesame seeds for a shot of added fibre, vitamins, minerals and omega-3 fatty acids. It's a simple combination based on a 1:10 ratio that goes to the heart of what makes the Midlife Kitchen tick: bumping up the health benefits, pumping up the flavour and trying something new that takes mere seconds to prepare. The Japanese call this seasoning *gomashio*; try adding ground nori seaweed sheets to the mix if your taste for umami stretches that far.

Midlife Sesame Seasoning

MAKES APPROX. 4 TBSP

10 tsp black (or white) sesame seeds
1 tsp sea salt flakes

Using a pestle and mortar, pound the sesame seeds until lightly crushed (alternatively, whizz in a blender), then combine with the salt.

Transfer the mixture to a jar and use as an alternative to salt.

Try This...
* On dark green salads
* With French beans
* Sprinkled on an omelette or scrambled eggs

Midlife Hack: Semi-salts can really reduce your salt consumption, while adding dazzling nutrient-rich flavour to any number of dishes.

Health Tip
For such an unassuming little seed, sesame brings quite a lot to the Midlife party: protein, fibre, B vitamins, calcium and iron are just some of their nutrient line-up, guarding against health issues such as high cholesterol and osteoarthritis. They are also a source of phytoestrogens, which can promote the cardiovascular health of menopausal women.

WHY WE LOVE IT

Our go-to vinaigrette: olive oil is the undisputed king of fats – it's heart healthy and can raise the good cholesterol in your bloodstream, while lowering the bad. Choose extra virgin, which has more flavour, nutrients and antioxidants than refined pressings (it tastes more interesting too – grass-green and vivid – which makes it the perfect choice for a vinaigrette). As for apple cider vinegar, choose a raw, unfiltered variety with a recognizable cloudy swirl known, rather fittingly, as 'the mother' – a living ball of enzymes and friendly bacteria.

Midlife Salad Dressing

MAKES APPROX. 10 TBSP

4 tbsp extra virgin olive oil

2 tbsp apple cider vinegar

1 tbsp lemon juice

1 tbsp Dijon mustard

2 tsp clear honey

2 tsp dried thyme

sea salt flakes and freshly ground black pepper

Place all the ingredients in a jar, seal with the lid and shake well to emulsify.

The dressing keeps well in the fridge for up to 2 weeks.

Try This...
Our Midlife Dressing works as a great base for other flavours, so try it with:

* A handful each of finely chopped parsley and tarragon for a great green dressing
* A crushed garlic clove, a finely chopped spring onion and a dash of chilli flakes for a punchy version
* Replace the mustard and thyme with 1 tablespoon of tamari and 2 teaspoons of grated fresh root ginger, for an Asian-style dressing
* Replace the mustard and thyme with 1 tablespoon of tahini, 2 teaspoons of sesame seeds and 2 tablespoons of natural yogurt for a creamier dressing

Midlife Hack: Keep extra virgin olive oil and apple cider vinegar in a cool, dark place to prevent them losing potency.

Health Tip
Olive oil is high in mono- and polyunsaturated fats which, when consumed alongside a diet low in saturated fat and sugar can help reduce cholesterol levels. This is especially important post-menopause.

WHY WE LOVE IT

This curry paste is called *bumbu kuning*, or 'yellow spice', in Indonesian, thanks to the amount of fresh turmeric root it contains. Blessed with impressive health-giving properties, turmeric has long been used in India to soothe the liver, and in China to treat depression – but in the Midlife Kitchen, we love it equally well for its decadent golden colour and subtle, earthy flavour. This gorgeous, aromatic paste forms the basis of several of our recipes, so it's well worth the bit of contemplative effort required to peel and pulse. As you would expect, it has a southeast Asian vibe rather than an Indian one, so think ginger and lemon grass rather than cumin and curry powder.

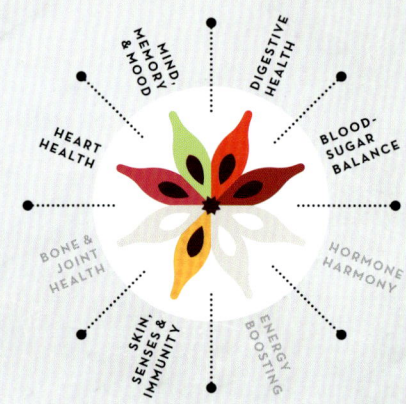

Midlife Curry Paste

MAKES APPROX. 10 TBSP

1 star anise

3 cloves

10 small shallots, roughly chopped

15 garlic cloves, roughly chopped

5cm (2in) piece of fresh turmeric root, peeled and roughly chopped

5cm (2in) piece of fresh root ginger, peeled and roughly chopped

5cm (2in) piece of galangal, peeled and roughly chopped

1 lemon grass stalk, tough outer layers removed and thinly sliced

3 lime leaves, sliced

2–3 hot red chillies, deseeded and sliced, to taste

1 tsp Midlife Spice Mix, see page 24

4 tbsp coconut oil, melted if solid

½ tsp sea salt flakes

freshly ground black pepper

Put the star anise and cloves in a coffee grinder or spice mill and pulse until finely ground. Alternatively, pound using a pestle and mortar.

Tip the ground spices into a food processor or blender, add the remaining ingredients and pulse to a coarse paste.

Store in an airtight container in the fridge for up to 2 weeks.

Health Tip
Turmeric is right up there in the Midlife Hall of Fame, boasting an astonishing array of health benefits. One of the active compounds in turmeric, curcumin, is currently being researched for it's potential in treating Alzheimer's disease.

WHY WE LOVE IT

Yogurt is the original A* health food – in fact, full-fat yogurt is bursting with nutrients, and provides a big hit of gut-loving bacteria in the live culture. What you're really after, though, are the clever little bacteria in the live culture. Probiotic literally means 'for life': these microorganisms can help improve your immune function and strengthen your digestive system. Taking antibiotics can disrupt the normal balance of bacteria in the gut, as can the menopause or any period of stress – so eating plenty of live yogurt will help rebalance and restore your inner world. Probiotics don't hang around for long, so replenish them regularly by eating yogurt often – it's well worth considering the outlay for a yogurt maker.

Midlife Yogurt

MAKES APPROX. 1 LITRE (1¾ PINT)

1 litre (1¾ pint) UHT whole milk

2 tbsp skimmed milk powder

2 tbsp live yogurt from previous batch, or shop-bought live yogurt

½ tsp vanilla seeds from a pod or a good grind of vanilla bean from a mill, see Midlife Hack on page 211

Place all the ingredients in a large jug and mix together well. Pour into a clean sterilized 1 litre (1¾ pint) jar or several smaller jars and secure the lid.

Place the jar/s in a yogurt maker and leave to incubate for 8–12 hours, or according to the manufacturer's instructions.

Chill the yogurt in the fridge for a few hours or overnight before serving.

Some tips for successful yogurt making:
* Use jars straight from the dishwasher to ensure they are scrupulously clean
* Using whole milk and adding milk powder will make a super-creamy (though more calorific) yogurt. It will also be higher in vitamin A
* Probiotics are delicate Goldilocks types, so they will only flourish at the right temperature – which is where a maker comes in handy
* If you prep the yogurt in the morning, incubate during the day and chill overnight, it's ready to go for breakfast the following day
* Remember to keep a little yogurt back from each batch to start the next
* After a few weeks of recycling, the taste of your yogurt may become a bit sour and funky; that's when to start afresh with a new shop-bought live yogurt

Health Tip
Recent research has found that people who eat yogurt every day have a lower risk of developing type-2 diabetes, while it also might help to reduce blood pressure.

BREAKFAST & BRUNCH

WHY WE LOVE IT

We first came up with the idea for *The Midlife Kitchen* at the Yoga Barn in Ubud, eating bowls of this dense, dark rice porridge, so this dish is particularly close to our hearts. Known as 'bubur injin' in Bali, it has a unique silken texture, combines the glories of sweetness and saltiness, and looks fabulously dramatic, especially when coupled with shards of fresh white coconut and the bright orange of tropical fruit.

Sweet & Salty Balinese Black Rice

SERVES 4

400ml (14fl oz) can coconut milk

150g (5½oz) black sticky rice, soaked overnight and rinsed clean

400ml (14fl oz) water

2 tbsp date syrup

½ tsp vanilla extract

sea salt flakes, to taste

TO SERVE

1 mango (or other tropical fruit), peeled, stoned and chopped

1 tbsp finely chopped fresh coconut or desiccated coconut

Reserve 2 tablespoons of the coconut milk and set aside.

Place all the other ingredients in a saucepan and bring to the boil, then reduce the heat and simmer gently for about 30 minutes, stirring often, until the rice is tender, plump and has absorbed most of the liquid.

Serve warm, with the reserved coconut milk and topped with the chopped fruit and coconut.

Try This...
* With blueberries and fresh figs instead of tropical fruit and coconut
* Served with natural yogurt for a black-and-white combo

Midlife Hack: Don't be put off by the prep required – you can buy black glutinous rice from Amazon and other online suppliers, and pre-soaking is not essential, it simply lessens the cooking time. Make plenty, keep it overnight and eat for breakfast the next day too.

Health Tip
Black rice, as you might expect, contains high levels of health-boosting antioxidants called anthocyanins, which are free-radical scavengers, helping to guard against cellular damage.

WHY WE LOVE IT

The very point of porridge is that it's a big hug in a bowl – warming, filling, as comforting as a fairy tale on a dark night. This version ticks all of those boxes and then gives you an additional autumnal cuddle. As you might expect, given their depth of colour, blackberries and black plums have some of the highest antioxidant powers of any fruit. Make this with plain oats, or with our Power Porridge for extra Midlife clout.

Hedgerow Spiced Porridge
WITH BLACKBERRIES, PLUMS, FIGS & HAZELNUTS

SERVES 2

- 50g (1¾oz) Midlife Power Porridge, see page 28, or jumbo oats
- 250ml (9fl oz) shop-bought or homemade unsweetened almond milk, see page 296 (or milk of your choice)
- a pinch of sea salt flakes
- ½ tsp vanilla extract
- 1 tbsp Midlife Sweetener, see page 31, or 2 tsp date syrup, plus extra to serve (optional)
- ¼ tsp ground cinnamon
- ¼ tsp ground ginger
- a grating of nutmeg
- 40g (1½oz) soft dried figs, chopped
- 40g (1½oz) fresh or frozen blackberries, plus extra to serve

TO SERVE

- 2 fresh figs, quartered
- 2 black plums, halved, stoned and sliced
- 20g (¾oz) hazelnuts, roughly chopped

Place all the porridge ingredients, except the dried figs and blackberries, in a saucepan and cook over a low heat for 3 minutes, stirring frequently, until the mixture starts to thicken.

Add the dried figs and blackberries and gently simmer for a further 2–3 minutes, breaking open the berries to release their juices, until thickened to your liking.

Serve with the fresh figs, black plums and hazelnuts, extra blackberries and a further drizzle of Midlife Sweetener or date syrup to taste.

Midlife Hack: Frozen berries are cheaper and arguably better than fresh, as they are frozen quickly and higher in vitamin C than berries that have been sitting on supermarket shelves.

Health Tip
It's the purple anthocyanins that give blackberries their Midlife badge of honour: dark berries are particularly high in heart-healthy antioxidants.

CARROT CAKE PORRIDGE

CHERRY CHOCOLATE PORRIDGE

SPICED PUMPKIN PORRIDGE

SALTED ALMOND PORRIDGE

SUPER GREEN PORRIDGE

WHY WE LOVE IT

Who doesn't adore the comforting taste of carrot cake? This brilliant breakfast take on a classic is super healthy and has no added sugar, with all the sweetness coming from the banana, carrot and sultanas. It maxes out the spices too, so the antioxidant level zooms up.

Carrot Cake Porridge

SERVES 2

50g (1¾oz) Midlife Power Porridge, see page 28, or jumbo oats

250ml (9fl oz) full-fat milk (or milk of your choice)

1 tsp flaxseeds

1 small carrot, about 50g (1¾oz), peeled and grated

½ tsp ground cinnamon

½ tsp ground nutmeg

½ tsp allspice

½ tsp peeled and grated fresh root ginger or ground ginger

2 cardamom pods

1 tsp vanilla extract

½ ripe banana, mashed

20g (¾oz) sultanas

20g (¾oz) goji berries (optional)

a pinch of sea salt flakes

TO SERVE

1 tbsp Midlife Raw Seed Mix, see page 25

a handful of walnuts, chopped (optional)

Place all the ingredients in a saucepan and cook over a low heat for about 5 minutes, stirring frequently, until thickened to your liking.

Remove the cardamom pods and serve with a scattering of Midlife Raw Seed Mix and/or walnuts.

The recipe also works well if you soak the mixture overnight for a super-quick bircher-style breakfast.

See photograph on page 42.

Health Tip
Carrots are brilliant orange because they're high in beta-carotene – a pigment converted to vitamin A in the body, promoting good vision and immune function. Its absorption is improved (up to 6.5 times) if the carrots are cooked.

BREAKFAST & BRUNCH

WHY WE LOVE IT

A pumpkin's gorgeous orange colour is a telltale sign that it's full of health-boosting carotenoids, so adding it to your morning porridge will spike your breakfast with good things. Think of this as an autumnal Thanksgiving special – deliciously warming for a cold day – and the good-carb hit will keep you feeling full for hours.

Spiced Pumpkin Porridge

SERVES 2

50g (1¾oz) Midlife Power Porridge, see page 28, or jumbo oats

200ml (7fl oz) semi-skimmed milk (or milk of your choice)

100g (3½oz) canned pumpkin purée

1 tsp runny honey, plus extra to serve (optional)

1 tsp finely grated orange zest

½ tsp ground cinnamon

¼ tsp grated nutmeg

a pinch of sea salt flakes

TO SERVE

1 tbsp walnuts or pecan nuts, chopped

1 tbsp pumpkin seeds

1 tsp finely grated orange zest

Combine all the ingredients in a saucepan. Cook over a low heat for about 5 minutes, stirring frequently, until thickened to your liking.

Serve scattered with the nuts, seeds and orange zest, adding a drizzle of honey, if required.

See photograph on page 43.

Midlife Hack: A can of pumpkin works just as well as fresh, and avoids the faff of prep; use the remainder to thicken a root veg soup, or it will keep in the fridge for up to a week.

Health Tip
Pumpkin is incredibly high in beta-carotene which gets converted to vitamin A – this is needed by the body for maintaining good skin and eyesight.

WHY WE LOVE IT

Almonds and cherries are perfect dance partners, and both happen to be key Midlife ingredients. Almonds have been basking in the limelight for a while now and this subtle super porridge uses them in four different forms – milk, butter, extract and flakes – which covers all the bases (the almond butter is calorific, so go easy). Cherries, meanwhile, are bursting with antioxidant power. Keep them in the freezer for a cheap and constant supply.

Salted Almond Porridge
WITH WARM CHERRY CHIA JAM

SERVES 2

50g (1¾oz) Midlife Power Porridge, see page 28, or jumbo oats

250ml (9fl oz) shop-bought or homemade unsweetened almond milk, see page 296 (or milk of your choice)

1 tbsp almond butter

1 tsp vanilla extract

1 tsp almond extract

a pinch of sea salt flakes

1 tbsp flaked almonds, to serve

FOR THE WARM JAM

50g (1¾oz) frozen cherries, defrosted

1 tsp chia seeds

First make the jam. Put the cherries and chia seeds in a microwaveable bowl and mash together, then microwave on full power for 2 minutes to make a warm raw jam. Allow to sit while you make the porridge.

Place all the porridge ingredients in a saucepan and cook over a low heat for about 5 minutes, stirring frequently, until thickened to your liking.

Serve the porridge with a dollop of the jam and a sprinkle of flaked almonds.

See *photograph on page 43.*

Health Tip
Almonds are nutrient dense, high in vitamin E, fibre and essential fats which can help improve heart health, lower cholesterol and aid digestion. This is important during perimenopause as our cardiovascular risk increases and our gut microbiota diversity falls.

WHY WE LOVE IT

This is definitely a wild card, but give it a chance – it's packed with Midlife goodies and is unexpectedly delicious. There should be enough sweetness in the ripe banana, but if the green-tea taste is a little strong for you, moderate it with an extra teaspoon of honey to serve.

Super Green Porridge

SERVES 2

50g (1¾oz) Midlife Power Porridge, see page 28, or jumbo oats

2 tsp runny honey, plus 1 tsp to serve (optional)

1 small courgette, about 40g (1½oz), grated

a pinch of sea salt flakes

250ml (9fl oz) water

1 tsp pure matcha powder

1 small ripe banana, mashed

a handful of blueberries, to serve

Place all the ingredients, except the matcha and banana, in a saucepan and cook over a low heat for about 5 minutes, stirring frequently, until the mixture starts to thicken.

Dissolve the matcha powder in a little boiling water and stir well, then add to the porridge with the mashed banana and heat through.

Serve the porridge topped with the blueberries and drizzled with extra honey to taste.

See photograph on page 43.

Midlife Hack: It's worth hunting down the 'ceremonial grade' Japanese matcha, which is the purest form with the greatest potency. It's an acquired taste, so persevere!

Health Tip
Matcha is loaded with powerful antioxidants that may help lower the risk of heart disease and type 2 diabetes, earning it our vote as the healthiest drink on the planet. Consuming green tea is even thought to enhance memory and reduce anxiety.

BREAKFAST & BRUNCH

WHY WE LOVE IT

If you're having trouble getting your kids interested in porridge, try this unexpectedly healthy chocolate version. You don't even need to tell them that it's packed with gut-friendly fibre and protective resveratrol. Of course, you can eat it too, for all the same benefits.

Cherry Chocolate Porridge

SERVES 2

50g (1¾oz) Midlife Power Porridge, see page 28, or jumbo oats

250ml (9fl oz) milk

1 tsp unsweetened cocoa powder

1 tbsp Midlife Sweetener, see page 31, or date syrup

50g (1¾oz) dark chocolate, broken into small pieces

50g (1¾oz) fresh or frozen pitted cherries

raw cacao nibs, to serve (optional)

Place the oats, milk, cocoa powder and Midlife Sweetener or date syrup in a saucepan and cook over a low heat for about 5 minutes, stirring frequently, until thickened to your liking.

Stir in the chocolate and cherries and cook for a further 3 minutes until the cherries and chocolate have softened.

Serve the porridge topped with raw cacao nibs.

See photograph on page 42.

Health Tip
Resveratrol, which is found in dark chocolate, is a powerful antioxidant thought to have cardio-protective benefits. Research continues, but we don't need any more persuasion to eat it!

WHY WE LOVE IT

Depth of colour is a clue to the antioxidant power of any fruit or vegetable, so you can tell just by looking at this yogurt combo that it is bursting with health-boosting merit. The pomegranate molasses treads a fine line between sweet and sour, which is just right here – but of course you can use date syrup, honey or maple syrup if you don't happen to have any molasses to hand.

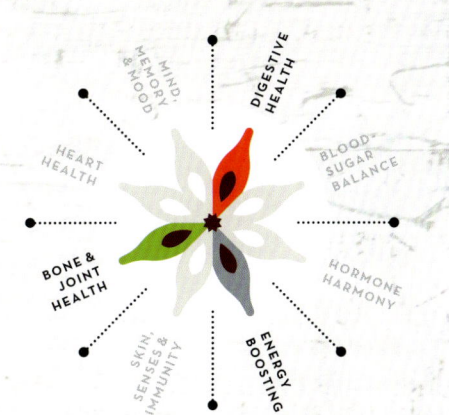

Yogurt with Figs & Pomegranate Molasses

SERVES 2

100g (3½oz) natural yogurt

4 ripe fresh figs, quartered

seeds of 1 pomegranate (see the Midlife Hack on page 98 for a quick way to deseed pomegranates)

1 tbsp pomegranate molasses

Divide the yogurt between 2 bowls, then top with the figs and pomegranate seeds.

Drizzle with the pomegranate molasses, grab a spoon and dive in.

See photograph on page 50.

Health Tip
The punicalagins in pomegranates have been shown to reduce inflammation, one of the leading drivers for many age-related diseases.

BREAKFAST & BRUNCH

YOGURT WITH FIGS & POMEGRANATE MOLASSES

APPLE STRUDEL YOGURT

ST CLEMENT'S YOGURT

YOGURT WITH HOT MEGA-BERRY SAUCE

TROPICAL YOGURT

WHY WE LOVE IT

Here, you get all the delicious flavours of a good strudel – soft apples, fat sultanas, plenty of cinnamon. We've added nuts and dates, increasing the nutrient and energy count to power you through to lunchtime.

Apple Strudel Yogurt

SERVES 2

100g (3½oz) natural yogurt

4 tbsp Midlife Apple Sauce, see page 244, or 1 small apple, grated

1 tbsp Midlife Sweetener, see page 31, or date syrup

1 tsp ground cinnamon, plus extra to serve

2 tbsp walnuts, chopped

1 tbsp flaked almonds

1 tbsp sultanas

1 tbsp Medjool dates, pitted and chopped

Place the yogurt in a bowl and swirl in the apple sauce or apple, Midlife Sweetener or date syrup and cinnamon.

Spoon the mixture into 2 bowls, top with the nuts and dried fruit and a light dusting of cinnamon, then serve.

See photograph on page 50.

Health Tip
We all want to reduce refined and added sugar in our diets, and fruit compotes like apple sauce are a great way to add sweetness in a healthier way. Apples are, of course, high in fibre and vitamin C, but they also contain potassium for heart health and an array of health-boosting antioxidants.

52   BREAKFAST & BRUNCH

WHY WE LOVE IT

This is a zingy, fresh, fabulous start to the day, banging with vitamin C and rich in calcium from the yogurt and nuts. You can use canned pink grapefruit segments instead of, or as well as, the orange segments to bring even more tang to the table.

St Clement's Yogurt

SERVES 2

1 large orange

100g (3½oz) natural yogurt

1 tsp finely grated lemon zest

1 tbsp pistachio nuts, lightly crushed

a few saffron threads (optional)

1 tsp runny honey

Finely grate the zest of the orange and set aside the zest. Using a sharp knife, remove the peel and pith from the orange, then cut out the segments, removing the membranes.

Divide the yogurt between 2 bowls, then top with the orange segments, orange zest, lemon zest, pistachios and saffron.

Drizzle with the honey and dig in.

See photograph on page 51.

Midlife Hack: Freeze citrus fruits whole, so they're always available to zest.

Health Tip
Lemon and orange peel contains around double the vitamin C of the fruit inside, so don't throw away those skins!

WHY WE LOVE IT

There's something completely irresistible about the combination of tropical fruit, coconut and lime – they somehow add up to an exotic holiday in a bowl. Here, we simply strew these glamour fruits on our thick, creamy yogurt... close your eyes and you can almost feel the sun on your face.

Tropical Yogurt

SERVES 2

100g (3½oz) natural yogurt

1 mango, peeled, stoned and chopped

1 papaya, peeled, deseeded and chopped

1 tbsp chopped fresh coconut or desiccated coconut

1 tsp finely grated or finely sliced lime zest

2 tsp runny honey

Layer all the ingredients, except the honey, in 2 glasses, finishing with a layer of fruit, coconut and lime zest.

Drizzle with the honey and enjoy.

See *photograph* on page 51.

Health Tip
Papayas contain an enzyme called papain that aids digestion. They are also low in calories compared with most tropical fruit, with just 39 calories per 100g.

WHY WE LOVE IT

This is a dynamite way to eat yogurt – a blissfully rich hot berry sauce, full of health-giving goodies. The pomegranate molasses, date syrup and dark star anise give the sauce a gorgeous, semi-spicy, grown-up flavour. It may be simple, but this would make a great dinner-party dessert, thanks to its complexity of tastes and sumptuous colour.

Yogurt with Hot Mega-berry Sauce

SERVES 2

100g (3½oz) natural yogurt

FOR THE SAUCE

a handful each of fresh or frozen blackberries, blueberries and pitted cherries

1 tbsp pomegranate molasses

1 tbsp date syrup

1 tsp water

1 star anise

Place all the sauce ingredients in a small saucepan and heat through until the berries have burst and released their juice.

Divide the yogurt between 2 bowls, then swirl in the sauce and spoon more on top.

Eat any remaining sauce with a spoon, direct from the saucepan!

See *photograph on page 51.*

Health Tip
A study of over 16,000 women showed that those eating just one serving of blueberries a week experienced less mental decline over time than those who did not. As they are so delicious, we can't think of any reason why you wouldn't!

WHY WE LOVE IT

Overnight oats are a perfect breakfast if you're in a hurry, and they're a great vehicle for all manner of Midlife brilliance. Here, the classic combo of cherries and chocolate makes for a decadent (and antioxidant) breakfast on the run.

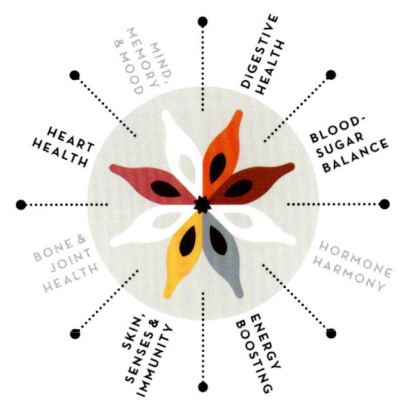

Black Forest Overnight Oats

SERVES 2

100g (3½oz) Midlife Power Porridge, see page 28, or jumbo oats

2 tsp chia seeds

2 tsp unsweetened cocoa powder

½ tsp ground cinnamon

½ tsp sea salt flakes

300ml (½ pint) shop-bought or homemade unsweetened almond milk, see page 296 (or milk of your choice), plus extra to serve (optional)

½ tsp vanilla extract

2 tsp date syrup

100g (3½oz) frozen pitted dark cherries

large handful of chopped pistachio nuts, to serve

Combine all the dry ingredients in a small Kilner jar or airtight plastic container. Stir in the milk, vanilla extract and date syrup, then top with the frozen cherries. Seal and leave to soak in the fridge for 8 hours or overnight.

In the morning, add extra milk if needed until you get the consistency you like. Add the pistachios and serve.

This can be made up to 3 days ahead and kept in the fridge.

Midlife Hack: Frozen cherries are readily available at most supermarkets, usually for a fraction of the price of the fresh fruit. They generally come ready-pitted too so are super easy to use.

Health Tip
Cherries are very rich in antioxidants, such as anthocyanins and catechins, which can help fight inflammation.

WHY WE LOVE IT

Bircher spends the night in the fridge, where its flavours and textures mingle and develop ready for a speedy, sensational breakfast the next morning. Most traditional birchers include yogurt, which can make them a little rich, but our tropical version uses coconut water to keep it really light.

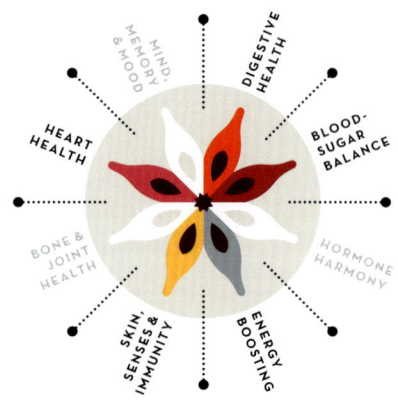

Nurture Bircher

SERVES 2–3

100g (3½oz) Midlife Power Porridge, see page 28, or jumbo oats

250ml (9fl oz) coconut water

2 tbsp desiccated coconut

1 tsp finely grated lemon zest

1 small apple, grated

5 pitted dates, chopped

1 tbsp flaked almonds

1 star anise

1 tsp peeled and finely grated fresh root ginger

TO SERVE

passion fruit or other chopped tropical fruit, such as mango, pineapple, melon or papaya

Put all the ingredients, except the tropical fruit, in an airtight plastic container and mix thoroughly. Seal and leave to soak in the fridge overnight.

In the morning, serve topped with tropical fruit of your choice.

Health Tip
Coconut water is great for hydration – indeed, it is often referred to as 'nature's sports drink', replenishing the body with vital nutrients including potassium which helps maintain a healthy balance of fluids in the body.

WHY WE LOVE IT

What's not to love about avocado toast? It's our fall-back breakfast (and lunch... and supper) in the Midlife Kitchen. The trick is to keep the toppings simple but intensely savoury, a foil for the mellow avocado beneath. This version is utterly mouth-watering, with the spiced crunch of the nuts set off by a tang of crumbled goat's cheese or feta.

Nutty Goat Avo Toast

SERVES 2

light olive oil spray

1 tsp Midlife Spice Mix, see page 24

½ tsp chilli flakes

50g (1¾oz) raw almonds, roughly crushed

sea salt flakes and freshly ground black pepper

4 slices of Seedy Soda Bread, see page 209, or rye or multigrain bread, toasted

1 ripe avocado, peeled, stoned and roughly mashed

100g (3½oz) goat's cheese or feta, crumbled

Heat a small nonstick frying pan and spray with a little olive oil. Add the Midlife Spice Mix, chilli flakes, crushed almonds, salt and pepper and fry for a few minutes until the nuts start to colour, taking care not to burn them.

Top each slice of toast with the mashed avocado, then sprinkle with the nut mix and the cheese.

This works brilliantly with our Zehug (Coriander, Chilli & Tomato Relish), see page 238.

See photograph on page 62.

Health Tip
Avocados contain 'heart-healthy' fatty acids, plenty of fibre and more than 20 essential nutrients; these clever little pears can also boost your body's ability to absorb fat-soluble nutrients from other fruit and vegetables.

WHY WE LOVE IT

This is cheese-on-toast with a twist, but with far less saturated fat than the traditional teatime version. Choose a good-quality seeded bread (try it with our Seedy Soda Bread on page 209) for a guilt-free tower of taste. The basis here, as with any avo toast, is a perfectly ripe avocado – don't even try to get anything glorious from an avocado bullet.

Welsh Rarebit Avo Toast

SERVES 2

100g (3½oz) mature Cheddar cheese, grated

2 tsp grainy Dijon mustard

1 tsp milk

a good dash of Worcestershire sauce

4 slices of Seedy Soda Bread, see page 209, or rye or multigrain bread, toasted

1 tomato, thinly sliced (optional)

1 ripe avocado, peeled, stoned and roughly mashed

a grating of nutmeg

Combine the Cheddar, mustard, milk and Worcestershire sauce to form a thick paste.

Top each toast with a couple of slices of tomato, if using, then a quarter of the mashed avocado.

Divide the cheese mix over the avocado and grate with a little nutmeg.

Cook under a preheated hot grill for about 3 minutes until the topping bubbles and starts to brown, then serve.

See photograph on page 62.

Midlife Hack: Keep avocados in the fruit bowl, not in the fridge. If you want one to ripen quickly, place it in a brown paper bag with a banana; both give off ethylene gas, which speeds up the ripening process.

Health Tip
Avocados contain vitamins B, C and K, together with lots of potassium which helps support healthy blood pressure. They're rich in mono- and polyunsaturated fats which can help manage cholesterol levels – especially important in menopause.

BREAKFAST & BRUNCH

SESAME STREET AVO TOAST

BEANS ON (AVO) TOAST

WHY WE LOVE IT

Here, we've taken avocado toast on a journey to Japan and we think it's a match made in heaven. Sesame and avocado make excellent toast partners, while bean sprouts and thinly sliced spring onions bring a snappy crunch to the deal. If you are a tofu fan you can include some here for extra protein; add a scatter of Midlife Sesame Seasoning and you've got yourself a fabulous, umami-packed start to the day.

Sesame Street Avo Toast

SERVES 2

¼ tsp wasabi paste

1 tbsp tahini

1 tsp sesame oil or extra virgin olive oil

4 slices of Seedy Soda Bread, see page 209, or rye or multigrain bread, toasted

1 ripe avocado, peeled, stoned and roughly mashed

juice of 1 lime

100g (3½oz) tofu, diced (optional)

2 spring onions, finely sliced

a handful of bean sprouts

4 tsp Midlife Sesame Seasoning, see page 32, or sesame seeds

pickled ginger, to serve (optional)

Combine the wasabi, tahini and oil to form a paste, then spread this on each slice of toast.

Top with the mashed avocado, drizzle with the lime juice and add the tofu, if using, the spring onions and bean sprouts.

Sprinkle each toast with the sesame seasoning or seeds and serve with pickled ginger.

See photograph on page 63.

Health Tip
Tahini, made from sesame seeds, is a rich source of B vitamins, which have been shown to provide iron and support immune and cognitive function.

WHY WE LOVE IT

Simplicity is, we've found, the key to avo toast – it should be a tasty, speedy something to rustle up when time is tight. This Mexican-inspired version has the added Midlife magic of fresh tomatoes and pinto beans. Sombrero optional.

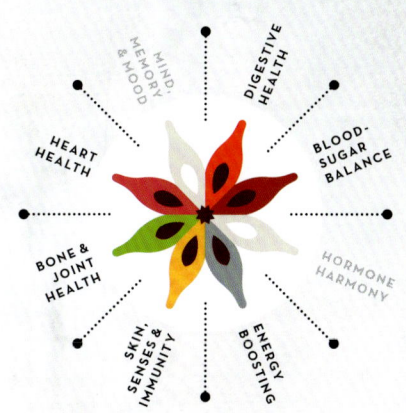

Beans on (Avo) Toast

SERVES 2

200g (7oz) canned pinto beans, rinsed and drained

2 ripe tomatoes, diced

10 jalapeño pepper slices from a jar, diced

4 slices of Seedy Soda Bread, see page 209, or rye or multigrain bread, toasted

1 ripe avocado, peeled, stoned and roughly mashed

2 tbsp natural yogurt

sea salt flakes and freshly ground black pepper

Place the pinto beans in a bowl and mash lightly with a fork. Add the tomatoes and jalapeño slices and mix well.

Top each slice of toast with the mashed avocado, the tomato mixture and a spoonful of yogurt. Season and serve.

See photograph on page 63.

Health Tip
Red beans, such as these pretty, speckled pinto beans, are rich in protein, gut-friendly fibre, antioxidant anthocyanins and slow-release carbs, making them making them the perfect food for perimenopause and particularly menopause.

BREAKFAST & BRUNCH

WHY WE LOVE IT

Chia seeds – tiny, tasteless, ever-so trendy – are also exceptionally healthy, providing protein, fibre, bone-protecting minerals and all-important omega-3 fatty acids. They can (almost miraculously, when you see them for the first time) absorb up to ten times their weight in liquid, producing a gelatinous texture that works brilliantly in combination with fresh fruit or compote for a quick, sustaining breakfast.

Chia-up Pots

MAKES 4 POTS

2 small ripe bananas

300ml (½ pint) shop-bought or homemade unsweetened almond milk, see page 296, or coconut milk

50g (1¾oz) chia seeds

1 tsp vanilla extract

Place the bananas in a bowl and mash with a fork. Stir in the milk, then add the chia seeds and vanilla, combining well.

Divide the mixture between 4 small bowls, glasses or ramekins, filling to about halfway.

Chill in the fridge until completely cold, ideally overnight (they'll be fine there for up to 3 days).

Try This...
Top your Chia-up Pots with:

* Chopped strawberries, passion fruit, kiwifruit and orange zest (pictured)
* Chopped mango, strawberries, kiwifruit and mint leaves
* Midlife Apple Sauce, see page 244
* Fresh blueberries and Midlife Grown-up Granola, see page 29
* Raspberries and mint leaves
* Sliced banana and chopped pecans
* Desiccated coconut, pineapple and chopped dates

Health Tip
Chia seeds were prized by the Aztecs and Mayans as a source of sustainable energy (in fact, 'chia' is the ancient Mayan word for 'strength') – and science is now catching up; a recent study found that chia seeds may have a stabilizing effect on blood sugar in people with type 2 diabetes.

BREAKFAST & BRUNCH

WHY WE LOVE IT

We ate these gorgeous wraps after a class at the famous Yoga Barn in Bali and knew at once that they warranted a starring role in the Midlife Kitchen, thanks to their fabulous flavour and impressive cast of nutritional goodies. This is definitely a brunch option as it takes a little longer to make than your usual breakfast, but the effort is well worth it. Don't be put off by the egg white bit – we aren't getting all LA on you; an egg white omelette just goes better with the strong pickle and spices. This is best made with our Easy Chapatis (they really are).

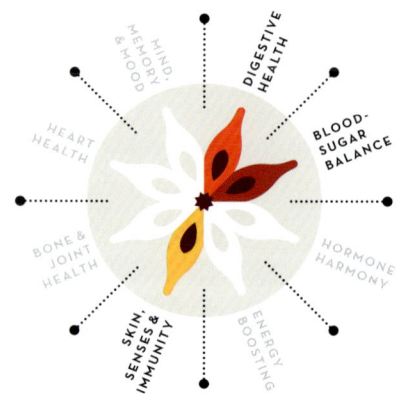

Yoga Barn Wraps
WITH GINGER PICKLE

SERVES 2

4 egg whites

1 tsp Midlife Spice Mix, see page 24

a pinch of sea salt flakes

a splash of water

light olive oil spray

FOR THE GINGER PICKLE

1 small carrot, peeled and grated

a thumb-sized piece of fresh root ginger, peeled and finely grated

2 tsp Midlife Sweetener, see page 31, or 1 tsp clear honey

½ tsp ground cumin

a squeeze of lemon juice

100ml (3½fl oz) water

sea salt flakes and freshly ground black pepper

TO SERVE

2 Easy Chapatis, see page 206, or shop-bought seeded wraps

2 tbsp natural yogurt

Place all the pickle ingredients in a small saucepan and simmer for 5 minutes until reduced to a chutney consistency, then set aside to cool for at least 5 minutes.

Using a fork, whisk together the egg whites, spice mix, salt and a splash of water in a bowl until well combined.

Heat a medium nonstick frying pan and spray with a little olive oil to just coat the base. Pour in half the egg mixture and roll it around to thinly cover the base of the pan. Cook for a couple of minutes until lightly golden, then flip and cook on the other side. Remove from the pan and set aside. Repeat with the remaining mixture to make a second omelette.

Place the omelettes on the chapatis or wraps and roll up. Cut each roll in half and serve with Ginger Pickle and yogurt.

Health Tip
We use a lot of ginger in the Midlife Kitchen; among its many health benefits it's traditionally used to help ease the gut – which explains why ginger is a traditional remedy for seasickness.

WHY WE LOVE IT

We always welcome a new way to eat eggs, as they are nutritionally the best possible start to the day; here, they come in the guise of fluffy, omelette-y mini-muffins. As the base is simply whisked eggs, you can add whatever your taste buds (or your children) desire, but we've done some of the work for you in suggesting a few tasty, healthy power-combos – just choose your favourite and add to the tin.

Egg Muffins
WITH AVOCADO SALSA

MAKES 10–12 MUFFINS

light olive oil spray

6 eggs

sea salt flakes and freshly ground black pepper

FOR THE FLAVOUR COMBINATIONS

crumbled feta, olives and finely chopped fresh chilli or chilli flakes

grated Parmesan, finely chopped spring onions and diced tomato

smoked fish (trout, mackerel or salmon), chopped into small pieces, chopped dill and natural yogurt

FOR THE SALSA

1 large ripe avocado

1 spring onion, finely chopped

a handful of flat leaf parsley, chopped

2 tsp lemon juice

½ tsp runny honey

Preheat the oven to 190°C (375°F)/Gas Mark 5. Spray 10–12 holes of a muffin tin with olive oil, brushing each hole to coat really well, then place in the oven.

Whisk the eggs in a jug with a splash of water and salt and pepper.

Take the hot tin out of the oven and pour in the egg mixture to fill halfway up each hole, then top each one with your chosen ingredients. Bake for 20 minutes, or until cooked through and golden.

Meanwhile, peel, stone and dice the avocado, then combine in a bowl with the spring onion and parsley, adding the lemon juice and a little honey to balance the acidity. Season to taste.

Remove the muffins from the oven and leave to cool for a minute or two. Remove from the tray – they may stick a bit so use a palette knife to release the sides. Serve with the avocado salsa.

Health Tip
Eggs contain a little of almost every nutrient we need for a mere 75 calories. They are especially good for countering perimenopausal and post-menopausal muscle loss, making them perfect midlife food.

WHY WE LOVE IT

This is one of those dishes that is so much more than the sum of its parts. On the face of it, a comfortingly retro dish of baked eggs, tomatoes and paprika but, with a few Midlife tweaks such as adding peppers and red onions, the antioxidant content is pumped, transforming it into a delicious and nutritious brunch-time feast.

Midlife Shakshouka

SERVES 2

light olive oil spray

1 small red onion, diced

1 garlic clove, crushed

2 small peppers (1 red, 1 yellow), cored, deseeded and chopped

400g (14oz) can chopped tomatoes

½ tsp chilli flakes, or more to taste

½ tsp ground cumin

½ tsp paprika

½ tsp soft brown sugar

a squeeze of lemon juice

4 eggs

sea salt flakes and freshly ground black pepper

2 tbsp natural yogurt, to serve

a handful of flat leaf parsley, chopped, to serve

Heat a medium-sized frying pan over a medium heat and spray with a little olive oil. Add the onion and sauté for a few minutes until it begins to soften, then add the garlic and continue to sauté for a minute. Add the peppers and cook for a further 5 minutes until softened.

Stir in the tomatoes, chilli flakes, spices, sugar and lemon juice and simmer for 5–7 minutes until the mixture starts to thicken.

Make 4 evenly spaced wells in the tomato mixture, then crack an egg into each one. Season well and cover the pan with a lid. Cook for 10 minutes, or until the egg whites are firm and the yolks still runny.

Serve with the yogurt and scatter with parsley.

Health Tip
Studies have shown that lycopene, a potent antioxidant found in tomatoes, is boosted by cooking, so by slowly simmering this rich, red sauce you are also maximizing the nutritional benefit.

BREAKFAST & BRUNCH

WHY WE LOVE IT

A muffin, we can all agree, is a marvellous thing and these bouncy bran muffins are better yet as they combine plenty of health-giving fibre with very little refined sugar (the sweetness comes instead from date syrup, banana and pineapple). Make a big batch of the mix and it will keep happily in the fridge for up to 3 days – you can add different berries, chopped apple or pear, nuts or seeds to your mix each morning. We've found that they're best straight from the oven on a Sunday morning, eaten warm with a dab of cold butter.

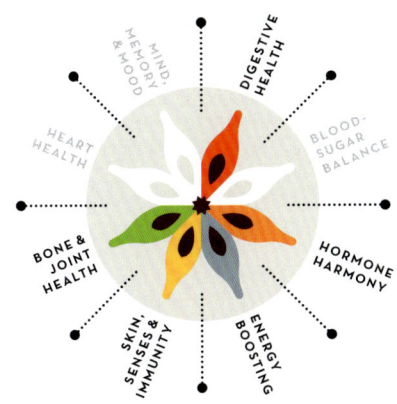

Breakfast Bran Muffins

MAKES 12-16

- 100g (3½oz) bran flake breakfast cereal
- 100g (3½oz) wholemeal flour
- 50g (1¾oz) Midlife LSA, see page 27, or ground almonds
- 100g (3½oz) sultanas
- 100g (3½oz) canned crushed pineapple
- 100g (3½oz) natural yogurt
- 2 eggs
- 1 tsp ground cinnamon
- 1 tsp mixed spice
- 1 tsp ground ginger
- 1 ripe banana, mashed
- 1 tbsp olive oil
- 1 tbsp Midlife Sweetener, see page 31, or date syrup
- 1 tsp vanilla extract
- 1 tsp baking powder
- a pinch of sea salt flakes

Preheat the oven to 170°C (340°F)/Gas Mark 3½. Line 1 or 2 muffin tins with paper muffin cases.

Combine all the ingredients in a large bowl and stir well – the mixture will be lumpy.

Spoon the mixture into the muffin cases and bake for 20 minutes until just firm. Eat warm.

Try this...
* Add chopped dried apricots, pitted and chopped dates and top with Midlife Raw Seed Mix, see page 25
* Add frozen berries and ground cardamom
* Add a grated carrot, dried cranberries, and top with oats

Health Tip
Fibre can help reduce the risk of all manner of age-related illnesses, but most of us don't eat nearly enough. A bran muffin is a brilliant way to get your fix.

BREAKFAST & BRUNCH

WHY WE LOVE IT

Once you cook these little beauties, you'll wonder why you didn't discover them years ago. We think of them as pancakes without the guilt trip because they're packed with protein and fibre, and they're also naturally gluten-free. Serve with fresh fruit, spices and seeds for an ideal way to start the day, giving your digestion and energy levels a breakfast boost.

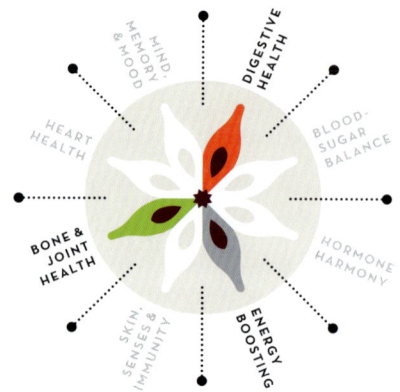

No-flour Banana Pancakes

MAKES 6–8 PANCAKES

2 large ripe bananas
2 large eggs
light olive oil spray

OPTIONAL EXTRAS

1 tbsp Midlife Raw Seed Mix, see page 25, or seeds of your choice

1 tbsp raisins, chopped ready-to-eat dried apricots or other dried fruit

½ tsp ground cinnamon

1 tbsp dark chocolate chips (kids love this one!)

Place the bananas in a bowl and mash with a fork, then whisk in the eggs and combine well. Stir in a combination of your choice of seeds, dried fruit, cinnamon or chocolate.

Heat a nonstick frying pan and spray with a little olive oil. Add small scoops of mixture to the pan, enough to make pancakes about 8cm (3¼in) across (if you make them too big they will be hard to flip).

Cook for about 3 minutes on each side until golden and just cooked through.

Try This...
Serve the pancakes warm with your choice of toppings:

* Fresh orange segments, natural yogurt and grated orange zest (pictured)
* A drizzle of maple syrup and chopped papaya
* Grated coconut and chopped mango

Health Tip
Bananas are an excellent source of potassium, a mineral that is essential for heart health, especially blood pressure control.

WHY WE LOVE IT

These are posh pancakes really – so why 'angel cakes'? Well, they're light, fluffy and truly virtuous. The ricotta is less of a taste and more of a texture, making the angel cakes deliciously rich and dreamy. We've chosen to use hemp milk here, just to embrace something new – but semi-skimmed cow's milk would work equally well. This is one for a lazy Sunday: hot coffee, warm angel cakes, fresh fruit, pure heaven.

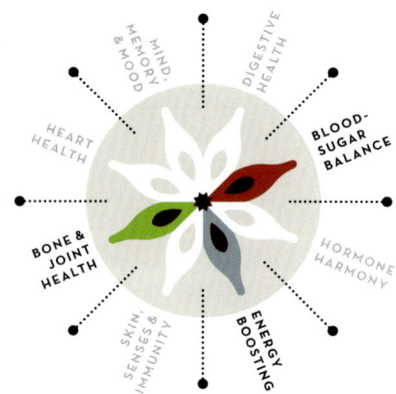

Ricotta Angel Cakes

MAKES 12–15 CAKES

- 4 eggs, separated
- 4 tbsp ricotta cheese
- 2 tbsp Midlife LSA, see page 27, or ground almonds
- 2 tbsp plain flour
- 1 ripe banana, mashed
- 4 tbsp semi-skimmed milk
- 1 tsp ground cinnamon
- 1 tsp vanilla extract
- 1 tsp baking powder
- 1 tsp maple syrup
- a pinch of sea salt flakes
- light olive oil spray

Whisk the egg whites in a clean bowl until soft peaks form.

Combine all the remaining ingredients, except the olive oil, in a separate bowl, including the egg yolks (don't worry about a few lumps), then add the whisked egg whites and fold in gently to retain a soufflé texture.

Heat a nonstick frying pan or griddle and spray with a little oil. Ladle on spoonfuls of the mixture and spread them out slightly with the back of a spoon (an 8cm (3¼in) diameter for each cake is about right). When bubbles start to appear, carefully flip the cakes and cook gently on the other side until golden and just set, with a bit of interior wobble. Remove the angel cakes from the pan and keep warm in a low oven. Repeat with the remaining batter.

Try This...
Serve the Angel Cakes warm with your choice of toppings:

* Fresh sliced strawberries, mint leaves, a little extra ricotta and a drizzle of maple syrup (pictured)
* Fresh orange segments and blueberries
* Sliced banana and Midlife Raw Seed Mix, see page 25

Health Tip
Ricotta is an excellent source of calcium – this helps protect against menopausal bone loss which can increase our risk of osteoporosis.

BREAKFAST & BRUNCH

WHY WE LOVE IT

This is a real wake-up in a bowl, a happy salad full of sunshine and good things. Stick to orange and pink fruits to get the prettiest effect. The ginger is the ace card here, elevating it from the mundane to the truly tasty and adding masses of antioxidant power. Use plenty of dressing – the idea is that the fruit should be drenched and the ginger should be strong enough to leave a tingle on the tongue.

Morning Fruit Salad
WITH GINGER & ORANGE

SERVES 2

orange and pink fruits – enough for 2 people, choose from apricot, nectarine, peach, melon, mango, papaya, guava or orange or pink grapefruit segments, cut into bite-sized pieces

zest of 1 lime, grated or thinly sliced

FOR THE DRESSING

juice of 1 orange

a thumb-sized piece of fresh root ginger, peeled and finely grated

1 tsp runny honey (optional)

2 star anise

Place all the dressing ingredients in a jar, seal with the lid and shake well.

Arrange the fruit in a serving bowl, then add the dressing and sprinkle with lime zest. Serve immediately.

Health Tip
What we have here is an abundance of vitamin C which is crucial for collagen production. This helps to support skin health from the inside.

BREAKFAST & BRUNCH

WHY WE LOVE IT

Smoothie bowls are a bit of a thing at the moment – and there's good reason: not only do they look enticing, they also combine the triple glories of natural yogurt, fresh fruit and satiating carbs to give you a supercharged breakfast. We first spotted this version in a little beach café in Bali and it's just brimming with tropical zing. You can use whatever fruits you have to hand, but do include the coconut flakes and mint leaves – they bring something interesting, tasty and special to the bowl.

Bali Beach Smoothie Bowl

SERVES 2

10 blueberries

10 strawberries

10 blackberries

3 tbsp natural yogurt

mint leaves, to serve

maple syrup or Midlife Sweetener, see page 31, to serve (optional)

FOR THE TOPPINGS

2 tbsp Midlife Grown-up Granola, see page 29, or muesli

assorted fresh fruit, such as bananas, strawberries, mango and blueberries

2 tsp chia seeds

4 tsp coconut flakes or desiccated coconut

Whizz the berries and yogurt in a blender to produce a smoothie consistency.

Pour the mixture into a bowl, leaving space for the toppings, then line up the granola or muesli, fruit, chia seeds and coconut on the top.

Decorate with mint leaves and, if you like extra sweetness, drizzle with a little maple syrup or Midlife Sweetener.

Health Tip
The focus here is the wide range of colourful plant foods you are getting in one bowl. Remember, more colours = more nutrients!

82   BREAKFAST & BRUNCH

SALADS & SOUPS

WHY WE LOVE IT

We love this simple, sparky salad showcasing the healthy lightness that is the hallmark of Japanese cuisine. This makes a perfect lunch alongside a bowl of miso soup; you'll feel full of energy for the rest of the afternoon. *Itadakimasu!*

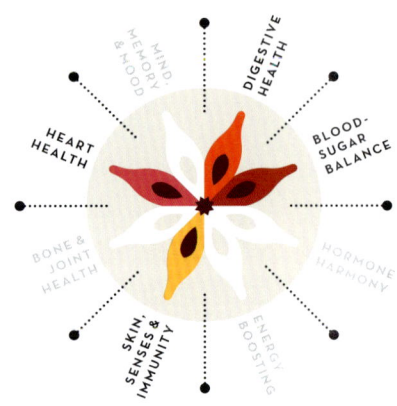

Hijuki Salad

SERVES 2

1 large or 2 small sheets of nori seaweed, cut into 1cm (½in) thin strips

½ a cucumber, deseeded and cut into thin strips

1 carrot, peeled and cut into thin strips

2 spring onions, thinly sliced

a palm-sized piece of fresh coconut, finely grated, plus extra to serve

25g (1oz) unsalted cashew nuts, lightly crushed

1 tsp Midlife Sesame Seasoning, see page 32, or sesame seeds, to serve

FOR THE DRESSING

juice of ½ a lemon

1 tsp miso paste

1 tsp soy sauce

1 tsp sesame oil

Put all the salad ingredients into a bowl and combine. (The dressing will soften the nori seaweed, so there's no need to presoak.)

Mix the dressing ingredients and pour over the salad, tossing well.

Divide the salad between 2 large bowls and serve sprinkled with the sesame seasoning or seeds and extra grated coconut.

Midlife Hack: It's worth investing in a 'julienne' tool for making Asian-style salads, where veggies are often prepared in thin strips. It is so quick and lends a pretty look to the dish.

Health Tip
Seaweed is a plant-based source of iodine which is needed for thyroid support, skin and cognitive function.

WHY WE LOVE IT

Possibly the prettiest plate of food you'll ever make. Choose a good, wobbly buffalo mozzarella for the best results – it's the combination of that wobble and the soft, sweet peaches that make this dish such a hit. If you have really sweet summer peaches, there's no need to grill them.

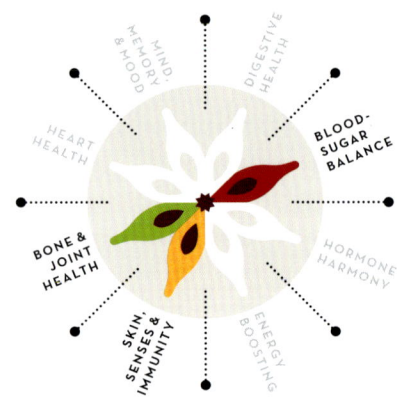

Peach & Mozzarella Salad
WITH PISTACHIO PESTO

SERVES 2–3

2 peaches, stoned and each cut into 8 slices

100g (3½oz) buffalo mozzarella cheese, torn into pieces

a handful of pomegranate seeds

FOR THE PESTO

a handful of basil leaves

a handful of coriander leaves, plus extra to serve

30g (1oz) pistachio nuts, lightly crushed, plus extra to serve

grated zest and juice of ½ a lemon

1 garlic clove, peeled and halved

2 tbsp extra virgin olive oil

sea salt flakes and freshly ground black pepper

Cook the peach slices under a preheated hot grill for 5 minutes until they start to soften and colour. Leave to cool.

Put all the pesto ingredients into a food processor and blitz until almost smooth (you want to retain a bit of texture). The pesto will keep in the fridge for up to 2 days.

Arrange the torn mozzarella and grilled peach slices on a plate and drizzle generously with the pesto. Scatter with the pomegranate seeds, extra pistachios and coriander leaves, then serve.

Midlife Hack: If you find yourself with extra pistachio pesto, keep it in the fridge to have another day with spaghetti, or as a topping for roasted veggies or steamed broccoli.

Health Tip
This bone-friendly salad contains plentiful protein and calcium, two key nutrients for a healthy menopause.

SALADS & SOUPS

WHY WE LOVE IT

One of our Midlife mantras is to embrace variety – and the sheer abundance of flavour, texture and colour here will clearly do wonders for you. It's a rainbow of raw excellence, brought together with a terrific tangy dressing guaranteed to transport you to a Koh Samui beach. You'll need a bit of time to chop and slice, but otherwise it's a doddle. Add cubes of tofu or cooked prawns for a more substantial meal.

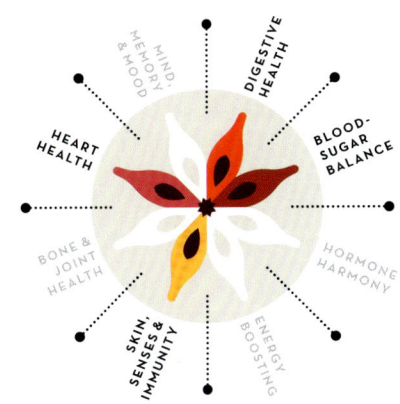

Raw Pad Thai

SERVES 2

1 small carrot, peeled and cut into thin strips, shaved or shredded

1 small courgette, finely sliced or cut into thin strips

50g (1¾oz) red cabbage, very thinly sliced

50g (1¾oz) sugar snap peas, sliced

½ a pepper (orange, yellow or red), deseeded and thinly sliced

2 spring onions, sliced diagonally

1 mild red chilli, deseeded and thinly sliced

a handful of bean sprouts

a handful of coriander leaves

a handful of mint leaves, plus sprigs to serve

FOR THE DRESSING

2 tbsp coconut milk

finely grated zest and juice of 1 lime

1 tbsp crunchy peanut butter (100 per cent peanuts, no sugar)

2 tsp soy sauce

2 tsp tahini

1 tsp Thai fish sauce (nam pla)

1 tsp sesame oil

1 tsp maple syrup

1cm (½in) piece of fresh root ginger, peeled and finely grated

1 garlic clove, crushed

1 lemon grass stalk, tough outer layers removed, finely chopped

TO SERVE

20g (¾oz) peanuts, crushed

2 tsp Midlife Sesame Seasoning, see page 32, or sesame seeds

1 tsp Midlife Spiced Seed Mix, see page 26 (optional)

Place all the vegetables and herbs in a large bowl and mix well.

Place all the dressing ingredients in a jar, seal with the lid and shake well until combined.

Pour the dressing over the salad and toss well, then arrange on a serving plate. Top with the peanuts, seeds and extra mint sprigs and serve.

Health Tip
Peanuts are not, in fact, a nut but a legume. In addition to their 'good' fat content, peanuts contain an array of other nutrients that have been shown to promote heart health.

SALADS & SOUPS

WHY WE LOVE IT

So much more than a salad, this is a veritable taste sensation, thanks to the layering of flavours (sweet, sharp, savoury), textures (creamy, crunchy) and colours (deep ruby reds, pale pinks, vibrant greens). You don't need a huge quantity of Stilton in this salad – regard it as a seasoning rather than a protein fix. The tangy dressing brings the whole lot together for a dish that looks a total treat and requires nothing more for a fabulous lunch.

Pink Salad

WITH STILTON CRUMB & POMEGRANATE MOLASSES GLAZE

SERVES 4

2 heads of red chicory, leaves separated

1 small head of radicchio, leaves torn

2 handfuls of baby salad leaves, such as Lollo Rosso and rocket

2 ripe figs, each cut into 8 slices

1 ripe red pear, quartered, cored and sliced into thin crescents

30g (1oz) walnut pieces

100g (3½oz) Stilton or other hard blue cheese, crumbled

a handful of pomegranate seeds

FOR THE GLAZE

1 tbsp pomegranate molasses

1 tbsp balsamic glaze (or use balsamic vinegar for a sharper dressing)

1 tbsp date syrup

1 tbsp extra virgin olive oil

1 tbsp water

sea salt flakes and freshly ground black pepper

Arrange the salad ingredients, as decoratively as you like, in a lovely serving bowl.

Mix all the glaze ingredients and drizzle over the salad.

Midlife Hack: You can prep all the ingredients in advance and keep in the fridge. Dress the pear slices with lemon juice to prevent browning if you are not serving the salad straight away.

Health Tip

Eating just a small handful of walnuts a day can provide significant levels of the heart healthy fatty acid ALA (alpha-linolenic acid), which may help to lower 'bad' cholesterol levels in the blood.

WHY WE LOVE IT

This has a little bit of French style and a whole lot of punchy flavour, the leaves functioning as a ferry for a cargo of pure deliciousness. It's ridiculously easy to make and tastes wonderfully decadent, without any undue heaviness, as the blue cheese dressing is moderated with a dollop of yogurt. It's messy to eat, so you'll need a napkin.

Red Chicory & Walnuts
WITH A WARM ROQUEFORT DRESSING

SERVES 4

2 heads of red chicory, leaves separated

30g (1oz) walnut pieces

100g (3½oz) Roquefort cheese, crumbled

2 tbsp natural yogurt

Arrange the chicory leaves to sit like boats on a serving plate, then sprinkle the walnuts into each.

Place the Roquefort and yogurt in a small saucepan and heat gently for about 2 minutes, stirring to eliminate the lumps, until it has a soup-like consistency.

Pour the sauce liberally into the chicory boats and eat immediately.

Health Tip
Chicory is rich in phytonutrients, including folate, fibre and vitamins A, C and K; the red cultivar has high levels of antioxidant anthocyanins that can protect the cells in our body.

WHY WE LOVE IT

This is just one of those perfect marriages: sweet beetroot, peppery watercress, creamy goat's cheese, the pop of blueberries and the crunch of hazelnuts. It looks pretty as a picture too. Roasting the beetroot slowly will release its gorgeous natural stickiness. We like it with a walnut oil and lemon dressing, which manages to be both delicate and flavourful.

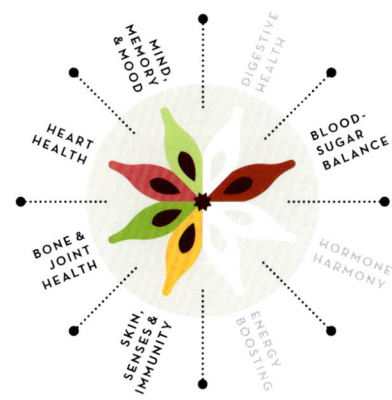

Beetroot & Blueberry Salad
WITH HAZELNUTS & GOAT'S CHEESE

SERVES 4

- 3 raw beetroot (including stems and leaves)
- 1 tsp extra virgin olive oil
- sea salt flakes and freshly ground black pepper
- a handful of watercress, thicker stems removed
- a handful of salad leaves, such as rocket, lamb's lettuce or mixed baby leaves
- 1 tbsp hazelnuts, lightly crushed
- 50g (1¾oz) blueberries
- 50g (1¾oz) goat's cheese, broken into small pieces
- edible flowers, to serve (optional)

FOR THE DRESSING

- 1 tbsp walnut oil or extra virgin olive oil
- juice of ½ a lemon
- 1 tsp maple syrup
- sea salt flakes and freshly ground black pepper

Preheat the oven to 160°C (325°F)/Gas Mark 3. Reserve some of the tender beetroot leaves and slice a few of the stems. Scrub the beetroot and cut into 8 or 12 pieces, depending on their size.

Place the beetroot in a small baking tin, drizzle with the olive oil and season with salt and pepper. Bake for about 20–25 minutes until tender. Set aside to cool.

Place all the dressing ingredients in a small jar, seal with the lid and shake well until combined.

Arrange the watercress, salad leaves and reserved beetroot stems and leaves on a serving plate. Add the nuts, blueberries and cheese, then drizzle liberally with the dressing and top with edible flowers.

Health Tip
Don't throw away the leafy tops and slim ruby-red stems of beetroot; they can be steamed or stir-fried or, as here, eaten raw. They are particularly rich in vitamin C, needed for healthy gums, while beetroot leaves also contain iron, folate and beta-carotene, which converts to vitamin A for healthy eyes.

WHY WE LOVE IT

This is a lovely, delicate salad, sophisticated even, but it takes a bit of time and care to properly segment the fruit. Why Pom Pom? Well, pomegranate of course, but the other star of this show is pomelo, which is really just a mega-grapefruit with a slightly firmer texture. It is widely eaten as a snack in Southeast Asia, often with a dusting of salt and sugar; if you have trouble finding one, use grapefruit instead. Here, the citrus tang and sharpness of the fennel and lime are offset brilliantly by the sweetness of the orange juice and pomegranate seeds.

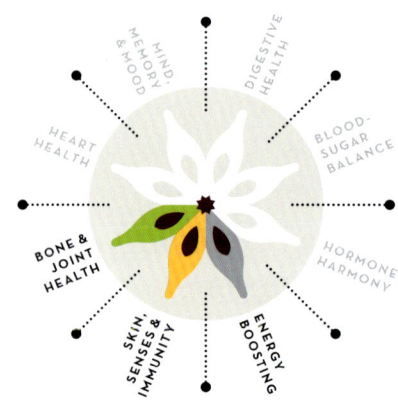

Pom Pom Salad

SERVES 2–3

1 fennel bulb, trimmed and thinly sliced
2 tsp runny honey
2 tsp extra virgin olive oil
1 pomelo or pink grapefruit
100g (3½oz) mixed baby salad leaves
a handful of dill, chopped
seeds of 1 pomegranate, see Midlife Hack

FOR THE DRESSING
juice of 2 limes
juice of 1 small orange
1 tbsp extra virgin olive oil
sea salt flakes and freshly ground black pepper

Preheat the oven to 200°C (400°F)/Gas Mark 6. Place the fennel on a baking sheet and drizzle with the honey and olive oil. Roast for 15 minutes, or until tender.

Meanwhile, using a sharp knife, remove the peel and pith from the pomelo or grapefruit, then cut out the segments, removing the membranes and place in a bowl with the salad leaves and dill.

Place all the dressing ingredients in a large jar, seal with the lid and shake well until combined.

Pour the dressing over the salad and toss well, then transfer to a serving plate. Top with the roasted fennel and serve sprinkled with the pomegranate seeds.

Midlife Hack: To deseed a pomegranate, cut it in half across the middle. Take each half and hold over a bowl with the seed side down in your palm. Whack the back of the pomegranate with a wooden spoon to release the seeds. Magic!

Health Tip
Grapefruits are full of fibre and skin-supporting vitamin C; eating half a grapefruit before a meal has also been associated with improved insulin sensitivity, which can help lower the risk of type 2 diabetes.

WHY WE LOVE IT

There's something uniquely moreish about salty, squeaky halloumi cheese, and here it's coated in sesame seeds, elevating it to another level of yum. A fennel, lentil and pear base for this salad makes for a substantial meal, packed with Midlife magnificence.

Fenneloumi Salad

SERVES 2

50g (1¾oz) dried green or brown lentils or ½ a pouch (about 125g (4½oz)) ready-cooked lentils

1 fennel bulb, trimmed and sliced into 5mm (¼in) strips

1 tbsp extra virgin olive oil

1 tsp Midlife Spice Mix, see page 24, or ½ tsp ground cumin and ½ tsp ground coriander

sea salt flakes and freshly ground black pepper

juice of ½ a lemon

150g (5½oz) halloumi cheese, thinly sliced

light olive oil spray

a pinch of chilli flakes

2 tsp sesame seeds

1 small Romaine lettuce, shredded

½ quantity of Midlife Salad Dressing, see page 33

1 small pear, cored and sliced

½ a small red onion, thinly sliced

If using dried lentils, place them in a saucepan of water and bring to the boil, then reduce the heat and simmer for 25 minutes until tender but still holding their shape. Drain.

Meanwhile, place the fennel in a bowl and coat with the extra virgin olive oil, spice mix or ground spices, salt and pepper. Leave to marinate while you prepare the rest of the dish.

Tip the drained lentils or pouch of lentils into a bowl and dress with the lemon juice, salt and pepper. Chill in the fridge for 15 minutes.

Spray the halloumi slices with a little olive oil, then dust with the chilli flakes and sesame seeds.

Heat a frying pan, add the marinated fennel and cook for about 5 minutes on each side until it softens and colours at the edges. Set aside.

Wipe the pan with kitchen paper to remove any liquid, then dry-fry the halloumi for a few minutes on each side until the sesame seeds are toasted and the cheese is beginning to crisp and brown.

To assemble the dish, toss the lettuce leaves in the Midlife Salad Dressing and place in a serving bowl. Sprinkle the chilled lentils over the lettuce, top with the fennel, halloumi, pear slices and red onion rings. Drizzle with a little more dressing and serve.

Health Tip
Eating plenty of dairy in midlife means you'll help protect your bones; halloumi, usually made from sheep or goat's milk, is a rich source of calcium and protein, which is important in perimenopause and particularly post-menopause.

WHY WE LOVE IT

There are good Greek salads... and then there are great Greek salads, and this one is packed with health-loving extras. We've added green pepper, cornichons and sunflower seeds for crunch, and handfuls of fresh herbs to give a dear old classic a vibrant update. Make sure your red onion is sliced in almost transparent shards to keep its influence beautifully subtle.

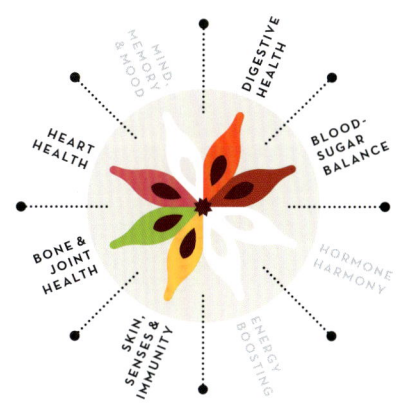

The Mother of all Greek Salads

SERVES 2

½ a head of Romaine lettuce, torn into pieces

10 cherry tomatoes, halved

5cm (2in) piece of cucumber, halved and sliced

½ a small red onion, thinly sliced

1 small green pepper, cored, deseeded and thinly sliced

10 Kalamata olives, pitted

10 cornichons, sliced

50g (1¾oz) feta cheese, crumbled

a handful each of oregano, mint and coriander leaves

1 tsp Midlife Sesame Seasoning, see page 32, or sesame seeds

2 tsp sunflower seeds

sea salt flakes and freshly ground black pepper

FOR THE DRESSING

1 tbsp extra virgin olive oil

1 tbsp lemon juice

1 tbsp red wine vinegar

1 garlic clove, crushed

1 tsp dried oregano

1 tsp runny honey

Place all the dressing ingredients in a jar, seal with the lid and shake well until combined.

Assemble all the salad ingredients in a bowl and dress liberally, season well with plenty of black pepper and dig in.

Health Tip
Olives contain phenolic compounds that are natural antioxidants and which also give them their distinctive taste. Olives and olive oil, when eaten as part of a healthy Mediterranean diet, can lead to a reduced risk of heart disease and cancer.

WHY WE LOVE IT

Our Midlife Spiced Seed Mix brings a delicious crunch and a whole realm of flavour to an otherwise simple salad. Add the burst of blueberries and a few shards of almond and you have a little bowl of Midlife magic. There's so much going on that you barely need a vinaigrette – just a squeeze of lemon and a hint of extra virgin olive oil and you're done.

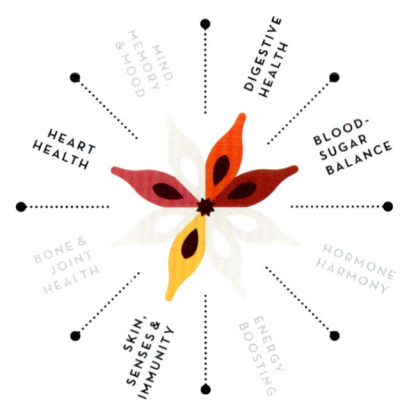

Herb Salad

WITH BLUEBERRIES & SPICED SEEDS

SERVES 2

a handful of salad leaves, such as herbs, rocket and baby spinach

a handful of blueberries

1 tbsp Midlife Spiced Seed Mix, see page 26

2 tsp extra virgin olive oil

juice of ½ a lemon

2 tsp flaked almonds

Place the leaves, blueberries and seed mix in a salad bowl, and toss with the olive oil and lemon juice.

Sprinkle with almonds, then serve and devour.

Health Tip
Blueberries are a great source of fibre, vitamin C and K, and cancer-protective antioxidants. This is a perfect summer salad when blueberries are in season.

WHY WE LOVE IT

If we were pressed to name our top Midlife ingredient, a humble broccoli floret would be right up there in pole position; it really is the king of veg, full of mighty vits, minerals and fibre. So broccoli is the rightful star of this crunchy, colourful salad, first eaten at the Cafe Batujimbar near Sam's home in Bali. It's the mix that makes it brilliant, but there's hidden magic too: the mustard seeds will help boost the broccoli's protective health benefits.

Brilliant Broccoli Salad

SERVES 2

- 1 small head of broccoli, cut in to bite-sized florets; slice the tender stems too
- sea salt flakes
- 50g (1¾oz) flaked almonds
- 100g (3½oz) cooked chilled quinoa, see Midlife Hack
- 2 tbsp dried cranberries

FOR THE DRESSING

- juice of 1 lime
- 1 tsp runny honey
- a thumb-sized piece of fresh root ginger, peeled and finely grated
- 2 tsp extra virgin olive oil
- 1 tsp apple cider vinegar
- 1 tsp mustard seeds

Cook the broccoli florets and sliced stems in a saucepan of salted boiling water for 1–2 minutes. They need to stay crunchy so take care not to overcook them. Refresh in cold water, drain well, pat dry with kitchen paper and set aside.

Heat a frying pan until hot, add the almonds and dry-fry until lightly toasted (this is a very quick process, so do not leave unattended or you will have charcoal flakes). Tip on to a plate and leave to cool.

Combine all the dressing ingredients in a small bowl, stirring well.

Place the broccoli and quinoa in a serving bowl and spoon over some of the dressing. Scatter with toasted almonds and cranberries, finish with a little more dressing and serve.

Midlife Hack: This is an ideal opportunity to bust out a pouch of pre-cooked quinoa; it will save you around 15 minutes cooking time and one less pan in the sink!

Health Tip

A diet rich in cruciferous veg such as broccoli can help reduce the risk of many chronic diseases associated with ageing; some of the nutrients in broccoli have been linked to a reduced risk of cancer and heart disease, as well as improved eye health.

SALADS & SOUPS

WHY WE LOVE IT

This colour-combo salad is a total taste-fest; with avocado for 'good' fats and black rice for 'good' carbs, it promises to fill you up and give you a satisfying lunchtime energy boost. The recipe features our Spiced Red Cabbage Pickle, so you need to have made this in advance, but it's a delicious Midlife staple that can be kept happily in the fridge for several weeks.

RGB Salad

RED, GREEN & BLACK SALAD

SERVES 2

50g (1¾oz) black or wild rice, or a 150g (5½oz) pouch of ready-cooked rice (Tilda's Black and Red Lucky Rice is our pouch of choice)

sea salt flakes

1 small avocado, stoned, peeled and sliced

1 small bag (about 90g (3¼oz)) rocket leaves

8 radishes, thinly sliced

½ quantity Midlife Salad Dressing, see page 33

6 tbsp Spiced Red Cabbage Pickle, see page 240

freshly ground black pepper

If you're not using a ready-cooked rice pouch, cook the rice in a saucepan of boiling salted water for 20–30 minutes until tender. Rinse under cold running water and drain well. Chill in the fridge for about 15 minutes.

Place the rice, avocado, rocket and radishes in a large bowl, add the dressing and combine well.

Transfer to a large serving plate and top with the Spiced Red Cabbage Pickle and a good grind of black pepper.

Health Tip
Radishes are surprisingly high in fibre. Adding fibre to your diet lowers your risk of diabetes and heart disease and improves digestion.

WHY WE LOVE IT

We came across the idea of Kale Caesar and, frankly, just loved the name. We found, though, that using only kale was a little too dark and demanding – but it works a treat if you mix half-and-half kale and the more traditional Romaine. The dressing, though rich, is used sparingly; we've added Midlife power by using flaxseed oil (high in polyunsaturated fats), while the anchovies provide a further omega-3 hit. Instead of the usual croutons, we use roasted chickpeas – simple, sassy and full of beneficial insoluble fibre.

Midlife Caesar

SERVES 4

400g (14oz) can chickpeas, drained and rinsed

sea salt flakes and freshly ground black pepper

200g (7oz) kale, tougher stems removed and leaves shredded

200g (7oz) Romaine lettuce, shredded

30g (1oz) Parmesan cheese, shaved with a vegetable peeler

FOR THE DRESSING

1 egg yolk

1 tsp Dijon mustard

1 small garlic clove, crushed

2 anchovy fillets, roughly chopped

2 tsp capers, chopped

50ml (2fl oz) flaxseed oil

finely grated zest and juice of ½ a lemon

freshly ground black pepper

2 tsp water, plus extra if needed

Preheat the oven to 200°C (400°F)/Gas Mark 6. Place the chickpeas in a baking tin and season with salt and pepper. Bake for 20 minutes until golden and crisp. Leave to cool.

Meanwhile, make the dressing. Put the egg yolk, mustard, garlic, anchovies and capers into a bowl and mix together, then add the oil to the mixture drop by drop, whisking as you go. Add the lemon juice and zest, season with pepper and add a little water to form a coating consistency.

Place the kale and lettuce in a bowl, add the dressing and combine well with your fingers. Transfer to a serving plate, top with the Parmesan shavings and crispy chickpeas and serve. For a more substantial meal, add quartered hard-boiled eggs or sliced, grilled chicken breast.

Health Tip
Flaxseed oil will give your diet a nice little omega-3 boost in the form of ALA (alpha-linolenic acid). The body doesn't process ALA quite as effectively as the fatty acids found in fish and fish oils – but it's still a decent addition to your diet.

WHY WE LOVE IT

Fennel, despite its delicate demeanour, is a truly high-powered vegetable, and a Midlife must: it's stacked with phytonutrients and vitamins that can benefit your bones and immune response. But that's just by the by: the point is that slivers of crunchy, aniseedy fennel, spiked with yogurt, lemon, Parmesan and mint, are a little forkful of joy.

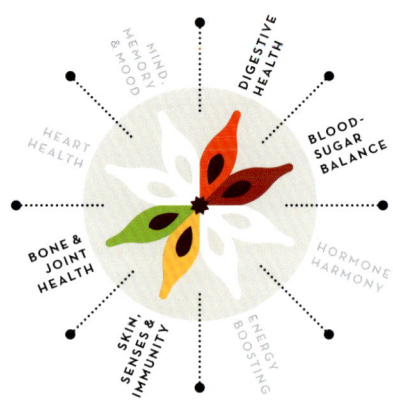

Fennel Carpaccio
WITH LEMON, YOGURT & MINT

SERVES 2

½ a fennel bulb (with fronds)

a handful of small mint leaves

a squeeze of lemon juice

1 tsp extra virgin olive oil

2 tbsp natural yogurt

60g (2¼oz) Parmesan cheese, thinly shaved with a vegetable peeler

sea salt flakes and freshly ground black pepper

½ tsp cumin seeds (optional)

Reserve the fronds from the fennel, then trim the bulb and slice very thinly using a sharp knife or a mandoline.

Place the fennel slices on a pretty plate and scatter with some of the fennel fronds. Add the mint leaves and drizzle generously with the lemon juice and olive oil.

Add a drizzle of yogurt and scatter with Parmesan shavings. Season with salt and pepper and, if you like the flavour, a sprinkling of cumin seeds.

Health Tip
Fennel is a wonderful midlife ingredient thanks to the prebiotics it contains. Perfect for keeping those all-important gut bacteria well fed.

WHY WE LOVE IT

Could this salad be any greener? Or any more delicious? We adore these glistening just-cooked peas, beans and asparagus, shot through with wisps of red chilli, lemon zest and red onion. Yotam Ottolenghi is the inspiration here, but we've added a few Midlife tricks, including skinny, *al dente* asparagus for added oomph. This is one you can prep in advance and assemble quickly, so it makes a great dinner-party showstopper. And, as this salad is leaf-free, it's brilliant for a picnic as it will stay perfectly crunchy even when dressed.

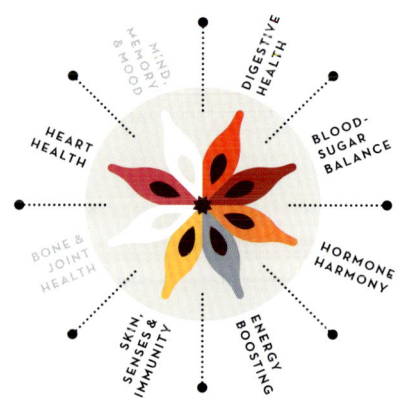

Green Bean & Asparagus Salad

WITH MIDLIFE SPICED SEEDS, TARRAGON & CHILLI

SERVES 4

- 250g (9oz) fine green beans, trimmed
- 250g (9oz) frozen petits pois
- 250g (9oz) mangetout
- 250g (9oz) fine asparagus
- 1 tbsp Midlife Spiced Seed Mix, see page 26

FOR THE DRESSING

- 2 tsp coriander seeds, crushed
- 3 tbsp extra virgin olive oil
- 1 tsp nigella seeds
- ½ a small red onion, finely diced
- 1 garlic clove, crushed
- 1 mild red chilli, deseeded and finely sliced
- finely grated zest of 1 lemon
- a good handful of tarragon leaves, chopped
- sea salt flakes and freshly ground black pepper

Cook all the green vegetables in a large saucepan of boiling water until just tender (green beans for 4 minutes, then add the peas, mangetout and asparagus to the boiling water for the final minute). Refresh in very cold water and drain well. Pat the vegetables dry with kitchen paper.

Place the crushed coriander seeds in a small saucepan with the olive oil and heat gently until the seeds begin to pop and release their aroma. Leave to cool, then add the nigella seeds, red onion, garlic, chilli and lemon zest. Leave to stand while you assemble the veggies in a bowl.

Add the tarragon to the dressing and season well. Pour the dressing over the vegetables, sprinkle with the seed mix and serve.

Health Tip
Asparagus is an excellent source of B vitamins, and play a key role in the metabolism of sugars and starches, which is needed for energy release and to help reduce fatigue.

WHY WE LOVE IT

It's Monday night, the kids are out and you're hungry. In the fridge: a hunk of red cabbage, some radishes. Figs. A lonely jar of pickled baby beetroot and a bunch of dill left over from the weekend pasta. Three minutes slicing and a dollop of lemony yogurt later and you've got yourself a crunchy bowl of salad bliss – sweet, savoury, positively pink with joy and buzzing with antioxidant potential. Lesson? Have good things to hand, recognize happy flavour and texture combinations and don't overthink it.

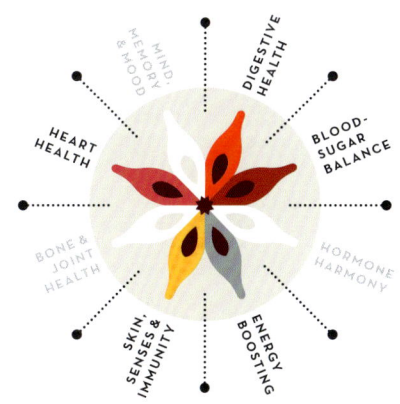

Red Cabbage Coleslaw
WITH BEETS, FIGS, RADISH & DILL

SERVES 1

50g (1¾oz) red cabbage, thinly sliced

8 long radishes, thinly sliced

2–3 pickled beetroot, cut into thin strips

2 ripe figs, each sliced into 4 or 8 pieces

a handful of dill, roughly chopped

FOR THE DRESSING

2 tbsp natural yogurt

a squeeze of lemon juice

2 tsp extra virgin olive oil

sea salt flakes and freshly ground black pepper

Combine the dressing ingredients in a small bowl.

Place the vegetables, figs and dill in a bowl or on a plate, then drizzle with the yogurt dressing.

Eat in front of the telly (optional).

Health Tip
From it's vibrant hue you can tell that beetroot is bursting with antioxidants. It also contains folate and potassium which are hearty healthy nutrients.

WHY WE LOVE IT

Chris Salans, the inspirational chef behind the beautiful Mozaic restaurant in Bali, gave us this recipe after we visited his café Spice in Ubud. This salad takes a bit of prep, but it's a real show-off dish and the perfect platform for tempeh, a cousin of tofu that has a firmer, and we think much nicer, texture. There is an alchemy that happens here that we can't quite explain; you'll just have to try it for yourself.

Ubud Spice Salad

SERVES 2

FOR THE SALAD

a large handful of mixed salad leaves

a small handful of coriander leaves

1 spring onion, thinly sliced diagonally

5 radishes, thinly sliced

1 small mango, peeled, stoned and cubed

1 small avocado, peeled, stoned and cubed

5 cherry tomatoes, quartered

1 tbsp toasted sesame seeds, to serve

FOR THE TEMPEH

1 tbsp coconut oil

100g (3½oz) tempeh, cut into 2cm (¾in) cubes

sea salt flakes and freshly ground black pepper

FOR THE DRESSING

2 tbsp Thai sweet chilli sauce

2 lemon grass stalks, tough outer layers removed, very finely sliced

2 garlic cloves, finely chopped

2 tsp chopped coriander leaves (include the plant roots if possible)

1 tsp Thai fish sauce (nam pla)

a squeeze of lime juice

Arrange all the salad ingredients in a large bowl.

Heat the coconut oil in a frying pan, add the tempeh cubes and fry for about 5 minutes, turning occasionally to ensure the cubes are golden on all sides. Season well and allow to cool slightly, then add the tempeh to the salad.

Combine the dressing ingredients in a separate bowl. Dress the salad and toss to coat (this salad needs plenty of dressing, so don't worry if it seems too much).

Sprinkle with the toasted sesame seeds and serve.

Health Tip
Tempeh is a highly nutritious soya bean product popular in Indonesia and elsewhere in Asia. Unlike tofu, tempeh is fermented, which allows easier digestion of its protein. It contains isoflavones able to mimic some effects of oestrogen, making it potentially beneficial for symptoms of the menopause.

Four Great Salad Dressings

We all have our favourite everyday dressing, the one that lives in the fridge to be called up for duty every time a salad hits the table; you'll find our Midlife version on page 33. But sometimes, a particular combination of salad ingredients demands something creamier, spicier, more complex or exotic. Here, then, are four more super-healthy dressings, each one boasting key Midlife ingredients and guaranteed to make your salad sing.

AVOCADO & TURMERIC

MAKES APPROX. 10–12 TBSP

juice and finely grated zest of 1 lemon

3 tbsp extra virgin olive oil

3 tbsp water, plus extra if needed

3 tsp ground turmeric

½ a small ripe avocado

1 garlic clove, crushed

2 tsp runny honey

sea salt flakes and freshly ground black pepper

Put all the ingredients into a food processor or blender and blitz until you have a smooth, pourable dressing, adding a little more water if the dressing is too thick. Store in a sealed jar in the fridge for up to 2 days.

Try This…
* Inside Little Gem 'boats'
* Drizzled on Romaine lettuce leaves
* As a dip for crudités

TAHINI, LIME & CUMIN

MAKES APPROX. 6 TBSP

juice and finely grated zest of 1 lime

2 tbsp tahini (stir well first)

3 tbsp water, plus extra if needed

1 tsp runny honey

1 tsp ground cumin

1 tsp cumin seeds

2 tsp white sesame seeds

sea salt flakes and white pepper

Combine the lime juice, tahini and water in a bowl and whisk until the mixture becomes smoother and creamier. Add the remaining ingredients and stir well. The thickness is up to you – add a little more water if you prefer a runnier dressing. Store in the fridge for up to 3 days.

Try This…
* Poured into half an avocado
* Drizzled over couscous with grilled chicken
* As a dressing for a falafel pitta

CHILLI & HERB

MAKES APPROX. 6–8 TBSP

a handful of coriander leaves, finely chopped

a handful of parsley, finely chopped

1 garlic clove, crushed

1 red chilli, deseeded and finely chopped, or to taste

3 tbsp extra virgin olive oil

juice of 1 lemon

2 tbsp water

1 tsp runny honey

1 tsp sweet paprika

sea salt flakes and freshly ground black pepper

Place all the ingredients in a jar, seal with the lid and shake well until combined. Store in the fridge for up to 3 days.

Try This…
* On a herb leaf salad with grilled halloumi
* As a dip with toasted pitta bread
* Drizzled on warm grilled veggies

MISO, SESAME & GINGER

MAKES APPROX. 6 TBSP

2 tsp miso paste

2 tsp runny honey

2 tbsp rice vinegar

2 tbsp sesame oil

1 tbsp soy sauce

1 garlic clove, crushed

a thumb-sized piece of fresh root ginger, peeled and finely grated

2 tsp black sesame seeds

1 spring onion, white part only, finely sliced

Place all the ingredients in a jar, seal with the lid and shake well until combined. Store in the fridge for up to 3 days.

Try This…
* With Chinese leaf cabbage, pak choi, sugar snap peas, bean sprouts, shredded white cabbage and grated carrot
* As a marinade for fish or chicken
* As a dipping sauce for rice paper spring rolls

Health Tip
An oil-based dressing will make a salad taste great, but research also shows that it can improve the body's absorption of the fat-soluble antioxidant carotenoids in veggies. The same study found that chopping and shredding helps, too.

WHY WE LOVE IT

Peru has recently established itself as a global health-food capital, due to its unique and nutrient-dense array of produce, much of it hauled from the Amazon and the high Andes. This soup includes quinoa, Peru's famous protein-packed super seed, and lean chicken breast; with plentiful coriander, a hint of chilli and a zing of lime, it's a fortifying mini meal in a bowl.

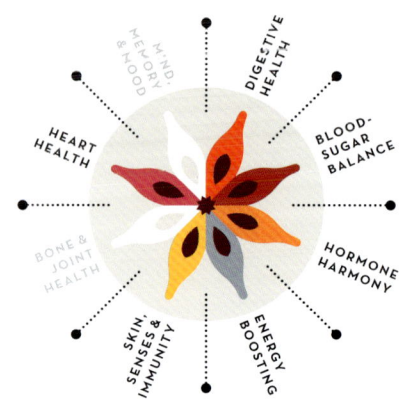

Aguadito
PERUVIAN CHICKEN & CORIANDER SOUP

SERVES 2

- 50g (1¾oz) coriander (leaves and stalks), plus extra leaves to serve
- 1 small onion, roughly chopped
- 1 garlic clove, peeled
- 1 green chilli, deseeded
- 1 celery stick, roughly chopped
- 1 tbsp extra virgin olive oil
- 500ml (18fl oz) chicken stock
- 50g (1¾oz) quinoa, well rinsed
- 1 boneless, skinless chicken breast, about 150g (5½oz), cut into about 4 pieces
- 50g (1¾oz) frozen peas
- juice of ½ a lime
- sea salt flakes and freshly ground black pepper
- lime wedges, to serve

Put the coriander, stalks and all, and the onion, garlic, chilli, celery and olive oil into a food processor and blitz until you get a pesto-like consistency.

Tip the mixture into a saucepan and fry gently for several minutes, then add the stock and rinsed quinoa. Bring to a simmer and cook for 15 minutes.

Add the chicken and cook for a further 15 minutes until the chicken and quinoa are cooked through. Transfer the chicken from the pan to a plate, then shred with a fork. Return the chicken to the pan with the peas and bring to a simmer. Add the lime juice and cook for a few minutes until the peas are tender.

Season and serve scattered with extra coriander leaves and lime wedges on the side.

Midlife Hack: Lazy... but smart: buy ready-diced onion and keep it in the freezer to speed up soup recipes.

Health Tip
Technically a seed but eaten like a grain, quinoa is one of the few plant foods that contains all nine essential amino acids, including lysine and isoleucine, which most other grains lack. Naturally high in fibre, quinoa is a slowly digested carbohydrate, making it a great low-GI option.

WHY WE LOVE IT

Forget green juice or anything that tastes remotely of garden clippings, *the* perfect way to get your fill of leafy greens is in a soup – and this is the best we've tasted. Pile in the veg, simmer it down, give it a quick pulse in the blender and there you have it: a delightful bowl of antioxidant goodness. Add a generous spoonful of natural yogurt for a creamy tang.

All-green Soup

SERVES 4

- 1 tbsp extra virgin olive oil
- 3 garlic cloves, crushed
- 5cm (2in) piece of fresh root ginger, peeled and sliced
- 1 tsp ground coriander
- 5cm (2in) piece of fresh turmeric root, peeled and grated, or 1 tsp ground turmeric
- 1 star anise
- sea salt flakes and freshly ground black pepper
- 500ml (18fl oz) vegetable stock
- 2 courgettes, sliced
- 1 head of broccoli (including tender stalks), chopped
- 2 large handfuls of kale leaves (tougher stems removed), chopped
- juice of 2 limes
- a handful of flat leaf parsley, roughly chopped
- 2–3 tbsp natural yogurt, to serve

Heat the olive oil in a large saucepan, add the garlic, ginger, coriander, turmeric, star anise, salt and pepper and fry over a medium heat for 2 minutes, then add 3 tablespoons of the stock to add a little moisture to the spices.

Add the courgettes, mixing well to coat in the spice mixture, then pour in the remaining stock, bring to a simmer and cook for 5 minutes.

Add the broccoli, kale and lime juice and simmer for a further 3–4 minutes until all the vegetables are softened (you may have to add a little water depending on the volume of greens, but plenty of moisture will be released from the vegetables).

Remove the pan from the heat and add the chopped parsley. Remove the star anise, then pour the soup into a blender and blitz until almost smooth. Reheat the soup, if necessary.

Ladle the soup into bowls and serve each with a swirl of yogurt and a grind of pepper.

Health Tip

Think of kale as a leafy multivitamin – it contains iron, calcium and magnesium which are key midlife minerals, especially in post-menopause when we need extra bone support. An 80g (2¾oz) serving contains more vitamin C than an orange, and seven times the recommended dietary allowance (RDA) for vitamin K – an important nutrient for bone health.

SALADS & SOUPS

WHY WE LOVE IT

This super-savoury soup has a great depth of flavour, thanks to the leeks and Parmesan. The Midlife LSA thickens and adds a welcome nutty, nutritious dimension. You can blitz it to a smooth soup or leave it chunkier for a good rustic bowlful.

Chickpea, Leek & Parmesan Soup

SERVES 4

1 tbsp olive oil

1 tsp butter

2 leeks, trimmed, cleaned and sliced

1 small red onion, diced

2 garlic cloves, chopped

sea salt flakes

400g (14oz) can chickpeas, drained and rinsed

2 tbsp Midlife LSA, see page 27, or ground almonds

800ml (1½ pint) chicken or vegetable stock

freshly ground black pepper

70g (2½oz) Parmesan cheese, grated, plus extra to serve

TO SERVE

a grating of nutmeg

a small handful of parsley, chopped

Heat the olive oil and butter in a large heavy-based saucepan, add the leeks, onion, garlic and a pinch of salt and sauté gently for about 5 minutes until tender.

Add the chickpeas and cook for a further minute, then add the LSA or ground almonds and the stock and simmer for 15 minutes. Season and stir in the Parmesan.

If you prefer a smooth soup, blitz in a blender or use a stick blender. Reheat the soup, if necessary.

Ladle the soup into bowls and add a grating of nutmeg, a scatter of parsley and extra grated Parmesan.

Midlife Hack: Add the rind of the Parmesan to the stock as it simmers to kick up the flavour in this soup. Just remember to remove it before you blitz...

Health Tip
Leeks contain significant amounts of the flavonoid kaempferol, together with plenty of the B vitamin folate and antioxidant polyphenols – all known to protect and support the cardiovascular system.

WHY WE LOVE IT

Hippocrates is thought to have used watercress to treat his patients, and, we now know, with very good reason: this peppery powerhouse contains more calcium than milk, more vitamin C than an orange, and more absorbable iron than spinach. Here's a simple, speedy soup to bring all of that health-giving goodness direct to your spoon.

Watercress Powerhouse Soup

SERVES 2

1 tsp butter

1 onion, roughly chopped, or 1 leek, trimmed, cleaned and roughly chopped

1 potato, peeled and chopped

1 bunch of watercress, about 120g (4¼oz), larger stems removed

500ml (18fl oz) chicken or vegetable stock

a grating of nutmeg

sea salt flakes and freshly ground black pepper

2 tbsp natural yogurt, to serve

Melt the butter in a saucepan, add the onion or leek and sauté gently for a few minutes until starting to soften. Add the potato and watercress and cook over a low heat for 5 minutes until the watercress has wilted.

Add the stock and nutmeg and season well, then bring to a simmer and cook for about 15 minutes until the potato is tender.

Remove the pan from the heat and blitz the soup in a blender (or use a stick blender) until smooth. Reheat the soup, if necessary.

Ladle the soup into bowls and serve each with a swirl of yogurt.

Health Tip
Recent research has put watercress at the top of the Aggregate Nutrient Density Index, which measures vitamin, mineral and phytonutrient content in relation to calorific content. The sulphur-containing compounds, which give cruciferous vegetables such as watercress their bitter, peppery bite, are also what give them their cell-protecting power.

WHY WE LOVE IT

This soup is a new take on a recipe from Mimi's *The Fast Diet Recipe Book*. It was included there because of its brilliantly low calorie count (around 116 calories per serving), but it's here now on account of its amazing health credentials. It's full of the good stuff – beetroot, apples, star anise, yogurt and seeds – adding up to a rich, warming bowl to fend off the autumn chill.

Beetroot & Apple Soup
WITH STAR ANISE

SERVES 4

500g (1lb 2oz) raw beetroot, scrubbed

1 tbsp olive oil

2 onions, roughly chopped

1 tbsp water

2 Bramley apples

1.5 litres (2½ pints) chicken or vegetable stock

2 star anise

sea salt flakes and freshly ground black pepper

TO SERVE

1 tbsp natural yogurt

Midlife Spiced Seed Mix, see page 26 (optional)

Preheat the oven to 180°C (350°F)/Gas Mark 4. Place the beetroot on a baking tray standing in 1cm (½in) of water. Cook for 45 minutes until tender. Leave until cool enough to handle, then peel and roughly chop.

Heat the olive oil in a heavy-based saucepan, add the onions and the tablespoon of water and cover with a lid. Sweat over a medium heat, without colouring, for about 5 minutes until the onions are softened and translucent.

Peel, quarter and core the apples and add to the pan along with the chopped beetroot. Pour in the stock, add the star anise and season with salt and pepper. Bring to a simmer and cook for 15 minutes until the apples are soft.

Remove the pan from the heat and take out the star anise, then blitz the soup in a blender or with a stick blender until smooth. Reheat the soup, if necessary.

Ladle the soup into bowls and serve each with a swirl of yogurt and a sprinkling of Spiced Seed Mix. A crumble of feta and some chopped flat leaf parsley would be good too.

Health Tip
Beetroot is known for it's deep, earthy flavour, but it also contains lots of lovely fibre, around 2-3 grams per 100g. Great for your gut health.

SOTO AYAM

WHY WE LOVE IT

For Sam, one of the many joys of living in a tropical country is the abundance of fresh, fragrant ingredients, which are put to great use in this classic Indonesian chicken soup. In Bali we have this at least once a week and, with your Midlife Curry Paste to hand, it's a doddle to whip up for a quick lunch or light, family-friendly supper.

Soto Ayam

BALINESE CHICKEN BROTH

SERVES 2–3

- a large handful of coriander (with roots if possible)
- 1 tbsp coconut oil
- 1 heaped tbsp Midlife Curry Paste, see page 34
- 1 boneless, skinless chicken breast, thinly sliced
- 1 litre (1¾ pint) chicken or vegetable stock
- sea salt flakes
- 1 large egg
- 100g (3½oz) mangetout or sugar snap peas
- 100g (3½oz) broccoli, cut into small florets
- a squeeze of lime juice

Rinse the coriander well, then finely slice the roots, if using, and set aside. Remove the leaves from the stalks and reserve a few to serve, then roughly chop the remainder.

Place a saucepan over a medium heat and add the coconut oil, the curry paste and sliced coriander roots and fry gently for a few minutes. Add the chicken and stock and stir well. Bring to a simmer and cook for about 25 minutes until the chicken is tender and cooked through. Taste the soup and add a pinch of salt, if necessary.

Meanwhile, cook the egg in a small saucepan of simmering water for 10 minutes until hard-boiled, then plunge into a bowl of cold water and leave to cool. Peel and quarter the egg.

Add the vegetables, chopped coriander leaves and lime juice to the soup and simmer for a further 2–3 minutes. The vegetables should be *al dente*, so don't overcook them.

Serve the soup immediately, with the boiled egg nestled among the veggies and the reserved coriander leaves scattered over the top.

See photograph on pages 130–1.

Midlife Hack: Much of the flavour in fresh coriander comes from the roots (Asian recipes often use only the roots) so, if you can, buy the whole plant. Wash the roots thoroughly and finely slice.

Health Tip
Coriander is an excellent source of vitamin A – which helps with immune function and healthy vision – and vitamin K, important for bone health.

SALADS & SOUPS

WHY WE LOVE IT

Lentil soup is an absolute health classic, and with our Midlife upgrades in this recipe you'd be hard pushed to pack more nutrition into a bowl. Lentils provide protein, vits and minerals, and are also a great source of 'prebiotics', which fuel the good flora in the gut. Add carrots, onions, garlic and an array of brilliant spices and there's no part of your body that won't feel the sunshine in this sensational soup.

Sunshine Soup
RICH LENTIL SOUP WITH MINTY YOGURT

SERVES 2 GENEROUS PORTIONS OR 4 AS A STARTER

1 tbsp olive oil

1 small red onion, finely diced

2 garlic cloves, crushed

3 tsp Midlife Spice Mix, see page 24

2 tsp paprika

1 tsp ground cinnamon

200g (7oz) canned chopped tomatoes

500ml (18fl oz) chicken or vegetable stock

100g (3½oz) dried green or brown lentils, rinsed

2 carrots, peeled and grated

sea salt flakes and freshly ground black pepper

FOR THE TOPPING

a large handful of mint leaves

3 tbsp natural yogurt

a squeeze of lemon juice

Heat the olive oil in a large saucepan, add the onion, garlic, spice mix, paprika and cinnamon and fry gently for about 5 minutes until the onion is softened.

Add the tomatoes, stock, lentils and carrots, bring to a simmer and cook for 20–30 minutes until the lentils are tender. Depending on how much liquid the lentils absorb, you may need to top up with water if it gets too thick. Season well with salt and pepper.

Transfer the soup to a blender (or use a stick blender) and pulse until fairly thick and coarse-textured. If possible, leave the soup to stand for a couple of hours to let the flavours develop further (or even better, chill overnight in the fridge).

To make the topping, put all the ingredients into a food processor or blender and pulse until the mint is finely minced and the yogurt turns a lovely pale green.

Reheat the soup, then ladle into bowls and serve each with a generous spoonful of minty yogurt on top.

Health Tip
Lentils have a low GI and the ability to increase satiety, which means your blood-sugar levels will stay steady and you won't feel like eating for hours after your bowl of Sunshine.

SALADS & SOUPS

WHY WE LOVE IT

If you have never made miso soup before, now is the time to try. This steaming infusion, gloriously spiked with fresh ginger, is brimming with veggies and delicately poached pale-pink salmon. The fresh cucumber pickle, served here on the side, elevates this Japanese classic to heady new heights: when our friend Nicky told us about this Japanese-style pickle we knew it would be a Midlife winner. Hydrating cucumber, fragrant dill and sharp rice vinegar combine to create a fresh and tangy palate cleanser – the perfect sidekick to any fish dish.

Salmon Miso Soup
WITH NICKY'S PICKLED CUCUMBER

SERVES 4

2 salmon fillets, about 125g (4½oz) each

2 tsp soy sauce

1.5 litres (2½ pints) water

6 tbsp brown miso paste

a thumb-sized piece of fresh root ginger, peeled and finely grated

4 spring onions, finely sliced

10 mushrooms, quartered

2 carrots, peeled and finely sliced or cut into thin strips

2 heads of baby pak choi, sliced in half lengthways

4 tsp sesame seeds, to serve

FOR NICKY'S PICKLED CUCUMBER

½ a cucumber, halved, deseeded and sliced into crescents

2-3 dill fronds, chopped

100ml (3½fl oz) rice vinegar

1 tsp runny honey

a pinch of sea salt flakes

To make the Pickled Cucumber, combine all the ingredients in a bowl. Transfer to the fridge and chill for 30 minutes before serving.

Meanwhile, brush the top of the salmon fillets with the soy sauce. Bring 1 litre (1¾ pints) of the water to a gentle simmer in a large saucepan, then add the salmon fillets and poach for 10 minutes until cooked through, turning once. Remove the salmon from the pan, retaining the cooking water, and leave to cool. Remove any skin and bones from the fish, then flake the flesh into large pieces.

Sieve the poaching water into a clean, large saucepan, discarding any bits. Add the miso paste and ginger and stir until any lumps have dissolved (a mini hand whisk is good for this). Add the remaining 500ml (18 fl oz) water and bring to the boil.

Add the spring onions, mushrooms, carrots and pak choi, then reduce the heat and simmer gently for about 5 minutes until the veg are tender.

Ladle the broth into bowls, add the salmon flakes and sprinkle with the sesame seeds. Serve with the Pickled Cucumber.

Try This...
Pickled Cucumber is also good served with:

* Swish Rösti with Gravadlax, see page 165
* Fast Falafel, see page 151
* Asian Salad Nori Wraps, see page 182

Health Tip
Salmon is a healthy source of the omega-3 fatty acids EPA and DHA which have benefits for the heart and brain. It's also protein-rich to support muscle mass during the menopausal years.

SALADS & SOUPS

HEALTHY MAINS

WHY WE LOVE IT

Although this sweet-savoury tagine has an extensive list of ingredients, it really couldn't be simpler – just simmer in a pan for an hour, then ladle over lemony couscous. It's a great one to whip up on a Sunday ahead of a busy week as it keeps well in the fridge (like all of us, its character just improves as time goes by). If you have any left over, blitz it with a little more stock to make a moreish Moorish soup.

Rich Chickpea Tagine
WITH ORANGE & APRICOTS

SERVES 4

- 1 tbsp olive oil
- 1 red onion, thinly sliced
- 3 garlic cloves, crushed
- 2 tsp ground turmeric
- 2 tsp ground cumin
- 1 tsp ground cinnamon
- 1 cinnamon stick, broken in two
- 1 tsp cayenne pepper
- 1 small aubergine, cut into bite-sized chunks
- 2 carrots, peeled and chopped
- 400g (14oz) can cherry tomatoes
- 400g (14oz) can chickpeas, drained and rinsed
- 75g (2¾oz) dried apricots, halved
- grated zest and juice of 1 orange
- juice of ½ a lemon
- 400ml (14fl oz) vegetable stock
- 1 tbsp honey or date syrup
- sea salt flakes and freshly ground black pepper
- 200g (7oz) spinach leaves
- a handful of flat leaf parsley, roughly chopped

FOR THE COUSCOUS

- 200g (7oz) wholegrain couscous
- a large handful of flat leaf parsley, chopped
- grated zest and juice of 1 lemon

FOR THE HARISSA YOGURT

- 2 tbsp natural yogurt
- 2 tsp harissa paste

Heat the olive oil in a large, ovenproof heavy-based pan, add the onion and fry gently for a few minutes until softened, then add the garlic and spices. Cook for 2–3 minutes, adding a splash of water after the first minute or so. Add the aubergine and carrots, stir to coat well in the spiced onion mixture and cook for a further 2 minutes, stirring occasionally.

Add the tomatoes, chickpeas, apricots, orange juice and zest, lemon juice, stock and honey or date syrup. Season with salt and pepper and stir well, then bring to a simmer and cook very gently for 45–60 minutes until the vegetables are tender. Alternatively, bake in a preheated oven, at about 160°C (325°F)/Gas Mark 3, for 1 hour.

Prepare the couscous according to the packet instructions and leave to stand, then fluff up with a fork. Season with salt and pepper, then stir in the parsley and lemon juice. Sprinkle with the lemon zest.

Add the spinach and parsley to the tagine 5 minutes before the end of the cooking time and simmer until the spinach just wilts. Mix the yogurt and harissa paste in a bowl.

Serve the tagine with the couscous and the harissa-swirled yogurt on the side.

Health Tip
There's a lot to shout about when it comes to chickpeas: they contain protein and insoluble, gut-loving fibre – helping to boost your gut microbial diversity and maintain muscle – both vital in perimenopause and beyond.

WHY WE LOVE IT

Beans are brilliant bolts of goodness: their high protein content + plentiful fibre = top-notch nutrition. Black beans, though, are magic beans, the dark undiscovered pick of the bunch, featuring a host of health-giving quirks that mean they really should feature more heavily in our lives. They also taste wonderful, not unlike mushrooms, with a delicious, velvety texture that demands mopping up with a soft, seedy tortilla wrap. Our promise: you won't be hungry again for hours.

Black Bean Mess
WITH SOFT BAKED EGGS

SERVES 2

1 tbsp olive oil

1 small red onion, finely diced

1 garlic clove, crushed

1 celery stick, finely diced

1 small red pepper, cored, deseeded and finely diced

1 red chilli, deseeded and finely sliced, or to taste

1 tsp smoked paprika

a handful of coriander (leaves and stalks), separated and finely chopped

400g (14oz) can black beans, drained and rinsed

1 bay leaf

400ml (14fl oz) vegetable or chicken stock

sea salt flakes and freshly ground black pepper

2 eggs

TO SERVE

a handful of chopped parsley

2 warm seeded tortilla wraps

Heat the olive oil in a medium frying pan, add the onion and fry gently for several minutes until it starts to soften. Add the garlic, celery, red pepper, chilli, paprika and coriander and cook for a further 10 minutes until everything softens.

Add the black beans, bay leaf and stock. Stir, bring to a simmer and cook for 30–35 minutes until thickened. Remove the pan from the heat and mash the beans a little with a fork (aim for the consistency of a thick dhal).

Season and stir, then make 2 wells in the mixture. Crack an egg into each hollow, cover the pan with a lid and cook over a medium heat for a further 3–4 minutes, or until the eggs are cooked to your liking.

Scatter with the parsley and serve with warm tortillas.

Health Tip
Black beans are high in phytonutrient anthocyanins, those all-important antioxidants that can help guard against disease. In fact, they have more antioxidant activity, gram for gram, than other beans.

HEALTHY MAINS

WHY WE LOVE IT

The idea of digging into a big bowl of soulfood may seem a bit trendy, but it's a great, no-fuss way to get a balanced burst of slow-burn carbs, lots of veggies and just enough protein in every bite. This first Nourish Bowl (there are 2 more on the following pages) has got the lot: sweet, nutty, earthy…there's plenty going on here, with very little effort. We're all pressed for time, so the 'shove it in the oven' approach rules in the Midlife Kitchen!

Butternut, Butter Bean & Red Onion Roast

WITH FETA & PINE NUTS

SERVES 2

350g (12oz) bag ready-diced butternut squash and sweet potato

1 large red onion, cut into 8 wedges

6 garlic cloves, peeled

a squeeze of lemon juice

sea salt flakes and freshly ground black pepper

2 tbsp olive oil

400g (14oz) can butter beans, drained and rinsed

TO SERVE

a small handful of thyme, leaves picked and chopped

50g (1¾oz) feta cheese, crumbled

2 tbsp toasted pine nuts

a handful of pomegranate seeds

Preheat the oven to 190°C (375°F)/Gas Mark 5.

Place the squash, sweet potato, onion, garlic and lemon juice in a roasting tin, season with salt and pepper and drizzle with the olive oil. Bake for 40 minutes until softened and starting to caramelize.

Add the butter beans, giving everything a shove around with a wooden spoon to release the sticky bits. Return to the oven and bake for a further 5–10 minutes.

Divide between 2 bowls and serve sprinkled with the thyme, feta, toasted pine nuts and pomegranate seeds.

Midlife Hack: If there are any leftovers, this mix makes a great soup. Just add stock, blend, heat and serve.

Health Tip
Butter beans are a tasty way in which to eat more plant protein, which will keep you fuller for longer as well as support muscle mass.

ROASTED BEETROOT WITH SPICED ORANGE, RAS EL HANOUT & GOAT'S CHEESE

BUTTERNUT, BUTTER BEAN AND RED ONION ROAST WITH FETA & PINE NUTS

ROASTED PUMPKIN WITH QUINOA & LABNEH

WHY WE LOVE IT

'Ras el hanout' is Arabic for 'head of the shop', suggesting a mixture of the best spices a seller has to offer. Well, we're all about spices here in the Midlife Kitchen, and this aromatic, antioxidant North African blend works wonderfully with the sticky beetroot, sweet carrot and curls of roasted red onion in this sublime bowlful. You'll get a little protein and dairy dynamite from the goat's cheese too. The mint isn't just for show: it brings another layer of lovely to the dish.

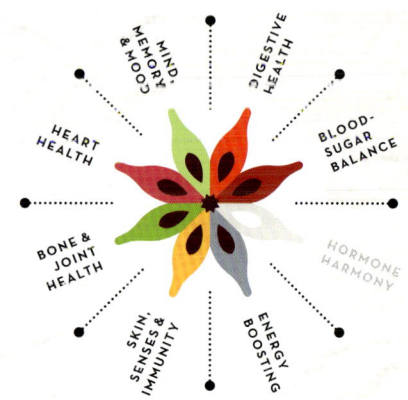

Roasted Beetroot
WITH SPICED ORANGE, RAS EL HANOUT & GOAT'S CHEESE

SERVES 2

1 large carrot, peeled and cut into batons

4 ready-cooked beetroot, about 250g (9oz) in total, halved or quartered

1 red onion, cut into 8 wedges

juice of 1 orange

2 tbsp olive oil

sea salt flakes and freshly ground black pepper

1 tbsp ras el hanout

1 tsp cumin seeds

TO SERVE

1 carrot, peeled and shaved into ribbons

a handful of mint leaves

50g (1¾oz) goat's cheese, crumbled

Preheat the oven to 200°C (400°F)/Gas Mark 6.

Place the carrot batons, beetroot and red onion in a roasting tin and add the orange juice and olive oil. Season well and sprinkle with the ras el hanout and cumin seeds. Bake for 40 minutes until the vegetables are softened and sticky.

Divide the roasted veg, either warm or at room temperature, between 2 ample bowls, then add the shaved carrot ribbons, scatter with the mint and top with the goat's cheese.

See photograph on page 143.

Health Tip
Beetroot is a good source of the B vitamin folate which is not only heart healthy, it also aids immune function.

WHY WE LOVE IT

Pumpkin is a storehouse of vitamins, minerals, fibre and antioxidants, so it made sense to give it the starring role in this gathering of the glorious, the great and the good. Almost every ingredient in this brilliant bowl is a Midlife winner. If you haven't made labneh before, give it a go – it's a simple, strained, garlicky yogurt that hails from the Middle East and it really brings something special to the show here. Otherwise, a little crushed garlic mixed with yogurt makes a great understudy.

Roasted Pumpkin
WITH QUINOA & LABNEH

SERVES 4

- 1 tbsp olive oil
- 2cm (¾in) piece of fresh root ginger, peeled and grated
- 2 tsp ground cinnamon
- 1 tsp chilli flakes
- 500g (1lb 2oz) pumpkin, peeled, deseeded and sliced into 3cm (1¼in) pieces
- 1 red onion, cut into 8 wedges
- sea salt flakes and freshly ground black pepper
- 2 tsp maple syrup
- a squeeze of lemon juice
- 2 tsp Midlife Sesame Seasoning, see page 32, or black sesame seeds
- a handful of baby spinach leaves and/or baby watercress
- a handful of coriander leaves, roughly chopped
- a handful of mint leaves, roughly chopped
- 20 cherry tomatoes, halved
- 250g (9oz) pouch ready-cooked quinoa
- 50g (1¾oz) walnuts, chopped
- 30g (1oz) pumpkin seeds

FOR THE DRESSING

- 3 tbsp extra virgin olive oil
- 2 tbsp apple cider vinegar
- 1 tbsp pomegranate molasses
- 2 tsp date syrup
- 1 tsp Dijon mustard
- juice of ½ a lemon

FOR THE LABNEH

- 150g (5½oz) thick Greek yogurt
- 1 garlic clove, crushed
- 2 tsp cumin seeds
- sea salt flakes and freshly ground black pepper

Health Tip
Pumpkin is the perfect food for midlifers. The orange pigment comes from beta-carotene, which is converted to vitamin A in the body and supports eyes, immune function and skin.

To make the labneh, strain the yogurt through a piece of muslin or a new all-purpose cloth over a bowl (secured with a rubber band). Transfer to the fridge and leave overnight for the yogurt to release its liquid and become firm and cheese-like. The next day, tip the strained yogurt into a clean bowl, add the garlic and cumin and season with salt and pepper. Chill in the fridge until ready to serve.

Preheat the oven to 190°C (375°F)/Gas Mark 5. Warm the olive oil in a small saucepan, then add the ginger, cinnamon and chilli flakes.

Place the pumpkin in a roasting tin and baste with the warm oil. Add the red onion and season, then drizzle with the maple syrup and lemon juice. Bake for 15 minutes until the pumpkin is tender and starting to caramelize. Sprinkle with the sesame seasoning (or seeds) and set aside.

Combine all the dressing ingredients and whisk to emulsify.

When ready to serve, assemble the spinach and/or watercress, the herbs and tomatoes in a large bowl, then add the cooked quinoa and the dressing. Top with the pumpkin slices and sticky red onion, then add generous dollops of the garlicky labneh. Scatter with the walnuts and pumpkin seeds and serve.

See photograph on page 143.

HEALTHY MAINS

WHY WE LOVE IT

These incredible veggie burgers were inspired by a visit to the Soul in a Bowl café in Sanur, one of those laid-back beachside places that have made Bali such a culinary hot spot. If you usually reach, in bored, bovine fashion, for meat when you think of burgers, our veggie version should convince you to ring the changes. Every ingredient has Midlife cred, from the lentils and squash, to the subtle spicing and the super-crisp coating of dukkah and red quinoa. You don't even need a bun – rest your burger instead on a bed of Little Gem lettuce and feel the bliss.

Bliss Burgers
WITH A RED QUINOA & DUKKAH CRUST

MAKES 4 BURGERS

- 250g (9oz) butternut squash, peeled, deseeded and sliced
- 1 tsp olive oil
- 1 tsp cumin seeds
- sea salt flakes and freshly ground black pepper
- 100g (3½oz) red lentils, rinsed
- 300ml (½ pint) water
- 1 bay leaf
- 200g (7oz) firm tofu, cubed (optional)
- 2 spring onions, finely sliced
- 1 garlic clove, crushed
- 1 tsp Midlife Spice Mix, see page 24, or 1 tsp ground coriander and 1 tsp ground cumin
- 1 tsp chilli flakes
- a handful of coriander (leaves and stalks), finely chopped
- 1 egg, beaten (if necessary)
- light olive oil spray

FOR THE CRUST

- 2 tbsp uncooked red quinoa
- 2 tbsp Midlife Dukkah, see page 30, or 1 tbsp ground almonds and 2 tsp sesame seeds

TO SERVE

- Little Gem lettuce leaves
- Uchucuta, see page 226 (optional)

Preheat the oven to 200°C (400°F)/Gas Mark 6. Place the squash in a small roasting tin, drizzle with the olive oil, add the cumin seeds and season. Bake for 20–30 minutes until softened and beginning to colour at the edges. Leave to cool, then chop into small pieces.

Meanwhile, place the lentils, the water and bay leaf in a saucepan, bring to a simmer and cook for 10 minutes until tender but not overcooked. Remove the bay leaf, drain and leave to cool.

Place the cooled lentils, roasted butternut, tofu (if using), spring onions, garlic, spices and coriander in a large bowl and mix together. Season well, then divide the mixture into 4 and shape into burgers. If you find the mixture is too crumbly, add a beaten egg to bind.

Mix the crust ingredients in a shallow bowl. Coat each burger in the mixture, pressing gently. Chill in the fridge for at least 30 minutes.

Heat a large nonstick frying pan and spray with a little olive oil. Fry the burgers for 5–6 minutes on each side until golden and cooked through. Serve the burgers on Little Gem leaves, perhaps with Uchucuta on the side.

Midlife Hack: These are great eaten cold, making them ideal for packed lunches and picnics, so make a big batch to chill or freeze.

Health Tip
Butternut squash is chock-full of the plant form of vitamin A, which plays an important role in maintaining the health of all body tissues, including skin, immune function and vision.

WHY WE LOVE IT

Gado gado, meaning 'medley' or 'mix', is a hugely popular Indonesian dish found on the menu at most street-side *warungs* (restaurants). The basis is just-cooked vegetables served with a chilli-hot peanut pouring sauce, but here we add shredded omelette, transforming it from a mere sideshow into a substantial (and beautiful) main event. You can use all or just a selection of the vegetables listed here.

Gado Gado
WITH SHREDDED EGG

SERVES 2–3

FOR THE GADO GADO

1 large carrot, peeled and cut into thin batons
100g (3½oz) bean sprouts
100g (3½oz) green beans, cut into 3cm- (1¼in-) long pieces
100g (3½oz) mangetout or sugar snap peas
100g (3½oz) baby sweetcorn, halved
1 small white cabbage, thinly sliced
1 head of pak choi, sliced
sea salt flakes

FOR THE PEANUT SAUCE

3 tbsp crunchy peanut butter (100% peanuts, no sugar)
2 tsp soy sauce
2 tsp soft brown sugar
1 garlic clove, finely chopped
a thumb-sized piece of fresh root ginger, peeled and grated
juice of 1 lime
½–1 tsp chilli flakes, to taste
75ml (5 tbsp) boiling water

FOR THE SHREDDED EGG

3 eggs
a splash of water
freshly ground black pepper
light olive oil spray

TO SERVE

2 spring onions, finely sliced
1 red chilli, deseeded and finely sliced
a handful of coriander leaves
a handful of unsalted peanuts
lime wedges

To make the peanut sauce, place all the ingredients, except the boiling water, in a bowl. Gradually add the water, slowly combining with a fork until everything is well mixed. The sauce should be runny enough to pour, so add more boiling water as necessary. Set aside.

Bring a large saucepan of salted water to the boil. Cook each vegetable in turn for a minute or so, then remove with a slotted spoon and drain on kitchen paper. Season with a little salt.

Whisk the eggs with a splash of water in a jug, then season with salt and pepper. Heat a large nonstick frying pan and spray with a little olive oil. Pour in half the egg mixture and roll it around to thinly cover the base of the pan. Cook for 1–2 minutes until lightly golden, then flip and cook on the other side. Remove from the pan and repeat with the remaining mixture to make a second omelette. Roll up the omelettes and slice across the rolls to form long, thin lengths.

Arrange the vegetables in a serving dish and drizzle with the peanut sauce. Drape with the shredded egg and top with the spring onions, chilli, coriander and peanuts. Any extra peanut sauce can be served on the side, along with the lime wedges.

Health Tip
In recent studies, peanuts were found to be just as effective at reducing the risk of heart disease as tree nuts – good news as they generally cost about half as much as premium nuts such as walnuts and almonds.

WHY WE LOVE IT

There's something irresistible about the crunchy exterior and yielding centre of a good falafel – but the shop-bought versions often aren't that inspiring. There's no faff to making falafel at home: our version is quick and easy, using ingredients that can be grabbed in a rush from the kitchen cupboard. We've coated them in a few of our favourite things – dukkah, sesame seeds, LSA – for that all-important Midlife lift.

Fast Falafel

MAKES 8 SMALL OR 6 LARGE FALAFEL

FOR THE FALAFEL

400g (14oz) can chickpeas, drained and rinsed

1 tbsp Midlife Spice Mix, see page 24, or 1 tsp ground coriander and 1 tsp ground cumin

1 egg

a large handful of flat leaf parsley

juice of ½ a lemon

sea salt flakes and freshly ground black pepper

1 tsp olive oil

FOR THE COATINGS

1 tbsp Midlife Sesame Seasoning, see page 32, or sesame seeds

or 1 tbsp Midlife Dukkah, see page 30

or 1 tbsp Midlife LSA, see page 27, or ground almonds

TO SERVE

2 wholemeal pitta breads

2 carrots, peeled and grated

2 tbsp hummus

2 tbsp Zehug, see page 238 (optional)

Place all the falafel ingredients, except the olive oil, in a food processor and blitz to a coarse paste. Shape the mixture into 8 small or 6 large patties. Coat each in your chosen coating, patting so it sticks well. They can be chilled at this point, and cooked later.

When ready to cook, heat the olive oil in a large frying pan, add the falafels and fry for 5–7 minutes on each side until golden brown on the outside and cooked through.

Serve in warm pittas, with the grated carrots, Zehug and hummus.

Try This...
Add any of the following to your falafel mix:

* 2 teaspoons grated lemon zest
* 1 teaspoon chilli flakes
* 1 teaspoon cumin seeds
* More chopped herbs, such as mint or coriander leaves
* Instead of Zehug and hummus, serve with: Beetroot Raita, see page 230; Wholly Guacamole, see page 220 or Roasted Red Pepper Hummus with Almonds & Paprika, see page 221

Health Tip
Chickpeas are a really affordable source of protein, perfect for peri- and post-menopausal bones, muscles and guts... and you can make falafel with them!

HEALTHY MAINS

WHY WE LOVE IT

A staple Ayurvedic healing food, this complete-protein meal nourishes and soothes the digestive system. It's essentially a Midlife take on kedgeree – traditionally made just with rice, but here we have added red lentils to improve the texture and boost the health credentials.

Red Lentil & Smoked Mackerel Kitchri

SERVES 2

1 tbsp olive oil or coconut oil

1 tsp mustard seeds

1 tsp nigella seeds

1 tbsp mild curry powder

2 tbsp Midlife Spice Mix, see page 24, or 3 tsp ground cumin, 2 tsp ground turmeric and 2 tsp ground coriander

1 small red onion, finely chopped

a splash of water

100g (3½oz) red lentils, rinsed

500ml (18 fl oz) vegetable stock

1 bay leaf

1 cinnamon stick, broken in 2

2 eggs

125g (4½oz) cooked basmati rice or ½ a pouch ready-cooked rice

150g (5½oz) smoked mackerel fillets, flaked

juice of ½ a lemon

sea salt flakes and freshly ground black pepper

coriander leaves, to serve

lemon wedges, to serve

Heat the oil in a large frying pan, add the mustard seeds and nigella seeds and fry for a couple of minutes, taking care not to burn them. Add the remaining ground spices and Spice Mix and fry for a further 30 seconds. Add the onion with a splash of water and fry gently for 2–3 minutes until softened.

Stir in the lentils and coat with the fragrant spice mixture, then add the stock, bay leaf and cinnamon stick. Bring to a simmer and cook for about 15 minutes until the lentils are tender.

Meanwhile, cook the eggs in a small saucepan of simmering water for 10 minutes until hard-boiled, then plunge into a bowl of cold water and leave to cool. Peel and quarter the eggs.

Stir the cooked rice into the lentils, then add the fish flakes and gently heat through. Add the lemon juice and season.

Spoon the kitchri into 2 bowls and top with the hard-boiled eggs. Scatter with coriander leaves, season with pepper and serve with lemon wedges.

Health Tip
Substituting mackerel for the more conventional haddock increases the omega-3 fatty acid content in this dish – great for your heart and joints.

WHY WE LOVE IT

We're forever on the hunt for speedy suppers that are just a bit special – and this fits the bill perfectly. It's one of those dishes that tastes as though it's been hours in the making, but in fact the prep couldn't be easier, and most of the ingredients (bar the fish) are probably already lurking in your fridge. Simply add a sturdy white fish – we've used monkfish here, but halibut would be equally delicious – or calamari and king prawns, and eat with a warm wholemeal pitta to mop up the densely savoury juices. Very little could improve it, but Sam says a glass of chilled Sancerre works a treat.

Monkfish & Fennel
WITH HERBS, TOMATOES & ANCHOVIES

SERVES 2

2 tsp olive oil

½ a fennel bulb, trimmed and thinly sliced

4 ripe tomatoes, quartered

4 anchovy fillets, chopped

sea salt and freshly ground black pepper

250g (9oz) monkfish fillet or tail, membrane removed and cut into 3cm- (1¼in-) thick medallions

a handful of Greek olives, pitted and chopped

a handful of coriander leaves, chopped

a handful of basil leaves

a handful of dill, chopped

Heat the olive oil in a medium frying pan, add the fennel and sauté for several minutes until softened, then add the tomatoes and anchovies. Season and simmer for 10–15 minutes until the tomatoes start to soften (see Midlife Hack).

Add the monkfish medallions and olives, cover with a lid and simmer for a further 5–10 minutes until the fish is cooked through. Stir through the herbs and serve.

Midlife Hack: You can cook the recipe to this point, then cool and refrigerate until required.

Health Tip
Monkfish is a wonderful source of iodine – this is key to support thyroid function which regulates metabolism.

HEALTHY MAINS

WHY WE LOVE IT

This zingy green sauce pays homage to the fabulous flavours of Thailand and is the perfect partner for a piece of oily fish. Our favourite is a pale-pink and delicate trout fillet, flash-fried to give it a crisp skin, but the dressing would work well with any fish fillet: salmon, snapper, sea bass or sea bream would all be excellent. For maximum Midlife points, try it with fresh grilled mackerel or sardines.

Crispy Trout
WITH ASIAN SALSA

SERVES 2

2 trout fillets, about 125g (4½oz) each, with skin on

a little olive oil

sea salt flakes and freshly ground black pepper

coriander leaves, to serve

FOR THE SALSA

a handful of coriander (leaves and stalks), roughly chopped

a thumb-sized piece of fresh root ginger, peeled and chopped

a thumb-sized piece of fresh turmeric, peeled and chopped

1 garlic clove, peeled and halved

2 spring onions, roughly chopped

1 large red chilli, deseeded and roughly chopped, or to taste

juice of 1 lime

2 tsp sesame oil

2 tsp soy sauce

2 tsp runny honey

1 tsp Thai fish sauce (nam pla)

Place all the salsa ingredients in a food processor and pulse to form a coarse paste.

Heat a griddle pan or large frying pan over a high heat until it is hot enough to crisp the trout skin. Drizzle the fish with a little olive oil and season well, then place, skin-side down, in the hot pan, pressing lightly. Cook for 3–4 minutes until the skin turns crisp. Gently flip the fillets, reduce the heat and cook for a further 2–3 minutes until the fish is cooked through and opaque (the timing will depend on the thickness of the fish).

Serve immediately, drizzled with a good amount of the zingy salsa.

Health Tip

There is an ever-increasing body of evidence to suggest that regular consumption of fish, and in particular oily fish like trout, reduces the risk of cardiovascular disease. They're also a good source of vitamin D, the 'sunshine vitamin', which benefits the bones and immune system.

WHY WE LOVE IT

Ginger is a staple ingredient in the Midlife Kitchen, and here we use the pickled version more commonly found sitting alongside sushi and wasabi. We adore its delicate flavour and elegant ballerina-pink colour, an unexpected complement to the clean crunch of sugar snaps in this quick, bright dish. We've used king prawns here, but chicken would work well for a great low-cal, high-flavour lunch.

Miso King Prawns
WITH SESAME & PICKLED GINGER SUGAR SNAPS

SERVES 2

8 large raw peeled king prawns

1 tsp coconut oil

2 tbsp rice vinegar or mirin

FOR THE MARINADE

2 tbsp brown miso paste

2 tbsp soy sauce

2 tsp sesame oil

2cm (¾in) piece of fresh root ginger, peeled and finely grated

juice of 1 lime

FOR THE SALAD

100g (3½oz) sugar snap peas

100g (3½oz) mangetout

sea salt flakes

2 tbsp pickled ginger, from a jar

2 tbsp sesame seeds

Combine all the marinade ingredients in a bowl and add the prawns. Cover with clingfilm and leave to marinate in the fridge for at least 10 minutes, or several hours if you have time.

Cook the sugar snaps and mangetout in a saucepan of salted boiling water for 2 minutes until just tender. Drain and refresh in very cold water (this will help retain their colour and crunch). Drain well and pat dry with kitchen paper, then slice on the diagonal and transfer to a bowl. Combine with the pickled ginger and sesame seeds.

Heat a griddle pan until hot, add the coconut oil and prawns, including the marinade, and fry for 1 minute or so on each side until they turn pink and are cooked through. Remove the prawns from the pan and keep warm. Add the rice vinegar or mirin to the pan, stirring in any sticky bits from the base of the pan.

Serve the prawns with the pretty salad and drizzled with the pan juices.

Health Tip
Prawns are a source of zinc, iodine and selenium which are hard to find, so they're a real powerhouse for the brain and body.

WHY WE LOVE IT

A simple piece of fish is a glorious thing – low in calories, high in protein – and it's better still when given the Midlife treatment with this collection of antioxidant super spices. Here, we've paired haddock loin with 'sabji', an Indian-style vegetable stir-fry. We've chosen asparagus for our sabji – a glorious addition to the Midlife menu thanks to its anti-inflammatory saponins, gut-friendly prebiotic inulin and B-vits, which help with blood-sugar management. Cook the asparagus quickly in lemon and spice, keeping it deliciously *al dente*, with the petits pois adding sweetness.

Indian Spiced Fish
WITH ASPARAGUS & PEA SABJI

SERVES 2

2 tsp ground cumin

1 tsp hot curry powder

½ tsp ground cinnamon

½ tsp ground turmeric

sea salt and freshly ground black pepper

2 tbsp vegetable oil

2 skinless loins of white fish (haddock, cod, hake or pollock), about 125g (4½oz) each

FOR THE SABJI

light olive oil spray

½ tsp coriander seeds

½ tsp fennel seeds

250g (9oz) fine asparagus, trimmed and cut into 4cm (1½in-) long pieces

60ml (4 tbsp) water

juice of ½ a lemon

1 tsp peeled and finely grated fresh root ginger

sea salt and freshly ground black pepper

100g (3½oz) frozen petits pois

FOR THE YOGURT TOPPING

4 tbsp natural yogurt

a handful of mint leaves, thinly sliced

Place the cumin, curry powder, cinnamon and turmeric in a small bowl with a pinch of salt and a grind of black pepper. Add the vegetable oil to make a paste.

Marinate the fish in the spice paste for at least 15 minutes in the fridge, to allow the flavours to develop.

Preheat the oven to 180°C (350°F)/Gas Mark 4. Place the marinated fish in a foil-lined baking tray and bake for 15–20 minutes until the fish is cooked through and flakes easily.

Meanwhile, make the sabji. Heat a nonstick frying pan and spray with olive oil. Add the coriander and fennel seeds and when they start to pop, add the asparagus and fry for 1 minute, then add the water, lemon juice and ginger.

Season and simmer for 2 minutes, then add the peas and cook for a further 2 minutes until most of the liquid has evaporated and the vegetables are just cooked.

Combine the yogurt and mint in a small bowl.

To assemble the dish, transfer the sabji to a serving plate, top with the fish and the minty yogurt.

Health Tip
Common or garden peas are an incredible source of vitamin C and they also contain the B vitamin folate, which helps to release energy from food.

HEALTHY MAINS

WHY WE LOVE IT

This peppy mustard marinade brings a whole new angle to any white fish – almost as if it's dressed in the perfect condiments from the get-go. Halibut, a delicate oily fish that is simplicity itself to cook, makes a great heart-healthy alternative to the usual cod fillets, though this marinade and method would work equally well with any fish or meat.

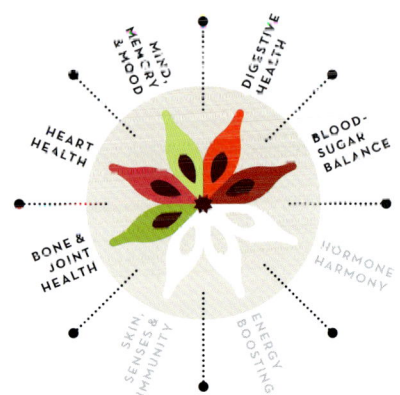

Grilled Mustard & Herb Halibut

SERVES 2

- 2 shallots, roughly chopped
- 2 garlic cloves, peeled and halved
- 2 tbsp Dijon mustard
- 2 tsp dried Herbes de Provence
- a squeeze of lemon juice
- 1 tsp apple cider vinegar
- 1 tsp mustard seeds
- sea salt flakes and freshly ground black pepper
- 2 halibut fillets, 150–200g (5½–7oz) each, skin removed
- watercress salad, to serve (optional)

Put the shallots, garlic, mustard, herbs, a squeeze of lemon juice and apple cider vinegar in a food processor and whizz to produce a smooth paste, making sure the shallots have been well blitzed so that they cook quickly under the grill. Stir in the mustard seeds and season.

Place the fish in a dish and coat with the paste. Cover with clingfilm and leave to marinate in the fridge for at least 30 minutes, or preferably overnight to ensure a good depth of flavour.

Transfer the marinated fish to a foil-lined baking tray and cook under a preheated hot grill for 3–5 minutes on each side until the fish is cooked through and flakes easily (the timing will depend on the thickness of the fish).

Serve immediately, perhaps with a simple watercress salad.

Midlife Hack: Quickly peel shallots by placing them in a bowl of boiling water for 5 minutes first to help release the skins. Let them cool a bit before you embark!

Health Tip
Halibut is a lovely firm-fleshed white fish that is a good source of protein, as well as providing omega-3s, B vits and essential minerals phosphorus and selenium – great for energy and for keeping bones and joints strong.

WHY WE LOVE IT

These are definitely a bit swish, but the name comes from our Swedish spin on a Swiss classic, the much-loved rösti. Our Midlife makeover uses gravadlax, a Nordic smoked salmon packed with omega-3s, and replaces half the regular potato with sweet potato to increase the vitamin A content; retaining the potato skins will increase the amount of fibre in your rösti and help with the all-important crunch.

Swish Rösti

WITH GRAVADLAX & DILL YOGURT

MAKES 6–8 RÖSTI

250g (9oz) white potatoes, scrubbed and cut into large pieces

250g (9oz) sweet potatoes, scrubbed and cut into large pieces

sea salt flakes

150g (5½oz) gravadlax slices

2 spring onions, finely sliced

freshly ground black pepper

2 tsp olive oil

1 tsp butter

green salad, to serve (optional)

lemon wedges, to serve

FOR THE DILL YOGURT

4 tbsp natural yogurt

juice of ½ a lemon

a handful of dill, finely chopped

Cook the potatoes and sweet potatoes in a large saucepan of salted boiling water for 10 minutes until they are starting to soften but not cooked through. Drain, then leave to cool. Place in the fridge and chill for a few hours or overnight (or place in the freezer for 15 minutes).

When chilled, grate the potatoes using the coarse side of a grater. Cut 100g (3½oz) of the gravadlax into ribbons.

Using your fingers, combine the grated potato, gravadlax ribbons, spring onions and salt and pepper in a large bowl until everything is well mixed. Take handfuls of the mixture and shape into 6–8 palm-sized rösti. Aim for thin patties, squeezing to compress them into shape.

Heat the olive oil and butter in a large frying pan, add the rösti, about 4 at time depending on the size of your pan. Cook over a medium heat for about 10 minutes on each side – press down with a spatula to flatten and ensure they are crisp and golden brown. Remove from the pan and repeat with the remaining rösti mixture.

Meanwhile, combine the dill yogurt ingredients in a bowl.

When cooked, place the rösti on a large plate and top with the remaining slices of gravadlax. Serve with the dill yogurt, a green salad and lemon wedges on the side.

Health Tip

Both regular potatoes and sweet potatoes deserve a place in your diet, but orange sweet potatoes are vitamin A superstars; they also tend to be higher in potentially helpful phytochemicals, such as the antioxidant defensin.

WHY WE LOVE IT

The tuna and bean salad is an all-time classic – a harmonious marriage of healthy ingredients that just happen to be lurking in the larder. Tuscans are sometimes referred to as *mangiafagioli* or 'bean eaters', and the prevalence of beans in their cooking is one of the reasons that an Italian diet is considered so healthy. Beans are primed with good things: protein, fibre, vats of vits, while the tuna and red onion of the classic dish bring bold flavour to the gathering.

Classic Tuna Fagioli

SERVES 2

2 x 200g (7oz) cans different beans, such as kidney, haricot, cannellini or butter beans, or a 400g (14oz) can mixed beans, drained and rinsed

½ a small red onion, thinly sliced

160g (5¾oz) can tuna in olive oil, drained

a handful of parsley, chopped, plus extra to serve

4 tbsp Midlife Salad Dressing, see page 33

finely sliced lemon zest, to serve

Place the beans, onion, tuna and parsley in a bowl. Add the dressing, mix well and chill for at least 30 minutes in the fridge to allow the flavours to mingle and develop.

Serve sprinkled with lemon zest and chopped parsley.

WHY WE LOVE IT

Given this is such a standard, we've created an alternative version starring peppered smoked mackerel, fennel and dill to take your fagioli fork in a whole new direction. The extra virgin olive oil in the Midlife Dressing is crucial here – you'll want the tang of a really good, grass-green oil; you also need plenty of lemon juice and zest to add a note of acidity (and more antioxidant goodness).

Midlife Mackerel Fagioli
WITH FENNEL & DILL

SERVES 2

2 x 200g (7oz) cans different beans, such as kidney, haricot, cannellini or butter beans or a 400g (14oz) can mixed beans, drained and rinsed

½ a small red onion, thinly sliced

150g (5½oz) peppered smoked mackerel fillets, skin removed, torn into bite-sized pieces

½ a small fennel bulb, trimmed and thinly sliced

a handful of dill, plus extra to serve

4 tbsp Midlife Salad Dressing, see page 33

finely sliced lemon zest, to serve

Place the beans, onion, mackerel, fennel and dill in a bowl. Add the dressing, mix well and chill for at least 30 minutes in the fridge to allow the flavours to mingle and develop.

Serve sprinkled with lemon zest and chopped dill.

Health Tip
Adding beans to a salad is an easy and thrifty way to increase your fibre intake, helping to improve gut health and regulate appetite.

WHY WE LOVE IT

Think of this aromatic bowlful as moules marinière meets tom yum soup. It's incredibly simple and ready in minutes, which belies its sophisticated appearance, making for a pretty impressive dinner-party starter or light lunch.

Thai Midlife Mussels

SERVES 2

1kg (2lb 4 oz) fresh mussels

1 tsp coconut oil

a thumb-sized piece of fresh root ginger, peeled and finely grated

a thumb-sized piece of fresh turmeric root, peeled and finely chopped

4 shallots, thinly sliced

2 garlic cloves, crushed

1 lemon grass stalk, tough outer layers removed, finely minced

1 large red chilli, deseeded and finely chopped, or to taste

500ml (18fl oz) fish or vegetable stock

1 tsp runny honey

1 tbsp Thai fish sauce (nam pla)

juice of 1 lime

a small handful of coriander leaves, chopped

a small handful of mint leaves, chopped

Rinse and scrub the mussels thoroughly, removing the beards and discarding any that are cracked or aren't tightly shut.

Heat the coconut oil in a wide saucepan or wok, add the ginger, turmeric, shallots, garlic, lemon grass and chilli and fry gently for about 3 minutes until softened. Add the stock, honey and fish sauce and bring to a simmer.

Add the mussels, cover with a lid and cook for 5 minutes, or until all the mussels have opened. Discard any that remain closed.

Stir in the lime juice and herbs and it's ready to eat.

Midlife Hack: If you crave carbs, or want a more filling meal, this works really well with cooked brown rice added to the bowl once you've eaten the mussels, to soak up the lovely golden broth.

Health Tip
Mussels have an impressive nutritional profile, containing long-chain fatty acids that can improve brain function and help reduce inflammatory conditions such as arthritis.

HEALTHY MAINS

WHY WE LOVE IT

This is a light, fragrant curry, alive with the flavours of Southeast Asia. Using our Midlife Curry Paste speeds up the process considerably, so, apart from the time it takes for the chicken to cook through, it requires no more than 15 minutes effort on your part to produce something pretty spectacular.

Balinese Yellow Chicken Curry

SERVES 4

- 1 tbsp coconut oil
- 5 tbsp Midlife Curry Paste, see page 34
- 2 lemon grass stalks, bashed with a rolling pin
- 4 kaffir lime leaves, crushed
- 2 tsp tamarind paste
- 1kg (2lb 4oz) boneless chicken thighs and drumsticks, skin removed
- 350ml (12fl oz) chicken stock
- 400ml (14fl oz) can coconut milk
- juice of 2 limes
- a large handful of coriander leaves, left whole, to serve
- sea salt flakes and ground white pepper

Heat the coconut oil in a large wok or deep saucepan, add the curry paste and fry over a high heat for about 1 minute until fragrant. Reduce the heat, add the lemon grass, lime leaves and tamarind paste and cook, stirring, for a further minute.

Add the chicken and cook for a couple of minutes on each side to get a little colour, then add the stock. Bring to the boil, then reduce the heat, cover with a lid and simmer gently for 40 minutes, or until the chicken is cooked through.

Add the coconut milk and lime juice and simmer for a further 5 minutes. Season and scatter with the coriander leaves, then serve. Brown or red rice is an excellent partner for this dish and, as with most curries, it tastes even better reheated the next day.

Midlife Hack: Keep any leftover coconut milk in the fridge to stir into your morning porridge with chopped banana, a pinch of salt and a dash of date syrup.

Health Tip
Chicken is a high-quality protein that delivers vitamin B6 which is heart healthy, supports the immune system and can regulate hormones. A midlife winner.

WHY WE LOVE IT

This is one-pot Midlife cooking at its best: lots of lean protein, plenty of slow-burn carbs, bags of herby flavour and a solitary pan to wash up at the end. Make this your new Sunday roast and you'll be able to stick it in the oven, play a game of tennis or tiddlywinks and return to a complete family meal. Job done.

Pot-roast Chicken
WITH LENTILS, PARSLEY, SAGE, ROSEMARY & THYME

SERVES 4

- 1 tbsp vegetable oil
- 2 onions, diced
- 4 garlic cloves, peeled and halved
- 2 rosemary sprigs, leaves picked and chopped
- 225g (8oz) red lentils, rinsed
- a handful of thyme sprigs, tied with string
- 5 sage leaves
- 750ml (1¼ pint) chicken stock, plus extra if needed
- juice of 1 lemon (retain the squeezed lemon halves)
- 1 medium free-range chicken, about 1.5–1.8kg (3lb 5 oz–4lb)
- 2 tsp butter, softened
- sea salt flakes and freshly ground black pepper
- a handful of flat leaf parsley, chopped

Preheat the oven to 180°C (350°F)/Gas Mark 4.

Heat the oil in a large casserole dish, add the onions and cook over a medium heat for a few minutes until softened. Add the garlic and rosemary and cook for a further 3 minutes, then stir in the lentils, thyme, sage leaves and stock. Stir in the lemon juice and add the squeezed lemon husks.

Smear the chicken with the butter and season well. Nestle it into the lentil mix and bring to a simmer, then transfer to the oven. Bake, uncovered, for 1 hour 15 minutes until the chicken is golden brown and the juices run clear when the thickest part of the thigh is pierced with a knife. Check occasionally that the lentils aren't too dry (if they are, add a little more stock or boiling water and give it a stir). Remove the chicken from the casserole and leave to rest.

Check the lentils for seasoning, remove the lemon husks, stir in the sticky bits from the side of the dish and add plenty of chopped parsley. Carve the chicken and serve with the lentils.

Midlife Hack: If you crave leafy greens with this, try some oven-baked kale. Empty a bag of sliced kale into a roasting tin, toss in a teaspoon or two of olive oil and a scatter of sea salt flakes, then pop in the oven about 15 minutes before the chicken comes out.

Health Tip
Herbs are a wonderful way to add multi-layered flavour without resorting to salt, sugar or fat. And, by adding herbs to meals, you are increasing your intake of those all-important plant foods.

HEALTHY MAINS

WHY WE LOVE IT

If you're feeding a gang, nothing beats a slow-roasted joint – the kind of meal you can prep quickly in advance, whack in a low oven and forget until the aromas entice you back to the kitchen for the final hurrah. It's a great Italian and Middle Eastern tradition, based on the provocative principle that slow-cooked meat becomes gorgeously tender, requiring little more than a tug to carve. This is our Midlife version, packed with our favourite garlic and Midlife Spice Mix. A roasted fig on the side simply adds another divine dimension to something that is already heavenly.

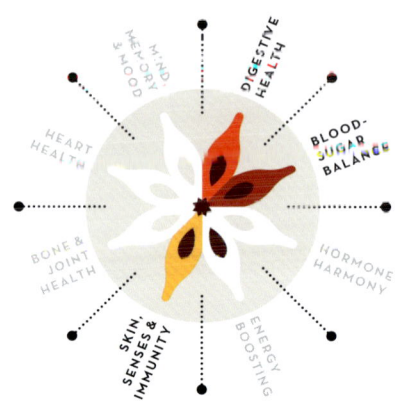

Slow-roasted Lamb
WITH STICKY FIGS

SERVES 8

1 large leg of lamb (on the bone), about 2.5kg (5lb 8oz)

juice of 1 lemon

FOR THE PASTE

75g (2¾oz) butter, softened

4 tbsp Midlife Spice Mix, see page 24

1 tbsp cumin seeds

1 tsp chilli flakes

1 tsp ground turmeric

2 tsp dried mixed herbs

5 garlic cloves, crushed

1 tbsp sea salt flakes

freshly ground black pepper

FOR THE FIGS

12–16 ripe fresh figs, scored with a cross

1 tbsp pomegranate molasses

1 tbsp extra virgin olive oil

sea salt flakes and freshly ground black pepper

Preheat the oven to 150°C (300°F)/Gas Mark 2. Score the lamb deeply with a sharp knife and place it in a large roasting tin. Combine all the paste ingredients in a bowl to make a spicy, herby garlic butter. Rub the paste into the lamb, pressing well into the incisions.

Roast for 4–5 hours (it will depend on the lamb, and even on the season), basting every so often to keep it moist, until the meat is dark golden and sticky. Remove from the oven, leaving the oven on, and place on a platter, cover loosely in foil and leave to rest for up to 30 minutes.

About 10 minutes before serving, turn the oven up to 200°C (400°F)/Gas Mark 6. Place the figs in a small baking tin, drizzle with the pomegranate molasses and olive oil, then season. Bake for 10 minutes until just softened and blistered.

Meanwhile, remove the excess oil from the lamb roasting tin, leaving the sticky deposits. Place the tin on the hob and add the lemon juice. Stir well over a medium heat to release the caramelized, almost burnt bits from the base of the tin, adding a little water if it needs more liquid (you're looking for a few tablespoons of reduction, not a gravy).

Serve the warm lamb with the juices, and the roasted figs hot from the oven. A green salad with pomegranate seeds is a good accompaniment.

> **Health Tip**
> Figs contain prebiotics, a type of fibre that passes through the gut undigested and stimulates the growth of 'good' bacteria, improving digestive health.

WHY WE LOVE IT

Another of our Midlife observations is that our appetite for red meat has declined dramatically – so this main meal gives spiced veg the starring role. What you get is a sticky bed of sweet veggie goodness, with the slender slivers of seared steak introduced as a decadent garnish. On a more prosaic note, it's a cheap way to make a steak go around.

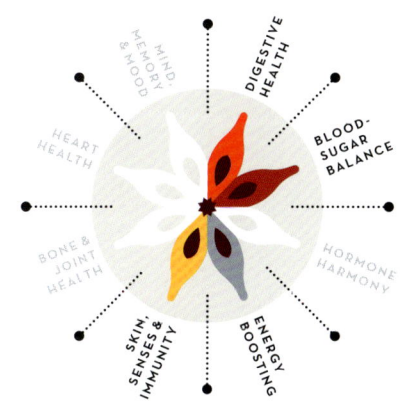

Seared Sirloin on Pan-roasted Veg

WITH A SPICED BALSAMIC GLAZE

SERVES 4

300g (10½oz) sirloin steak, about 2.5cm (1in) thick

sea salt flakes and freshly ground black pepper

1 tsp vegetable oil

FOR THE GLAZED VEG

1 tbsp olive oil

2 tsp nigella seeds

2 tsp mustard seeds

2 tsp coriander seeds

3 small peppers (red, orange and yellow), deseeded and cut into chunks

1 courgette, cut into 2cm (¾in) chunks

1 small aubergine, cut into 2cm (¾in) chunks

4 shallots, peeled and halved

4 garlic cloves, crushed

1 red chilli, deseeded and finely sliced, or to taste

a handful of oregano leaves (or herbs of your choice)

juice of 1 lemon

1 tbsp balsamic vinegar

125g (4½oz) baby spinach leaves

Preheat the oven to 180°C (350°F)/Gas Mark 4.

First prepare the glazed veg. Heat the olive oil in a small frying pan, add the seeds and fry for several minutes until they start to colour and pop, taking care not to burn them.

Place the veggies, shallots, garlic and chilli in a large roasting tin, dress with the warm spiced oil, then add the oregano, lemon juice and balsamic vinegar. Bake for 30 minutes until the veg are softened and lightly charred. Add the spinach to the tray, return to the oven and bake for a further 5 minutes until wilted.

Meanwhile, generously season the steak with salt and pepper. Heat the vegetable oil in a small frying pan, add the steak and fry until cooked to your liking: 1½ minutes on each side for rare; 3 minutes on each side for medium; 4 minutes on each side for well done. Leave to rest for at least 5 minutes, then thinly slice.

Divide the baked veggies among 4 bowls, then top with the steak and serve.

Health Tip

Red meat is, of course, a great source of iron, which is important for preventing anaemia and boosting energy. The iron found in meat is called haem iron, more easily absorbed by the body than the iron found in plants.

HEALTHY MAINS

WHY WE LOVE IT

One of the joys of writing a cookbook is that you get to eat *a lot* of food, often several times in one sitting, just to finesse a recipe. So it was that we found ourselves tucking into these kick-ass pork chops at 8.30 one morning. We finished the lot, and then popped a few more under the grill, just to *make sure* – a bit like Pooh with his honey pots. Meat doesn't feature heavily in the Midlife Kitchen, so when you do eat it, try to buy the best you can and treat it like a king: give it gorgeous accessories and allow it to rest well before it hits the plate.

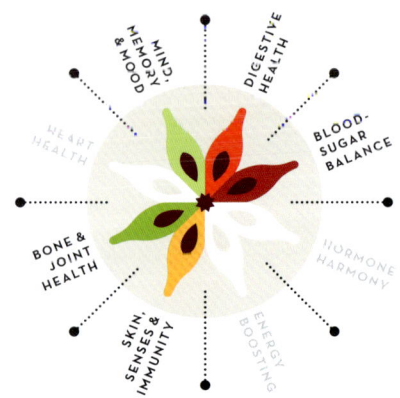

Uchucuta Pork

SERVES 4

4 thick pork chops, about 250g (9oz) each, trimmed

1 quantity (approx. 8 tbsp) Uchucuta, see page 226, plus extra to serve (optional)

Marinate the chops in the Uchucuta for a couple of hours or overnight in the fridge.

Place the chops, doused in plenty of the sauce, on a foil-lined baking tray. Cook under a preheated hot grill for 4–5 minutes on each side until the meat is cooked through and the fat is gently charred. Remove from the heat and leave to rest for 5 minutes.

Serve the chops with the juices from the foil and a spoonful of extra Uchucuta on the side (don't use any uncooked sauce that has been in contact with the raw meat).

These chops would sit very nicely alongside our Zesty Tenderstem with Midlife Dukkah & Chilli, see page 193.

Midlife Hack: These chops also cook brilliantly on a barbecue; try an Uchucuta marinade with pork loin (really slather it on and roast quickly) or with lamb chops, rack of lamb or chicken wings.

Health Tip
Lean protein is essential for muscle growth and maintenance. After the age of 30, we lose up to 8 per cent of our muscle mass each decade, so include lots of protein in your daily diet to maintain muscles and bones through the menopause and beyond.

WHY WE LOVE IT

These are essentially thin omelettes laced with spinach, which serve as a great green wrap to be filled with whatever takes your fancy. Here we keep it simple with tomato and avocado, but it works just as well with sautéed vegetables, crumbled cheese, smoked salmon, caramelized onions, guacamole and jalapeños – you name it. They are a brilliantly versatile alternative to bread or wheat wraps for lunch and it goes without saying that they make a superb breakfast.

Green Egg Wraps

MAKES 2

2 large eggs

a splash of water

sea salt flakes and freshly ground black pepper

light olive oil spray

a large handful of spinach leaves

FOR THE FILLING

1 ripe tomato, diced

1 small ripe avocado, peeled, stoned and chopped

1 spring onion, finely sliced

a squeeze of lemon juice

1 tbsp Midlife Spiced Seed Mix, see page 26, to serve (optional)

Place the eggs in a bowl, add a splash of water and whisk together, then season with salt and pepper.

Heat a medium nonstick frying pan and spray with a little olive oil. Add a small handful of the spinach (just a few leaves in a single layer in the pan) and cook for about 20 seconds until just starting to wilt. Pour in half the egg mixture and roll it around to thinly cover the base of the pan. Cook until golden (it will take no more than a minute), then flip and cook on the other side. Remove from the pan and set aside. Repeat with the remaining egg mixture and spinach to make a second wrap.

Fill the wraps with the tomato, avocado and spring onion, adding a squeeze of lemon juice to give some acidity. Roll up the wraps, top with the spiced seeds and serve.

Health Tip

When buying spinach, the greener the better – it indicates higher levels of health-giving carotenoids, which are important for eye health, guarding against macular degeneration, a leading cause of vision loss in the over 50s.

WHY WE LOVE IT

This is a brilliant, brilliant little lunch idea. Brilliant because we use seaweed as a healthy alternative to a traditional wheat wrap – the nori provides fibre, iron, calcium and other essential minerals, so it's an excellent choice to help protect your heart and bones – and brilliant again because it uses up any leftovers you may have in the fridge. Surplus rice, quinoa, cooked chicken, prawns and salad all come together in Japan-easy, sushi-style rolls, thanks to the yummy sesame soy dressing.

Asian Salad Nori Wraps

SERVES 2

a small handful of coriander leaves, chopped

1 small carrot, peeled and very finely sliced

½ a cucumber, deseeded and very finely sliced

1 small Little Gem lettuce, finely sliced

2 spring onions, finely sliced on the diagonal

100g (3½oz) cooked chicken or prawns or firm tofu (optional)

2 tbsp Miso, Sesame & Ginger Dressing, see page 119, plus extra to serve

1 tsp Midlife Sesame Seasoning, see page 32, or sesame seeds

4 dried nori seaweed sheets (the kind used for sushi)

250g (9oz) cooked rice or quinoa, or a ready-cooked pouch of either

Place the coriander, vegetables and your choice of chicken, prawns or tofu in a bowl and combine. Add the dressing, sprinkle with the sesame seasoning or seeds and toss well.

Lay a nori seaweed sheet on a chopping board, add a thin layer of cooked rice or quinoa, leaving a strip at the end to seal the wrap. Layer a small handful of the vegetable mix over the rice and roll up as tightly as you can without tearing the nori sheet. Moisten the edge with a little water or dressing and finish rolling to create a cigar shape. Repeat with the remaining ingredients to form 4 wraps.

Cut the wraps in half diagonally and serve with extra dressing as a dipping sauce.

Health Tip
Sesame seeds are a good source of fibre, B vits and magnesium, which can help to keep blood pressure healthy.

WHY WE LOVE IT

We've yet to meet anyone who doesn't adore rice paper wraps, but we tend to eat them on the rare occasions we go to a Vietnamese restaurant – which is a shame, because they're so easy to make at home. You can use whatever you like as a filling, but our absolute favourite is this crab and avocado duo, served with an authentic sweet-and-sour dipping sauce.

Vietnamese Crabocado Wraps

WITH SWEET & SOUR DIPPING SAUCE

MAKES 8

8 rice paper roll wrappers

1 large carrot, peeled and very finely sliced

½ a cucumber, deseeded and very finely sliced

3 spring onions, very finely sliced

FOR THE FILLING

100g (3½oz) fresh white crabmeat

finely grated zest and juice of 1 lime

1 tbsp natural yogurt

½ a ripe avocado, peeled and sliced

a handful of coriander leaves, chopped

a handful of mint leaves, chopped

sea salt flakes and freshly ground black pepper

FOR THE DIPPING SAUCE

juice of 2 limes

2 tsp runny honey

2 tbsp Thai fish sauce (nam pla)

2 tbsp rice vinegar

1 tbsp finely chopped coriander leaves

1 garlic clove, crushed

1 large red chilli, deseeded and very finely chopped

Combine all the filling ingredients in a bowl, then cover with clingfilm and chill in the fridge.

Mix all the dipping sauce ingredients in a separate bowl, stirring well. Set aside.

Lay a rice paper wrapper on a chopping board. Using a pastry brush, moisten the sheet lightly with warm water so that it softens. Place a few lengths of carrot, cucumber and spring onion horizontally at the top of the wrapper, then spread 1 heaped tablespoon of the filling in a line beneath the veggies, so that a third of the rice paper is covered.

Take the top edge of the wrapper and fold it down over the filling. Fold the edges in from the left and right and keep rolling, tucking in the edges as you go, as if you are wrapping a present. It's a little fiddly, but aim to create a fairly tight cylinder – the rice paper is quite elastic when wet so it can be stretched and manhandled fairly easily. Repeat with the remaining ingredients to make 8 wraps.

Serve with the dipping sauce on the side.

Health Tip
Crabmeat is crammed with essential nutrients including protein, healthy fats, B vits and important minerals such as zinc, selenium and iodine; it contains phosphorus, too. Alongside calcium, it's a real peri- and post-menopausal treat for hormones, muscles and bones.

HEALTHY MAINS

SIDES & SNACKS

WHY WE LOVE IT

Spinach is the original power veg, the ninja of the salad drawer, loaded with nutrients in a glorious low-calorie package. Its health credentials are in no doubt, so it's great to find some new weekday ways to prepare it. A comforting combo of spinach, onion and mushrooms is given a twist with dill, and stirred through with yogurt for a silky finish. Though great as a side dish, this would also be gorgeous on toasted seedy bread, crowned with a poached egg.

Wilted Spinach
WITH SAUTÉED MUSHROOMS & DILL

SERVES 2

250g (9oz) spinach leaves

2 tbsp water

1 tsp extra virgin olive oil or butter

1 small red onion, finely diced

1 garlic clove, crushed

250g (9oz) chestnut mushrooms, sliced

a handful of dill, roughly chopped

sea salt flakes and freshly ground black pepper

2 tbsp natural yogurt

1 tbsp lemon juice

½ tsp paprika

Place the spinach in a large frying pan over a medium heat, add the water and cook for 2–3 minutes until wilted. Transfer to a sieve and press with the back of a spoon to remove any moisture, then pat dry with kitchen paper and roughly chop.

Heat the olive oil or butter in a small frying pan, add the onion and garlic and fry gently for about 3 minutes until softened. Add the mushrooms and fry for 3 minutes, then stir in the chopped spinach and dill and cook for a further 3 minutes. Season as necessary.

Combine the yogurt, lemon juice and paprika in a small bowl, then swirl into the spinach mix, heat through and serve.

Health Tip
Foods rich in vitamin A, such as spinach, are known to be beneficial for the skin, immunity and eye health, so eat them in abundance during midlife.

WHY WE LOVE IT

This is a great dish to make in advance as the flavours develop when given a little time to sit and get to know each other. Puy lentils are a very fine thing indeed – nutty, punchy, protein-packed and unbelievably easy to prepare – particularly if, like us, you use a ready-cooked pouch.

Puy Lentils
WITH FETA & ROASTED TOMATOES

SERVES 4

250g (9oz) pouch ready-cooked Puy lentils, or 200g (7oz) dried Puy lentils plus 1 litre (1¾ pint) water

sea salt flakes and freshly ground black pepper

20 cherry tomatoes on the vine

1 tsp olive oil

1 tbsp apple cider vinegar

1 garlic clove, finely chopped

1 small red onion, finely diced

1 tsp runny honey

1 tbsp extra virgin olive oil

60g (2¼oz) feta cheese, crumbled

1 tbsp lemon juice

a handful of mint leaves, chopped

If using dried lentils, place them in a pan with 1 litre (1¾ pint) of water, bring to the boil, then reduce the heat and simmer until tender. Drain, season with a little salt and pepper and set aside to cool.

Preheat the oven to 170°C (340°F)/Gas Mark 3½.

Place the tomatoes in a small baking tin, drizzle with the olive oil and season with salt and pepper. Bake for 10–15 minutes until blistered and soft.

Meanwhile, put the remaining ingredients into a serving bowl with the lentils and mix well. Add the roasted tomatoes and juices from the tin, stir through and it's ready to serve.

Health Tip
Eat more lentils! Not only are they packed with beneficial fibre, protein, minerals and vitamins, they support peri- and post-menopausal guts, muscles and bones. And they taste great too.

SIDES & SNACKS

WHY WE LOVE IT

Here's a fresh and fragrant Balinese staple that's usually served as one of the components of 'nasi campur', a pick-and-mix of rice, meat, salads and sambals. Urab is a simple but incredibly tasty combination of green beans and fresh coconut, with a chilli kick coming from our Midlife Curry Paste. If you're a bit bored with green beans, this will give them a whole new lease of life.

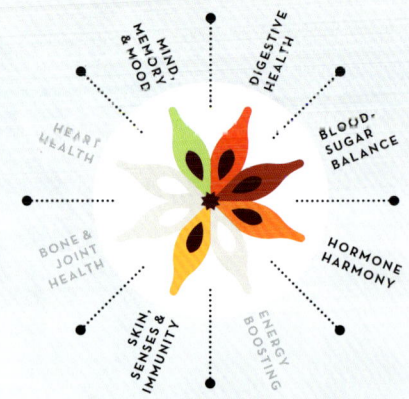

Urab

BALINESE GREEN BEAN & COCONUT SALAD

SERVES 4

- 300g (10½oz) fine green beans, trimmed and halved
- 1 tsp coconut oil
- 1 tbsp Midlife Curry Paste, see page 34
- 1 tsp runny honey
- 1 tbsp water
- 4 shallots, finely sliced
- a squeeze of lemon juice
- 100g (3½oz) fresh coconut, grated
- 50g (1¾oz) roasted, unsalted peanuts, crushed
- a pinch of sea salt flakes

Cook the green beans in a saucepan of boiling water for a few minutes until just cooked but still *al dente*. Drain, then plunge them into a bowl of cold water (this will help retain their colour and crunch). Drain well and pat dry with kitchen paper.

Heat the coconut oil in a frying pan, add the curry paste and honey and fry gently for 2–3 minutes. Add the water and cook for a further few minutes. Transfer the paste mixture to a bowl and leave to cool slightly.

Combine the just-cooked beans, the shallots, lemon juice and grated coconut in a serving bowl, add the paste mixture and toss well. Season and sprinkle with the crushed peanuts, then serve.

Health Tip
Green beans contain a good amount of folate, a B vitamin that is heart healthy – this helps to reduce fatigue and supports immune function.

SIDES & SNACKS

WHY WE LOVE IT

Broccoli rightly deserves its place in the Veggie Hall of Fame. Beyond its impeccable health profile, broccoli is easy to prep, inexpensive and versatile – and it responds well to a bit of primping. Here, you get added nutritional value from lemon zest, chilli, mustard seeds and our fabulous Midlife Dukkah, which really is a mega-food in its own right. We also like the fact that you can make this in advance and set it aside. That's the Midlife Kitchen message in a single mouthful.

Zesty Tenderstem
WITH MIDLIFE DUKKAH & CHILLI

SERVES 4

200–250g (7–9oz) Tenderstem broccoli, trimmed

a drizzle of extra virgin olive oil

2 tbsp Midlife Dukkah, see page 30

1 tsp mustard seeds

1 small red chilli, deseeded and finely sliced, or to taste

zest of 1 lemon

sea salt flakes and freshly ground black pepper

Cook the broccoli in a saucepan of boiling water for 2 minutes. It should be *al dente*, so take care not to overcook it. Drain, then plunge it into a bowl of very cold water (this will help retain its colour and crunch). Drain well and pat dry with kitchen paper.

Transfer the broccoli to a serving bowl, drizzle with a little olive oil and sprinkle over the dukkah, mustard seeds, chilli and lemon zest. Season and serve at room temperature.

Health Tip
A diet rich in cruciferous vegetables such as broccoli may help guard against many chronic diseases associated with ageing. Broccoli is also a good source of fibre and flavonols, which helps reduce the risk of many diseases.

SIDES & SNACKS

WHY WE LOVE IT

A proper Makhani dhal is a rich, unctuous bowl of lentil-y bliss and we genuinely feel that there are times when the full butter and cream version is exactly what you are after. For day-to-day eating, though, a lighter option is welcome – so here we provide a luxe and a lean version. There's enough depth and layering of flavour in either if you want to make this a meal in itself, with a wholemeal pitta or one of our Easy Chapatis on the side.

Luxe or Lean Makhani Dhal

SERVES 4

400g (14oz) can kidney beans, drained and rinsed

40g (1½oz) butter (luxe) or 1 tbsp coconut oil (lean)

2 small red onions, diced

1 large green chilli, deseeded and sliced

2cm (¾in) piece of fresh root ginger, peeled and finely grated

3 garlic cloves, thinly sliced

½–1 tsp hot chilli powder, to taste

2 tsp ground turmeric

1 tbsp ground cumin

1 tbsp ground coriander

1 tsp garam masala

4 cardamom pods, crushed

400ml (14fl oz) vegetable or chicken stock

2 bay leaves

250g (9oz) pouch ready-cooked Beluga lentils

1 ripe tomato, finely diced

sea salt flakes and freshly ground black pepper

3 tbsp double cream (luxe) or 3 tbsp natural yogurt (lean)

a handful of coriander leaves

Easy Chapatis, see page 206, or wholemeal pitta breads, to serve

Tip the kidney beans into a bowl and mash lightly with a fork. Set aside.

Heat the butter or coconut oil in a saucepan, add the onions and chilli and fry gently for 5 minutes until softened. Add the ginger, garlic, chilli powder and spices and cook for a further minute or two.

Add the water, the bay leaves, mashed beans, lentils and tomato. Bring to a simmer and cook for about 20 minutes, or until thickened.

Season with salt and pepper, then add the cream or yogurt and stir well. Scatter with the coriander, then serve with chapatis or pittas.

Midlife Hack: It's worth making a double batch of this as it freezes brilliantly – or add vegetable stock to turn it into a hearty soup, then just heat and eat.

Health Tip
Kidney beans are mighty big on fibre, which is key for keeping your digestive system in tip-top condition, and with their dark red skins, they're rich in cell-protecting antioxidants too.

WHY WE LOVE IT

Roasting whole garlic sweetens and mellows its flavour and produces an unctuous stickiness that makes for a delicious spread or topping. New-season garlic will give you the finest result.

Roasted Garlic...

AND PLENTY OF WAYS TO USE IT

MAKES 6

6 good, fat garlic bulbs, outer leaves removed

1 tbsp extra virgin olive oil

sea salt flakes and freshly ground black pepper

Preheat the oven to 180°C (350°F)/Gas Mark 4.

Slice off the tops of the garlic and place in a small roasting tin. Drizzle with the olive oil, season and cover with foil. Roast for 30–40 minutes until the garlic is butter-soft and golden.

Serve whole as a side dish, or squeeze the cloves to release the glory within.

Try This...
* Mashed into a salad dressing for a smooth, sweet flavour
* Squeezed into soups, sauces and stews for added savoury depth
* Swirled through mashed potato, sweet potato or White Bean Mash, see page 205
* Spread as a first layer on any Midlife Avo Toast, see pages 60–65
* Stirred through steamed asparagus or fine green beans
* Squeezed over roasted veg
* Mashed into softened butter with some chopped parsley, for a great garlic butter to add to steaks or bread
* Added to natural yogurt for a delicious dip
* Rubbed on to corn on the cob with a smear of butter

Midlife Hack: It's worth throwing a couple of garlic bulbs into the tin whenever you roast meat, ready to flavour the gravy for Sunday lunch.

Health Tip
Garlic is full of Midlife beauty, including vitamin B6, which enables the energy in food to be utilized by the body, making it great for keeping energy levels up. It also helps regulate hormones and supports the immune system.

SIDES & SNACKS

WHY WE LOVE IT

'Mata sapi' means bull's eye, which is how Indonesians describe a fried egg, but this is no ordinary egg. Cumin is in the spotlight here, the fragrant seeds decorating our bull's eye and the ground version flavouring the dressing, which, all in all, transforms a pouch of mixed grains into a mouth-watering mini-meal.

Mixed Grain Mata Sapi

SERVES 2

- 250g (9oz) pouch ready-cooked mixed grains
- a handful of coriander leaves, chopped
- a handful of mint leaves, chopped
- 2 spring onions, finely sliced
- 50g (1¾oz) feta cheese, crumbled
- freshly ground black pepper
- light olive oil spray
- 2 tsp cumin seeds
- 2 eggs
- 3 tbsp natural yogurt
- 1 tsp ground cumin
- 4 tbsp Wholly Guacamole, see page 220, or 1 ripe avocado, peeled, stoned and diced

Place the mixed grains in a large bowl and fluff up with a fork. Add the herbs, spring onions and feta and season well with pepper (using feta means that you shouldn't need to add salt).

Heat a large nonstick frying pan and spray with a little olive oil. Add the cumin seeds and cook for a couple of minutes until they start to colour and pop, taking care not to burn them, then remove from the pan. Fry the eggs, sunny side up, sprinkling with the toasted cumin seeds as they cook.

Meanwhile, combine the yogurt and ground cumin in a small bowl, then add to the grain mixture, mixing well.

Divide the grains between 2 shallow bowls, add 2 spoonfuls of Wholly Guacamole or half the avocado to each bowl and top with the cumin-fried eggs.

Health Tip
Whole grains are an essential part of a healthy diet in midlife. A large study, looking at data from 786,000 individuals, found that people who ate 70g (2½oz) of whole grains a day had a 22 per cent lower risk of mortality compared with those who ate few or no whole grains.

WHY WE LOVE IT

This is proper Midlife comfort food – satisfying, tasty and off-the-charts good for you. With your quinoa pouch to hand you can have this on the table in about 10 minutes, and it works well hot or cold, so any leftovers happily serve as tomorrow's lunch.

Red & White Quinoa
WITH MUSHROOMS, RED CHARD & PARMESAN

SERVES 4

- 1 tsp butter
- 1 tsp olive oil
- 200g (7oz) chestnut or button mushrooms, sliced
- 250g (9oz) pouch ready-cooked red and white quinoa
- 100g (3½oz) red chard, tough stems removed
- a handful of mint leaves, chopped
- a handful of flat leaf parsley, chopped
- juice of ½ a lemon
- 1 tbsp natural yogurt
- 1 tsp grainy mustard
- 50g (1¾oz) Parmesan cheese, grated, plus shavings to serve
- sea salt flakes and freshly ground black pepper

Heat the butter and olive oil in a large frying pan, add the mushrooms and fry gently for a few minutes until softened and starting to brown. Add the quinoa, chard and herbs and cook for 3–4 minutes until the leaves have wilted.

Combine the lemon juice, yogurt and mustard in a bowl, then stir into the quinoa. Remove the pan from the heat, mix in the Parmesan, season well and serve with extra Parmesan shavings on top.

Health Tip
Unsurprisingly, red and white quinoa have very similar nutritional profiles, but red quinoa has extra riboflavin (vitamin B2), which works as an antioxidant to help prevent cell damage.

SIDES & SNACKS

WHY WE LOVE IT

As you might expect, Beluga lentils are named after the caviar they resemble – we adore them because they're such a beautiful jet black, and they have a rich flavour and velvety texture that works perfectly in this good-carb bowl. Like all lentils, they're high in protein and fibre, so they make for a filling meal, particularly when paired with roasted sweet potato, toasted pine nuts and this sweet, dark dressing.

Black Beluga Lentils
WITH SWEET POTATO, BALSAMIC & POMEGRANATE

SERVES 4

1 sweet potato, about 250g (9oz), peeled and sliced

1 tsp olive oil

sea salt flakes and freshly ground black pepper

250g (9oz) pouch ready-cooked Beluga or Puy lentils

1 small red onion, very finely diced

1 tbsp toasted pine nuts

a handful of pomegranate seeds

FOR THE DRESSING

1 tbsp balsamic vinegar

1 tbsp pomegranate molasses

1 tbsp extra virgin olive oil

1 tsp date syrup

Preheat the oven to 200°C (400°F)/Gas Mark 6. Place the sweet potato slices in a small roasting tin, drizzle with the olive oil and season with salt and pepper. Bake for 10 minutes until just softened and starting to brown. Leave to cool, then cut or tear into 1cm (½in) pieces.

Tip the lentils into a serving bowl, add the cooled sweet potato and the onion.

Combine all the dressing ingredients in a bowl and stir well, then season. Pour half of the dressing over the lentils and toss together.

Top the lentils with the toasted pine nuts and pomegranate seeds and serve with the remaining dressing on the side.

Midlife Hack: Use the lentil and sweet potato mix (undressed) as the base for a stunning soup – just add veg stock, heat through and blend.

Health Tip
Unlike green lentils, black lentils possess anthocyanins, the same potent antioxidants found in dark berries such as blueberries and blackberries, offering added protection against age-related disease.

WHY WE LOVE IT

Almost too pretty to eat, this super side takes rice to another level with the addition of the bright greens and pinks of sweet broad beans, peas, crisp radish and spring onion. We quite like the name too…. Try it with a combination of rices – the ready-cooked wild and wholegrain rice pouches come in handy here, although they generally already contain some oil, so taste first to get the balance right. Top with shredded cooked chicken if you're after a more substantial meal.

Midlife Rices

SERVES 4

- 100g (3½oz) fresh or frozen broad beans
- 100g (3½oz) frozen petits pois
- 250g (9oz) pouch ready-cooked wholegrain, wild or black and red rice, or 150g (5½oz) wholegrain or wild rice, cooked and cooled
- 1 ripe avocado, peeled, stoned and sliced
- 10 long radishes, thinly sliced
- 3 spring onions, thinly sliced on the diagonal
- a small handful of flat leaf parsley, chopped
- sea salt flakes and freshly ground black pepper

FOR THE DRESSING

- 1 tbsp extra virgin olive oil
- finely grated zest and juice of 1 lime
- 1 tsp chilli flakes
- 1 garlic clove, crushed
- sea salt flakes and freshly ground black pepper

Cook the broad beans and peas in a saucepan of boiling water for 3 minutes until tender. Drain and refresh in cold water. Pop the beans from their outer skins and transfer to a serving bowl with the peas.

Combine all the dressing ingredients in a bowl and stir well.

Add all the remaining ingredients to the peas and beans, add the dressing and stir gently to combine. Season and serve.

Health Tip
Wholegrain rice is not milled, which means it retains much of its constituent B vits and essential minerals, together with lots of lovely fibre and fatty acids. Replacing white rice in your diet with an unrefined variety is good for the heart and may reduce the risk of developing type 2 diabetes.

WHY WE LOVE IT

It's so vividly, vibrantly green that you can just tell that this sublime mash-up of peas and beans is packed with goodies. What you get for a bit of effort shelling the broad beans is a supremely versatile crush: brilliant served warm beside grilled lamb chops or cold as a salad at a barbecue, it works equally well as a great dip or as a spread for bruschetta and crostini – although there's a real risk you'll polish this off before it even hits the table.

Broad Bean, Pea & Mint Smash

SERVES 4

150g (5½oz) fresh or frozen broad beans
150g (5½oz) frozen peas
sea salt flakes
1 small garlic clove, peeled and halved
a handful of mint leaves
2 tsp extra virgin olive oil
a squeeze of lemon juice
freshly ground black pepper

Cook the broad beans and peas in a saucepan of salted boiling water for 3 minutes until tender. Drain and refresh in cold water. Spend a mellow moment removing the white outer shells of the broad beans to get at the vivid green beans within.

Put three-quarters of the peas and beans into a food processor with the garlic, mint leaves, olive oil and lemon juice. Season well and blitz to a coarse pesto texture.

Transfer to a bowl and stir in the remaining whole peas and beans. Serve either warmed through or at room temperature.

Try This...
* Topped with a scatter of pine nuts or crumbled feta cheese
* Sprinkled with grated Parmesan and chilli flakes for a jumped-up version

Health Tip
Low-GI broad beans are a good source of protein, fibre and vitamins A and C; they also contain L-dopa, a chemical the body uses to produce dopamine. So they could make you feel good too!

WHY WE LOVE IT

This is truly a mash made in heaven. In fact, it's a mash made in the Midlife Kitchen, so you know it's going to be bursting with good things and utterly delicious to boot. It is fabulous served hot with fish (a piece of poached smoked haddock on top would be lovely) – or try it chilled as a dip, or as a protein-packed, slow-burn, tasty topping for Seedy Soda Bread, see page 209. The riffs on this theme are endless, so we've included some of our best variations below.

White Bean Mash
WITH LEMON & SAGE

SERVES 2

2 tbsp extra virgin olive oil

3 garlic cloves, crushed

10 sage leaves, finely sliced

400g (14oz) can white beans (try cannellini or butter beans), drained and rinsed

3 tbsp water

2 tbsp natural yogurt

a squeeze of lemon juice

zest of ½ a lemon

sea salt flakes and freshly ground black pepper

Health Tip
Pulses, like these silky white beans, are packed with protein and fibre, a combo which promises to keep you fuller for longer.

Heat the olive oil, garlic and sage in a medium saucepan over a low heat and cook for a minute or so until the garlic has softened. Add the beans and mash lightly with a fork.

Add the water, bring to a simmer, then cook for 3–4 minutes until the liquid has reduced almost completely. Remove the pan from the heat and set aside.

Mix the yogurt, lemon juice and zest in a bowl and season well (this benefits from plenty of black pepper).

Stir the yogurt mixture through the beans and serve. The mash will keep in the fridge for several days.

Try This...
Replace the garlic, sage and lemon juice and zest with:

* 1 teaspoon of ground cumin, a handful of chopped coriander and the juice of 1 lime
* A handful of chopped tarragon and thyme and 1 teaspoon of grainy Dijon mustard
* 1 tablespoon of Midlife Dukkah, see page 30, and the juice of 1 lime
* A handful of chopped flat leaf parsley and a few soft Roasted Garlic cloves, see page 190

WHY WE LOVE IT

Our favourite flatbread is that basic of Indian cuisine: the humble chapati. Happily, they are also extremely easy to make, as neither of us are natural-born kneaders. This recipe is so ridiculously simple – a little flour, a splash of water, a mere 5 minutes' work – that you will feel a disproportionate amount of satisfaction as you tuck in to your own healthy homemade wraps.

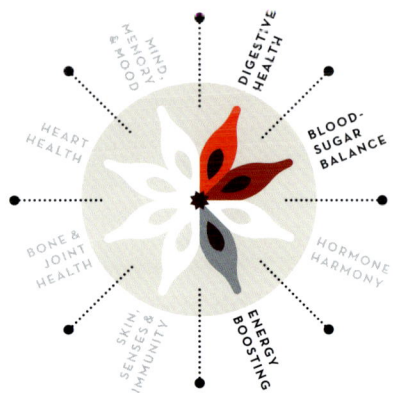

Easy Chapatis

MAKES 4

120g (4¼oz) wholemeal flour or half rye, half white flour, plus extra for dusting

a pinch of sea salt flakes

100ml (3½fl oz) lukewarm water

light olive oil spray

Sift the flour into a bowl, adding any fibre that remains in the sieve. Add the salt, then slowly incorporate the water with your hands to make a soft dough. Knead for a minute or two on a lightly oiled surface to make a smooth and pliable ball. The longer you knead, the softer the chapatis will be, but there is no need to knead for more than a couple of minutes. Cover the dough with a damp cloth or clingfilm and leave to rest for at least 10 minutes.

Divide the dough into 4 equal pieces, then roll into smooth balls and press flat. Press both sides of the flattened balls on to a floured surface (this makes them easier to roll), then roll out each ball to form a 25cm- (10in-) diameter circle (they should be quite thin – just a millimetre or two (approx. 1/16in).

Heat a large nonstick frying pan over a high heat and spray with olive oil. Place a chapati in the pan and spray the top of the chapati with a little more oil.

When it starts to puff up, flip it (there will be some golden brown spots on the cooked side).

Using a spatula, press lightly on the puffed parts, cooking for a further minute until it has light golden brown spots on both sides. Remove from the pan and repeat with the remaining chapatis.

Serve immediately. Alternatively, if you make a big batch, they will keep for a couple of days in an airtight container in the fridge. Simply reheat in a frying pan to serve.

Health Tip
We generally use wholemeal flour in the Midlife Kitchen because it includes the highly nutritious bran and germ of the wheat grain, source of most of the vitamins, minerals and fibre found in flour.

WHY WE LOVE IT

We'd love to be bread makers, really we would – the smell of freshly baked dough, flour up to our elbows, shafts of light through the farmhouse windows… the reality is, however, that very few of us (and absolutely neither of us) have the time or the inclination to embark on proper yeast-knead-prove bread making, especially when the end product lasts for half a day before turning into a doorstop. So this is the bread we swear by – a simple soda bread with a Midlife seedy twist. This excellent healthy loaf can be on the table within half an hour; better yet, it's impossible to muck up.

Seedy Soda Bread

MAKES 1 LOAF

225g (8oz) wholemeal flour, plus extra for dusting

225g (8oz) plain flour

1 tsp caster sugar

1 tsp bicarbonate of soda

½ tsp sea salt flakes

3 tbsp Midlife Raw Seed Mix, see page 25, or 2 tbsp sunflower seeds and 1 tbsp pumpkin seeds

200g (7oz) natural yogurt

200ml (7fl oz) milk

2 tsp rolled oats

Preheat the oven to 200°C (400°F)/Gas Mark 6. Place a lidded casserole dish in the oven to warm.

Place all the dry ingredients in a large bowl and mix together. Add the yogurt and milk and combine to make a soft, pliable dough, gathering any escaping seeds back into the mix.

Working quickly, shape into a round loaf and carefully place in the hot casserole, topping with a little more flour. Using a sharp knife, score the top with a cross and scatter with the oats.

Replace the lid and bake for 20 minutes, then remove the lid and bake for a further 5 minutes until nutty brown. When the bread is cooked, it should sound hollow when tapped on the base.

Turn out and leave to cool slightly before tucking in.

Health Tip
Wholemeal flour contains different types of fibre which help with many aspects of our digestion. Most of us don't eat enough, so this loaf is the simple answer.

SIDES & SNACKS

WHY WE LOVE IT

'Sooooooo good!' That's what our families think of this yummy snack mix. We love a Snickers bar, but they have now been replaced in our hearts by this far healthier grown-up reinvention. The familiar peanuty, chocolatey flavours are there, and we've added Brazils and walnuts, which add up to a nutritious, energy-packed snack.

Midlife Mega Mix
WITH PEANUTS & DARK CHOCOLATE

MAKES 200G (7OZ)

- 75g (2¾oz) roasted, salted peanuts
- 50g (1¾oz) walnut pieces
- 25g (1oz) Brazil nuts, each chopped into 3 pieces
- 50g (1¾oz) organic dark chocolate chips

Combine all the ingredients, then store in an airtight container. The mix will keep for weeks, but honestly it won't hang around that long!

Midlife Hack: Look for a 'bitter-sweet' choc chip containing 70% cocoa solids. Some choc chips contain stabilizers to allow them to retain their shape in cooking, which can make them taste waxy, so choose your chips with care.

Health Tip
Nuts contain protein, fibre and healthy fats, but they're calorific, too (the NHS recommends half a handful a day as the optimum portion size). Brazils bring selenium to this mix – great for skin, hair and nails, as well as thyroid function.

WHY WE LOVE IT

As you might have noticed, we're nuts about nuts in the Midlife Kitchen. They're our go-to high-protein snack when we are having a busy day. A small handful will stave off hunger pangs and keep your energy and blood-sugar levels on an even keel. This mix is equally awesome for breakfast, scattered over Midlife Yogurt and chopped fruit.

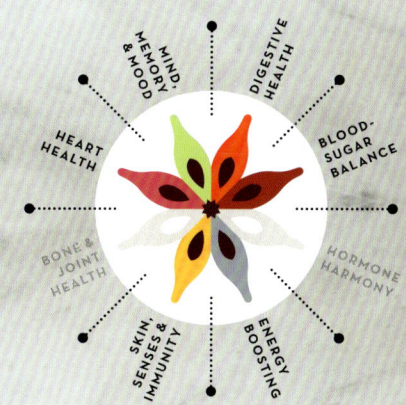

Midlife Toasted Trail Mix

MAKES 500G (1LB 2OZ)

300g (10½oz) shelled nuts, choose from: walnuts, Brazils, peanuts, cashews, almonds, hazelnuts, pistachios, coconut chips

100g (3½oz) dried fruit, choose from: apricots, figs, raisins, dates, pineapple, mango, pear, apple, cranberries, goji berries, blueberries, cherries

100g (3½oz) seeds, choose from: pumpkin seeds, sunflower seeds, sesame seeds, flaxseed

2 tbsp coconut oil, melted if solid

2 tsp ground cinnamon

a grind of vanilla bean, see Midlife Hack, or ½ tsp vanilla extract

Health Tip
There is plenty of evidence that people who regularly eat nuts and seeds in the context of an overall healthy diet have a lower risk of developing heart disease, type 2 diabetes and obesity.

Preheat the oven to 160°C (325°F)/Gas Mark 3. Line a large baking tray with nonstick baking paper.

Chop the larger ingredients (Brazil nuts, walnuts, apricots and figs) into smaller pieces, aiming for 1cm (½in) pieces.

Put the nuts, seeds and dried fruit into a bowl. Add the coconut oil, cinnamon and vanilla and mix well. Spread the mixture out on the prepared baking tray and bake for 20 minutes until crisp and golden, turning the mixture after 10 minutes.

Leave the mix to cool, then store in an airtight container for up to 1 week.

Midlife Hack: We often use a vanilla bean grinder rather than a whole pod, essence or extract – it's the quickest way to add pretty flecks of vanilla to porridge, yogurt or bakes.

WHY WE LOVE IT

Our perennial dilemma is what to eat when the Midlife munchies call; we're looking for sweet, salty, crunchy and spicy... but ultimately healthy. Here, we square the circle by coating almonds – full of protein, fibre, vitamin E, essential minerals and antioxidants – with an irresistible combination of super spices and a touch of honey, crisped to perfection in the oven.

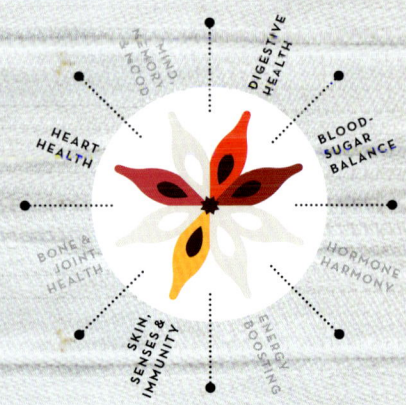

Hot Tapas Almonds
WITH HONEY & CINNAMON

MAKES 200G (7OZ)

- light olive oil spray
- 2 tsp ground cumin
- 1 tsp ground cinnamon
- ¼ tsp cayenne pepper, or more to taste
- ½ tsp sea salt flakes
- 200g (7oz) whole almonds, with skins on
- 1 tbsp runny honey

Preheat the oven to 180°C (350°F)/Gas Mark 4. Line a baking tray with nonstick baking paper and spray with a little olive oil.

Combine the spices and salt in a bowl. Put the almonds into another bowl, drizzle with the honey and mix well to ensure they are all coated. Add the spice mixture and stir until the almonds are evenly coated.

Spread out the almonds on the prepared baking tray and bake for 25 minutes until crisp and golden, turning the nuts after about 15 minutes to prevent them sticking.

Leave to cool for 20 minutes before serving, or cool completely and store in an airtight container for up to 1 week.

Health Tip
Whole almonds, including the skins, are loaded with flavonoids – plant nutrients that help to maintain a healthy heart and protecting the body from the effects of ageing.

WHY WE LOVE IT

If you fancy a healthy little savoury something to accompany a good glass of wine, these excellent cheesy biscuits do the business. They're buttery and crunchy, as is only fitting for a shortbread, but they also contain a decent haul of Midlife goodness – from the olive oil, pistachios, almonds and mustard to the sesame seeds, cumin seeds, dried oregano or chilli flakes used as a topping.

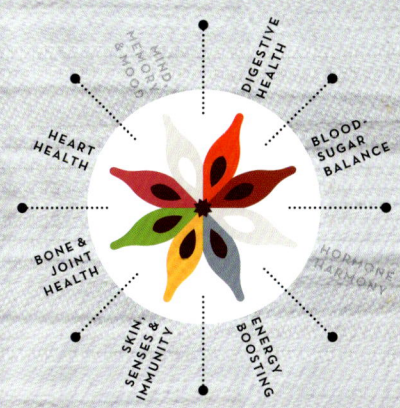

Parmesan, Almond & Pistachio Sables

MAKES 30

100g (3½oz) Parmesan cheese, grated
50g (1¾oz) blanched almonds
50g (1¾oz) pistachio nuts
100g (3½oz) butter, softened
50ml (2fl oz) extra virgin olive oil
50g (1¾oz) semolina
100g (3½oz) self-raising flour
1 heaped tsp English mustard powder
sea salt flakes and freshly ground black pepper

FOR THE TOPPINGS
crushed pistachio nuts
sesame seeds, poppy seeds and/or cumin seeds
dried oregano and/or chilli flakes

Preheat the oven to 180°C (350°F)/Gas Mark 4. Line a large baking sheet with nonstick baking paper.

Place all the ingredients, except for the toppings, in a food processor and whizz to form a coarse dough. Tip the dough on to a piece of clingfilm and shape into a long sausage, using the film to help with the rolling. Secure the ends of the roll and place in the freezer for at least 30 minutes.

When chilled, use a sharp knife and slice the dough into slim discs about 3mm (⅛in) thick.

Place the discs on the prepared baking sheet and sprinkle over the toppings of your choice (some of each looks pretty). Bake for 15 minutes until golden brown and crisp. Transfer to a wire rack and leave to cool.

The sables will keep for up to 2 days in an airtight container.

Midlife Hack: Keep the dough 'sausage' in the freezer and it will be ready to bake at a moment's notice if you need a quick savoury snack for parties.

Health Tip
The unique green and purple colour of the pistachio kernel is a result of its lutein and anthocyanin content. Lutein is often referred to as the 'eye vitamin' as it can help reduce the risk of eye problems including age-related macular degeneration.

SIDES & SNACKS

WHY WE LOVE IT

Not really a recipe, just a really good idea. Chop some of your favourite fruit, add a few berries and a handful of dates and pop the lot in the freezer. Then later, when you need a sweet fix, you have lovely chewy chunks of fruity goodness. Needless to say, this is universally adored by kids too.

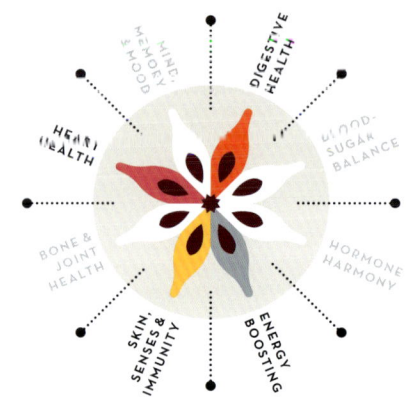

Freezer Fruit

MAKES AS MUCH AS YOU LIKE!

mixed fruit, such as banana, mango, papaya, pineapple and kiwifruit, cut into bite-sized chunks

mixed whole fruit, such as blueberries, raspberries and grapes

pitted Medjool dates

Put your selection of fruit in a plastic container and freeze for a few hours or overnight.

Eat straight from the freezer.

Try This...

∗ As a fruit smoothie, combined with natural yogurt or a splash of coconut water

Health Tip
Some people think that because added sugars are bad for you, the same must apply to fruit. While fruit *does* contain fructose, it is also packaged with fibre and a host of vital nutrients, making it a natural, healthy snack.

MIDLIFE EXTRAS

WHY WE LOVE IT

This super spread does the job of hummus but with a Midlife twist – replacing the more usual chickpeas with butter beans and spinach to give a lighter texture. We've kept it simple, so you can whizz it up at a moment's notice to have on stand-by in the fridge. It's perfect as a dip for raw veggies, or spread thickly on toast topped with a handful of Midlife Spiced Seed Mix, see page 26.

Middle-aged Spread

MAKES 500G (1LB 2OZ)

250g (9oz) spinach leaves

400g (14oz) can butter beans, drained and rinsed

2 tbsp extra virgin olive oil

juice of ½ a lemon

a small handful of flat leaf parsley, roughly chopped

1 tbsp Midlife Spice Mix, see page 24, or 1 tsp ground coriander and 1 tsp ground cumin

2 tbsp natural yogurt

1 garlic clove, crushed

sea salt flakes and freshly ground black pepper

Rinse the spinach, then cook in a large frying pan with the residual water over a low heat for 2 minutes until wilted. Drain well and pat dry with kitchen paper to remove any moisture.

Put the spinach into a food processor, add the remaining ingredients and pulse to a semi-smooth texture.

This can be served warm, or cold from the fridge, where it will keep in an airtight container for up to a week.

Health Tip
Beans take centre stage in perimenopause and beyond because their protein supports muscles and bones while their fibre boosts microbial diversity in the gut.

WHY WE LOVE IT

We might just have created the ultimate dip. But it's not just a dip, it's a spread, it's a sauce, it's breakfast, lunch and dinner. As we know, avocados are positively full of the good stuff – but we've added so much more to this that you *need* to have it in your fridge: seeds, peas, edamame, mint, lime juice, garlic... it's a roll call of Midlife excellence.

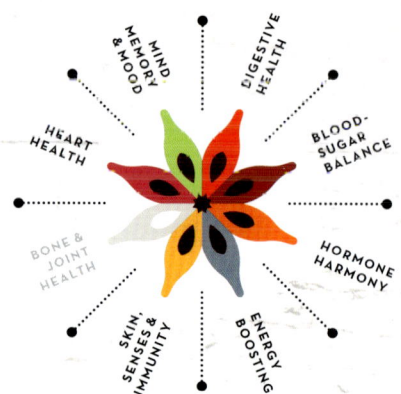

Wholly Guacamole

MAKES 500G (1LB 2OZ)

- 100g (3½oz) frozen edamame beans
- 100g (3½oz) frozen peas
- 3 tbsp Midlife Raw Seed Mix, see page 25, or pumpkin seeds
- 2 perfectly ripe avocados
- 2 garlic cloves, crushed
- 2 spring onions, sliced
- a handful of mint leaves, chopped
- a handful of flat leaf parsley, chopped
- juice of 2 limes
- finely grated zest of 1 lime
- 2 tbsp extra virgin olive oil
- ½ tsp sea salt flakes
- freshly ground black pepper
- 1 ripe tomato, finely diced

Cook the edamame beans and peas in a saucepan of boiling water for 3 minutes until tender. Drain and refresh in cold water. Pop the beans from their outer skins and set aside with the peas.

Place the seed mix in a small, shallow frying pan and dry-fry over a medium heat for a few minutes until just starting to colour and pop, taking care not to burn them. Leave to cool for a few minutes, then tip into a coffee grinder or spice mill and pulse until coarsely ground. Alternatively, pound the seeds using a pestle and mortar.

Peel and stone the avocados, then put into a food processor with the ground seeds. Add all the remaining ingredients, except the tomato, and pulse to a semi-chunky texture. Add the diced tomato and stir well. Transfer the guacamole to a bowl and chill for 30 minutes before serving.

Try This...

* As a sauce for pan-fried fish or fishcakes
* As a dip for toasted pitta bread with crumbled feta cheese
* As a base for Avo Toast, see pages 60–65
* Spooned on to an omelette

Midlife Hack: Fresh shelled edamame beans are available at most supermarkets; just boil for a few minutes and they are ready to go.

Health Tip
Studies show that eating sources of unsaturated fats, like avocados, nuts and seeds, can help lower heart-disease risk factors, improving your cholesterol profile as well as lowering blood triglycerides.

WHY WE LOVE IT

Hummus is a reliable staple in the fridges of the nation; we know it's a fine thing because it's full of plant protein, fibre and lip-smacking flavour. But the commercial versions are often dosed with high levels of salt (research recently found that some pots contain as much salt as four bags of crisps), while you can't always be sure of the quality of oil that goes in. Making your own is the answer. In this case, there's added buzz from roasted red peppers, almonds and paprika, and only as much salt as you choose to add.

Roasted Red Pepper Hummus

WITH ALMONDS & SMOKED PAPRIKA

MAKES 500G (1LB 2OZ)

1 large red pepper

400g (14oz) can chickpeas, drained and rinsed

2 tbsp Midlife LSA, see page 27, or ground almonds

2 tbsp tahini

2 tbsp extra virgin olive oil

2 tbsp lemon juice

3 tbsp warm water

1 garlic clove, crushed

1 tsp smoked paprika

sea salt flakes and freshly ground black pepper

Cook the red pepper under a preheated hot grill for 5 minutes, turning occasionally, until softened and slightly charred. Leave to cool a little, then remove the stalk, deseed and roughly chop.

Place the red pepper in a food processor, add the remaining ingredients and pulse to a coarse paste (or make it smoother if you prefer).

The hummus will keep in an airtight container in the fridge for up to 3 days.

Health Tip
100g (3½oz) of red pepper contains more than three times the recommended dietary allowance (RDA) for vitamin C, making it one of the richest sources of this essential nutrient, vital for cell protection and immunity.

MIDLIFE EXTRAS

WHY WE LOVE IT

If you're looking for a quick lunch, this healthy fallback recipe is simply delicious. The oily fish provides omega-3s, there's vitamin C from the dill, lemon juice and zest, and excellent digestive benefits from the yogurt. Add chilli flakes if you like a kick. Be warned though, it's addictive!

Smoked Mackerel & Dill Pâté

SERVES 2

300g (10½oz) smoked mackerel fillets, skin removed

2 tbsp thick Greek yogurt

finely grated zest and juice of ½ a lemon

1 spring onion, finely sliced

a handful of dill, chopped

sea salt flakes and freshly ground black pepper

½ tsp chilli flakes (optional)

Place the mackerel fillets in a bowl and mash gently with a fork. Add the remaining ingredients and mix well. Alternatively, if you prefer a smoother pâté, whizz the ingredients together in a food processor.

Chill for at least 30 minutes before serving. This works wonderfully as a dip for veggies, on toasted Seedy Soda Bread, see page 209, or with oatcakes.

The pâté will keep in the fridge for several days.

Health Tip
We ❤ oily fish and, happily, oily fish loves your ❤. Studies have found that eating oily fish can lower blood pressure and reduce fat build-up in the arteries.

WHY WE LOVE IT

This five-minute wonder, stacked with must-have omega-3s, makes a lovely light starter served on warm crisp wholemeal toast, grainy bagels or rye bread, or a healthy canapé spread on to pumpernickel rye toasts. You want a pungent punch of fresh horseradish here, while plenty of black pepper, snipped chives and antioxidant lemon zest make it a truly magic mouthful.

Smoked Trout Pâté

WITH LEMON & HORSERADISH

SERVES 4

- 300g (10½oz) hot-smoked trout fillets, skin removed
- 2 tbsp natural yogurt
- 2 tsp fresh horseradish root, peeled and grated, or ready-grated horseradish in a jar (not horseradish sauce)
- grated zest and juice of ½ a lemon
- a pinch of sea salt flakes
- freshly ground black pepper
- 1 tbsp snipped chives

Place 150g (5½oz) of the smoked trout in a food processor, add the yogurt, horseradish, lemon juice and zest. Season, then pulse until smooth.

Transfer to a bowl and break in the remaining fish. Add the chives and check the seasoning, then stir and serve.

Midlife Hack: Fresh horseradish root, like ginger or turmeric, freezes well. If you are having trouble finding fresh or grated horseradish, use English mustard instead.

Health Tip
Horseradish has long been used as a traditional remedy for sinusitis and colds, and recent research suggests that it has antibacterial properties to help fight infections naturally.

WHY WE LOVE IT

If there's one food that can really contribute to health in midlife, it has to be oily fish. Sardines may have fallen out of fashion, but they are a nutritional knockout, almost a 'perfect food', with benefits for the entire body. So we've given these overlooked little fish an update in this rich, savoury pâté – just the thing for high tea, spread generously on warm toasted pitta bread triangles. They'd make an excellent canapé too.

Sardinade

SERVES 2

- 100g (3½oz) tin sardines in olive oil
- ½ a small red onion, very finely diced
- a small handful of parsley, chopped
- 6 black Greek olives, pitted and finely chopped
- juice of ½ a lemon
- a few drops of Tabasco, or to taste
- 20g (¾oz) butter, melted
- freshly ground black pepper

Drain the sardines, reserving 1 tablespoon of the oil. Place the fish in a bowl and mash well with a fork.

Add the onion, parsley, olives, lemon juice, Tabasco, reserved olive oil and half the melted butter. Season with black pepper and mix well.

Press the mixture into 2 ramekins and pour over the remaining butter. Chill for at least 30 minutes before serving. The sardinade will keep in the fridge for up to 3 days.

Midlife Hack: This dish works best with tinned sardines, which are a cheap store-cupboard staple in the Midlife Kitchen. Look for sardines in extra virgin olive oil – it will add to the omega-3 content of your pâté.

Health Tip
Small oily fish like sardines can be eaten whole, which provides maximum nutritional benefit, particularly good for the bones and joints. Sardines are very high in heart-healthy fatty acids, which may also boost the brain and mood.

WHY WE LOVE IT

Uchucuta is the Peruvian equivalent of Argentinian chimichurri – a herby, garlicky sauce usually served with meat. This, however, includes cheese, which makes for a smoother and more complex sauce. In Peru, the cheese of choice is 'queso fresco' (fresh cheese); our nearest cousin is feta. Charring the chillies over a naked flame only takes a moment and introduces a warm, rounded note. The result is pretty fiery, so play around with the amount of chilli to suit your tolerance – we prefer to deseed the charred chillies to turn down the dial a bit.

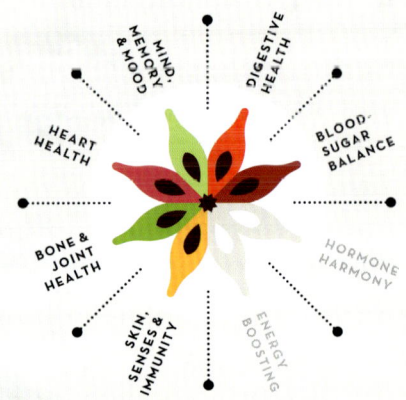

Uchucuta

SERVES 5
MAKES APPROX. 250G (9OZ)

1 long green jalapeño chilli
1 Scotch bonnet chilli
150g (5½oz) feta cheese, crumbled
1 tbsp extra virgin olive oil
2 tbsp natural yogurt
a squeeze of lemon or lime juice
1 garlic clove, peeled and halved
a handful of flat leaf parsley, roughly chopped
a handful of coriander (leaves and stalks), roughly chopped
sea salt flakes and freshly ground black pepper

Cook the chillies under a preheated hot grill until slightly blackened and beginning to soften. Alternatively, using tongs, char over an open flame. Leave to cool, then remove the stalk and deseed, if you prefer a less intense heat.

Put the charred chillies and all the remaining ingredients into a food processor and blitz until smooth. Store in an airtight container in the fridge for up to 3 days.

Try This...
* As a marinade for a whole chicken
* As a fabulous dip for corn chips
* On a baked potato
* As a condiment to slop generously over barbecued meat
* For Uchucuta Pork, see page 178

See photograph on page 229.

Health Tip
The pungent heat of chillies comes from the plant alkaloid capsaicin, which has been shown to have antioxidant and anti-inflammatory properties and can contribute to a lower risk of cancer and heart disease.

WHY WE LOVE IT

We always love finding a new recipe that's healthy, easy and can be made in advance – and this one fits the bill perfectly. Matbucha is a versatile, lightly spiced Israeli tomato salad, usually eaten at room temperature as a side dish, spread or dip. The health heroes here are the tomatoes and red peppers, both of which are rich in lycopene, which protects the skin and supports healthy heart function.

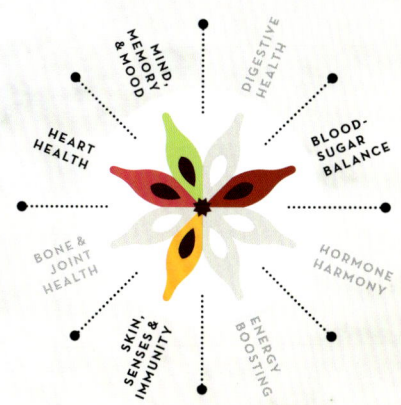

Matbucha

ISRAELI SPICED TOMATO SALSA

SERVES 10
MAKES APPROX. 500G (1LB 2OZ)

- 1 tbsp extra virgin olive oil
- 3 garlic cloves, crushed
- 2 tsp Midlife Spice Mix, see page 24
- a pinch of cayenne pepper
- 5 ripe tomatoes, roughly diced
- 1 large red chilli, deseeded and finely sliced (optional)
- 1 red pepper, cored, deseeded and roughly diced
- sea salt flakes

Heat the olive oil in a saucepan, add the garlic and fry gently for 1 minute, then stir in the spices and fry for a further 2 minutes.

Add the tomatoes, chilli (if using) and the red pepper, then pour in enough water to just cover the mix. Add a pinch of salt and bring to the boil. Reduce the heat to low and simmer gently for 1½ hours, stirring occasionally and adding more water if it becomes too thick. The final consistency should resemble a chunky salsa.

Matbucha is best served at room temperature, but it can be stored in the fridge for up to 3 days.

See photograph on page 229.

Midlife Hack: Matbucha makes an excellent bruschetta topping; try it on some lightly toasted Seedy Soda Bread, see page 209.

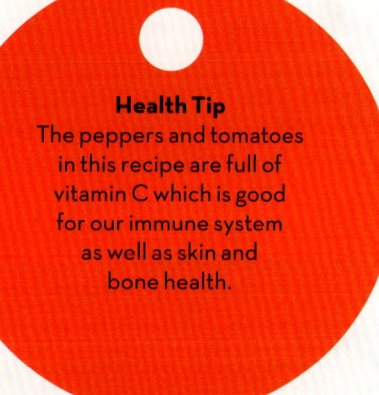

Health Tip
The peppers and tomatoes in this recipe are full of vitamin C which is good for our immune system as well as skin and bone health.

WHY WE LOVE IT

When we discovered 'mole verde', it quickly became a firm favourite at Midlife Central. For a start, it's based on three A* ingredients – broccoli, asparagus and pumpkin seeds – whizzed up with even more top-grade goodness from cumin, olive oil, chilli and a hint of garlic. But it's the flavour that makes this Mexican staple so addictive. It's rich, complex, sweet/savoury and almost nutty, bringing something seriously good to a meal.

Mole Verde

SERVES 6
MAKES APPROX. 500G (1LB 2 OZ)

6 fat asparagus spears, trimmed and roughly chopped

sea salt flakes

50g (1¾oz) pumpkin seeds, plus extra to serve (optional)

1 tsp ground cumin

a pinch of ground cinnamon

2 tbsp olive oil

150g (5½oz) broccoli (including stalks), roughly chopped

1 banana shallot or ½ an onion, diced

225ml (8fl oz) boiling water

a handful of coriander (leaves and stalks), roughly chopped

1 small green chilli, deseeded and roughly chopped

1 garlic clove, peeled and halved

freshly ground black pepper

cumin seeds, to serve (optional)

Cook the asparagus spears in a saucepan of salted boiling water for 1 minute until al dente. Drain, then plunge them into a bowl of cold water (this will help retain their colour). Drain well and pat dry with kitchen paper.

Place the pumpkin seeds, ground cumin and cinnamon in a large, shallow frying pan and dry-fry over a medium heat for 2–3 minutes until the seeds start to colour and pop, taking care not to burn them. Tip into a bowl and set aside.

Heat the olive oil in the pan, add the broccoli, shallot or onion and blanched asparagus and cook for 1 minute, stirring. Add the boiling water and simmer, uncovered, for 5 minutes, then stir in the coriander, chilli, garlic and spiced pumpkin seeds and cook for a further 5 minutes. Season to taste and leave to cool slightly.

Blend the vegetable mixture in a food processor or blender, then pour into a bowl and chill before serving. If you really can't wait, eat it warm from the bowl topped with extra pumpkin seeds and cumin seeds.

Try This...
* As a marinade for chicken
* With grilled meat or prawns
* As a dip with toasted pitta breads

Midlife Hack: With the addition of a little stock this makes a hearty, heart-loving and extremely tasty soup.

Health Tip
Pumpkin seeds, or *pepitas* in Spanish, contain a whole realm of nutrients, including protein, iron, vitamin K, magnesium and zinc – plus fibre and essential fatty acids, which support heart health. They contain phytoestrogens too, which have been found to help reduce menopause symptoms.

WHY WE LOVE IT

The astonishing pink of this raita will bring Midlife brilliance to the side of any plate, thanks to the abundant betacyanin, an antioxidant found in beetroot. The addition of aromatic garam masala, apple and fresh mint add extraordinary depth of flavour and even more nutritional rewards.

Beetroot Raita
WITH APPLE & GARAM MASALA

SERVES 5
MAKES APPROX. 250G (9OZ)

60g (2¼oz) cooked beetroot, finely diced

150g (5½oz) thick Greek yogurt

1 heaped tsp garam masala

a small handful of mint leaves, finely sliced, plus extra to serve

1 tsp lemon juice

½ an apple, cored and grated

sea salt flakes and freshly ground black pepper

Combine all the ingredients in a bowl.

Chill for at least 30 minutes. Scatter with extra chopped mint and serve. The raita will keep in the fridge for up to 2 days.

Midlife Hack: A garam masala grinder, which contains the whole spices, will deliver a potent blast of fresh flavour every time.

Health Tip
Garam masala, a combination of cumin seeds, cinnamon, black pepper, nutmeg, cardamom and cloves, has traditionally been used in Ayurvedic medicine for its health-giving properties; indeed, there is some evidence to suggest it can aid digestion.

WHY WE LOVE IT

Taking a basic, like pesto, and reinventing it in the interests of better health is the name of the game in the Midlife Kitchen. To pimp our pesto we've used walnuts, which are excellent heart helpers, and watercress, a nutritional blockbuster that brings a peppery new bite to an old favourite.

Walnut, Watercress & Pecorino Pesto

SERVES 4 (WITH PASTA)

50g (1¾oz) walnut pieces

1 small garlic clove, peeled and halved

2 tbsp extra virgin olive oil

zest and juice of ½ a lemon

150g (5½oz) watercress, rinsed

30g (1oz) Pecorino cheese, grated

a small pinch of sea salt flakes

freshly ground black pepper

Put all the ingredients into a food processor and blitz to a coarse consistency.

Best served stirred through pasta the same day it's made, while the pesto is at its freshest.

Health Tip
Watercress is particularly nutrient-dense and contains magnesium, iron and fibre that could boost bone, heart and cognitive health.

WHY WE LOVE IT

This great pesto boasts gutsy powerhouse nutrients – from pumpkin, nuts, citrus and sage – which are all high in vitamins and antioxidants to help protect against colds and flu. Think of it as an immunity booster, to adorn an everyday pasta with good-for-you glory.

Pumpkin, Pecan & Sage Pesto

SERVES 6 (WITH PASTA)

50g (1¾oz) pecan nuts

50g (1¾oz) pumpkin seeds

200g (7oz) canned pumpkin purée

30g (1oz) Parmesan cheese, grated

juice of 1 lemon

1 tbsp extra virgin olive oil

sea salt flakes and freshly ground black pepper

10 sage leaves, finely sliced

Put the pecans and pumpkin seeds into a food processor and blitz to a coarse crumb. Add the pumpkin purée, Parmesan, lemon juice and olive oil and blitz again.

Transfer to a bowl, season and stir in the thin slivers of sage.

Serve stirred through your favourite pasta. The pesto can be stored in the fridge for up to 2 days.

Try This...
* On wholewheat linguine, topped with extra Parmesan and herbs
* As a filling for homemade ravioli, drizzled with warm sage butter

Health Tip
Pecans, along with walnuts, contain the highest antioxidant value of all edible nuts, and provide healthy fats to benefit the heart and brain. A recent study found that people who eat nuts daily are 20 per cent more likely to live longer (and are slimmer too).

MIDLIFE EXTRAS

WHY WE LOVE IT

If we had to shut our eyes and jot down the Midlife Kitchen's top-performing ingredients, the list would look a lot like...this recipe for Salsa Verde! Parsley is clearly the main event here, bolstered by a supporting cast of goodness from the apple cider vinegar, lemon juice, anchovies, mustard and garlic, resulting in a bold and brilliant spoonful. Purists argue that every ingredient in a salsa verde should be chopped by hand. Be our guest. If pushed for time, though, blitz away; you'll still get an authentic sauce – it will just be a little more uniform in texture.

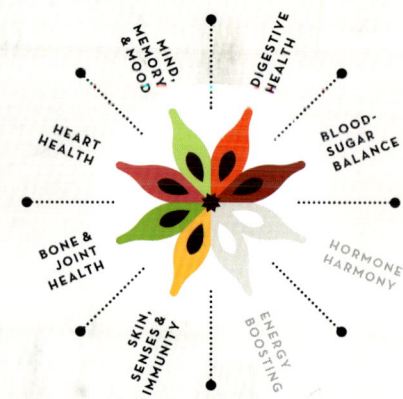

Midlife Salsa Verde

SERVES 4
MAKES APPROX. 200G (7OZ)

a large handful of parsley
4 anchovy fillets, rinsed
1 tbsp capers, rinsed
1 garlic clove, peeled and quartered
4 tbsp extra virgin olive oil
1 tbsp lemon juice
grated zest of ½ a lemon
1 tsp apple cider vinegar
2 tsp Dijon mustard
freshly ground black pepper

Finely chop the parsley, anchovies, capers and garlic by hand, which gives a sauce with more texture, then transfer to a bowl. Add the olive oil, lemon juice and zest, vinegar and mustard and season with plenty of pepper.

Alternatively, blitz all the ingredients in a food processor. It's best served fresh, when the green colour is most vivid, but it will keep in the fridge for a couple of days.

Try This...
* As a dip for crusty bread
* Dolloped on to a baked sweet potato
* Drizzled over new potatoes
* Served with scrambled eggs
* The classic Italian way, served alongside grilled or poached fish

See photograph on page 237.

Midlife Hack: This also works well with other soft herbs, such as mint, tarragon or basil.

Health Tip
Parsley is a good source of vitamins A, C and K, plus folate and iron – delivering bags of goodies to support immunity, bones, joints and skin. But why stop there? It's also loaded with phytochemicals, flavonoids and antioxidants.

WHY WE LOVE IT

Of all the lovely foods we have discovered in Bali this is our absolute favourite. It's the ultimate pick-me-up for any simply grilled piece of meat or fish – a heady combination of lemon grass, chilli, lime and terasi shrimp paste, the Indonesian equivalent of Thai fish sauce (which you can use instead, if terasi eludes you).

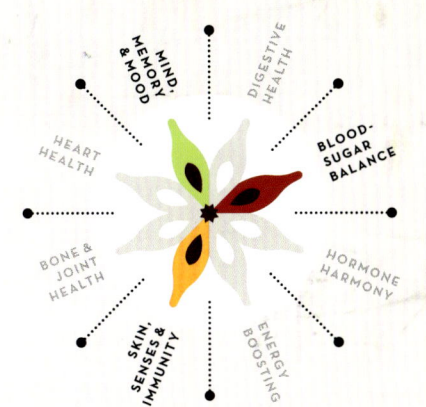

Sambal Matah

SERVES 3
MAKES APPROX. 150G (5½OZ)

- 3–4 shallots, peeled and finely chopped
- 1 spring onion, finely chopped
- 2 small red chillies, deseeded and finely chopped
- 2 lemon grass stalks, tough outer layers removed, finely minced
- ½ tsp terasi shrimp paste or Thai fish sauce (nam pla)
- 2 tbsp olive oil
- juice of 2 limes
- a pinch of sea salt flakes

Combine all the ingredients in a bowl. Leave to stand for 10 minutes or so to allow the flavours to marry.

Serve at room temperature.

Try This….
* Served with grilled sardines or any oily fish
* Alongside barbecued meat
* Simply spooned over wholegrain rice

See photograph on page 237.

Midlife Hack: Authentic dried terasi (also known as belacan) can be found in Asian supermarkets and needs to be fried before use. You can also buy shrimp paste in a jar, which is ready to use; just be sure to check the instructions before you embark.

Health Tip
Lemon grass, beyond having the most gorgeous aroma, has antibacterial and anti-inflammatory properties. Onions are also a useful source of prebiotics which can improve our gut microbiome diversity.

WHY WE LOVE IT

A light, bright, pretty salsa, which will happily jazz up a simple piece of grilled fish. We love it with smoked mackerel, grilled sardines or pan-fried trout.

Radish, Cucumber & Herb Salsa

SERVES 4
MAKES APPROX. 200G (7OZ)

150g (5½oz) salad radishes, finely diced

¼ of a cucumber, finely diced

a handful of mint leaves, finely chopped

a handful of coriander leaves, finely chopped

1 spring onion, finely diced

juice of 1 lime

sea salt flakes and freshly ground black pepper

Combine all the ingredients in a bowl and serve.

Health Tip
Radishes are packed with a dizzying array of plant-based antioxidant compounds which can protect our cells from damage, provide heart healthy benefits and potentially reduce our risk of cancer.

STRAWBERRY SALSA WITH AVOCADO & GREEN CHILLI

ZEHUG

MIDLIFE SALSA VERDE

RADISH, CUCUMBER & HERB SALSA

SAMBAL MATAH

WHY WE LOVE IT

Who can resist anything with 'hug' in the name? This delicious, fresh relish is originally from Yemen and positively explodes with the flavours of the Middle East. It takes mere minutes to make, and promises to transform a simple piece of fish, chicken or meat into something really rather special.

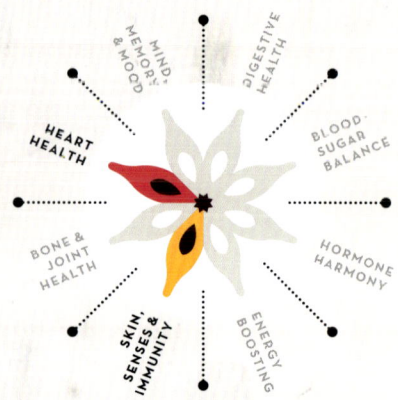

Zehug

CORIANDER, CHILLI & TOMATO RELISH

SERVES 5–6
MAKES APPROX. 250–300G (9OZ–10½OZ)

2 cloves

5 cardamom pods, crushed

1 garlic clove, crushed

3 tbsp extra virgin olive oil

1 ripe tomato, diced

1 green chilli, finely diced, including seeds

a large handful of coriander leaves, roughly chopped

½ tsp ground cumin

½ tsp cumin seeds

sea salt flakes and freshly ground black pepper

Place the cloves and the seeds from the cardamom pods into a pestle and mortar and crush to release their aroma.

Tip the crushed seeds into a bowl, add the remaining ingredients and season. Mix well, then cover with clingfilm and leave to steep in the fridge for about 30 minutes before serving. It's best eaten immediately.

See photograph on page 237.

Midlife Hack: Deseeding cardamom pods means that you'll get a fresher flavour; simply smash the pods to release the black seeds within.

Health Tip
Some studies have shown that coriander may help lower blood sugar levels. While more research is needed, it certainly can't hurt to include it in your diet.

WHY WE LOVE IT

Good old-fashioned apple sauce is a fantastic sweetener which has staged a comeback in the Midlife Kitchen. Eat it straight from the pot for an immediate sweet fix, spread it on a crêpe or stir it into porridge or yogurt (see Apple Strudel Yogurt on page 52). Date syrup will give you a rich, dark caramel colour, rather than the insipid pale-green of a shop-bought apple sauce.

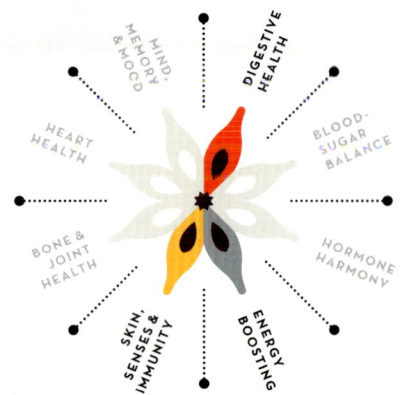

Midlife Apple Sauce

MAKES APPROX. 500G (1LB 2OZ)

2 Bramley apples, about 500g (1lb 2oz) in total, peeled, cored and roughly chopped

2 tbsp water

1 tsp ground cinnamon

2 cloves

2–3 tbsp Midlife Sweetener, see page 31, or 2 tbsp date syrup or maple syrup

Place all the ingredients in a saucepan and bring to a simmer, stirring. When the mixture begins to bubble, reduce the heat and cook gently, stirring occasionally, until the apples have disintegrated.

Remove the pan from the heat and give it a good stir to make a smooth sauce, or leave it chunkier if you prefer. Leave to cool, then chill. The sauce will keep in the fridge for up to a week.

Midlife Hack: This is easier still if you cook it in the microwave – just give it 2–3 minutes, covered, on full power. Make a batch, cool and then freeze in ice-cube trays; it defrosts in minutes for a quick breakfast bonus.

Health Tip

Apples really are nutritional superstars. In numerous epidemiological studies, they have been associated with a decreased risk of chronic diseases, such as cardiovascular disease, asthma and diabetes, which may be due to their high antioxidant activity.

WHY WE LOVE IT

Our Caramel Sauce delivers all the unctuous gooeyness of a traditional toffee sauce, but (amazingly) with no butter at all, and coconut sugar replacing the usual caster. Of course, sugar is sugar whatever the form – and we all know that eating too much of it is no good thing; but coconut sugar does have a lower GI score than conventional table sugar, which means less of a blood-sugar spike when you do choose to indulge.

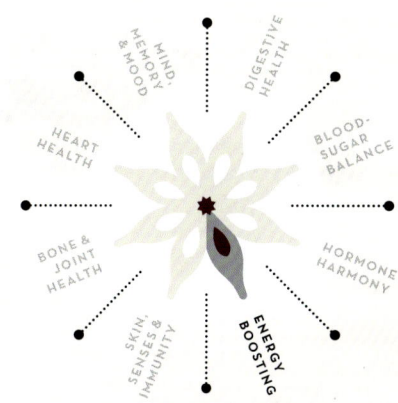

Caramel Sauce

SERVES 2

50g (1¾oz) coconut sugar

a splash of water

50ml (2fl oz) coconut milk

½ tsp vanilla extract

a pinch of sea salt flakes (optional)

Mix the coconut sugar with a splash of water in a small saucepan, then bring to a simmer. Add the coconut milk, vanilla and salt (if using); bring to a simmer and cook for 10 minutes, stirring occasionally, until the sauce is reduced and darkened.

Leave to cool slightly, then chill – it benefits from 30 minutes in the fridge to thicken before serving, but it can also be served warm. The sauce will keep in the fridge for up to a week.

Try This...
* With Midlife Sticky Toffee Puddings, see page 262
* Swirled into porridge
* As an alternative to date syrup to sweeten Apple Strudel Yogurt, see page 52

Health Tip
Coconut sugar tastes similar to brown sugar, but contains some nutrients and has a lower GI score. This sauce is slightly less sweet than conventional toffee sauces, but a spoonful still goes a long way...

MIDLIFE EXTRAS   **245**

GOOD SWEET STUFF

WHY WE LOVE IT

This gorgeous spiced syrup would work with any fruit you have to hand, but we love it with a combination of delicate white and pale-green exotic fruit. The crushed coriander seeds are a revelation, bringing an aromatic burst to every bite. The xylitol is an experiment for us; we're always keen to find natural sugar substitutes that deliver sweetness without a chemical aftertaste, and here we think it works really well. If in doubt, substitute a light clear honey, such as acacia.

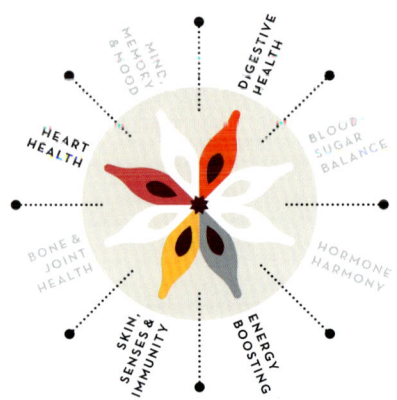

White Fruit Salad
WITH CORIANDER SEED & LIME SYRUP

SERVES 4

1 nashi pear

1 apple

½ a white dragon fruit, peeled

2 mangosteen, peeled and segmented

10 fresh or canned lychees

10 white seedless grapes

FOR THE SYRUP

juice of 2 limes

2 tbsp xylitol or runny acacia honey

2 tsp coriander seeds, crushed

2 cloves

a grind of vanilla bean, see page 211, or the seeds from a pod

Place all the syrup ingredients in a small saucepan, bring to a simmer and cook for 5 minutes until reduced and slightly thickened. Leave to cool, then chill in the fridge.

Peel, quarter and core the pear and apple, then cut all the fruit into bite-sized pieces and place in serving bowls. Dress liberally with the fragrant chilled syrup and serve.

Midlife Hack: Some of the fruits we use can be tricky to find, so substitute fruits of your choice – for example, white melon or pear.

Health Tip
Xylitol is a natural substance extracted from corn cobs or birch bark – it has the same sweetness as sugar, but 40 per cent fewer calories, a lower GI and it won't damage your teeth. It even feeds friendly microbes in the gut.

WHY WE LOVE IT

Most of the fruit salad ingredients are store-cupboard items that, with the addition of ricotta and oranges, can be transformed into this delicious, decadent dessert in a matter of minutes. It's a grown-up mouthful – not overly sweet, richly spiced and darkly aromatic, like Christmas in a bowl.

Warm Winter Fruit Salad
WITH ORANGE RICOTTA

SERVES 4–6

- 80g (2¾oz) soft dried apricots
- 80g (2¾oz) soft dried figs
- 60g (2½oz) soft prunes
- 60g (2½oz) dried pears
- 60g (2½oz) dried cherries
- 30g (1oz) dried cranberries
- 60g (2½oz) ready-cooked and peeled chestnuts from a packet
- 300ml (½ pint) Earl Grey tea
- juice of 1 orange
- 2 strips of orange peel, each about 7cm (2¾in) long
- 1 cinnamon stick, broken in 2
- 2 star anise

FOR THE ORANGE RICOTTA

- 100g (3½oz) ricotta cheese
- 2 tsp orange zest
- 1 tbsp fresh orange juice

Place all the fruit salad ingredients in a large saucepan, bring to a simmer and cook, uncovered, for 10 minutes until the fruit has plumped up. Remove the fruit from the pan and set aside.

Return the pan to the heat and simmer the liquid for a further 5 minutes until reduced, then pour over the fruit and leave to cool.

Meanwhile, combine all the orange ricotta ingredients in a bowl.

Serve the warm fruit salad with the orange ricotta on the side.

Midlife Hack: Remove the star anise and cinnamon stick and pulse the cooled fruit in a food processor or blender to make a gorgeous healthy marmalade to stir into your morning yogurt, or a great chutney to serve alongside a good strong Cheddar.

Health Tip
Dried fruit is a good source of iron, is nutrient dense and a convenient source of fibre, excellent for digestive health.

GOOD SWEET STUFF

WHY WE LOVE IT

Simple, fresh, healthy and interesting – you'll know by now that these are our watchwords in the Midlife Kitchen, and this ingenious idea is all of those things. Include anything from your fruit bowl and experiment – the spring rolls are great pepped up with a hint of finely sliced chilli, or with soft herbs such as mint or basil. Nuts, seeds and dried fruit add another dimension.

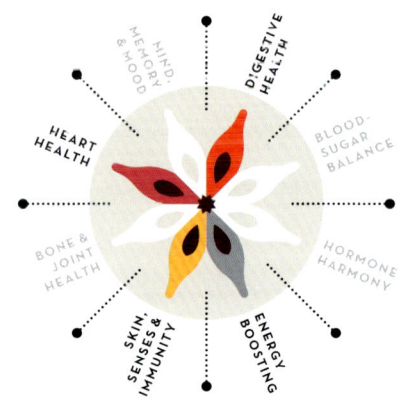

Fresh Fruit Spring Rolls

MAKES 6 ROLLS

FOR THE ROLLS

2 or 3 strawberries, sliced
½ kiwifruit, peeled and sliced
½ banana, peeled and sliced
a few pieces of pineapple, chopped
a few pieces of mango, chopped
6 rice paper wrappers
warm water
a few mint leaves, finely sliced
6 walnut halves, chopped
3 Medjool dates, pitted and chopped
2 tsp desiccated coconut
1 tsp finely grated lime zest

FOR THE DIPPING SAUCE

juice of 3 limes
1 tbsp runny honey, maple syrup or date syrup
1 star anise

Combine all the dipping sauce ingredients in a small bowl and set aside.

Pat the prepared fruit dry with kitchen paper to prevent the rolls becoming too slippery.

Lay a rice paper wrapper on a chopping board. Using a pastry brush, moisten the sheet lightly with warm water so that it softens. Place some of the fruit on the top third or so of the wrapper and scatter with your choice of the remaining ingredients (our 3 favourite combos are mango, pineapple, desiccated coconut and lime zest; strawberry, kiwi and mint; banana, walnut and date).

Taking the top edge of the wrapper, fold it down over the filling. Fold the edges in from the left and right and keep rolling up, tucking in the edges as you go, as if you are wrapping a present. It takes a little practice, but aim to create a fairly tight cylinder. Repeat with the remaining ingredients to make 6 rolls.

Serve immediately, doused with plenty of dipping sauce.

Health Tip
The NHS recommends that we eat five 80g (2¾oz) portions of a variety of fruit and vegetables every day as they are an excellent source of vitamins, minerals and fibre. These fresh fruit rolls are a delicious way to do it.

WHY WE LOVE IT

This is a glorious pot of plummy flavour and nutty crunch. The secret to a good crumble is a really crisp topping – guaranteed with our Midlife Grown-up Granola, which doesn't just deliver crunch and speed, but is also full of stealth health from the Brazils, almonds, cashews, oats and amaranth. Serve with warm plum juice for an autumn treat.

Elderflower & Granola Plumble

SERVES 2

350g (12oz) fresh or frozen plums or damsons, halved and stoned

1 tbsp elderflower cordial

1 tbsp maple syrup

a grind of vanilla bean, see page 211, or the seeds from a pod

4–6 tbsp Midlife Grown-up Granola, see page 29

1 tbsp coconut flakes (optional)

2 tsp demerara sugar (optional)

Preheat the oven to 180°C (350°F)/Gas Mark 4.

Place the plums or damsons in a saucepan, add the elderflower cordial, maple syrup and vanilla, bring to a simmer and cook for 5 minutes until the plums are just beginning to soften.

Use a slotted spoon to divide the warm plums between 2 ramekins or a small copper pan (pictured), leaving any extra juice to serve on the side. The plums should be moist, but not swimming in liquid.

Cover the fruit with the granola and sprinkle with the coconut flakes and sugar, if using.

Bake for 15 minutes until the tops are golden brown, toasty and crunchy, and the fruit is bubbling through. Serve with the reserved juice on the side.

Health Tip
Thanks to their high vitamin C content, plums fortify the immune system (useful, as autumn chills generally arrive at the same time as the plum glut). Vit C will also assist iron absorption in the body, which helps boost energy as the days get shorter.

WHY WE LOVE IT

This delicate dessert makes a lovely light end to a meal. The tender pears sit prettily in a honeyed syrup, with ginger and cardamom lending a warm bass-note buzz. Add a drizzle of melted dark chocolate for a more indulgent pud.

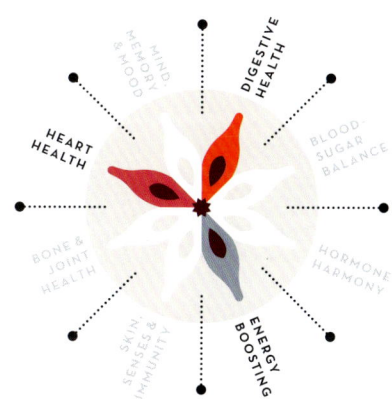

Drenched Cardamom & Ginger Pears

WITH AMARETTI & ALMOND CRUMB

SERVES 4

750ml (1¼ pint) perry or cider

6 cardamom pods, crushed

a thumb-sized piece of fresh root ginger, peeled and sliced

1 cinnamon stick, broken in half

1 strip of lemon peel, about 6cm (2½in) long

2 tbsp runny acacia honey

4 firm but just ripe Comice or Williams pears

a squeeze of lemon juice

TO SERVE

50g (1¾oz) dark chocolate, melted (optional)

a handful of almonds, with skins on, thinly sliced

2 Amaretti biscuits, crushed

Put the perry or cider, cardamom, ginger, cinnamon stick, lemon peel and honey into a deep, lidded saucepan and bring to the boil, then reduce the heat and simmer for 5–10 minutes, stirring occasionally.

Meanwhile, peel the pears, leaving the stalks intact, then squeeze with a little lemon juice to prevent discolouration.

Lay the pears on their sides in the poaching liquid, cover with a lid and simmer for 20–30 minutes (the timing will depend on the pear variety and ripeness), turning occasionally, until evenly poached and softened. The thickest part of each pear should be tender when pierced with a sharp knife. Remove the pears from the pan, place in a bowl and leave to cool, then transfer to the fridge.

Return the pan to the heat and bring the poaching liquid to a strong simmer and cook for 10 minutes until reduced by about half. Pour the syrup over the pears and leave to cool, then chill in the fridge for an hour or more.

When ready to serve the pears, add a drizzle of melted dark chocolate (if using), and scatter with almond slivers and crushed Amaretti.

Health Tip
In addition to dispensing a good dose of antioxidants and potassium, pears contain soluble fibre (pectin) which can help aide digestion.

WHY WE LOVE IT

'"A Handful of Blueberries Can Improve Memory in Older Adults" – it's a stark headline, and well worth remembering next time you're planning what's for dessert. A fruit soup sounds oddly anachronistic, but a Blueberry Gazpacho? Irresistible. A garnish of black pepper really does work – give it a go – while edible flowers are gorgeously pointless. Never underestimate the power of pretty.

Blueberry Gazpacho

SERVES 4

- 300g (10½oz) fresh or frozen blueberries
- 200g (7oz) fresh or frozen raspberries
- 3 tbsp date syrup
- a splash of water
- juice of 2 oranges
- grated zest of 1 orange
- 1 tbsp lemon juice
- a grind of vanilla bean, see page 211, or the seeds from a pod

TO SERVE (OPTIONAL)

- freshly ground black pepper
- edible flowers

Place half the berries in a saucepan with the date syrup and a splash of water, bring to a simmer and cook for 3 minutes until the berries burst and release their juices. Remove from the heat, leave to cool, then chill.

Put the remaining berries into a food processor or blender with the orange juice and zest, lemon juice and vanilla. Blitz until smooth, then combine with the chilled cooked berries.

Chill again, then serve with a grind of black pepper and edible flowers.

Midlife Hack: For a sensational sorbet, freeze this gazpacho mix, stirring occasionally with a fork to break up the ice crystals. Strawberries and blackcurrants work well in this gazpacho too.

Health Tip
A 2009 study found that cooking blueberries for a short burst, as we do here, increases antioxidant activity, probably because it breaks down cell walls.

WHY WE LOVE IT

Who doesn't love cheesecake? Sam loves it so much that she had one as her wedding cake, so it was a top priority for us to devise a healthier way to enjoy this divine dessert. Our version is lightened with ricotta and yogurt and underpinned by a nutty base – with pumpkin purée, fresh ginger and cinnamon as the Midlife trump cards. The result is a rather spectacular and wholesome centrepiece, great for any get-together.

Pumpkin & Ginger Cheesecake

WITH HONEY & FRESH RASPBERRIES

SERVES 8

125g (4½oz) Midlife LSA, see page 27, or ground almonds

2 tsp ground ginger

75g (2¾oz) Medjool dates, pitted and finely chopped

2 tbsp coconut oil, melted if solid

1 egg white, lightly whisked

a handful of fresh raspberries, to serve

FOR THE FILLING

250g (9oz) ricotta cheese

150g (5½oz) thick Greek yogurt

400g (14oz) can pumpkin purée (100 per cent pumpkin)

60ml (4 tbsp) runny honey, plus extra to serve

2 large eggs

2 tbsp lemon juice

2 tsp ground cinnamon

1 tbsp peeled and finely grated fresh root ginger

Preheat the oven to 180°C (350°F)/Gas Mark 4. Line a 20cm (8in) springform cake tin with greaseproof paper.

To make the base, combine the LSA or ground almonds, ground ginger, dates and coconut oil in a bowl. Mix well, using your fingers to create a crumb, ensuring the dates are evenly distributed. Press the mixture firmly into the bottom of the prepared tin, then brush it with egg white (this keeps the base layer crisp) and bake for 10 minutes. Remove from the oven and leave to cool completely.

Reduce the oven temperature to 160°C (325°F)/Gas Mark 3.

To make the filling, put the ricotta cheese into a food processor or blender and whizz until completely smooth. Add the remaining filling ingredients and blend until combined.

Pour the filling over the cooled base, then bake for 50 minutes until the cheesecake is cooked through but still has a bit of a wobble in the middle. Turn off the oven, leaving the cake inside to cool completely. Transfer to the fridge and chill for at least 2 hours to firm up.

To serve, remove the cheesecake from the tin, place on a serving dish and top with the raspberries. Drizzle with honey just before serving. This cheesecake is deliberately not overly sweet so, for those with a sweeter tooth, serve with a little extra honey on the side.

Health Tip
This recipe is lower in sugar and saturated fat than most other cheesecakes, yet here you won't be compromising on taste.

GOOD SWEET STUFF

WHY WE LOVE IT

A 10-minute mini marvel, these little puddings are completely fat-free, with the sweetness coming from our favourite Medjool dates. You get a real lift from the whisked egg white, resulting in a very light but wonderfully sticky mouthful.

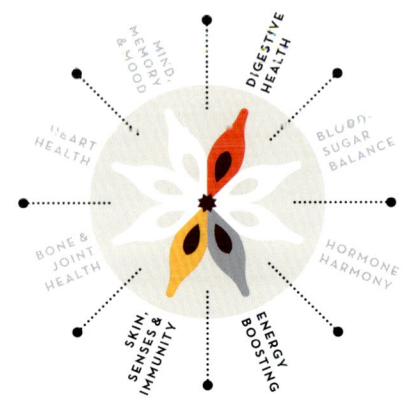

Midlife Sticky Toffee Puddings

SERVES 4

175g (6oz) Medjool dates, pitted

175ml (6fl oz) water

2 tbsp maple syrup

1 tsp vanilla extract

2 large eggs, separated

85g (3oz) self-raising flour

a pinch of sea salt flakes

1 tsp bicarbonate of soda

4 tbsp date syrup

Health Tip
Dates are a great source of gut-friendly fibre - plus iron which helps support the immune system.

Preheat the oven to 160°C (325°F)/Gas Mark 3.

Place the dates and water in a saucepan and bring to a simmer, then cook for 3-4 minutes until softened. Leave to cool slightly, then transfer to a food processor or blender, add the maple syrup and vanilla extract and blitz until almost smooth. Tip into a bowl and stir in the egg yolks. Sift in the flour, add the salt and bicarbonate of soda and stir well.

Whisk the egg whites in a clean bowl until stiff peaks form, then fold into the date mixture, ensuring they are fully incorporated.

Put 1 tablespoon of the date syrup into each of 4 pudding moulds or ramekins, then divide the mixture between them. Transfer the moulds to a roasting tin and pour hot water into the tin to reach halfway up the moulds.

Bake for 25-30 minutes, or until a skewer inserted into the puddings comes out clean (the timing will depend on the depth of the moulds or ramekins). Run a knife around the edge of the moulds, then invert the puddings on to individual plates. Serve immediately.

These puddings don't require any extra sweetness, but if you're keen to add a sauce, try our Caramel Sauce (pictured), see page 245.

WHY WE LOVE IT

This is the kind of pudding to serve straight from oven to table, so that picky fingers can get at the sticky edges as a stand-in for seconds. It's a take on a crumble, of course – but this streusel version is made in a shallow dish with the topping in clusters, delivering a crisp crunch over a layer of oozy black fruit, which manages the clever Midlife trick of being both healthy and opulent in equal measure. Our Power Porridge mix brings LSA and oat bran to the table, nuts and seeds add their health dividend, and date syrup stands in for much of the sugar in a conventional crumble topping.

Black & Blue Berry Streusel

SERVES 8

100g (3½oz) butter, melted

75g (2¾oz) Midlife Power Porridge, see page 28, or jumbo oats

40g (1½oz) flaked almonds

30g (1oz) sunflower seeds

70g (2½oz) wholemeal flour

1 tsp ground cinnamon

50g (1¾oz) soft light brown sugar

3 tbsp date syrup

300g (10½oz) fresh or frozen blackberries

200g (7oz) fresh or frozen blueberries

Preheat the oven to 180°C (350°F)/Gas Mark 4.

For the streusel topping, mix all the ingredients, except the berries, in a large bowl.

Place the berries in a single layer in a shallow baking dish and scatter with the topping. Place it in clusters rather than trying to cover all of the fruit, to form a patchwork of streusel and berries.

Bake for 20–25 minutes until the fruit is sticky and bubbling and the topping is crisp.

Midlife Hack: You can make this with fresh or frozen fruit; if you're raiding the freezer, a handful of frozen black cherries, black plums or blackcurrants could easily be added to bump up the berry bonanza.

Health Tip
Blackberries, like all dark berries, are among the healthiest fruit, thanks to their plant pigments. A study for the American Cancer Society found that those who eat the most berries are significantly less likely to die from cardiovascular disease.

GOOD SWEET STUFF

WHY WE LOVE IT

Deliciously decadent, and not a drop of double cream in sight! This quickie mousse uses natural yogurt for its voluptuous creaminess, and whisked egg whites for lift. Yes, there's some sugar – use 3 tablespoons if you prefer a truly dark spoonful, or 4 if you have a sweet tooth. Do serve in small bowls or glasses, though; this is surprisingly rich and indulgent and will easily satisfy six chocoholics.

Five-minute Chocolate Mousse

SERVES 6

200g (7oz) dark chocolate (70% cocoa solids), broken into pieces

4 egg whites

3-4 tbsp caster sugar, to taste

150g (5½oz) natural yogurt

fresh raspberries, to serve

Melt the chocolate in a heatproof bowl set over a saucepan of gently simmering water, making sure the bowl does not touch the water, stirring occasionally. Alternatively, melt the chocolate in a microwave. Leave to cool slightly.

Meanwhile, whisk the egg whites in a clean bowl until stiff peaks form. Gently fold in the sugar, a spoonful at a time.

Mix the yogurt into the melted chocolate (it will start to thicken immediately, so work fairly quickly), then fold in the egg white mixture, a third at a time.

Spoon the mousse into 6 small bowls or glasses and serve immediately or chill to serve later (we give you 5 minutes!). Serve with fresh raspberries and small spoons.

Health Tip
According to a study by the University of Copenhagen, dark chocolate is far more satisfying than milk chocolate, lessening our cravings for sweet, salty and fatty foods. It's also a source of iron.

WHY WE LOVE IT

Let's face it, there are times when only cake will do. But not all cakes are created equal; with a bit of Midlife manipulation, they can be a healthy indulgence, particularly when the quantity of sugar is limited and the main ingredients are, instead, yogurt, olive oil and almonds. This moist, golden cake works well as a dessert, served warm with a dollop of yogurt, slivers of almond and fresh orange segments.

Yogurt, Almond & Orange Drizzle Cake

MAKES 8 SMALL CAKES OR 1 LARGE CAKE

- 150g (5½oz) natural yogurt
- 150g (5½oz) ground almonds
- 150g (5½oz) self-raising flour
- 75g (2¾) soft brown sugar
- 100ml (3½fl oz) olive oil
- 3 eggs
- 1 tsp vanilla extract
- 1 tbsp clear honey
- 1 tsp saffron threads, soaked in 1 tsp boiling water
- grated zest of 1 orange
- 2 tsp baking powder
- a pinch of sea salt flakes
- a grating of nutmeg

FOR THE SYRUP

- juice of 2 oranges
- 1 tbsp runny honey

Preheat the oven to 170°C (340°F)/Gas Mark 3½. Line an 8-hole mini loaf tin with individual cases, or use a nonstick liner in a 450g (1lb) loaf tin.

Combine all the ingredients either using a stand mixer or hand-held mixer and beat well to form a smooth batter. Pour the mixture into the prepared tin and bake for 30 minutes for small cases or 40–45 minutes for a large loaf, until firm and golden and a skewer inserted into the centre comes out clean.

To make the syrup, heat the orange juice and honey in a small saucepan over a low heat.

Remove the cake or cakes from the oven, pierce a few times with a skewer and drizzle with the honey syrup. Leave to cool in the tin. Serve warm or at room temperature, with a spoonful of yogurt, almond slivers or fresh orange segments.

Try This...

Replace the saffron, orange zest and nutmeg with:

* the grated zest of 1 lemon, 1 teaspoon of poppy seeds and drizzle with a lemon and honey syrup
* 2 tablespoons crushed pistachios, the zest of 1 lime, a grind of vanilla bean, or the seeds from a vanilla pod, and drizzle with a lime and honey syrup

Midlife Hack: If you are gluten intolerant, this cake works with 300g (10½oz) ground almonds – you'll just get a denser crumb.

Health Tip

Swapping half of the flour in a regular cake recipe for ground almonds doesn't just bring flavour and texture: there's protein in those nutritious little nuts, plus vitamin E and magnesium.

WHY WE LOVE IT

The perfect antidote to those pale and sugary fairy cakes that make your teeth ache, this devilishly dark ginger cake packs a real punch, thanks to its mighty trio of gingers: ground, fresh and stem. A slick of black treacle and warming spices add more depth, and, while the hint of chilli is optional, it's well worth adding if you like a full-on flavour sensation. The upshot is a very grown-up cake, best eaten in small, sticky, sumptuous squares – perhaps on a cold day with a strong cup of tea and a smile on your face.

Three-ginger Fire Cake

MAKES ABOUT 16 SQUARES

- 50g (1¾oz) butter
- 100g (3½oz) black treacle
- 100g (3½oz) date syrup
- 80g (2¾oz) dark muscovado sugar
- 60ml (4 tbsp) milk
- 60g (2¼oz) stem ginger, roughly chopped
- 1 egg, beaten
- 2 tsp peeled and grated fresh root ginger
- 200g (7oz) self-raising flour
- 5 tsp ground ginger
- 1 tsp ground cinnamon
- 1 tsp allspice
- 1 tsp chilli powder, or less to taste (optional)
- a pinch of sea salt flakes
- 1 tsp bicarbonate of soda
- 2 tbsp stem ginger syrup (from the stem ginger jar)

Preheat the oven to 160°C (325°F)/Gas Mark 3. Line a baking tin, about 30 x 30cm (12 x 12in), with nonstick baking paper.

Place the butter, treacle, syrup and sugar in a large saucepan and melt over a medium heat, stirring gently to combine. Remove the pan from the heat and leave to cool slightly.

Add the milk and stem ginger, then stir in the beaten egg and root ginger. Sift all the dry ingredients into the mixture and combine.

Spoon the mixture into the prepared tin and bake for 30–35 minutes until cooked through and a skewer inserted in the centre comes out clean. While still warm and in the tin, prick the cake a dozen times with a skewer, then spoon the stem ginger syrup over the top. Leave to cool.

Cut into 16 smallish squares to serve. Store in an airtight container for up to a week.

Health Tip
Gingerol, the main bioactive compound in ginger, is thought to have immunity-boosting, anti-inflammatory and antioxidant effects.

WHY WE LOVE IT

This book is, of course, devoted to healthy eating in midlife, with the explicit aim of living longer... But we reckon there's little point living longer if there's no cake in your life. So, one of our prime preoccupations at the Midlife Kitchen has been to develop cake recipes that taste truly scrumptious, but don't serve up a mouthful of guilt with every bite. This moist cake easily made the cut: familiar, comforting and tasty, but we've kept the butter and sugar quota to a minimum, while the introduction of apples, cranberries and spicing brings a happy health hit to teatime.

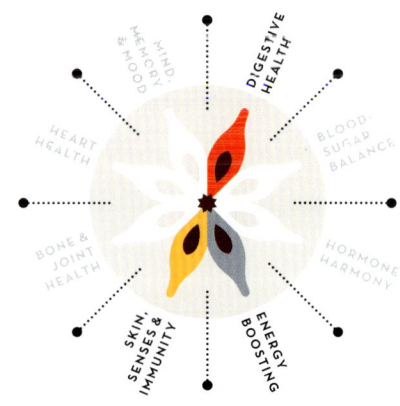

Spiced Apple & Cranberry Cake

MAKES A 20CM (8IN) CAKE

200g (7oz) self-raising flour

2 tsp ground cinnamon

a grating of nutmeg

a grind of vanilla bean, see page 211, or the seeds from a pod

1 tsp baking powder

a pinch of sea salt flakes

100g (3½oz) cold butter, diced

100g (3½oz) soft light brown sugar

2 eggs, beaten

125ml (4fl oz) milk

½ tsp vanilla extract

225g (8oz) Bramley apples, peeled, cored and roughly diced into 2cm (¾in) cubes

80g (2¾oz) dried cranberries

2 tbsp sunflower seeds

1 tsp demerara sugar

Midlife Apple Sauce, see page 244, to serve (optional)

Preheat the oven to 160°C (325°F)/Gas Mark 3. Line a 20cm (8in) diameter springform cake tin with nonstick baking paper.

Place the flour, cinnamon, nutmeg, grind of vanilla bean, baking powder and salt in a food processor. Add the diced butter and pulse until the mixture resembles fine breadcrumbs. Add the soft brown sugar and pulse again.

Whisk the eggs, milk and vanilla extract in a jug, then pour into the processor and pulse to form a smooth, thick batter. Add the chopped apples to the batter with the cranberries and stir to combine (without breaking down the apples too much).

Spoon the mixture into the prepared tin and scatter with the sunflower seeds and demerara sugar. Bake for 40 minutes until golden brown and a skewer inserted in the centre comes out clean.

Leave to cool in the tin for a few minutes, then transfer to a wire rack. Serve warm or at room temperature, perhaps with Midlife Apple Sauce on the side. Store in an airtight container for up to 3 days.

Midlife Hack: Add a handful of frozen cranberries to the Midlife Apple Sauce recipe for a tart, pink, pretty accompaniment to this cake.

Health Tip
Apples are, as we all know, super shots of fibre – but they also contain numerous potent phytochemicals, including quercetin and catechins, which studies have found can help reduce risk of chronic disease risk, particularly cardiovascular disease, asthma and type 2 diabetes.

WHY WE LOVE IT

We're quite partial to a slice of carrot cake – but our enjoyment is always tempered by the knowledge that there's nothing particularly healthy about it (apart from the word 'carrot' in the title). So, we set ourselves the task of coming up with a truly healthy carrot cake for the Midlife Kitchen: all the magic of the cake, but with the nutritional value bumped up, the sat fats reduced and portion control built in. Using Midlife Power Porridge brings our nutty LSA into the mix, while the oats, carrots, walnuts and cinnamon keep these heavenly chewy cookies on the right side of virtuous.

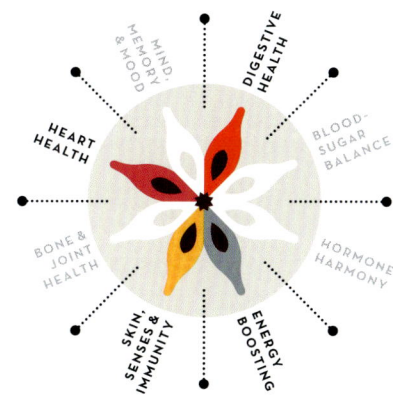

Carrot Cake Bites

MAKES 15-20

100g (3½oz) Midlife Power Porridge, see page 28, or jumbo oats

80g (2¾oz) wholemeal flour

1 tsp bicarbonate of soda

1 heaped tsp ground cinnamon

a pinch of sea salt flakes

50g (1¾oz) butter, melted

1 egg

1 tsp vanilla extract

75ml (5 tbsp) maple syrup or date syrup

100g (3½oz) carrots, peeled and roughly grated

50g (1¾oz) sultanas

50g (1¾oz) walnuts, chopped

chopped pecan nuts, to serve

FOR THE DRIZZLE

25g cream cheese

1 tbsp lemon juice

1 tbsp maple syrup

Health Tip
Carrots are a brilliant source of beta-carotene which is converted to vitamin A in the body for use in supporting eye health and immune function.

Combine the oats, flour, bicarbonate of soda, cinnamon and salt in a bowl. In a separate bowl, mix the melted butter, egg, vanilla extract and maple or date syrup, then stir in the carrots, sultanas and walnuts. Add the carrot mix to the flour and oats, stirring well to combine. Chill for 30 minutes.

Preheat the oven to 180°C (350°F)/Gas Mark 4. Line a baking sheet with nonstick baking paper.

Spoon 15-20 heaped tablespoons of the dough on to the baking sheet, fairly well spaced, then flatten slightly with the spoon. Chill again for 5 minutes.

Bake for 12-15 minutes until the cookies are crisp and golden on the outside. Leave to cool slightly on the sheet, then transfer to a wire rack to cool completely.

To make the drizzle topping, combine the cream cheese, lemon juice and maple syrup in a bowl and stir well until smooth. Using a teaspoon, gently drizzle a little over each cooled cookie and top with a scattering of chopped pecan nuts.

The cookies can be stored in an airtight container for up to 3 days.

Try This...
* For a more indulgent frosting to use in place of the drizzle topping, mix 50g (1¾oz) cream cheese, 25g (1oz) softened butter and 2 tablespoons of icing sugar in a bowl, beating with a spoon until smooth. Smear the frosting on to each cooled cookie.

WHY WE LOVE IT

A truly healthy cake is, we've found, a rare treasure – very often, the taste or texture is all wrong because the usual delicious alchemy of fats and sugars has been lost in translation. We put our minds to creating something that really works and tastes divine, and here it is: a Midlife marvel in a loaf tin, bursting with flavour, low on fat and with just the right amount of squidge. Perfect with afternoon tea.

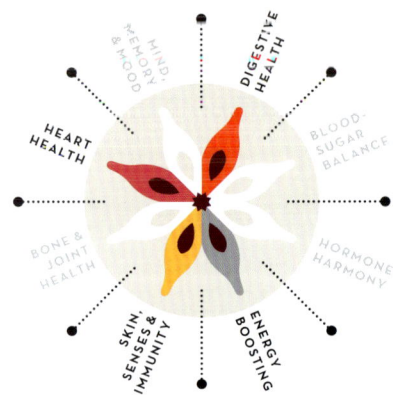

Teatime Walnut & Banana Loaf

MAKES 1 LOAF

- 40g (1½oz) butter, softened
- 150g (5½oz) wholemeal flour, plus extra for dusting
- 100g (3½oz) date sugar or soft light brown sugar
- 1 large egg
- 100ml (3½fl oz) milk
- 2½ tsp baking powder
- 2 tsp mixed spice
- 2 ripe bananas, roughly mashed
- 30g (2 tbsp) walnuts, chopped
- 30g (2 tbsp) pitted dates, chopped

Preheat the oven to 170°C (340°F)/Gas Mark 3½. Line a 450g (1lb) loaf tin.

Using a hand-held or stand mixer, cream the butter and sugar, then beat in the egg and milk. Sift in the flour, baking powder and mixed spice, then use a metal spoon to fold in until incorporated. Add the bananas, walnuts and dates and stir again.

Pour the batter into the prepared tin and bake for 1 hour or until a skewer inserted into the centre comes out clean. Leave to cool slightly in the tin, then turn out on to a wire rack. The cake is best served warm.

Midlife Hack: Date sugar is well worth seeking out as an alternative to regular sugar if you bake a lot. It's available from online retailers.

Health Tip
Date sugar came top in a study ranking 12 of the most popular sweeteners by their antioxidant content – not that surprising, as date sugar is simply whole, dried dates pulverized into a powder.

FIG, WALNUT & GINGER UNCOOKIES

RAISIN, COCONUT & CINNAMON UNCOOKIES

DATE, APRICOT & CARDAMOM UNCOOKIES

CHOCOLATE, ORANGE & BRAZIL NUT UNCOOKIES

WHY WE LOVE IT

We like the idea of an 'energy ball', a healthy way to get a sweet fix without too much refined sugar. This is our Midlife version: the delicious, nutritious little 'uncookie' – perfect for those 'I need something now' moments (usually around mid-afternoon or after an exercise class), they go impressively well with a shot of espresso.

Uncookies

Health Tip
Don't be put off nuts because they are relatively high in calories – they're full of protein and fibre to keep you feeling full, so you'll probably eat less overall. Studies have shown that people who consume nuts are less likely to be overweight than those who don't.

Put all the ingredients, except the coatings, into a food processor and whizz, scraping down the sides between pulses using a spatula if necessary, until the ingredients are fully incorporated and the 'dough' is as chunky or as smooth as you like (we prefer it a little chunky). If the mixture is too dry, add more water; if too wet, add more LSA or ground almonds – it should be soft but not too sticky.

Take a heaped teaspoon of the mixture and form into small cookie shapes, about 3–4cm (1¼–1½in) each in diameter, then coat with the coating ingredients. Chill for about 15 minutes to firm them up – this makes them deliciously chewy.

They will keep in the fridge in an airtight container for up to a week, but we can assure you that they won't hang around that long!

See photograph on pages 278–9.

FIG, WALNUT & GINGER

MAKES 10–12

2 tbsp Midlife LSA, see page 27, or ground almonds

200g (7oz) soft dried figs

2 tbsp cold water

juice of 1 lime

50g (1¾oz) walnuts, crushed

1 tsp peeled and finely grated fresh root ginger

1 tsp ground cinnamon

a pinch of sea salt flakes

FOR THE COATING

2 tbsp Midlife LSA, see page 27, or ground almonds

CHOCOLATE, ORANGE & BRAZIL NUT

MAKES 10–12

200g (7oz) Medjool dates, pitted

2 tbsp freshly squeezed orange juice

1 tsp orange zest

6 Brazil nuts, finely chopped

2 tbsp Midlife LSA, see page 27, or ground almonds

a pinch of sea salt flakes

FOR THE COATING

2 tbsp unsweetened cocoa powder

RAISIN, COCONUT & CINNAMON

MAKES 10–12

2 tbsp desiccated coconut

150g (5½oz) raisins

2 tbsp cold water

a squeeze of lemon juice

2 tbsp almond butter

3 tbsp Midlife LSA, see page 27, or ground almonds

1 tsp ground cinnamon

FOR THE COATING

2 tbsp desiccated coconut

DATE, APRICOT & CARDAMOM

MAKES 10–12

10–15 cardamom pods, to taste

150g (5½oz) Medjool dates, pitted

50g (1¾oz) dried apricots, chopped

2–3 tbsp water

finely grated zest of 1 lemon

3 tbsp Midlife LSA, see page 27, or ground almonds

2 tbsp desiccated coconut

FOR THE COATING

2 tbsp pistachio nuts, finely crushed

DRINKS

WHY WE LOVE IT

A refreshing and uplifting wake-up infusion; we've kept it super simple, because nobody wants to be messing around with heaps of ingredients first thing in the morning, and the honey is optional if you prefer a sugar-free start to the day.

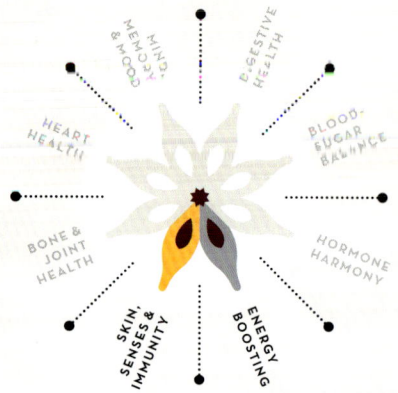

Sunrise Tea

SERVES 1

2 lemon grass stalks
a small handful of mint leaves
1 tsp runny honey

Bruise the lemon grass with a rolling pin and place in a mug. Add the mint and honey, then add boiling water.

Steep for 5 minutes, stirring with the lemon grass stalks.

Midlife Hack: Lemon grass stalks are hollow inside so they make great natural drinking straws.

Health Tip
The menthol component that gives mint its distinctive aroma stimulates the hippocampus area of the brain, which controls mental clarity and memory. Just the job first thing!

WHY WE LOVE IT

A refresher course of healthy vits, minerals and antioxidants, this hydrating tonic is a real eye-opener – who knew that simple celery could have so many health benefits? We love the delicate pale green combo of celery, cucumber and apple – all you need to do is gather them together and blitz away.

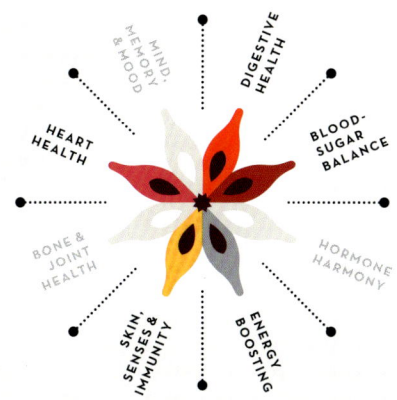

Wake-up Tonic

SERVES 2

½ a cucumber, peeled and roughly chopped

2 celery sticks, tougher strings removed, roughly chopped

1 apple, peeled, quartered and cored

juice of 1 lime

300ml (½ pint) chilled coconut water

Put all the ingredients into a blender and blitz well, then pour into 2 glasses and serve immediately (it will separate if left to stand).

Midlife Hack: The Midlife Kitchen requires little in the way of specialist cooking equipment – but we do love our NutriBullet 'extractors' because they can pulverize most fruit and veg without peeling or coring, which means more nutritional value, more fibre… and a lot less washing up.

Health Tip
Celery contains potassium, which can help maintain normal blood pressure, and vitamin K, which helps maintain bones (important in perimenopause and beyond), as well as a host of antioxidants.

WHY WE LOVE IT
Jamu is an intrinsic part of Balinese life, a daily ritual to ward off ill health, thanks to the amazing antibacterial and anti-inflammatory properties of its key ingredient, turmeric. It's something of an acquired taste, so to make it more approachable we've added the familiar citrus tang of lime and orange juice, which also boosts the vitamin C content, making this an immunity-boosting Midlife Elixir.

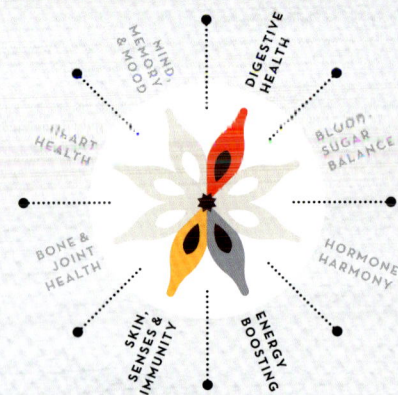

Jamu
INDONESIAN TURMERIC JUICE

SERVES 2

- 50g (1¾oz) fresh turmeric root, peeled and sliced
- 25g (1oz) fresh root ginger, peeled and sliced
- juice of 1 lime
- juice of 1 orange
- 150ml (¼ pint) chilled coconut water
- 1 tsp runny honey
- sea salt flakes and freshly ground black pepper
- ice cubes, to serve (optional)

Put all the ingredients into a blender with a small pinch of sea salt flakes and a grind of pepper, then blitz for 1 minute.

Strain the juice through a fine sieve or tea strainer into 2 glasses and serve, over ice if you prefer.

Midlife Hack: It's a good idea to use clingfilm as a barrier between your fingers and the turmeric when peeling and slicing as the staining can be difficult to remove.

Health Tip
Studies show that the curcumin found in turmeric may help fight infections and some cancers, reduce inflammation and treat digestive problems. The addition of black pepper, which contains piperine, increases the body's ability to absorb the curcumin.

WHY WE LOVE IT

A thick shake may not sound massively healthy, and that's exactly why we had such fun with this recipe. It tastes super indulgent, but every ingredient is happily working wonders: bananas for potassium and energy, avocado for good fats and cinnamon for antioxidant protection.

Bananacado Thick Shake

SERVES 1–2

1 banana, peeled, chopped and frozen

½ a ripe avocado, chopped

100ml (3½fl oz) semi-skimmed milk or unsweetened almond milk, see page 296

½ tsp ground cinnamon

Put all the ingredients into a blender and blend well for 1–2 minutes until the banana is completely incorporated.

Pour into 1 large or 2 smaller glasses and serve immediately.

Midlife Hack: If you have bananas that are past their best, just peel and freeze them, ready for shakes and smoothies.

Health Tip
Bananas are not only cheap and readily available, they are also an excellent energy source before, during or after exercise.

WHY WE LOVE IT

This dark, delicious juice looks – and tastes – deeply indulgent, yet takes mere minutes to make. You'll get a hit of vital minerals from the beetroot, powerful phytonutrients from the berries, plus a spicy antioxidant bass note from a pinch of cinnamon. Better yet, there's natural sweetness in the beets and berries, so there's no need to add a thing. If you choose frozen berries, you'll get an ice-cold frappé; with a little less apple juice, eat it with a spoon – or freeze for a couple of hours to make the perfect sorbet.

Beet the Blues Juice

SERVES 2

2 cooked beetroot, cut into chunks

150g (5½oz) fresh or frozen blackberries

100g (3½oz) fresh or frozen blueberries

300ml (½ pint) unsweetened apple juice or cold water

½ tsp ground cinnamon

Simply blitz all the ingredients in a blender until smooth, then pour into 2 glasses and serve.

Midlife Hack: No need to roast and peel fresh beetroot to get at the goodness. Buy ready-cooked (not in vinegar), grab from the fridge, rinse and go.

Health Tip
Beetroot is particularly high in natural nitrates which can help reduce blood pressure, when eaten regularly. As they also help to relax blood vessels, nitrates can improve the flow of oxygen to muscles which might improve exercise performance.

WHY WE LOVE IT

We know that we bang on about berries, but they really are a game-changer for anyone interested in midlife health – and cranberries are up there with the league champions for the impressive array of benefits they offer. The problem is that we rarely eat them raw; the cartons of cranberry juice we do consume tend to be over-processed, often containing as much sugar as cola. Our answer is this gorgeous Ruby Cooler, with the tart pop of frozen cranberries tempered by sweet watermelon, fresh mint and just a hint of honey.

Ruby Cooler

SERVES 2

100g (3½oz) frozen cranberries

100g (3½oz) watermelon, peeled and deseeded

6 mint leaves

200ml (⅓ pint) cold water

1 tsp runny acacia honey

TO SERVE

ice cubes

about 300ml (½ pint) sparkling water

Put all the ingredients, except the ice and sparkling water, in a blender and blitz until smooth.

Pour into 2 glasses over ice, then top up with the sparkling water. Serve immediately.

Health Tip
Vit-rich cranberries boast a raft of benefits, from improving gut, brain and urinary tract health, to helping balance blood sugars and lowering the risk factors for heart disease.

DRINKS

WHY WE LOVE IT

Hibiscus tea is thought to have been the drink of choice of the Pharaohs; the clever old sticks might well have understood that hibiscus can provide an array of vitamins and help to lower blood pressure and cholesterol. Known as 'karkade' in Arabic, the steeped flowers of hibiscus (or rosella) produce a deliciously cooling and astringent drink, perfect for a sunny afternoon. Traditional methods require boiling, but cold steeping works equally well and retains more of the vital vitamins.

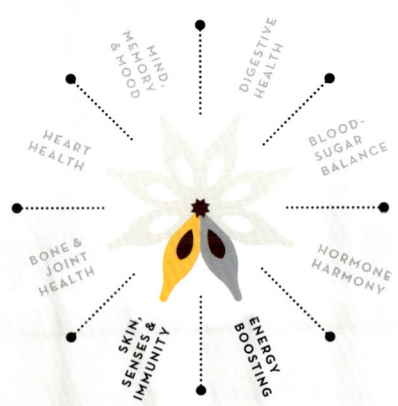

Karkade
HIBISCUS ICED TEA

SERVES 2

1 tbsp dried hibiscus flowers

500ml (18fl oz) cold water

a squeeze of lemon or lime juice

2 tsp runny acacia honey

crushed ice, to serve

Combine all the ingredients in a bottle or jug, mix well and chill for at least 1 hour, or overnight.

To serve, strain the tea through a fine sieve or tea strainer into 2 glasses over crushed ice. The iced tea keeps well in the fridge for up to a week.

Try This...
Perhaps add these optional extras to your tea:
* 1 teaspoon grated fresh root ginger
* 2 teaspoons orange blossom or rose water
* A grinding of vanilla bean and a small handful of mint leaves
* Cloves and ground cinnamon

Health Tip
Hibiscus tea is ranked 'number one beverage' for antioxidant content (beating green tea), and it contains vitamin C – which probably explains its traditional use as a herbal remedy to fight off colds and infections by strengthening the immune system.

WHY WE LOVE IT

A green and grassy lemon tea, mellowed with a spoonful of honey – it sounds simple enough, but don't be fooled: matcha green tea is an impressive power powder and is full of antioxidants which can reduce our risk of all sorts of diseases as we age. Choose the best-quality matcha you can – it's expensive, but a little goes a very long way. Persevere with this one; it's an unconventional taste, but once you've got it, you'll never let it go.

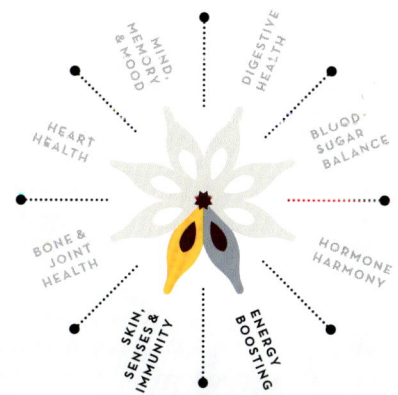

Chilled Matcha & Lemon Tea

SERVES 2

- 2 tbsp boiling water
- 1 tsp premium-grade matcha powder
- 500ml (18fl oz) cold water
- juice of ½ a lemon
- 1 tsp runny acacia honey
- ice cubes, to serve (optional)

Pour the boiling water over the matcha powder and stir well to eliminate any lumps.

Stir in the cold water, lemon juice and honey, then chill until required.

To serve, stir the tea well, then pour into 2 glasses, over ice if you like.

Midlife Hack: This is lovely hot too – a great green booster for chilly days when the flu season is upon us.

Health Tip
Matcha contains potent polyphenols – notably EGCG, an antioxidant linked to low rates of heart disease. Studies have shown that women who regularly drink green tea had a 22 per cent lower risk of developing breast cancer, while men had a 48 per cent lower risk of prostate cancer.

WHY WE LOVE IT

This grown-up lemonade has just a little honey and a mellow backdrop of ginger and mint. It really hits the spot when you need hydrating but want something more exciting than water. Perfect for summer barbecues.

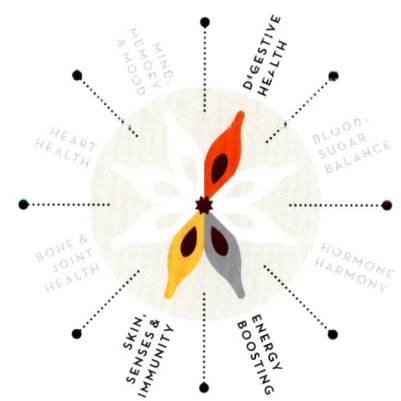

Ginger & Mint Muddle

SERVES 4

50g (1¾oz) mint leaves, chopped, plus extra to serve

100g (3½oz) fresh root ginger, rinsed and thinly sliced (no need to peel)

2 tbsp runny acacia honey

juice of 2 lemons

1 litre (1¾ pints) boiling water

TO SERVE

ice cubes

slices of lemon

Place the mint, ginger, honey and lemon juice in a large heatproof jug and add the boiling water. Stir well and leave to steep for 30 minutes. Strain into a clean jug, then chill until ice cold.

Serve over ice with extra mint leaves and lemon slices. The lemonade will keep in the fridge for a few days.

Health Tip
What we are getting here is plenty of gorgeous vitamin C, which can support skin health, immune function and energy release.

WHY WE LOVE IT

Switchel dates back to 19th-century American colonies, when it was apparently a favourite of thirsty farmers at harvest time. This is a great way to stay hydrated and can help replenish electrolytes after exercise. The thought of a vinegar drink may not immediately appeal, but it's all a matter of balance; adding honey, lemon and ginger – three more key Midlife ingredients – makes for an exceptionally delicious and refreshing drink.

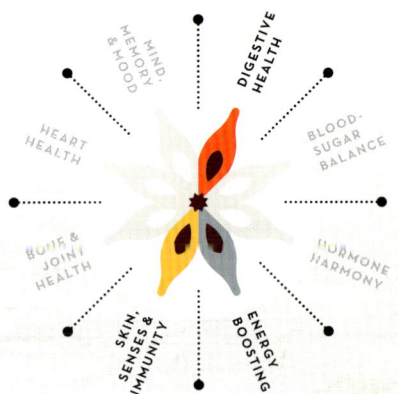

Switchel

SERVES 2

- 500ml (18fl oz) unsweetened cloudy apple juice or cold water
- 6cm (2½in) piece of fresh root ginger, peeled and grated
- 2 tbsp apple cider vinegar
- 1 tbsp runny acacia honey
- 1 tbsp lemon juice
- ice cubes, to serve

Heat all the ingredients in a saucepan and simmer gently for 2 minutes, stirring occasionally.

Strain the switchel through a fine sieve into 2 heatproof glasses or mugs and serve immediately. Alternatively, chill for an hour or more and serve over ice.

Midlife Hack: Try adding basil, lemon thyme or mint for a herby Switchel, or a cinnamon stick for a hint of spice.

Health Tip
Apple cider vinegar is a source of gut-friendly prebiotic plant compounds and has been shown to assist in blood-sugar control.

WHY WE LOVE IT

If you're a coffee addict (like us) then you'll know how great it is to have an alternative hot drink that you genuinely enjoy and, as in this case, is unbelievably good for you. This simple, aromatic infusion is a full-system reboot in a cup (if you inhale the steam it will give your head a good clear-out too). It makes a bright and refreshing morning brew, or a cleansing drink before bed.

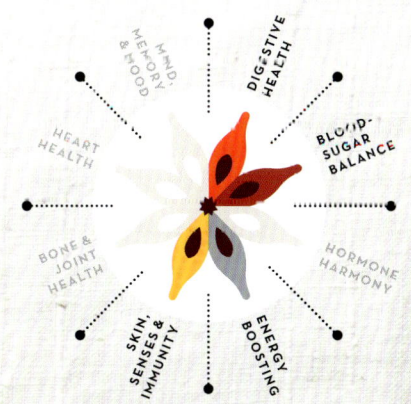

Lemon, Ginger & Star Anise Tea

SERVES 1

5cm (2in) piece of fresh root ginger, rinsed and sliced (no need to peel)

2 slices of lemon

1 star anise

Place the ginger, lemon slices and star anise in a mug and add boiling water. Leave to steep for 5 minutes before drinking.

Health Tip
Our emblem in the Midlife Kitchen, the star anise, has traditionally been used in Chinese medicine to support the immune system.

WHY WE LOVE IT

A goodnight cuddle in a cup, this mellow chai is full of good things to soothe you to sleep. Almonds are a great evening ingredient as they contain tryptophan, an essential amino acid required to synthesise serotonin (the 'happy hormone') and melatonin (the 'sleep hormone'). The dash of date syrup gives a slight insulin boost to help tryptophan to cross the blood-brain barrier, while the almonds and nutmeg both provide magnesium to improve tryptophan conversion... But, hey, don't worry about any of that now. It's bedtime.

Bedtime Chai

SERVES 2

1 quantity Almond Milk (see right) or 500ml (18fl oz) shop-bought unsweetened almond milk (see Midlife Hack)

4 cardamom pods, crushed

½ tsp ground cinnamon

a grating of nutmeg

a grind of vanilla bean, see page 211

1 tbsp Midlife Sweetener, see page 31, or date syrup

2 chai teabags

FOR THE ALMOND MILK

200g (7oz) whole almonds, with skins on

600ml (20fl oz) cold water, plus extra for soaking

sea salt flakes (optional)

To make the almond milk, soak the almonds overnight in water (this is important as it will produce a smoother, creamier milk, and it also activates enzymes which make the milk more nutritious).

The next day, drain and rinse the almonds. Put the nuts into a blender with the 600ml (20fl oz) cold water and blitz for 3 minutes to form an opaque liquid. Strain through muslin, a jelly bag or a specialist 'nut-milk bag' into a clean jug, squeezing to extract as much almond milk as possible. Add a pinch of salt, if using. The milk will keep in the fridge for up to 2 days.

To make the chai, place 500ml (18fl oz) of the almond milk in a small saucepan and bring to a simmer. Add the spices, vanilla and Midlife Sweetener or date syrup and simmer for a further minute or so. Remove the pan from the heat, add the chai teabags and leave to steep for 2–3 minutes.

Remove the teabags before serving, and use a milk frother if you fancy a frothy top.

Midlife Hack: Some commercial almond milks have a low almond content (as little as 2 per cent) and include added sugar, thickeners and emulsifiers such as carrageenan. If you do use shop-bought unsweetened almond milk, look for one with an almond content of 7 per cent plus.

Health Tip
A study published in the *Journal of Orthomolecular Medicine* found that when magnesium levels are too low, it's harder to stay asleep. Consuming magnesium-rich almonds and nutmeg (traditionally regarded as a cure for insomnia) could help you get good-quality sleep.

INDEX

A

aguadito 120–1
all-green soup 122–3
almonds 19
   avocado toast with feta 60, 62
   hot tapas 212
   milk 296
   Parmesan & pistachio sables 213
   red pepper hummus 221
   salted porridge 43, 46
   yogurt & orange drizzle cake 268–9
anchovies 109, 154, 234
apple cider vinegar 21, 33, 294
apples 16
   apple strudel yogurt 50, 52
   & beetroot raita 230–1
   & beetroot soup 128–9
   in Bircher 58
   sauce 244
   spiced apple & cranberry cake 272–3
   switchel 294
   wake-up tonic 285
   white fruit salad 248
apricots
   chickpea tagine 138
   date & cardamom uncookies 279–81
   in fruit salad 80–1, 250–1
   trail mix 211
Asian salad nori wraps 182–3
asparagus 17, 112–13, 160–1, 228–9
aubergine 138, 177
avocado 17
   bananacado thick shake 287
   green egg wraps 180
   guacamole 220
   midlife rices salad 202–3
   mixed grain mata sapi 198
   RGB salad 106–7
   salsa 770–1
   & strawberry salsa 239
   toasts 61–5
   & turmeric dressing 118
   Ubud spice salad 116
   Vietnamese crabocado wraps 185

B

Bali beach smoothie bowl 82–3
Balinese yellow chicken curry 170–1
banana
   bananacado thick shake 287
   bran muffins 75
   chia-up pots 66–7
   freezer fruit 214
   fruit spring rolls 252
   no-flour pancakes 76–7
   smoothie bowl 82–3
   super green porridge 47
   & walnut loaf 276–7
bananacado thick shake 287
basil 20, 88, 154
bean sprouts 90–1, 148–9
beans, black 140–1
beans, broad 202–3, 204
beans, butter 142–3, 166–7, 205, 218
beans, cannellini 166, 167, 205
beans, edamame 220
beans, green 112–13, 148–9, 192
beans, kidney 166, 167, 194–5
beans, pinto, on avocado toast 63, 65
bedtime chai 296–7
beef, sirloin steak on roast veg 176–7
beet the blues juice 288
beetroot 17, 115
   & apple soup 128–9
   & berry juice 288
   & blueberry salad 96–7
   raita with apple 230–1
   red cabbage coleslaw 115
   roasted, with orange, ras el hanout & goat's cheese 144
berries 16, 242, 265–6, 289
Bircher 58–9
black bean mess 140–1
blackberries
   beetroot & blueberry juice 288
   black & blue berry streusel 265–6
   hedgerow spiced porridge 40–1
   hot mega-berry sauce 55
   raw jam 242
   smoothie bowl 82–3
black beluga lentils with sweet potato, balsamic & pomegranate 200–1
black & blue berry streusel 264–5
black forest overnight oats 56–7
bliss burgers 146–7
blueberries 16, 55
   beetroot & blackberry juice 288
   & beetroot salad 96–7
   & blackberry streusel 265–6
   freezer fruit 214
   gazpacho 258–9
   herb salad 104
   hot mega-berry sauce 55
   raw jam 242
   smoothie bowl 82–3
blueberry gazpacho 258–9
bran muffins 74–5
Brazil nuts 19, 210, 211, 279, 280–1
breakfast bran muffins 74–5
brilliant broccoli salad 105
broad bean, pea & mint smash 204
broccoli 17
   all-green soup 122–3
   mole verde 228–9
   salad 105
   soto ayam 130, 132
   tenderstem with dukkah & chilli 193
burgers, squash and lentil 146–7
butternut, butter bean & red onion roast 142–3
butternut squash 17, 142–3, 146

C

cabbage
   gado gado 148
   red 17, 90–1, 106, 114–15, 240
Caesar salad, kale 108–9
cake 260–1, 268–9, 270–1, 272–3, 276–7
capers 109, 234
caramel sauce 245
cardamom 21, 195, 238, 240, 257, 281
carrot 17
   Asian salad nori wraps 182–3
   cake bites 274–5
   cake porridge 42, 44
   chickpea tagine 138
   with falafel 151
   gado gado 148–9
   hijuki salad 86–7
   pad Thai 90–1
   with roasted beetroot 144
   salmon miso soup 135
   sunshine soup 133
   Vietnamese crabocado wraps 185
carrot cake bites 274–5
cashews 19, 86–7
celery 120–1, 141, 285
chia-up pots 67
chapatis 206–7
chard, red 199
cheesecake, pumpkin & ginger 260–1
cherries
   Black Forest overnight oats 57
   chia jam 46
   chocolate porridge 42, 48
   hot mega-berry sauce 55
   warm winter fruit salad 250–1
chestnuts 250–1
chia seeds 19
   Black Forest overnight oats 57
   cherry chia jam 46
   chia-up pots 66–7
   raw jam 242–3
   smoothie bowl 82–3
chicken
   aguadito 120–1
   Asian salad nori wraps 182
   pot-roast with lentils & herbs 172–3
   soto ayam 130, 132
   yellow chicken curry 170–1
chickpea, leek & Parmesan soup 124–5
chickpeas 18
   Caesar salad 109
   falafel 150–1
   leek & Parmesan soup 124–5

red pepper hummus 221
rich chickpea tagine 138–9
chicory 92–3, 94–5
chilled matcha & lemon tea 291
chillies 17
 green bean & asparagus salad 112
 & herb dressing 119
 makhani dhal 195
 matbucha salsa 227
 mole verde 228–9
 pad Thai 90–1
 salsa criolla 241
 sambal matah 235
 strawberry & avocado salsa 239
 sweet & sour dipping sauce 185
 three-ginger fire cake 271
 uchucuta 226
 zehug 238
 & zesty tenderstem 193
chocolate, dark 21
 cardamom & ginger pears 257
 cherry porridge 42, 48
 five-minute mousse 266–7
 no-flour banana pancakes 76
 orange & Brazil nut uncookies 279–81
 & peanut mega mix 210
classic tuna fagioli 166
cinnamon 21, 261, 271, 272, 275, 281, 287
coconut
 & green bean salad 192
 hijuki salad 86–7
 milk 38–9, 170
 raisin & cinnamon uncookies 280–1
 smoothie bowl 82–3
 sugar 245
 tropical yogurt 54
 water 58, 285
coleslaw, red cabbage 114–15
coriander 20, 238
 aguadito 120–1
 Asian salad nori wraps 182
 Asian salsa 157
 black bean mess 141
 chilli & herb dressing 119

with gado gado 148
Greek salad 102–3
makhani dhal 195
mixed grain mata sapi 198
mole verde 228–9
with monkfish & fennel 154
pad Thai 90–1
pistachio pesto 88
radish, cucumber & herb salsa 236
with roasted pumpkin 145
soto ayam 130, 132
Ubud spice salad 116
uchucuta 226
Vietnamese crabocado wraps 185
yellow chicken curry 170
zehug 238
courgette 47, 90–1, 122–3, 177
couscous, chickpea tagine 138
crab, Vietnamese crabocado wraps 185
cranberries 105, 240, 250–1, 272–3, 289
crispy trout with Asian salsa 156–7
cucumber
 Asian salad nori wraps 182–3
 Greek salad 102–3
 hijuki salad 86–7
 Nicky's pickled 135
 radish & herb salsa 236–7
 Vietnamese crabocado wraps 185
 wake-up tonic 285
cumin 21, 118, 195, 198
curry paste 34, 170–1

D
dates 16
 apricot & cardamom uncookies 279–81
 in Bircher 58
 freezer fruit 214
 fruit spring rolls 252
 pumpkin & ginger cheesecake 260–1
 sticky toffee puddings 262–3
 syrup sweetener 31, 271
 walnut & banana loaf 276

dhal, makhani 194–5
dill 20, 115, 154, 165, 167, 188
dips 218, 220, 221, 226, 228–9
dragon fruit, white fruit salad 248
drenched cardamom & ginger pears 256–7
dukkah 30, 146, 151, 193

E
easy chapatis 206–7
egg muffins 70–1
eggs 20
 with black bean mess 140–1
 bran muffins 75
 egg white omelette 68–9
 with gado gado 148
 green wraps 180–1
 mixed grain mata sapi 198
 muffins 70–1
 no-flour banana pancakes 76–7
 ricotta angel cakes 78–9
 shakshouka 72–3
elderflower & granola plumble 254–5

F
fagioli 166, 167
falafel 150–1
fast falafel 150–1
fennel 17
 carpaccio 110–11
 fenneloumi salad 100–1
 mackerel fagioli 167
 & monkfish 154–5
 pom pom salad 98–9
fenneloumi salad 100–1
feta
 and avocado toast 60, 62
 butternut, butter bean & red onion roast 142
 Greek salad 102–3
 mixed grain mata sapi 198
 with Puy lentils & tomatoes 190–1
 uchucuta 226
figs 16
 hedgerow spiced porridge 40–1

pink salad 92–3
red cabbage coleslaw 115
sticky, with roast lamb 174–5
trail mix 211
walnut & ginger uncookies 278, 280–1
warm winter fruit salad 250–1
yogurt & pomegranate molasses 49, 50
fish 21, 157, 160–1
five-minute chocolate mousse 266–7
flaxseeds 19, 109
freezer fruit 214–5
fresh fruit spring rolls 252–3
fruit 16
 freezer 214–15
 raw jam 242
 salad 80–1, 248–9, 250–1
 smoothie bowl 82–3
 spring rolls 252–3

G
gado gado 148–9
garam masala 230
garlic 17, 142, 194–5, 196–7, 205
gazpacho, blueberry 258–9
ginger 21
 all-green soup 122–3
 Asian salsa 157
 & cardamom pears 257
 fig & walnut uncookies 278, 280–1
 lemon & star anise tea 295
 makhani dhal 195
 & mint muddle 292–3
 miso & sesame dressing 119
 & orange dressing with fruit salad 81
 pickled 68, 158
 & pumpkin cheesecake 260–1
 switchel 294
 three-ginger fire cake 270–1
ginger & mint muddle 292–3
goat's cheese 96–7, 144
granola, grown-up 29, 82–3, 254–5
grapefruit 53, 80–1, 98–9
grapes 214, 248

INDEX

gravadlax, with rösti & yogurt 164–5
Greek salad 102–3
green bean & asparagus salad 112–13
green egg wraps 180–1
green tea (matcha) 21, 47, 291
grilled mustard & halibut 162–3
guacamole 220

H
haddock, smoked, & lentil kitchri 153
halibut, mustard & herb 162–3
halloumi cheese, fenneloumi salad 100–1
harissa yogurt 138
hedgerow spiced porridge 40–1
herb salad 104
herbs 20, 104, 119, 162
hibiscus iced tea 290
hijuki salad 86–7
horseradish 224
hot tapas almonds 212
hummus, red pepper 221

I
Indian spiced fish 160–1

J
jam, raw 242–3
jamu 286

K
kale 17, 108–9, 122–3
karkade 290
kiwifruit 214, 242, 252

L
labneh 145
lamb, slow-roasted with figs 174–5
leeks 124–5, 126–7
lemon grass 235, 284
lemon, ginger & star anise tea 295
lemons 16
lentils 18
  black beluga, with sweet potato 200–1

burgers with quinoa & dukkah crust 146–7
fenneloumi salad 100–1
makhani dhal 194–5
with pot-roast chicken 173
Puy, with feta & tomatoes 190–1
& smoked mackerel kitchri 152–3
sunshine soup 133
lettuce 100–1, 102–3, 108–9, 182
lime
  all-green soup 122–3
  dipping sauce 252
  guacamole 220
  salsa criolla 241
  tahini & cumin dressing 118
  Vietnamese crabocado wraps 185
  wake-up tonic 285
LSA mix 27
lychees, white fruit salad 248
luxe or lean makhani dhal 194–5

M
mackerel 152–3, 157, 167, 222–3
mango
  with Bircher 58
  freezer fruit 214
  fruit salad with ginger & orange 80–1
  fruit spring rolls 252
  raw jam 242
  tropical yogurt 54
  Ubud spice salad 116
mangosteen 248
matbucha 227, 229
matcha 21, 47, 291
melon 58, 80–1, 289
middle-aged spread 218–9
midlife apple sauce 244
midlife caesar 108–9
midlife curry paste 34
midlife dukkah 30
midlife grown-up granola 29
midlife LSA 27
midlife mackerel fagioli 167
midlife mega mix 210
midlife power porridge 28
midlife raw seed mix 25

midlife rices 202
midlife salad dressing 33
midlife salsa verde 234
midlife sesame seasoning 32
midlife shakshouka 72–3
midlife spice mix 24
midlife spiced seed mix 26
midlife sticky toffee puddings 262–3
midlife sweetener 31
midlife toasted trail mix 211
midlife yogurt 35
mint 20
  broad bean & pea smash 204
  fennel carpaccio 110–11
  & ginger muddle 292–3
  Greek salad 102–3
  guacamole 220
  mixed grain mata sapi 198
  pad Thai 90–1
  with Puy lentils, feta & tomatoes 191
  radish, cucumber & herb salsa 236
  with roasted pumpkin 145
  smoothie bowl 82
  sunrise tea 284
  Vietnamese crabocado wraps 185
miso 86, 119, 134–5, 158
miso king prawns with sesame & pickled ginger sugar snaps 158–9
mixed grain mata sapi 198
mole verde 228–9
monkfish & fennel with herbs, tomatoes & anchovies 154–5
morning fruit salad 80–1
mother of all Greek salads, the 102–3
mozzarella & peach salad 88–9
muffins 70–1, 74–5
mushrooms 135, 188–9, 199
mussels, Thai 168–9

N
nectarines 80–1
no-flour banana pancakes 76–7
nurture bircher 58–9

nuts 19, 30, 210, 211
  see type of nut
nutty goat avo toast 60

O
oats 19
  Bircher 58–9
  black & blue berry streusel 265
  Black Forest overnight oats 56–7
  elderflower & granola plumble 254–5
  grown-up granola 29, 82–3
  see porridge
olive oil 21, 33, 268
olives 102–3, 154, 225
onion, red 18, 167
  butternut & butter bean roast 142–3
  fagioli 166, 167
  fenneloumi salad 100–1
  makhani dhal 194–5
  red cabbage pickle 240
  with roasted beetroot 144
  with roasted pumpkin 145
  salsa criolla 241
  wilted spinach & mushrooms 188
orange
  blueberry gazpacho 258–9
  chickpea tagine 138
  chocolate & Brazil nut uncookies 279, 280–1
  fruit salad with ginger & orange 80–1
  ricotta 251
  with roasted beetroot 144
  St Clement's yogurt 51, 53
  yogurt & almond drizzle cake 268–9

P
pad Thai 90–1
pak choi 133, 135
pancakes 76–7, 78–9
papaya 54, 58, 80–1, 214
Parmesan 109, 110, 125, 199, 213, 233

Parmesan, almond & pistachio sables 213
parsley 20
   all-green soup 122-3
   black bean mess 141
   chickpea tagine 138
   chilli & herb dressing 119
   guacamole 220
   middle-aged spread 218
   with pot-roast chicken 173
   salsa verde 234
   tuna fagioli 166
   uchucuta 226
passion fruit, with Bircher 58
pâté, fish 222-3, 224, 225
peach 80-1, 88-9
peach & mozzarella salad 88-9
peanuts 91, 148, 192, 210
pears 92-3, 100-1, 248, 250-1, 256-7
peas 112, 120, 160, 202, 204, 220
   mangetout 130, 132, 148-9, 158
   sugar snap 90-1, 158-9
pecan nuts 19, 233, 275
pecorino, walnut & watercress pesto 232
pepper, jalapeño 65
pepper, green, Greek salad 102-3
pepper, red 18, 72, 91, 141, 177, 221
pesto 88, 232, 233
pickle
   cucumber 135
   ginger 68
   red cabbage 106, 240
pine nuts 142, 200
pineapple 58, 75, 214, 252
pink salad 92-3
pistachio 88, 213
plums 40-1, 254-5
pom pom salad 98-9
pomegranate 16
   butternut, butter bean & red onion roast 142
   deseeding 98
   with lentils & sweet potato 200-1
   molasses 49, 50, 55, 93, 174
   peach & mozzarella salad 88-9
   pink salad 92-3
   pom pom salad 98-9
pomelo, pom pom salad 98-9
pork, uchucuta chops 178-9
porridge
   black & blue berry streusel 265
   carrot cake 42, 44
   carrot cake bites 275
   cherry chocolate 42, 48
   hedgerow spiced 40-1
   power porridge 28
   salted almond 43, 46
   spiced pumpkin 43, 45
   super green 43, 47
pot-roast chicken 172-3
potatoes 126-7, 164-5
prawns 91, 158-9, 182
prunes 250-1
puddings, sticky toffee 262-3
pumpkin 17
   & ginger cheesecake 260-1
   pecan & sage pesto 233
   roasted, with quinoa & labneh 145
   seeds 19, 145, 228-9, 233
   spiced porridge 43, 45
pumpkin, pecan & sage pesto 233
Puy lentils with feta & roasted tomatoes 190-1

Q

quinoa 19
   aguadito 120-1
   Asian salad nori wraps 182-3
   bliss burgers 146
   broccoli salad 105
   with mushrooms, chard & Parmesan 199
   with roasted pumpkin 145

R

radicchio 92-3
radish 106-7, 115, 116, 202-3, 236-7
radish, cucumber & herb salsa 236
raisins 76, 211, 240, 278, 280-1
raita, beetroot 230-1
ras el hanout 144
raspberries 214, 242, 258-9, 260-1, 267
raw jam 242-3
raw pad Thai 90-1
red cabbage 17, 90-1, 106, 114-15, 240
red cabbage coleslaw 114-15
red chicory & walnuts 94-5
red green & black salad 106-7
red lentil & smoked mackerel kitchri 152-3
red & white quinoa with mushrooms, red chard & Parmesan 199
rich chickpea tagine 138-9
rice 19
   Asian salad nori wraps 182-3
   lentil & mackerel kitchri 152-3
   midlife rices salad 202-3
   RGB 106-7
   sweet & salty Balinese black rice 38-9
Rice, Sam 6, 12, 304
ricotta 78-9, 251, 260-1
ricotta angel cakes 78-9
roasted beetroot with spiced orange, ras el hanout & goat's cheese 144
roasted garlic 196-7
roasted pumpkin with quinoa & labneh 145
roasted red pepper hummus 221
rocket, RGB salad 106-7
Roquefort dressing 94-5
rosemary 20, 173
rösti, gravadlax & dill yogurt 164-5
ruby cooler 289

S

sabji, asparagus & pea 160-1
sage 20, 173, 205, 233
St Clement's yogurt 51, 53
salad
   beetroot & blueberry 96-7
   broccoli 105
   Caesar 108-9
   dressings 33, 118-19, 200
   fennel carpaccio 110-11
   fenneloumi 100-1
   fruit 80-1, 248, 250-1
   Greek 102-3
   green beans & asparagus 112-13
   herb 104
   hijuki 86-7
   midlife rices 202-3
   peach & mozzarella 88-9
   pink salad 92-3
   pom pom 98-9
   raw pad Thai 90-1
   red cabbage coleslaw 114-15
   red chicory & walnuts with Roquefort dressing 94-5
   RGB 106-7
   Ubud spice salad 116-17
   urab 192
salmon miso soup 134-5
salsa
   Asian 157
   avocado 770-1
   criolla 241
   matbucha 227, 229
   radish, cucumber & herb 236-7
   strawberry, with avocado & green chilli 239
   verde 234
salted almond porridge 46
sambal matah 235
sardinade 225
sardines 157, 225
sauce
   apple 244
   caramel 245
   dipping 185, 252
   hot mega-berry 55
   peanut 148
   uchucuta 226, 229
seared sirloin on pan-roasted veg 176-7

INDEX

seasoning, sesame 32
seaweed 86-7, 182-3
seeds 19
   dukkah 30
   LSA mix 27
   no flour banana pancakes 76
   raw seed mix 25
   soda bread 208-9
   spiced seed mix 26
   toasted trail mix 211
seedy soda bread 208-9
sesame seeds 19
   avocado toast 63, 64
   miso & ginger dressing 119
   miso king prawns 158
   salmon miso soup 135
   seasoning 32, 182
   sunshine soup 133
   Ubud spice salad 116
sesame street avo toast 64
shakshouka 72-3
shallots, sambal matah 235
skin, senses & immunity 11
slow-roasted lamb with sticky figs 174-5
smoked mackerel & dill pâté 222-3
smoked trout pâté 224
smoothie bowl 82-3
smoothies 214, 285
soda bread 208-9
soto ayam 130, 132
soup
   aguadito 120-1
   all-green 122-3
   beetroot & apple 128-9
   blueberry gazpacho 258-9
   chickpea, leek & Parmesan 124-5
   salmon miso 134-5
   soto ayam 130, 132
   sunshine 133
   watercress powerhouse 126-7
soya 18
Spencer, Mimi 6, 12, 304
spiced apple & cranberry cake 272-3
spiced pumpkin porridge 45
spiced red cabbage pickle 240
spices 21
spinach 18, 138, 145, 180, 188, 218

spread, middle-aged 218
spring onion
   Asian salad nori wraps 182
   green egg wraps 180
   hijuki salad 86-7
   midlife rices salad 202-3
   mixed grain mata sapi 198
   pad Thai 90-1
   salmon miso soup 135
   Ubud spice salad 116
   Vietnamese crabocado wraps 185
spring rolls, fresh fruit 252-3
star anise 9-11, 21, 295
steak, sirloin, & pan-roasted veg 176-7
sticky toffee puddings 262-3
Stilton, with pink salad 93
strawberries 82-3, 239, 242, 252
strawberry salsa with avocado & green chilli 239
sultanas 75, 275
sunflower seeds 19, 265, 272
sunrise tea 284
sunshine soup 133
super green porridge 47
sweet & salty Balinese black rice 38-9
sweet potato
   butternut, butter bean & red onion roast 142
   with lentils & pomegranate 200-1
   rösti with gravadlax 164-5
sweetcorn, baby 148-9
swish rösti 164-5
switchel 294

T
tagine, rich chickpea 138-9
tahini 64, 91, 118, 221
tamarind 170
tea
   bedtime chai 296-7
   chilled matcha & lemon 291
   green 21, 47, 291
   hibiscus iced 290
   lemon, ginger & star anise 295
   sunrise 284

teatime walnut & banana loaf 276-7
tempeh, Ubud spice salad 116
Thai midlife mussels 168-9
three-ginger fire cake 270-1
tofu 63, 64, 91, 146-7, 182
tomatoes 18
   beans on (avo) toast 63, 65
   chickpea tagine 138
   Greek salad 102-3
   green egg wraps 180
   matbucha salsa 227, 229
   with monkfish & fennel 154
   with Puy lentils & feta 190-1
   with roasted pumpkin 145
   shakshouka 72-3
   sunshine soup 133
   Ubud spice salad 116
   zehug 238
trail mix, toasted 211
tropical yogurt 54
trout 156-7, 224
tuna, fagioli 166
turmeric 21
   all-green soup 122-3
   Asian salsa 157
   & avocado dressing 118
   juice (jamu) 286
   makhani dhal 195
   Thai mussels 169

U
ubud spice salad 116
uchucuta 178-9, 226, 229
uchucata pork 178-9
uncookies 278-81
urab 192

V
Vietnamese crabocado wraps 184-5

W
wake-up tonic 285
walnut, watercress & pecorino pesto 232
walnuts 19, 233
   & banana loaf 276-7
   carrot cake bites 275
   fig & ginger uncookies 278, 280-1

mega mix 210
pink salad 92-3
   with red chicory & Roquefort dressing 94-5
   with roasted pumpkin 145
trail mix 211
watercress & pecorino pesto 232
warm winter fruit salad 250-1
watercress 18, 96-7, 126-7, 232
watercress powerhouse soup 126-7
Welsh rarebit avo toast 61
white fruit salad 248-9
wholly guacamole 220
white bean mash 205
wilted spinach with sautéed mushrooms & dill 188-9

Y
yoga barn wraps 68-9
yogurt 20
   almond & orange drizzle cake 268-9
   apple strudel 50, 52
   bran muffins 75
   chocolate mousse 267
   dill 165
   fennel carpaccio 110-11
   figs & pomegranate molasses 49-50
   freezer fruit smoothie 214
   harissa 138
   with hot mega-berry sauce 51, 55
   making your own 36
   middle-aged spread 218
   with mint 133
   pumpkin & ginger cheesecake 260-1
   red cabbage coleslaw 115
   St Clement's 51, 53
   smoothie bowl 82-3
   tropical 51, 54
yogurt, almond & orange drizzle cake 268-9

Z
zehug 238
zesty tenderstem with midlife dukkah & chilli 193

AUTHORS' ACKNOWLEDGEMENTS

Producing *The Midlife Kitchen* has been the culmination of our long-held wish to work together – and it has been every bit as fun as we had hoped. Of course, creating a recipe book is a time-consuming affair, so our love and thanks go to our endlessly supportive husbands and kids: Paul, Lily and Ned (Mimi) and Rich, Rufus and Roxana (Sam).

We're lucky enough to have been surrounded by a uniquely talented team: our brilliant and wise agent Antony Topping at Greene & Heaton; our publisher Alison Starling, who shared our vision from the beginning and who led our dream team at Octopus – Jonathan Christie, Sybella Stephens, Caroline Brown, Matt Grindon and Saskia Sidey. We're incredibly proud of the photography on every page, so to our amazing shoot team – Issy Croker, Natalie Thomson, Linda Berlin, Stephanie McLeod and Nikky Richman – huge thanks for bringing our creations to life.

Thanks also to our consultants Dr Sarah Schenker and Claire Baseley, who made sure that everything we said was nutritionally sound.

Our original Midlife Kitchen star anise concept was brilliantly designed by Rachel Holtman at Surface Design www.surfacedesignconsultancy.com.

We'd also like to send a shout out to friends and places who have provided recipe thoughts and inspiration along the way: Nicola Williams, Michaela Van Nes, Debbie Spencer-Jones, Alex Hadfield, Avara Yaron, Chris Salans of the Mozaic Restaurant Group, the Yoga Barn Café, Café Batujimbar, Locavore and the many other great places we have eaten in Bali that sparked ideas for this book.

And finally, our special thanks to our inspirational mothers, Julie and Stephanie, because you can never show your mum enough gratitude (hear that, kids?).

First published in Great Britain in 2017 by Mitchell Beazley, an imprint of
Octopus Publishing Group Ltd
Carmelite House, 50 Victoria Embankment, London EC4Y 0DZ
www.octopusbooks.co.uk

An Hachette UK Company
www.hachette.co.uk

Revised edition published in 2025

The authorized representative in the EEA is Hachette Ireland, 8 Castlecourt Centre, Dublin 15, D15 XTP3, Ireland (email: info@hbgi.ie)

Text copyright © Mimi Spencer & Sam Rice 2017, 2025
Design and layout copyright © Octopus Publishing Group 2017, 2025
Photography copyright © Issy Croker 2017

Distributed in the US by Hachette Book Group, 1290 Avenue of the Americas, 4th and 5th Floors, New York, NY 10104

Distributed in Canada by Canadian Manda Group, 664 Annette St., Toronto, Ontario, Canada M6S 2C8

All rights reserved. No part of this work may be reproduced or utilized in any form or by any means, electronic or mechanical, including photocopying, recording or by any information storage and retrieval system, without the prior written permission of the publisher.

Mimi Spencer & Sam Rice assert their moral right to be identified as the authors of this work.

ISBN 978 1 84091 964 6

A CIP catalogue record for this book is available from the British Library.

Printed and bound in China

10 9 8 7 6 5 4 3 2 1

Nutritional Consultants:
Dr Sarah Schenker (first edition)
Claire Baseley (this edition)

Publisher: Alison Starling
Senior Managing Editor: Sybella Stephens
Copy Editor: Jo Murray
Creative Director: Jonathan Christie
Photographer: Issy Croker
Photographer's Assistant: Stephanie McLeod
Food Stylist: Natalie Thomson
Props Stylist: Linda Berlin
Senior Production Manager: Katherine Hockley

MIMI SPENCER

Mimi Spencer is best known for co-authoring *The Fast Diet* with Michael Mosley, which introduced the concept of 5:2 intermittent fasting to the world.

During a 30-year career in journalism, she wrote about 'all the good things in life' – fashion, beauty, food and travel – as a features writer and columnist for numerous national newspapers and magazines including *The Times*, the *Observer*, *Mail on Sunday* and the *Evening Standard*. She has written five cookbooks, including *The Midlife Kitchen*, focused on health and well-being as we age.

A lifelong devotee of yoga, Mimi trained as a yoga teacher in 2021, and she now runs regular retreats near her home in Sussex (therestisyoga.co.uk). When she's not on a yoga mat, Mimi can be found in her studio making pots, which she shows at the Two Kats and a Cow gallery in Brighton. @mimispencerceramics

SAM RICE

Sam's food journey began in 2012 following the shock death of her youngest brother, Ben, from type 1 diabetes. She spent the next few years experimenting in the kitchen, trying to find healthy foods she loved to eat, and quickly learned the power of the food we eat to heal and sustain.

The Midlife Kitchen was the culmination of everything she learned during those years, and her subsequent book, *The Midlife Method: How to Lose Weight and Feel Great After 40*, has also helped thousands of midlifers improve their health. Her latest book, *Supercharge Your Diet: Ten Easy Ways to Get Everything You Need from Your Food*, was written to give people back control over their nutrition in the increasingly complex food landscape we now live in.

Sam is the nutrition expert at the *Daily Telegraph*, where her writing centres on making good nutrition accessible to all. She's a recent graduate of Leiths Nutrition in Culinary Practice programme, the best training of its kind in the UK, which focuses on translating nutritional theory into practice in the kitchen. Her latest endeavour is an MSc in Clinical Nutrition at Aberdeen University, a tall order for those midlife brain cells!